Organizational effectiveness and improvement in education

COMPANION VOLUMES

The companion volumes in this series are:

Educational Management: Strategy, Quality and Resources, edited by Margaret Preedy, Ron Glatter and Rosalind Levačić

Professional Development for Educational Management, edited by Lesley Kydd, Megan Crawford and Colin Riches

Leadership and Teams in Educational Management, edited by Megan Crawford, Lesley Kydd and Colin Riches.

All four of these readers are part of a course, Effective Leadership and Management in Education, that is itself part of the Open University MA Programme.

THE OPEN UNIVERSITY MA IN EDUCATION

The Open University MA in Education is now firmly established as the most popular postgraduate degree for education professionals in Europe, with over 3,500 students registering each year. The MA in Education is designed particularly for those with experience of teaching, the advisory service, educational administration or allied fields.

Structure of the MA

The MA is a modular degree, and students are therefore free to select from a range of options the programme which best fits in with their interests and professional goals. Specialist lines in management and primary education are also available. Study in the Open Unviersity's Advanced Diploma and Certificate Programmes can also be counted towards the MA, and successful study in the MA programme entitles students to apply for entry into the Open University Doctorate in Education programme.

COURSES CURRENTLY AVAILABLE:

- Management
- Child Development
- Primary Education
- Curriculum, Learning and Assessment
- Special Needs
- Language and Literacy
- Mentoring

- Education, Training and Employment
- Gender
- Educational Research
- Science Education
- Adult Learners
- Maths Education

OU supported open learning

The MA in Education programme provides great flexibility. Students study at their own pace, in their own time, anywhere in the European Union. They receive specially prepared study materials, supported by tutorials, thus offering the chance to work with other students.

How to apply

If you would like to register for this programme, or simply to find out more information, please write for the *Professional Development in Education* prospectus to the Course Reservations and Sales Centre, PO Box 724, The Open University, Walton Hall, Milton Keynes, MK7 6ZS, UK (Telephone 01908 653231).

Organizational effectiveness and improvement in education

Edited by
ALMA HARRIS, NIGEL BENNETT AND
MARGARET PREEDY
at The Open University

OPEN UNIVERSITY PRESS
Buckingham · Philadelphia

Open University Press
Celtic Court
22 Ballmoor
Buckingham MK18 1XW

1058

and 1900 Frost Road, Suite 101
Bristol, PA 19007, USA

First published 1997
Reprinted 1998

A catalogue record of this book is available from the British Library

ISBN 0 335 19843 0 (pbk)   0 335 19844 9 (hbk)

Library of Congress Cataloging-in-Publication Data

Organizational effectiveness and improvements in education / edited by Alma Harris,
   Nigel Bennett, and Margaret Preedy.
      p.   cm. — (Leadership and management in education)
   Includes bibliographical references and index.
   ISBN 0-335-19843-0 (pbk)   ISBN 0-335-19844-9 (hbk)
      1. School management and organization—Great Britain.   2. School improvement
programs—Great Britain.   3. Educational evaluation—Great Britain.   4. Educational
change—Great Britain.   I. Harris, Alma, 1958–   II. Bennett, Nigel.   III. Preedy,
Margaret.   IV. Series.
LB2900.5.O74   1997
371.2'00941—dc20   96-42219
                                                                         CIP

Typeset by Type Study, Scarborough, North Yorkshire
Printed and bound in Great Britain by Redwood Books, Trowbridge

Contents

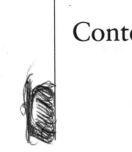

Acknowledgements

The chapters listed below come from the following sources, to whose publishers grateful acknowledgement is made.

2 Hanna, D. (1988) 'Understanding how organizations function', Chapter 1 in *Designing Organizations For High Performance*, pp. 8–31, © 1988 Addison-Wesley Publishing Company Inc. Reprinted with permission of Addison-Wesley Longman Inc.

3 Hales, C. (1993) 'Power authority and influence', Chapter 2 in *Managing Through Organisations*, London, International Thomson Business Press.

4 Meyerson, D. and Martin, J. (1987) 'Cultural change: an integration of three different views', *Journal of Management Studies*, 24: 623–47, © Blackwell Publishers Ltd and SAMS.

5 Bennett, N. (1995) 'Schools and management: ideas and action', Chapter 5 in *Managing Professional Teachers*. Reprinted with permission from the author, © 1995 Paul Chapman Publishing Ltd, London.

6 Fidler, B. 'Organizational structure and organizational effectiveness' (commissioned article).

7 Bush, T. (1995) 'Collegial models', Chapter 4 in *Theories of Educational Management*, 2nd edn. London, Paul Chapman. This material has been edited and has been reprinted with permission from the author, © 1995 Tony Bush.

8 Scheerens, J. (1992) 'Models of co-ordination in educational organizations', Chapter 2 in *Effective School Research, Theory and Practice*, pp. 18–22, London, Cassell.

9 Wallace, M. and Hall, V. (1994) 'Towards a cultural and political perspective', Chapter 2 in *Inside the SMT: Teamwork in Secondary School Management*. Reprinted with permission from the author, © 1994 Paul Chapman Publishing Ltd, London.

10 Scott, R.W. (1992) 'Organizational effectiveness', Chapter 13 in *Organizations:*

Rational, Natural and Open Systems, 3rd edn by Scott, © 1992. Reprinted by permission of Prentice Hall, Inc., Upper Saddle River, NJ.

11 Creemers, B.P. (1994) 'Towards a theory of educational effectiveness', in *The Effective Classroom*, London, Cassell.

12 Reynolds, D. *et al.* (1994) 'School effectiveness and school improvement in the United Kingdom', *School Effectiveness and School Improvement*, Conference paper, ICSESI (revised), The Netherlands, Swets and Zeitlinger.

13 Brown, S., Duffield, J. and Riddell, S. (1995) 'School effectiveness research: the policy makers' tool for school improvement', *European Education Research Association Bulletin*, 1(1) March: 6–15 and is reproduced with the kind permission of the European Educational Research Association.

14 Harris, A., Jamieson, I. and Russ, J. (1995) 'A study of effective departments', *School Organisation*, 15(3). Reprinted with permission of Carfax Publishing Company, PO Box 25, Abingdon, Oxfordshire OX14 3UE, UK.

15 Taylor, A. and Hill, F. (1993) 'Quality management in education', *Quality Assurance in Education*, 1(1): 21–8. Reprinted with permission MCB University Press Ltd, http: // www.mcb.co.uk

16 FEDA (1995) *Current Developments in Value Added*, May 1995. Open University Press is grateful for the contribution made by the Further Education Development Agency (FEDA) of its paper by Stella Dixon, Current Developments in Value Added.

17 McPherson, A. (1992) 'Measuring added value in schools', *National Commission on Education*, Briefing No 1, London, NCE. We are grateful to the National Commission on Education for their permission to use this extract.

18 Saunders, L. (1995) 'Value added principles, practice and ethical considerations' (NFER commissioned article).

19 Fullan, M.G. (1991) 'Planning, doing and copying with change', in *The New Meaning of Educational Change*, London, Cassell.

20 Blenkin, G.M., Edwards, G. and Kelly, A.V. (1992) 'Educational change: a theoretical overview' Chapter 2 in *Change and Curriculum*. Reprinted with permission from the authors, © 1992 Paul Chapman Publishing Ltd, London.

21 Sergiovanni, T.J. (1994) 'Organizations or communities? Changing the metaphor changes the theory', *Educational Management and Administration*, 30: 214–66. Reprinted by permission of Sage Publications Ltd, © 1994 Sage Publications Ltd and T. Sergiovanni.

22 Hargreaves, D.H. 'School culture, school effectiveness and school improvement', *School Effectiveness and School Improvement*, 6(1). Reprinted by permission of Swets and Zeitlinger Publishers, The Netherlands.

23 Reynolds, D. (1993) 'Linking school effectiveness knowledge and school improvement practice', in C. Dimmock (ed.) *School Based Management and School Effectiveness*, London, Routledge.

24 Hopkins, D., Ainscow, M. and West, M. (1996) 'School improvement – propositions for action' (commissioned article).

25 McMahon, A., Bishop, J., Carroll, R. and McInally, B. (1996) 'Fair Furlong Primary School', in National Commission on Education (ed.) *Success Against the Odds*, London, Routledge.

1 Introduction: organizational effectiveness and improvement in education

ALMA HARRIS, NIGEL BENNETT AND
MARGARET PREEDY

Educational effectiveness is very much on the political, research and practitioner agenda. Over the last few years there has been sustained pressure upon educational institutions to improve performance, to become more efficient and more effective. Familiar terms such as 'equal opportunities' and 'equality' have been extended to include words such as 'standards', 'ambition', 'diversity' and 'accountability'. These words are all part of the vocabulary of educational efficiency, effectiveness and improvement.

The arrival of the quasi-market has heightened competition between schools and colleges in the UK. Consequently, the measurement of institutional effectiveness and improvement has become increasingly more important. These developments have had far-reaching implications for the practice of educational management. Schools and colleges have been required to take increasing management responsibility and they have also experienced greater accountability in more varied and complex ways. The net result of this has been the demand for higher-level management skills within the educational sphere. Moreover, there has been a diffusing of management tasks and roles within educational institutions. As the management task becomes more complex, most teachers and lecturers have found themselves involved in some form of management activity.

A model of management premised upon hierarchical structures is no longer appropriate to the management tasks which most educational institutions currently face. Flatter organizations are emerging where responsibility is more widely shared. This implies that management is to be performed as part of the work of all staff in varying capacities. Therefore, effective management should be central to the professional development of all teachers and lecturers irrespective of their position within the organization.

The main aim of this book is to make management theory accessible and of practical use for teachers and lecturers. Consequently, the chapters collectively emphasize 'theory in practice' and focus upon ideas which are useful in the pursuit of effective educational management. This volume subscribes to the view that there are aspects of management in the work of all teachers and lecturers, not just in the work of those with designated management responsibility. Also, it takes as its premise the fact there are various perspectives on effective organizations and that these are important considerations for educational managers.

As the chapters in this volume illustrate, organizational effectiveness is not without some conceptual complexity and diversity. Definitions of organizational effectiveness and improvement are acknowledged to be dependent upon the particular theoretical position adopted. Consequently, a variety of different and sometimes competing theoretical views on management and organizational effectiveness are presented. This book aims to provide a broad theoretical base from which organizational effectiveness, organizational improvement and the management of change can be considered.

In educational policymaking and practice, the idea of an effective school/college is important because it offers the possibility of improving schools and colleges. Effectiveness is essentially related to goals in education. It deals with the reasons why schools, or colleges with initially comparable students differ in the extent to which they achieve their goals. As the chapter by Bert Creemers illustrates (Chapter 11), educational effectiveness can be seen as an integral theory about education which takes into account the inputs, processes and the contexts in which education takes place.

Organizational effectiveness has been found to incorporate a number of different levels within the organization. As Creemers shows, even though the classroom level is most important, other levels in the system, such as the organizational or faculty/department level, also provide the conditions for effective teaching and learning to take place. Consequently, an open-system model of management is central to the school and college effectiveness movements. This model emphasizes the effective transformation of inputs into outputs and underlines the importance of value-added measurement. In this open system model, a distinction is made between the input, context and processes, as well as the outcomes of education. The inputs consist of variables such as financial or personnel resources and the background of students. The context refers to the socio-economic, political and educational context of the school or college. The processes are those features, particularly at the classroom level, which affect the quality of teaching and learning.

Most models of school/college effectiveness distinguish between different levels in the organization. All models include the individual student level, the classroom level and the school level, and in most cases it is assumed that the higher-level models provide the conditions for what happens at the levels below. This multi-level effectiveness model emphasizes the interrelationship of all levels in affecting the quality of teaching and learning. The chapter by Creemers and that by Jaap Scheerens (Chapter 8) both emphasize the centrality of the classroom in the quest for educational effectiveness but also demonstrate the importance of other levels within the organization.

The model implies the dynamic nature of educational organizations and as such the necessary relationship between managing the organization and school/college effectiveness and improvement. It emphasizes the holistic nature of the management task and demonstrates the importance of individual, group and task-related concerns within the organization. In particular, the beliefs and values that guide organizational members and the means by which they are established, communicated and influenced are important.

Organizational culture is consequently an important unifying theme within this book. As the chapters by Meyerson and Martin (Chapter 4) Wallace and Hall (Chapter 9), Sergiovanni (Chapter 21) and Hargreaves (Chapter 22) all demonstrate, managing change is concerned with influencing the shared sets of meanings, values and beliefs that comprise school/college culture. Seen from this perspective, the management of institutional development cannot be an incremental 'stop–start' activity, reactively responding to specific internally, or externally identified needs, but instead, is a proactive process fundamentally concerned with developing a culture of change.

If we accept this dynamic model of educational effectiveness, some rather fundamental questions need to be addressed. First, how is educational effectiveness defined, conceived and measured? These particular issues are dealt with in the chapters by Scheerens (Chapter 8) and Creemers (Chapter 11). Second, what are the characteristics of an effective educational organization? Chapter 12 by Reynolds *et al.* outlines the empirical evidence base which addresses this issue. Finally, what are the implications for leadership and management practice emanating from the effectiveness/improvement research? The chapters by Hargreaves and Fullan (Chapter 19) explore the implications for educational management in some depth.

This book aims to address such questions in three interrelated parts which explicitly link school/college effectiveness and improvement to organizational/management theory. These three parts are as follows:

Part 1 Organizational theory and analysis.
Part 2 School/college effectiveness: theory, research and practice.
Part 3 Managing change for school/college improvement.

Part 1 provides a broad theoretical base for a consideration of organizational effectiveness within an educational context. The chapters therein reflect a range of perspectives on organizational effectiveness and demonstrate various conceptions of the management process. The prime purpose of Part 1 is to provide a broad theoretical overview, or framework, against which effective management and leadership practice can be considered.

Part 2 supplements the theoretical base of Part 1 with empirical findings from the literature on effectiveness. It looks at the relationship between organizational theory and the findings from research on school/college effectiveness. The implications for educational managers are at the centre of an analysis of this relationship. As this volume is primarily concerned with 'theory in practice', Parts 1 and 2 link organizational theory and effective organizational practice.

Building upon the association between Parts 1 and 2, Part 3 makes a further link between organizational theory, effective organizational practices and the management of change. It considers school/college improvement from this theoretical and empirical base. The central concern of Part 3 is to explore the implications for management and leadership of differing approaches to change and institutional improvement. The influence of organizational culture features predominantly in the discussion of the management of change presented in this part. Collectively, all three parts outline various perspectives on effective educational organizations and demonstrate how these various perspectives impinge upon the improvement task and the management of change process.

Part 1: Organizational theory and analysis

Part 1 introduces several major approaches to thinking about organizations and some of the key management theories and ideas involved. It provides an overview of systems theory which stresses the relation between inputs and outputs and the need for integration and coherence. This is a fundamental concept within the school and college effectiveness literature, within value-added analysis and total quality management. As the chapter by Scheerens illustrates (Chapter 8), models of school/college effectiveness are premised upon a relationship between student inputs/school/college processes and student outputs.

Chapter 2 by David Hanna focuses upon the organization as an open system. It discusses ways in which this theoretical model may help managers who wish to improve the effectiveness of their organizations. The basic premise of open-systems theory is that organizations have common characteristics with all other living systems: from microscopic organisms, to plants, to animals, to humans. It is suggested that understanding these characteristics allows us to work with the natural tendencies of an organization rather than struggle against them. Consequently, as well as considering structural factors, managers need to consider the interrelationships of the people involved, and the influences upon their work. In doing this, it is important to examine the basis upon which individuals are persuaded to act by others, since management is primarily concerned with ensuring that outputs meet expectations and that individuals work together in a coordinated way to achieve them.

If we accept that the management task is chiefly that of influencing or modifying the behaviour of others, then power is clearly important. Its attendant concepts are influence and authority which carry with them the willingness of others to acknowledge the ideas of individuals and grant them legitimacy. Chapter 3 by Hales discusses power and influence. It examines both concepts within the context of management: first, characteristics, types and dimensions of power resources; second, the modes of influence corresponding to these; and third, typical responses to different types of power and influence in terms of perceptions, evaluations and behaviour. The chapter outlines different types of power resource available to managers and describes their personal and positional forms. It is clear from this analysis that the behavioural responses to such forms of power depends upon the reactions of those over whom it is being exerted. Power and influence are real only if they are accepted by those over whom they are exercised. Consequently, just as power and influence must be analysed in relation to the responses made to them, so it would seem that a similar stance needs to be taken when considering management through institutionalized or organizational mechanisms.

Power and influence are important dimensions within the management of change process in any organization. If we accept that any organization is an open system which operates primarily on the interaction and interrelationship of people, then the power relations within that organization become important factors in affecting change. Similarly, culture is an important dimension of change. This is a theme which Hargreaves discusses at length (Chapter 22) and which Meyerson and Martin (Chapter 4) comment upon in their chapter. As both these chapters illustrate, organizational cultures can be resistant to change and depending upon their nature will require very different management approaches to bring about successful change. Despite the difficulty of considering change from a multi-paradigm approach it would seem that for effective management to take place a consideration of the complex multifaceted, dynamics of culture is imperative. This is a theme which is developed more fully in Part 3.

Chapter 5 by Bennett looks at the different cultures of schooling. Culture is acknowledged to be a powerful conceptual tool for analysing the extent to which it is possible to influence the work of others. It would appear that how change is brought about within an organization will be influenced by whether the culture of that organization is seen as integrative, or simply a distinctive identifying element. For example, there could be a distinctive culture of fragmentation, or ambiguity.

This set of ideas recurs with great frequency through the book, as an articulation and expression of individual values in a collective way. Thus, for example, the chapter by Wallace and Hall (Chapter 9) offers a power–culture model which reflects Meyerson and Martin's (Chapter 4) paradigm one view of culture. Alternatively, a paradigm two model would incorporate differentiation and multiple competing positions which are embedded in concepts of power. Wallace and Hall emphasize that there are limitations to holding a single perspective on management and demonstrate that cultural and political perspectives are important when considering school/college management.

Different views of change therefore, derive from different cultural paradigms. Meyerson and Martin clearly demonstrate this point in their chapter. In the chapter by Bush (Chapter 7), the collegial model is outlined. This model is predicated upon a culture of integration and a unified way of working. Indeed, much of the literature on effectiveness stresses cultures of integration rather than differentiation. This point is extended in Chapter 6 by Fidler who explores the relationship between organizational structure and organizational effectiveness. He argues that there is no single organizational structure which is most effective for a given situation but that there are a number of competing structures. This chapter, Chapter 10 by Scott and Chapter 21 in Part 3 by Sergiovanni, all illustrate how conceptions of organizational effectiveness are heavily dependent upon how the organization is conceived and understood. In particular, it emphasizes the importance of different metaphors for understanding the organization and organizational change.

The chapters by Scott and Scheerens both focus upon how organizational effectiveness might be measured and what criteria for determining organizational effectiveness might be set. There are many possible bases for generating criteria of effectiveness and the literature reveals that a vast number of criteria exist for this purpose. What remains clear however, is that in order for an evaluation of performance to occur, criteria must be selected. In order to judge organizational effectiveness therefore, standards need to be identified and indicators of performance need to be set. These indicators necessarily have to include outcome measures, as well as process and structural indicators.

The chapters in Part 1 demonstrate that, given the multiple possible meanings and measures of effectiveness and the complexity of organizations, a single set of factors to account for organizational effectiveness cannot be expected. While studies of organizational effectiveness provide valuable insights into new management techniques, other factors such as school context, teaching staff, pupil numbers, have been overlooked, or underemphasized. In summary, criteria for evaluating organizational effectiveness cannot be produced by some objective, apolitical process. They are always normative and often controversial and they are as varied as the theoretical models used to describe organizations.

Part 2: School and college effectiveness: theory, research and practice

Part 2 builds upon the theoretical base provided in Part 1 by introducing the empirical findings on school/college effectiveness. Drawing initially upon the organizational models outlined in Part 1, it provides the key ideas which have informed school effectiveness research. Chapter 11 by Creemers maps the theoretical base for educational effectiveness and its measurement. It acknowledges that the term 'effective' presupposes that some sort of judgement or measurement has been made but demonstrates the complexity of undertaking such measurement. The whole issue of trying to come to some objective judgement of school performance is shown to be both complex and difficult.

The concept of effectiveness is clearly related to a means–end relationship. When applied to educational phenomena, effectiveness refers to the degree to which educational means or processes result in the attainment of educational goals. In the language of a simple input-process–output systems model of education, effectiveness could be referred to as the transition of inputs by means of processes into desired outputs and outcomes. Although there are both conceptual and technical problems associated with measurement of this kind, none the less the entire school/college effectiveness movement is dependent upon being able to measure effectiveness.

In measuring educational effectiveness there has been a tendency to restrict the criteria for effectiveness to what can be achieved by schools and colleges and what schools and colleges are for. Research on school/college effectiveness has been criticized because it takes account of only a restricted set of outcomes, such as basic skills and knowledge. In his chapter, Creemers underlines the importance of having multiple outcomes as proposed criteria for effectiveness. In particular, given the importance of the classroom level within school/college effectiveness, it would appear particularly important to have more measures for classroom effectiveness. This is an issue taken up by Brown et al. in Chapter 13. They note that a narrow and top-down way of construing school effectiveness has had the effect of placing the primary emphasis on formal organizational variables with an assumption that matters of teaching and learning will follow. Their argument, like that of Creemers, is that the classroom level should be the central focus for school/college effectiveness studies. This viewpoint, that any serious attempt to innovate in the classroom should start from where teachers are and how they construe there own teaching, reinforces the messages concerning organizational culture in Part 1 and is returned to in Part 3 when issues of managing school improvement and change are discussed.

In their review of the empirical evidence on school effectiveness, Reynolds et al. (Chapter 12) accept that the field has its balance of strengths and weaknesses. They provide however, nine key factors of effective schooling which have been generated from the knowledge and research base. These factors include such dimensions as professional leadership, shared vision and goals and purposeful teaching. It is tempting to see these school/college effectiveness studies as producing some form of 'recipe' for school effectiveness as there is certainly consensus in the research concerning the features of effective schools. This chapter emphasizes the overlap between studies and the degree of duplication in many of the research findings on effectiveness.

However, in reality the take up of knowledge about school effectiveness by practitioners within the educational system has been limited. In part, this has been because research on school effectiveness has been dominated by high levels of abstraction and a lack of specific detail in some of the concepts used in the research. The knowledge base of research into school/college effectiveness is also not strong on teachers' focal concerns of the curriculum and the actual teaching and learning processes used within the classroom. Similarly, there is little consideration taken of the influence of the cultural or power dimensions of organizational effectiveness. As shown in Part 1, these dimensions influence the way in which we perceive organizational structures and bring about organizational change. Yet these dimensions are largely absent in any consideration of organizational effectiveness.

Effectiveness studies tend to focus upon the end result of being an effective school, or college. They do not outline how to get to the destination of 'effectiveness', or explore in any depth what might constitute barriers to effectiveness. The theoretical model favoured in these studies, as Brown et al. (Chapter 13) demonstrate, does not readily allow for different interpretations or constructs of organizational effectiveness. Indeed, the entire school/college effectiveness enterprise has tended to involve looking at effective schools and colleges to see what they have that ineffective schools and colleges do not have. In addition, the translation of the effectiveness findings into school improvement programmes has been generally poor. As Chapter 12 by Reynolds et al. reinforces, there has been a lack of synergy between British school effectiveness research and school improvement practice. This is an important debate which is returned to in Part 3.

Chapter 14 by Harris et al. demonstrates, however, that research on school effectiveness can provide an increasingly sensitive description of good practice. The chapter is an account of a small-scale study of effective school departments. It is an example of the synergy between measurement and improvement practice in school effectiveness which both Brown et al. and Reynolds endorse. The use of value-added measurement in this study reflects a more general trend towards using value-added measures in schools and colleges in recent years. The chapter by McPherson (Chapter 17) considers the use of value-added measurement in schools, while the Further Education Development Agency (FEDA) chapter (Chapter 16) looks at this process at work within further education. Chapter 15 by Taylor and Hill illustrates how value-added measurement has become part of the wider development of total quality management in education. The influence of market forces upon this development is stressed particularly in Chapter 18 by Saunders. This chapter concludes that value-added measures cannot improve anything without a careful consideration of how such data are used within organizations. Moreover, it is suggested that without the involvement and commitment of those within the organization, the potential for organizational improvement and change will be minimal. This is a theme which is explored in depth in Part 3.

Part 3: Managing change for school and college improvement

Part 3 draws upon the previous two parts by considering which theoretical models and empirical evidence can best assist the management of change for school/college improvement. Clearly, managing change, or innovation, is a central task in improving educational performance. As Hopkins et al. point out in Chapter 24, school/college improvement can be defined as a distinct approach to educational change that enhances student outcomes, as well as strengthening the organization's capacity for managing change.

Managing eductional change is a complex and long-term undertaking, involving at least four main stages: planning, implementation, establishing the change as part of the ongoing routine of the institution, and assessing outcomes and results. Managers within the institution have to deal with multiple externally and internally generated innovations which interact with each other and may not be mutually compatible. This entails balancing the tensions between external demands and internal needs and priorities. Also, decision-makers at various levels in the education system and within the school and college will have multiple and competing agendas, based on differing perspectives on the goals of education and the means of bringing these about. There is frequently a substantial mismatch between what is intended by policymakers and what is actually implemented in schools/colleges and classrooms.

Much of the literature on managing change portrays the process as a rational and systematic one, progressing through the four stages outlined above. However, studies of school improvement have cast doubt on the effectiveness of the rational model as a guide to planned change. Chapter 19 by Fullan explores some of the major problems in managing educational change and why rational models provide an inadequate guide to action. He proposes a flexible and interpretative approach to planning and implementing change, based on an analysis of the process which recognizes that complexity, uncertainty and conflict are inevitable in successful change.

Chapter 20 by Blenkin *et al.* identifies the factors within educational institutions that promote or hinder innovation, drawing on a range of perspectives or alternative analytical frameworks for understanding educational change. The authors highlight the factors within educational institutions that promote and hinder innovation, and hence need to be taken into account if planned change is to be successfully implemented. Chapter 21 by Sergiovanni argues that the prevailing rational technical perspective, centred around the organization as a machine, is inappropriate for schools and colleges. Instead he suggests we should change the metaphor and look at the school as a community, a culture of shared values, which would provide a more cooperative and consensual basis for the way we think about, organize and manage change.

Hargreaves in Chapter 22 explores the concept of organizational culture in some depth, examining the interactive relationship between culture and social structure. He notes that there are no clear cause-and-effect links between particular types of culture and school improvement, and that the effectiveness of various cultures depends upon the criteria for assessing effectiveness. The suggestion that schools with collegial, rather than more traditional bureaucratic cultures, are likely to be more supportive of school improvement is explored in this chapter. As Hargreaves notes, however, whether the collegial school will have more effective student outcomes has yet to be firmly established.

There is currently much work in progress which attempts to draw on what we know about managing change and school effectiveness and to apply this knowledge to practical development activities in schools and colleges. As Part 2 illustrated, school effectiveness studies have usually been large scale and quantitative in approach. They thus provide a broad picture of effective institutions and lists of factors which seem to be associated with positive outcomes. School improvement work, on the other hand, provides an in-depth picture of the change processes but often focused on teacher development, rather than student outcomes.

Chapter 23 by Reynolds explores the contribution of school effectiveness research to school improvement. He argues for a synthesis of the two separate traditions so that their findings can be applied more systematically to development work in schools and colleges. Reynolds assesses the strengths and weaknesses of both approaches and how they might fruitfully complement each other.

The final theme in Part 3 is concerned with how successful schools and colleges are in using insights from the two research fields to manage the process of ongoing development. Chapter 24 by Hopkins *et al.* reports on a project which attempts to do what Reynolds proposes, i.e. to take into account the lessons of previous effectiveness and improvement studies. This major school development project is premised upon a collaborative partnership between some 40 schools, their local education authorities and university research staff. The improvement strategy is focused on student learning and achievement outcomes, and simultaneously takes account of internal process factors of: culture, organization and management.

The final chapter by McMahon *et al.* (Chapter 25) illustrates improvement in practice. It is drawn from a collection of National Commission case studies of successful schools in disadvantaged areas. The authors highlight the major factors contributing to a school's 'success against the odds' which include positive leadership, a clear focus on learning and teaching and a collaborative management approach. As this chapter illustrates, 'improving' institutions are those which developed a culture for change that promotes ongoing learning and growth for staff as well as students. They are characterized by a clear sense of purpose and moving forward, a collaborative culture, a consistency of educational practice based on agreed approaches to teaching and learning, and positive staff–student relationships.

Conclusion

The literature on organizational theory, school/college effectiveness and the management of change is vast. It is hoped that the chapters in this book will provide an insight into the literature and illustrate the explicit linkages which exist between management theory, school/college effectiveness and the management of change. Moreover, it is intended that the concepts and frameworks discussed in this book will provide a helpful basis for the development of effective management practice in schools and colleges.

PART 1

Organizational theory and analysis

2 | The organization as an open system*

DAVID HANNA

The basic premise of Open Systems Theory is that organizations have common characteristics with all other living systems; from microscopic organisms, to plants, to animals, to humans. Understanding these characteristics allows us to work *with* the natural tendencies of an organization rather than struggle against them needlessly.

First let us define some terms. A *system* is an arrangement of interrelated parts. The words *arrangement* and *interrelated* describe interdependent elements forming an entity that is the system. Thus, when taking a systems approach, one begins by identifying the individual parts and then seeks to understand the nature of their collective interaction. It is the whole, not the parts alone, that counts.

All living systems are also classified as *open systems*. This means they are dependent on their external environment in order to survive and are, therefore, *open* to influences and transactions with the outside world as long as they exist.

The use of the word *open* in this context is frequently confused with open as in openness of communication and trust. It is important to keep these two meanings separate. *All organizations are open systems as defined here.* On the other hand, not every organization may have a climate of openness and trust.

If an open system is an arrangement of interrelated parts interacting with its environment, what are the various parts if we focus on an organization? These may be summarized as follows:

1 *Boundary.* All systems have a border or *boundary* that differentiates them from others. This boundary may be physical (e.g. a building), temporal (a work shift), social (a departmental grouping), or psychological (a steotyped prejudice).

Although the boundary tends to 'fence off' one system from another, it has openings to allow for interactions with the environment. The degree of permeability (or

*This material has been edited and was originally published as Chapter 1, 'Understanding how organizations function', in *Designing Organizations for High Performance*.

openness) in the boundary is critical for the system's survival. Too much permeability can overpower the system with external demands, too little can cut off the system from needed resources.

2 *Purpose/goals*. All living systems have a purpose, or a reason for existing. They are free to pursue their chosen course so long as they also fulfill certain expectations of their environment.

We see this in society every day. A great deal of latitude in personal values and life-styles is tolerated unless it leads to infringements on others, breaking laws, and so forth. We use the term *purpose* to refer to the organization's aim that meets its own, as well as environmental, needs. As such, the purpose is an implicit agreement or contract between the system and its environment that ensures the system's survival if fulfilled.

A corporate purpose statement, for example, would be incomplete if it focused solely on profits. Although this may be the main reason for existing (in the corporation's eyes), this is not the way the environment views it. The environment expects either goods or services that it values and it expects them to be delivered under certain conditions (ethical dealings, no pollution, etc.).

[. . .] Together, the purpose and goals provide two reference points for the organization to define the critical or core tasks of its operation.

3 *Inputs*. Materials and energy must be imported from the environment. Just as the body takes oxygen and food for its environment in order to survive and grow, so an organization draws on the outside world for raw materials, money, equipment, market data, ideas and people. Failure to import sufficient matter and energy resources leads to termination and death of the system.

4 *Transformation or throughput*. The inputs must be transformed into other forms (products, services) in preparation for transformation and return to the environment. Product specifications are developed, goods are manufactured, advertising copy is produced, orders are assigned – in other words, *work is performed*. The transformation is accomplished by the joint interaction of three core processes (*core* means something directly related to the purpose). These core processes are task, individual and group. The *task core process* refers to the tasks required to achieve the purpose. The term *individual core process* describes the process whereby an individual focuses his or her energy on the fulfillment of the core tasks. How well individuals and core tasks are linked together is a function of the *group core process*. This process refers to how individuals divide tasks, communicate, and interact with one another. Work (or more precisely, *core work*) is accomplished by the combination of these three core processes.

[. . .]

The challenge for any manager is to balance these three core processes to optimize results. This message may not seem new, but my experience suggests there are not many who are really successful at doing it. It is not enough to be aware of the core processes. What is required is a truly pragmatic way of balancing the core processes.

5 *Outputs*. Materials and energy (products, skills, services, etc.) are exported to the environment, hopefully fulfilling the purpose contract. Outputs also include undesirable by-products (pollution, scrap, rework, errors, etc.) in addition to those desired.

6 *Feedback*. Knowing whether or not the system is on target is a function of feedback. This term refers to information inputs that measure the acceptability of both outputs

and the purpose and goals. The terms *negative* and *positive* feedback, from the field of cybernetics, distinguish between two important types of feedback. Negative feedback measures whether or not the output is on course with the purpose and goals. It is also known as *deviation-correcting* feedback. Positive feedback measures whether or not the purpose and goals are aligned with environmental needs. It is sometimes called deviation-amplifying feedback.

As an example, let's suppose a rocket has been fired and is targeted to land in the Atlantic Ocean. The rocket's path could be carefully tracked in relation to the targeted destination. This tracking system is an example of negative feedback. As long as the rocket remained on track, no action would be called for. If the rocket were to deviate from its intended course, the feedback system would alert us immediately. Now let's assume the target were to be changed from the North Atlantic to the South Atlantic. The rocket would receive a new signal, indicating it should deviate from its present course and aim for a different target. This is an example of positive feedback. It's hard to separate the meanings of *negative* and *positive* feedback in systems theory from their everyday connotations of bad and good. If our promotion campaign has yielded targeted shipments to the trade, this is (in systems theory) negative feedback *because it monitors whether the target is met or not*. But a blind test result that shows our product to be at a disadvantage to competition (even though everything was executed as designed) is positive feedback. *It tells us our contract with the consumer must be renewed.*

Does it really make any difference whether we label feedback as positive or negative, or is it merely an intellectual exercise for scientists and theorists? The usefulness of the two concepts is that they demonstrate that it is not enough to merely measure our outputs versus the intended targets. Survival of the system is equally influenced by whether or not the targets themselves are appropriate. By monitoring both signals, we can avoid the pitfall of reaching our targets, only to find the output is no longer valued sufficiently to keep the system alive.

7 *Environment.* By definition, everything outside the system's boundary is the environment. The system must interface with various segments of the environment in order to survive. (An interface is an exchange of inputs or outputs.) This is the key difference between closed systems and open systems. Those who view an organization as a closed system make the major mistake of ignoring the environment. In reality, the environment provides the inputs, must accept the outputs, must support the purpose, and provides feedback to the system. Thus, its influence on the life of the system is critical.

[. . .] An organization may choose how it wishes to manage the key influences in its environment:

1 It may try to ignore the environment (e.g. closed systems thinking).
2 It may seek to control the environment (very difficult to do with *all* interfaces).
3 It may seek to balance the needs between itself and the environment.

Finding the 'right balance'– means the system may:

1 Cause changes in the influences/functions of some external groups.
2 Change its own operation in response to critical outside requirements.
3 Change its relationship with others by redefining workloads, expectations, purposes, communication patterns, etc.

The key point here is that managing the environment involves work – tasks that have to be planned, organized, and carried out just as internal tasks do. Managing the environment is also an iterative task due to the changing nature of today's environment. Thus, an organization needs to give constant attention to its relationships with environmental groups.

Dynamic processes of a system

The seven items described above are critical elements of an organization as viewed from a systems perspective. The diagram in Figure 2.1 offers a static model (a snapshot) of these elements in relation to each other. I said earlier, however, that an important part of a systems approach is to understand the *dynamic interaction* of the various elements.

In other words, this living open system (the organization) exists through time. As it exists, the parts of the system interact with one another. Thus, the systems approach helps us in viewing organization as a process – a moving, changing network of connections existing through time; a chain of events. Unfortunately this movement is impossible to diagram in a two-dimensional book. What I can do is describe some of the dynamic processes and leave you to imagine the motion picture effect this would have on the static model. Five fundamental systems processes are:

1 *Information coding.* The discussion of feedback indicated that a system needs information to know whether its outputs and purpose are acceptable or not. There is always information available to a system on these issues. The key here is for the system to select the critical elements about which to seek feedback and to devise ways of monitoring these information channels. The reception of input is selective – systems can react only to those signals to which they are attuned. This is information coding – the programming of the system to respond to certain signals and to ignore others.

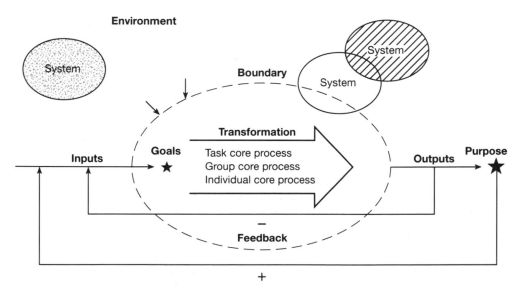

Figure 2.1   Model of an open system

Much like a computer, the organization is programmed to sift through data and present only what is desired. Coding also determines the permeability of the boundary. The coding process is evident as you go through your mail: some items are discarded immediately, whereas others are studied in great depth.

Information coding also explains, in part, why organizations seem to ignore signals from the environment that are readily apparent to others. The system's purpose initially leads to decisions about which inputs in the environment to be attuned to and which ones to ignore. Thus a shift in the environment's basic values toward the system's purpose may be missed; it may fall outside the original information code. Other systems, with different purposes, may spot the new development more easily.

[. . .]

2 *Steady state or dynamic homeostasis.* From homeostatic, meaning thing kept the same, steady state or dynamic homeostasis is the natural tendency for the system to stabilize its transformation processes within certain limits in order to survive. The goals and purpose provide 'peg points' for a system to define a path for effective operation. Although performance ideally would not deviate at all from the targets, the system usually can bear some minimal deviations without serious consequences to purpose and goal accomplishment. An initial disturbance in an organism results in mobilization of energy to restore the balance, and recurrent upsets lead to actions to anticipate the disturbance. This basic principle in an organization is the tendency toward *self-preservation of the character of the system.*

[. . .]

This characteristic of social systems also shows why it is so hard to change the way in which a particular organization unit functions: the unit will work toward maintaining its own character, which could well defeat the intended change. In other words, the system exerts so much energy to maintain stability, that it will oppose all forces that threaten it – even when radical change may be needed for the ultimate survival of the system. .

[. . .]

3 *Negative entropy.* To survive, open systems must move to arrest the entropic process. Entropy is a principle describing all systems' movement toward disorganization and death. Biological organisms break down and die. Complex physical systems move toward simple random distribution of their elements. The organization is no different unless it imports more energy from its environment than it uses both in keeping itself going and in exporting back to the environment. It can therefore store energy and arrest the entropic process: it achieves negative entropy. This is a key difference between an organization and other living systems. Plants, animals, and humans can only prolong the entropic process for a certain amount of time before they die. However, the organization may renew itself as long as its outputs generate sufficient new inputs from the environment.

Although all organizations have this potential, not all of them fulfill it. Many organizations follow a normal biological life cycle. Some even fail to outlive their founders. In such cases, their output becomes no longer valued by the environment, demand for their goods or services dwindles, and the system perishes. [. . .] The only way to prevent this decay from happening is to periodically monitor the system's outputs against what the environment needs (i.e. develop an effective positive feedback loop). Most product improvements are usually made in response to positive feedback from the environment.

4 *Equifinality*. The term *equifinality* refers to the fact that systems can reach the same final state from a variety of initial conditions and by a variety of paths. This adaptive capacity, or flexibility to get the job done, is evident in all living systems. Trees grow in different patterns, following various sunlight patterns for nourishment. Office workers cope in the short term when a flu epidemic knocks out a third of the work group. The key point here is that open systems are *self-regulating* in terms of organizing their core processes to achieve their purpose. Artificial attempts to regulate the system's performance from outside run the risk of thwarting the system's natural instinct for self-preservation. Does this mean that self-regulating systems *always* respond as needed to achieve their purpose? The answer is no. In some cases feedback systems are not adequate to alert the system to danger, or coding leads us to ignore the signals that are present. In other situations *individual purposes* may differ significantly from the organizational purpose. This explains why some individuals may not react as needed by the system. They will always do what is relevant for their purposes; this may or may not be what the system needs. External coercion and control may help improve things for the short term, but is always an unnatural, second-best option. The general principle still holds true: open systems are self-regulating in pursuing *their* purposes.

5 *Specialization*. As systems grow, they become more elaborate and form new specialized functions to cope with the growth and to maintain the steady state. Just as cells divide, multiply, and develop more specialized functions over time, so organizations create new departments and additional specialist roles as they grow. The inherent problem of highly specialized organizations is that they, like all systems, resist changes or disturbances that appear to threaten their steady state. Thus, specialized subsystems work to preserve themselves as systems in their own right – even if their purpose has changed and the environment has different needs from the parent system. [. . .]

Using the theory to improve results

With an understanding of the basic principles of Open Systems Theory, you are now in a position to think in terms of systems when analyzing organizational issues. We all face situations in which we would like our organizations to respond or perform better. Systems theory can help in planning such improvements. To understand any system's (or subsystem's) functioning, we might begin by asking a few fundamental diagnostic questions:

1 What is the apparent purpose or goal of the organization that causes activities to be coordinated into a pattern?
2 What are the key outputs and their major boundary transactions?
3 What are the key conversion or transformation processes and how effectively are they balanced in achieving the purpose?
4 What are the key inputs and their major boundary transactions?
5 What is the reactivating feedback being delivered, both positive and negative?

Reviewing these questions is like conducting a health checkup for the organization. If the parts of the system are found to be well defined and functioning properly, the initial diagnosis is encouraging. If something were missing or didn't fit properly, corrective action might be required. (*Fit* refers to the condition in which all organizational elements are congruent with the intended results.)

The next phase is to diagnose what happens when the system moves or exerts itself – do all of the parts still function properly? Examining the key processes would lead us to ask such questions as:

1 *Information coding.* Does the system obtain the needed information inputs (e.g. feedback) and appropriately block out unneeded items?
2 *Steady state.* Is the system able to maintain its operation within the limits of tolerance related to its targets?
3 *Negative entropy.* Is the system able to import more than it exports by changing purpose, goals, and practices to match emerging environmental demands?
4 *Equifinality.* Is there capacity for self-direction and spontaneous self-regulation by individuals and groups to achieve the needed results?
5 *Specialization.* Does the system grow and expand appropriately without becoming overspecialized?

Again, depending on any processes that were found to be off target, corrective action would be needed.

Once the entire analysis has been made, you will have a clearer idea of why the organization's performance and results may be falling short in a particular area or areas. The theory can also be useful in giving pointers on the types of interventions or solutions that may be required to achieve levels of high performance. Because Open Systems Theory describes actual characteristics of social organisms, any initiatives we attempt should be developed with these characteristics in mind.

Avoiding common fallacies

Above all, systems theory can help the manager avoid many of the common fallacies based on incorrect or incomplete notions of what an organization is. The most common fallacies individuals are guilty of when managing open systems are:

1 *Treating a living, organic system (an organization) as if it were a lifeless piece of machinery.* [. . .] Mechanistic procedures work against a living system's natural tendencies so as to limit its potential effectiveness and output. Improving this situation calls for a redesign of organizational patterns based on characteristics of living systems.
2 *Assuming that the organization's goals are also the goals of the individuals in the organization.* This is usually not the case, unless the goal-setting process somehow clearly identifies individual and organizational needs and then establishes end points that will cause one set of needs to be satisfied in the pursuit of the other.
3 *Ignoring the complex environment and looking only inside the system for planning and problem solving.* This overlooks important influences that the environment has on inputs, outputs, purpose, and feedback. The amount of complexity, interdependence, and uncertainty in the environment also has a major influence on the organizational structure required by the system to be successful. [. . .]
4 *Looking for one best way to handle a situation.* Generally there is no one best way. When evaluating action proposals, managers should pay more attention to whether

the proposed actions will lead to the desired results rather than insisting that different groups all follow the same plan.

5 *Believing in a singular cause and effect relationship between variables when in most cases there are many causal factors.* Systems thinking helps us identify multiple causes and effects and to understand the patterned relationships involved.

6 *Dealing with only a piece of the total system while ignoring the impact on the whole.* Too often the piece is not considered in context of the whole, nor is there consideration given to the total system. We have been taught to handle one thing at a time, instead of seeing and dealing with the big picture.

7 *Treating irregularities in the system as though they were errors in performance when in some cases they might be caused by changes in the environment.* Two distinct feedback loops are needed to clarify if performance is unacceptable because the target has been missed (negative feedback) or to a movement in the target (positive feedback).

8 *Forgetting that the reason for existence (purpose) of the organization is also determined by the environment, not by the organization alone.* Managers have to align the two sets of interests (system and environment) into an effective sense of purpose.

9 *Not realizing that people, as open systems, are also self-regulating and usually function in an optimal manner when the following items exist:*

- Goal clarity
- Goal commitment
- Reasonable autonomy
- Clear feedback

The challenge here is to design a work system so that these four elements are present for all members of the organization.

10 *Believing motivation is something to give others* (i.e. it is extrinsic), rather than something that is intrinsic to individual energy level and interests. The question is not so much how to motivate someone, but how to create the conditions so that the person's energy and interests are tapped by the work to be done.

11 *Assuming people are uncooperative, when in fact they may have different goals.* Cooperation and teamwork require clarity of joint goals and expectations and constant monitoring of outputs versus the agreed targets. Handling these tasks should be a primary concern of managers.

12 *Spending much time measuring the results versus the purpose, but too seldom questioning whether the purpose itself is still appropriate.* As already covered, an effective positive feedback loop will alert the system to environmental changes, which may make the current purpose obsolete.

13 *Ignoring the group core process by issuing directives and then depending on individuals to get the job done – somehow.* Ensuring that roles, activities, and communication patterns all fit together to accomplish the task is one of the functions of organization design.

14 *Not recognizing that resistance to change is almost always connected with the system's natural tendency to preserve its state of equilibrium* (homeostasis, information coding, etc.). Overcoming this requires a redefinition of purpose and goals and clear feedback.

15 *Failing to distinguish between accountability and responsibility.* [. . .] Accountability and responsibility are quite different as they occur in daily activities. Accountability

can never be delegated. A leader is accountable for everything that goes on within an organization. But that doesn't mean that responsibility for what is done can't (or shouldn't) be placed on those who actually do the work. Being held responsible for one's work simply means that the individual shares the fruits of success and is expected to correct any errors that are made. It is precisely this sense of responsibility that meshes individual purposes with the organization's purpose and establishes the condition where self-regulation can be harnessed.

16 *Getting caught up in the core work, rather than making management's unique contribution through 'boundary management'.* The predominant role for many managers through the years has been that of supervisor. A supervisor is immersed in core work, checking the work of employees, and issuing instructions to them on what needs to be done next.

There certainly are situations (e.g. when the core processes are not meshing) that require supervision. However, if that is all the manager does, the world of organizations will pass him or her by. Boundary management is a term that has been coined to describe the role of the manager in working interfaces with the environment, maintaining feedback channels, coordinating work with other departments, clarifying purpose, responding to change, and improving structures. Dr. W. Edwards Deming, the genius behind Japan's industrial juggernaut, has referred succinctly to the difference between boundary management and supervision as 'working *on* the system rather than working *in* the system'.

3 | Power, authority and influence*

COLIN HALES

Since management is, *inter alia*, the management of other people, so a critical, if not defining, management task is that of influencing or modifying the behaviour of others. Influence, in turn, presupposes some leverage or means for attempting to ensure that those being managed respond as intended. That leverage is power, and it is with types of power, the forms of influence to which they give rise and the kinds of responses which they typically evoke, that this chapter is concerned. [. . .]

The concept of power

Any attempt to distil a comprehensive and generally accepted conceptualisation, let alone definition, of power from existing writings on the topic is a difficult task. Diverse and often conflicting conceptualisations are offered by the major theorists. Most striking is the lack of agreement on how to distinguish among 'power', 'influence' and 'authority'. For some, power is essentially a resource or capacity, whilst for others it is something exercised and, therefore, indistinguishable from influence.

The view of power as a capacity is itself beset with debate about firstly, where that capacity may be located – in individual persons, social positions, social relationships or social structures – and, secondly, whether it is a generalised capacity or a specific capacity to prevail over others. Where power is seen as a process, there is debate about whether it is manifested only in positive actions or through negative/preventative action or non-action and whether it must be recognised only when it is effective.

Influence is either seen as synonymous with power or as a process, flowing from power resources. As a process, it is viewed, variously, as generalised or specific, intended or unintended.

* This material has been edited and originally appeared as Chapter 2 in *Managing Through Organisations*.

As for authority, this is variously defined as the formally constituted power of position, legitimate power in general, power which is inferred as legitimate, since commands are obeyed, or power legitimated by the pursuit of collective goals.

Our discussion here follows Bacharach and Lawler (1980) and Handy (1981) in distinguishing between power as a resource, and influence as the process of attempting to modify others' behaviour through the mobilisation of power resources. This permits the important distinction to be made, in the context of management, between the way in which people are managed (i.e. how behaviour is influenced) and what makes that 'management' possible.

A failure to maintain this distinction is characteristic of the classic 'A–B' models of power which Lukes (1974) has termed, respectively, 'one-', 'two-' and 'three-dimensional'. The one-dimensional model (Dahl 1957) asserts that A has power over B to the extent that A is able to get B to behave in a way that B would otherwise not have done. That is to say, power exists where A actively and wittingly modifies B's behaviour, despite B's opposition. The two-dimensional model (e.g. Bacharach and Baratz 1962) asserts that power additionally exists where A is able to prevent B from behaving in certain ways. Lukes' (1974) three-dimensional model asserts that A additionally has power over B to the extent that A can influence B's wants and, thereby, B's behaviour. A's power resides in B's failure to recognise that their actions are in accordance with A's wishes and would be very different if they were not influenced in this way. [. . .]

As well as conflating power and influence generally the three models conflate power with successful modification of others' behaviour. The circularity of this is clear. On the one hand, the power of A is inferred from B's response, yet on the other hand, B's response is explained by the existence of power. [. . .] This critically ignores the crucial distinction between, on the one hand, power and influence perceived as legitimate and, hence, responded to willingly and, on the other, power and influence perceived as nonlegitimate and, hence, responded to expediently and grudgingly. The second weakness of the A–B models of power is their use of the abstract entities, 'A' and 'B'. What is unclear is whether A and B are persons or occupants of particular positions. Thus, the models fail to clarify the distinction between positional power (the access to power resources enjoyed by A by virtue of holding a particular position) and personal power (A's personal possession of power resources). A third limitation of A–B models of power is that in focusing entirely upon power as 'power over', or the advantage of one party over another, they exclude other, and important senses of the term 'power'.

[. . .]

Power resources

One strength of the A–B model of power is that it draws attention to the fact that 'power over' is essentially relational and relative: A has power with respect to B. In that sense, power relations are always asymmetrical. A has 'more power' than B if A possesses or has access to more of certain kinds of resources than B. Moreover, these resources must be things which B wants. Therefore, a power relation is a dependency relationship, and it is this which affords A the leverage with which to influence B's behaviour. Power resources may be defined, therefore, as those things which bestow the means whereby the behaviour of others may be influenced and power relations arise out of the uneven distribution of these resources.

To create dependency through unequal possession, power resources must possess three key formal properties: scarcity, importance (or salience) and non-substitutability. Things become power resources when they are only available to some, when they are desired because they satisfy certain wants and when there are no alternatives available. Therefore, a power relationship exists where scarce and desired resources can only be obtained through the particular relationship. Furthermore, it is the perception of, rather than actual, scarcity, importance and non-substitutability of the resource, by the relatively powerless, which is important.

[. . .]

We distinguish four basic kinds of power resources:

1 Physical power resources, or the capacity to harm or restrict the actions of another, which others desire to avoid.
2 Economic power resources, or scarce and desired objects or the means of acquiring them (i.e. money).
3 Knowledge power resources, or scarce and desired knowledge and skill in the context of work. This knowledge and skill may be either:
   (a) administrative, concerned with how an institution operates; or
   (b) technical, concerned with how tasks are performed.
4 Normative power resources, or scarce and desired ideas, beliefs, values or affects.

Each of these power resources are, to varying degrees, available to managers – either as personal possessions or, more especially, by virtue of their position as managers. [. . .] Thus, to a large extent, managerial power is a function of the access which managerial positions afford to the economic, knowledge and normative resources of an organisation.

Two further refinements to the personal and positional power of managers can be made. Firstly, there is the distinction between ascribed and achieved elements of personal power; that is, between those power resources with which the individual is endowed (such as physical strength, inherited wealth, innate talent) and those which the individual has learned or acquired (such as accumulated wealth, knowledge and skill). Secondly, there is the distinction between permanent and contingent positional power; that is between access to power resources which a position permanently and routinely affords (e.g. control of a budget) and access to power resources which a position occasionally affords (e.g. *ad hoc* acquisition of information). With these distinctions in mind, the personal and positional forms of power resources available to a manager may be adumbrated.

Physical power resources are comparatively rare or little used in modern work organisations. For completeness, however, it may be noted that managers may possess physical power resources by virtue of their own physical strength, or 'presence', or have access to physical power resources (e.g. security personnel) by virtue of their position.

Economic resources are, perhaps, the definitive managerial power resource. In large organisations, personal economic resources, such as individual wealth or income, bestow relatively little power, except in the case of large individual shareholdings. More important are the organisational resources to which managers have access by virtue of their position and control of budgets and assets.

Another important power resource which managers may possess is knowledge, and this may, equally, be of either a personal or positional kind. 'Administrative' knowledge of how an organisation works may be personal, as with individual experience built up over time, or positional, in terms of access to or control over information about the operation and performance of an organisation which the manager's position affords. This information may be available through access to documents (reports, files) or to other people (experts). 'Technical' knowledge of particular work processes may, again, be either personal, in the form of individual expertise and skill acquired through education, training and experience, or positional, in terms of access to or control over technical information, the expertise of others or technology itself which the manager's position affords.

Lastly, normative power resources may be available to managers. On a personal level, managers may hold beliefs and values, espouse ideas or have qualities of character and personality which others find attractive and beguiling. Equally, managers may have access to and control over certain organisational values and ideas or acquire whatever 'aura of office' their position carries.

Modes of influence

Here, influence is defined as the attempt to modify others' behaviour through either the mobilisation of or reference to power resources. Hence, for each type of power resource, there are corresponding modes of influence.

Influence has a number of alternative formal properties. Influence may be either overt, where explicit use or reference to power resources is made, or covert, where the existence and possible use of power resources remain implicit. Overt influence divides into that which relies upon the actual mobilisation of power resources, and that which relies upon their provisional (i.e. promised or threatened) use. Thus, each type of power resource has, corresponding to it, an overt (actual), an overt (provisional) and a covert form of influence. It is possible to distinguish between the positive and negative use of power resources to influence, that is, between the provision, the withdrawal or the withholding of resources.

Thus, economic resources are amenable to the following modes of influence: actual provision of monetary rewards (e.g. bonuses, pay increases); actual withdrawal/withholding of monetary rewards (e.g. fines for lateness, dismissal); promised provision of rewards (e.g. future pay increases); threatened withdrawal of rewards (e.g. written warning of dismissal); implied possibility of rewards (e.g. the 'understanding' that pay increases will reflect company performance) and, finally, the implied possibility of withheld rewards (e.g. the 'understanding' that poor performance may bring dismissal).

Whereas economic resources are offered as rewards for being subject to influence, knowledge is used primarily as the justification for being influenced in particular ways. Thus knowledge resources are used to influence through: overt rational persuasion embodied in instructions or rules, which may be of an administrative/procedural kind (e.g. 'record all deliveries in goods received sheet') or a technical kind (e.g. 'drill to 3 mm diameter'); provisional suggestion (e.g. 'try it this way'); covert 'persuasion' in the form of unwritten rules and accepted practices ('how things are done here') or negatively, through withholding information (e.g. an absence of instructions on how to complete a particular task).

Use of normative power resources to influence others' behaviour reflects their dual character. Normative power resources in the form of meanings, values or ideologies are used primarily as the justification, rather than reward, for being subject to influence. However, normative power resources in the form of attractiveness of personality or aura of office are offered as forms of affective reward for being subject to influence. Therefore, normative resources are used to influence through: overt moral persuasion in the form of ideologies (e.g. 'for the good of the company') or the offer of affects (e.g. 'to please me'); provisional ideological suggestions (e.g. 'maybe this is the right thing to do') or promises of affects (e.g. 'I may think more highly of you as a result of this') and covert moral persuasion in the form of taken-for-granted ideological assumptions (e.g. 'a free market') or personal obligations (e.g. loyalty to a colleague). Failure to employ normative resources, such as an absence of moral persuasion (e.g. lack of company values) or affects (e.g. an absence of interpersonal bonds at work), may also influence behaviour.

[. . .]

It is also possible to distinguish among the different objects of the process of influence: that is, who and what are influenced. Briefly, managers may seek to influence subordinates, peers/other managers, senior managers and those outside the workplace. Furthermore, managers may attempt to induce positive behaviours (e.g. higher productivity), prevent certain behaviours (e.g. poor time-keeping), overcome resistance to their own actions (e.g. unwillingness to adopt new shift patterns), change attitudes and dispositions, hence influencing behaviour indirectly (e.g. instilling greater concern with product or service quality) or, lastly, alter the outcomes of others' behaviour, or exercise 'fate control' (e.g. manipulating the agenda of workers' consultative councils in order to lessen the impact of participation).

Thus, from a range of possible modes of influence, managers have, in fact, a more limited range of appropriate modes of influence. Influence is 'appropriate' in three respects. Firstly, it corresponds to the power resources available to managers. Influence without the leverage of power is unlikely to work: managers cannot promise pay increases if their companies are bankrupt or attempt, plausibly, to specify ways of working if they do not have the knowledge to do so. Secondly, a mode of influence is appropriate if it utilises a power resource in a way consistent with its nature. 'Promises' of non-restraint, or 'threats' of a withdrawal of affects are at odds with the nature of the power resource. Lastly, modes of influence must be appropriate to intended outcomes. What managers seek to bring about, in terms of the behaviour or disposition of others, determines how they seek to do so. This is because of the way different forms of power and influence are perceived and evaluated by those subject to them.

Responses to power and influence

Since power is relational, responses to the use of power and influence do not simply flow as predictable, inevitable consequences. Thus, force does not necessarily bring submission, rewards do not always entice, rationality may not persuade and moral exhortation may fail to inspire. Rather, the perceptions and evaluations of those subject to influence based on imbalances of power shape their behavioural responses to such attempts, responses which are underpinned by whatever countervailing power resources are available. Whether the attempt to use power in order to influence behaviour succeeds depends upon the reactions of those over whom it is being exerted.

As for perception, the key issue is whether power and influence are recognised by those subject to it, which in turn reflects the visibility of imbalances in power resources and how explicitly influence is exercised. The more obvious the attempt to influence and the more evident is the disparity in power resources underpinning it, the more a relationship is recognised as an unequal power relationship by those subject to it. This is important in two ways. Firstly, recognition is a prerequisite for any subsequent evaluation of power and influence. Secondly, where this recognition does not occur or is distorted, power and influence may, paradoxically, be at their most effective because they involve the unobtrusive manipulation of others. This is more likely with covert forms of influence such as implied force, agreed rewards, unwritten rules and accepted obligations.

Once power and influence are recognised as present, those subject to them evaluate, or form judgements, about them. Crucially, this entails judgement about the propriety, or legitimacy, of both the process of influence and the power resources upon which it is based. Those subject to power and influence ask, in effect, whether it is proper that others seek to influence their actions, whether they accept what they are required to do, whether it is proper that others possess or control more resources and whether they should use these to exert influence. The more these questions are answered in the affirmative, the more are power and influence deemed to be legitimate.

'Authority' may now be defined as the possession of power resources and attempts at influence which are deemed legitimate and, hence, acceptable by those subject to them. In contrast, 'naked power' is where power resources and influence are deemed non-legitimate. In principle, every type of power resource and corresponding mode of influence may be regarded as either legitimate or non-legitimate. In practice, however, physical power and influence by force or threats are almost always deemed non-legitimate by those subject to it (though not necessarily by third parties), whilst normative power and influence by moral persuasion are almost always deemed legitimate (except, perhaps, for a situation of helpless fatal attraction to a set of ideas or a person). In contrast, economic and knowledge power may be deemed either to be fairly held and acceptably used and, hence, legitimate, or the result of privileged possession or access, and hence regarded as non-legitimate.

What determines whether economic and knowledge power are judged as legitimate or not is a function of the attitudes, values and orientations of those subject to them, which are, in turn shaped by many social forces. What may be decisive, however, is the effect of competing ideologies of power. Diffuse attitudes are given sharper focus by the existence of coherent ideas offering either justification for or critique of the prevailing distribution of economic and knowledge resources. The extent to which economic and knowledge power are seen as legitimate, therefore, reflects the balance between competing sets of ideas. This balance in turn, reflects the distribution of normative power resources. The legitimacy of economic and knowledge power is underpinned (or undermined) by the balance of normative power.

The importance of different evaluations of the legitimacy of power and influence lies in their impact upon behavioural responses. There is considerable debate about whether power and influence are 'real' only if they are accepted by those over whom they are exercised, or whether the hard reality of power is quite independent of its evaluation. The debate is made more complex by a tendency to focus upon different issues. Firstly, there are different conceptions of 'effective' influence, particularly in terms of what kinds of behaviour are intended and how long those behaviours endure. For example, against the view that physical coercion (or its threat) is effective regardless of what those subject to it think of it, it is often argued that coercion merely evokes contingent 'compliance', in the sense of carrying out no more than is nominally required only as long as the threat of coercion remains. Thus, the extent to which power 'must' be legitimate depends upon the nature and duration of its intended effects. Secondly, different kinds of 'power setting' are cited to argue the importance of legitimate power.

Yet, clearly, the need for legitimacy in a high-security prison, where the aim is, predominantly, restraint, is very different from a religious order where nothing less than positive moral attachment will suffice. Between these two extremes, work organisations present a more complex and problematic setting.

The relationship between types of power and forms of response in different settings is traced by a number of writers. Etzioni (1961) distinguishes among alienative, calculative and moral involvement as responses to coercive, remunerative and normative power, respectively; Handy (1981) discerns compliance, identification and internalisation as responses to power and influence, and Fox (1985) distinguishes between compliance and consent. A model of responses to power and influence may be pieced together by synthesising these analyses (see Figure 3.1).

In this model, responses to power and influence lie along a continuum from positive to negative. Positive responses are consistent with the intentions of those exercising influence, and may be regarded as degrees of compliance. Following Etzioni (1961), however, it is argued that such compliance is qualified by different degrees of cognitive involvement, or the extent to which the individual not only behaves compliantly, but also feels positively about doing so. At one end of the continuum is behavioural compliance coupled with a positive cognitive or emotional attachment to that behaviour. This response may be termed 'commitment', or behaviour imbued with feelings of attachment and self-identification and with the energy and persistence associated with that. At the other end of the continuum is what may be termed 'alienative compliance', where behaviour is broadly consistent with the intention of those exercising influence, but where there is negative involvement in that the individual neither believes in nor feels positively about their behaviour, makes no investment of the self in it and seizes any available opportunity not to comply.

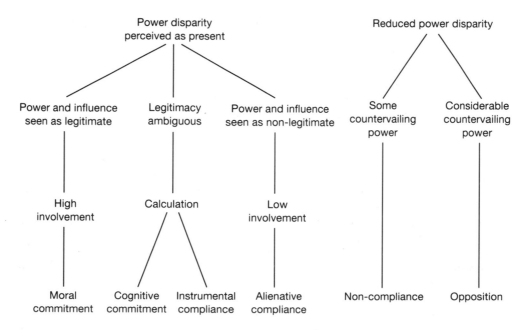

Figure 3.1   The spectrum of responses to power and influence

In between is a more contingent form of response which may be termed 'calculation', where those subject to influence weigh up, according to a rational calculus, the costs and benefits of compliance. The response is contingent in that the outcome is indeterminate. It may be either cognitive commitment, where the individual is persuaded that compliance is correct and has, therefore, some cognitive commitment to it, or instrumental compliance, where the individual sees only external advantages in complying. Whilst there is cognitive commitment in the first of these, in the second there is not. In neither response is there any affective commitment.

All the above represent forms of compliance, differing in how compliance is offered, which, in turn, reflects the extent to which power and influence are perceived as legitimate by those subject to them. Other things being equal, power resources and associated forms of influence which are viewed as legitimate evoke commitment, whereas those seen as non-legitimate produce only alienative compliance. Where the legitimacy of power resources and influence is ambiguous or contradictory, the likely response is a calculative one, the outcome of which is either cognitive commitment or instrumental compliance.

The lower the level of positive involvement, the more likely is compliance to become non-compliance at any available opportunity. If those responding to power and influence feel negatively about those responses, they are more likely to engage in different behaviour, given the opportunity. Of course, 'opportunity' is the important qualifier here. Behaviour remains compliant so long as disparities of power compel it. However, it may rapidly become non-compliant if the 'balance' of power shifts. This is the case when those subject to power and influence acquire, or realise that they possess, forms of 'negative' or 'countervailing' power. Indeed, as many have argued, the power to obstruct, avoid or create 'spaces' of autonomy free from power and influence is present in virtually all power relations. The amount of countervailing power available then determines different forms of non-compliant response, ranging from simple non-compliance (i.e. not doing what is required) to opposition or resistance (i.e. doing other than, or the reverse of, what is required).

We can now link these alternative forms of response to what has already been said about power, influence and legitimacy, by identifying typical combinations of power, influence, legitimacy and response.

1 The use of physical power resources to influence through the imposition or threat of physical harm or restraint is invariably seen by those subject to it as non-legitimate and therefore evokes a response which takes the form of alienative compliance.
2 The use of normative power resources to influence through the provision of meanings, affects and moral persuasion is invariably seen by those subject to it as legitimate and evokes a response which takes the form of moral commitment.
3 The use of economic resources to influence through the provision or promise of material rewards (or the threat of their withdrawal) may be seen as either legitimate or non-legitimate. It evokes a calculative response, which produces instrumental compliance (i.e. compliant behaviour contingent upon the continued perception that the benefits of that behaviour outweigh the costs).
4 The use of knowledge resources to influence through rational persuasion, rules and procedures may also be seen as either legitimate or non-legitimate. This, too, evokes a calculative response which produces a response in terms of rational commitment (i.e. compliant behaviour contingent upon the continued perception that the required behaviour is reasonable).

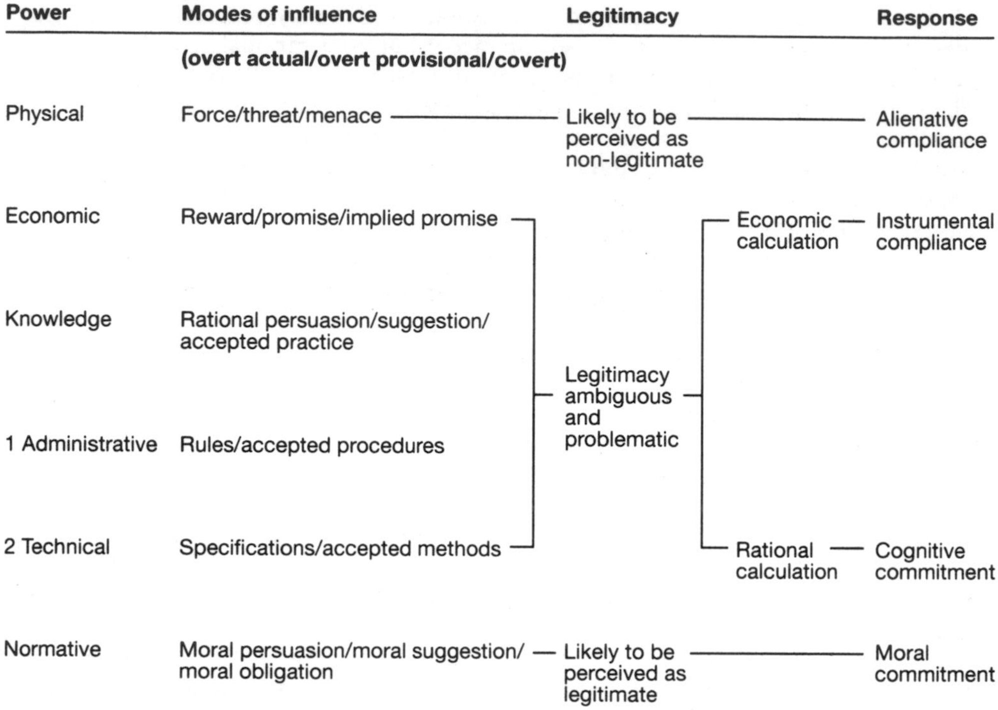

Power	Modes of influence	Legitimacy		Response
	(overt actual/overt provisional/covert)			
Physical	Force/threat/menace	Likely to be perceived as non-legitimate		Alienative compliance
Economic	Reward/promise/implied promise		Economic calculation	Instrumental compliance
Knowledge	Rational persuasion/suggestion/ accepted practice			
1 Administrative	Rules/accepted procedures	Legitimacy ambiguous and problematic		
2 Technical	Specifications/accepted methods		Rational calculation	Cognitive commitment
Normative	Moral persuasion/moral suggestion/ moral obligation	Likely to be perceived as legitimate		Moral commitment

Figure 3.2   Power, influence, legitimacy and response: a model

These links between power, influence, legitimacy and response are summarised in the model in Figure 3.2.

References

Bacharach, D. B. and Lawler, E. J. (1980) *Power and Politics in Organizations.* San Francisco: Jossey Bass.

Bachrach, P. and Baratz, M. S. A. (1962) Two faces of power. *American Political Science Review*, 56(4): 947–52.

Dahl, R. A. (1957) The concept of power. *Behavioural Science*, 2: 201–5.

Etzioni, A. (1961) *A Comparative Analysis of Complex Organizations.* New York: Free Press.

Fox, A. (1985) *Man Mismanagement*, 2nd edn. London: Hutchinson.

Handy, C. (1981) *Understanding Organizations*, 2nd edn. Harmondsworth: Penguin.

Lukes, S. (1974) *Power: A Radical View.* London: Macmillan.

4 Cultural change: an integration of three different views[1]*

DEBRA MEYERSON AND JOANNE MARTIN

Introduction

Organizational cultures are resistant to change, incrementally adaptive, and continually in flux. In this article we explain these seemingly contradictory statements about cultural change. Underlying our argument is the premise that cultures are socially constructed realities (Berger and Luckman 1966) and, as such, the definition of what culture is and *how cultures change* depends on how one perceives and enacts culture. Stated differently, what we notice and experience as cultural change depends directly on how we conceptualize culture. In accord with our opening statement, we will offer three very different ways – we believe equally compelling – of thinking about and enacting culture and cultural change.

We take the position that organizations *are* cultures. That is, we will treat culture as a metaphor of organization, not just as a discrete variable to be manipulated at will (Smircich 1983a). We view organizations, then, as patterns of meaning, values and behaviour (e.g. Weick 1979; Morgan, Frost and Pondy 1983).[2] By emphasizing different kinds of patterns, the three views of culture that we will describe shed light on different aspects of organizational change.

[. . .]

Because the three views of culture and cultural change are so different, we will refer to them as 'paradigms'. Paradigms, as we will use the term, are alternative points of view that members and researchers bring to their experience of culture. Paradigms serve as theoretical blinders for researchers and as perceptual and behavioural maps for cultural members. Paradigms determine the criteria and content of what we attend to, and as such, they determine what we notice and enact as cultural change. Below, these paradigms of culture and cultural change are described.

*This edited material was originally published in the *Journal of Management Studies*.

Paradigm 1: Integration

Culture is often defined as that which is shared by and/or unique to a given organization or group (e.g. Clark 1970; Smircich 1983b; Schein 1985). Culture, according to this definition, is an integrating mechanism (Geertz 1973; Schein 1983), the social or normative glue that holds together a potentially diverse group of organizational members. Given this definition of culture, paradigm 1 researchers use 'shared' as a codebreaker for identifying relevant manifestations of a culture, seeking, for example, a common language, shared values, or an agreed-upon set of appropriate behaviours. Paradigm 1 culture researchers differ in the types of cultural manifestations they study. Some paradigm 1 researchers focus on the espoused values of top management (e.g. Deal and Kennedy 1982; Peters and Waterman 1982). Other paradigm 1 researchers focus primarily on formal or informal practices, such as communication or decision-making norms (e.g. Ouchi 1981; Schall 1983), or the more obviously symbolic aspects of cultural life, such as rituals (Pettigrew 1979; Trice and Beyer 1984) or stories (e.g. Martin 1982; Wilkins 1983). Still others attend to deeper products of culture: basic assumptions (Schein 1983, 1985), codes of meaning (Barley 1983), or shared understandings (Smircich 1983b). Paradigm 1 portrayals of culture may emphasize different kinds and levels of cultural manifestations. Yet three characteristics are central in all these paradigm 1 portrayals of culture: consistency across cultural manifestations, consensus among cultural members, and – usually – a focus on leaders as culture creators.

An impression of consistency emerges because paradigm 1 views of culture focus only on manifestations that are consistent with each other. For example, Pettigrew (1979) examined the values and goals of school headmasters and then recounted ways in which these values and goals were reinforced by rituals. The second defining characteristic of a paradigm 1 view of culture is an emphasis on consensus. It is tacitly assumed, asserted, or (more occasionally) empirically demonstrated that cultural members drawn from various levels and divisions of an organizational hierarchy share a similar viewpoint. For example, Schein (1983) examined a top executive's commitment to the value of confronting conflicts and then cited evidence from fiercely argumentative group decision-making meetings to demonstrate that the leader's values were shared and enacted by lower level employees. Often, the ideas, values and behavioural norms that apparently generate consensus are highly abstract.

The third characteristic is that many, but by no means all, paradigm 1 portrayals focus on a leader as the primary source of cultural content (e.g. Clark 1970; Pettigrew 1979; Schein 1983, 1985). Cultural manifestations that reflect the leader's own personal value system are stressed, offering the possibility that the charisma of a particularly effective leader might be institutionalized, giving that leader an organizational form of immortality (e.g. Bennis 1983; Hackman 1984; Trice and Beyer 1984).

As a final defining feature, paradigm 1 portrayals of culture deny ambiguity. Such portrayals recognize only those cultural manifestations that are consistent with each other, and only those interpretations and values that are shared. In its quest for lucidity, paradigm 1 defines culture in a way that excludes ambiguity.

Because ambiguity will become an increasingly important concept in this article, a brief digression about its meaning is appropriate. By ambiguity we mean that which is unclear, inexplicable, and perhaps capable of two or more meanings (Webster 1985). Ambiguity is an internal state that may feel like confusion; individuals become confused when information that is expected is absent. This type of ambiguity is resolved when and if information becomes available. Another type of ambiguity from inherently irresolvable conflict or irreducible paradox may be inherently unsolvable. When individuals simultaneously embrace two or more irreconcilable meanings, they experience ambiguity.

[. . .]

According to paradigm 1, then, culture is a monolith. Integrating aspects – consistency, consensus, and usually leader-centredness – are emphasized. Ambiguity is denied. A picture of harmony emerges. Because of this promise of clarity and organizational harmony, according to many paradigm 1 researchers, culture offers the key to managerial control, worker commitment, and organizational effectiveness (e.g. Ouchi 1981; Pascale and Athos 1981; Deal and Kennedy 1982; Peters and Waterman 1982). Thus, Peters and Waterman's 'excellently managed' companies and Ouchi's Theory Z organizations, to name a few, celebrate cultural harmony as the source of organizational effectiveness. Implicit or explicit in such arguments is the managerial imperative of 'engineering', or at least partially controlling culture.

Researchers and cultural members[3] who endorse this paradigm 1 view of cultural change usually restrict their conception of culture to relatively superficial manifestations, such as the espoused values of top management. Those aspects of culture are, almost by definition, easier to control. Moreover, these advocates of cultural engineering usually think of culture as one of many organizational variables to manipulate, another managerial lever, (in contrast to Smircich's view of culture as something an organization is).

Other paradigm 1 researchers focus on deeper manifestations of culture, such as taken-for-granted assumptions and understandings that underlie behavioural norms or artefacts, such as stories (e.g. Barley 1983; Smircich 1983b; Schein 1983, 1985). Cultural persistence (Zucker 1977) and habit (Berger and Luckmann 1966) are implied in an approach that conceives of culture in terms of these deeper, taken-for-granted qualities. Thus, researchers who view culture in this institutionalized light accept persistence, inertia and thus resistance to change as part of their culture conception (e.g. Selznick 1957; Clark 1970; Sathay 1985). Yet, regardless of the revolutionary nature of this process, even these researches do admit (and some even advocate) the possibility of cultural change.

A paradigm 1 view of cultural change

Both sets of paradigm 1 perspectives – those based on relatively superficial manifestations and those rooted in deep assumptions – view cultural change in terms of a monolithic process, as an organization-wide phenomenon. Paradigm 1 researchers usually define cultural change in attitudinal or cognitive terms, to distinguish it from other forms of organizational change. [. . .] Perhaps because of their attitudinal or cognitive focus, most paradigm 1 views of cultural change are similar to models of individual learning (e.g. Rogers 1961; Bandura 1977).

Schein for example, describes individual and cultural change as a three-stage process (Schein 1968, 1985), requiring a temporary lapse in denial of ambiguity. First, individuals (and organizations) experience an unfreezing stage. The ambiguity of the unknown is acknowledged and disconfirming evidence is recognized. Schein argues that a critical part of this unfreezing stage is the creation of psychological safety. Such safety is essential for disconfirming information, and the resulting ambiguity, to be allowed into consciousness. In stage two change takes place. New behaviours and their meanings are learned. In stage three, which Schein calls 'refreezing', ambiguity is again denied and the new ways of behaving and interpreting become internalized. In this model, the acknowledgement of ambiguity is strictly a temporary, albeit necessary, stage in the change process. Schein's change model assumes that leaders can and do affect cultural change in organizations.

Other researchers agree that an essential (and possibly the only) function of leaders is the management of meaning in organizations (Clark 1972; Pfeffer 1981). [. . .] Paradigm 1 models of change (e.g. Brunsson 1985; Pettigrew 1985) offer a sequential portrayal of the organization-wide collapse and regeneration of a monolithic culture: clarity, the introduction of ambiguity, new clarity.

[. . .]

Paradigm 1 descriptions of the cultural change process focus attention on organization-wide changes in what is shared. A total world view is collapsed, to be replaced by an equally monolithic perspective. This is revolutionary change, similar in many ways to Kuhn's (1962) portrait of scientific revolutions. However, to varying extents, paradigm 1 researchers and practitioners assume that this process can (and several will argue *should*) be intentionally engineered or at least controlled by top management (Barnard 1938; Selznick 1957; Golding 1980). While important differences exist among paradigm 1 researchers, they generally emphasize these characteristics and share a common set of blind spots. These blind spots, and their importance, become evident if we look at culture and cultural change from alternative lenses.

Paradigm 2: Differentiation

In contrast to paradigm 1's emphasis on integration and homogeneity, a paradigm 2 approach to culture is characterized by differentiation and diversity. [. . .] Paradigm 2 researchers pay attention to inconsistencies, lack of consensus, and non-leader-centred sources of cultural content. This approach emphasizes the importance of various sub-units, including groups and individuals (Louis 1983; Nord 1985) who represent constituencies based within and outside the organization. In contrast to paradigm 1's relatively closed-system conception of culture, a paradigm 2 perspective is an open-system perspective; culture is formed by influences from inside and outside the organization.

According to paradigm 2, organizations are not simply a single, monolithic dominant culture. Instead, a culture is composed of a collection of values and manifestations, some of which may be contradictory. For example, espoused values may be inconsistent with actual practices (e.g. Meyer and Rowan 1977; Christenson and Kreiner 1984), or rituals and stories may reflect contradictions between formal rules and informal norms (e.g. Smith and Simmons 1983; Siehl 1984). Sometimes, the assumption of a common language must be suspended, as it becomes clear that the same words carry contrasting meanings in different contexts (e.g. Jamison 1985).

In part because of this stress on inconsistency, paradigm 2 portrayals of culture often emphasize disagreement rather than consensus. Complex organizations reflect broader societal cultures and contain elements of occupational, hierarchical, class, racial, ethnic, and gender-based identifications (Beyer 1981; Trice and Beyer 1984; Van Maanen and Barley 1984). These sources of diversity often create overlapping, nested subcultures.

Different types of subcultures can be distinguished (Louis 1983). For example, subcultural differences may represent disagreements with an organization's dominant culture, as in a counter-culture (Martin and Siehl 1983). Or, subcultural identifications may be orthogonal to a dominant culture, reflecting functional, national, occupational, ethnic, or project affiliations (e.g. Gregory 1983; Van Maanen and Barley 1984). Or still, a subculture might enhance a dominant culture. For example, members of one particular functional area may fanatically support the values espoused by top management (e.g. Martin, Sitkin and Boehm 1985).

Paradigm 2 emphasizes multiple, rather than leader generated, sources of cultural content. Gregory (1983), representing an extreme paradigm 2 position, argues that organizations are reflections and amalgamations of surrounding cultures, including national, occupational, and ethnic cultures. An organization, she argues, is simply an arbitrary boundary around a collection of subcultures. [. . .] Instead, we believe it is more informative to define organizational culture as a nexus where broader, societal 'feeder' cultures come together. What is unique, then, is the specific combination of cultures that meet within an organization's boundary (Martin 1986).

[. . .]

Some researchers combine a paradigm 2 with a paradigm 1 approach. For example, Lawrence and Lorsch (1967) argue that an organization's proper mix of integrating and differentiating forces is based, in part, on the nature of its environment. In cultural terms this means that an organization would probably be composed of a diverse set of subcultures that share some integrating elements of a dominant culture (e.g. Martin, Sitkin and Boehm 1985). As in formal structure, the mix of cultural integration and differentiation would depend in part on the nature of the organization and its environment. [. . .] Rather than only focusing on the integrating dominant umbrella, as from a purely paradigm 1 perspective, this hybrid view of culture also draws attention to the differentiated subcultures beneath it.

Some complications, due to the conceptual relationship between paradigms 1 and 2, merit discussion. Even if a paradigm 2 portrayal of an organizational culture includes an acknowledgement of elements of a dominant culture, the primary focus of attention is on inconsistencies and subcultural differentiation. This focus is complicated by considerations of levels of analysis. Any subculture is a smaller version of paradigm 1 integration, characterized within its boundaries by consistency and consensus. Thus, the contradictions and disagreements, characteristic of paradigm 2, become visible only at higher, organization-wide levels of analysis. In addition, at the individual level of analysis, a single person may be a member of several overlapping, nested subcultures, some of which may hold opposing views. For example, an organizational member may be a divisional manager, an engineer, a Stanford MBA, a New England Yankee, and a female. Each of these individual characteristics may be associated with membership in an organizational subculture, creating psychological inconsistency and conflict at the individual level of analysis. Thus, paradigm 2 has implications for organizational, subcultural, and individual levels of analysis.

Because of its awareness of these levels of analysis and its inclusion of sources of cultural content external to the organization, a paradigm 2 portrayal of cultural content is complicated. Yet these complications are still relatively clear, not ambiguous. Paradigm 2 reduces awareness of ambiguity by channelling it, and thereby limits its potentially bewildering and paralysing effects. [. . .] The potential complexities of the cultural domain are thereby reduced to dichotomies. Each subculture is an island of localized lucidity, so that ambiguity lies only in the interstices among the subcultures. Paradigm 2 channels ambiguity, as swift currents create channels around islands. This frees each subculture to perceive and respond to only a small part of the complexities and uncertainties of the organization's environment. Environmental complexity and uncertainty

Table 4.1 Contrasting the paradigms

Name	Paradigm 1: integration	Paradigm 2: differentiation	Paradigm 3: ambiguity
Degree of consistency among cultural manifestations	Consistency	Inconsistency and consistency	Lack of clarity (neither clearly consistent nor clearly inconsistent), and irreconcilable inconsistencies
Degree of consensus among members of culture	Organization-wide	Within, not between, subcultures	Issue-specific consensus, dissensus, and confusion among individuals
Reaction to ambiguity	Denial	Channelling	Acceptance
Metaphor for paradigm	Hologram; Clearing in jungle	Islands of clarity in sea of ambiguity	Web; jungle

is therefore experienced as manageable, rather than as overwhelming ambiguity. Table 4.1 summarizes these differences between paradigms 1 and 2.

A paradigm 2 view of cultural change

A paradigm 1 perspective draws attention to cultural changes that are often controlled by top management and shared throughout an organization. With a paradigm 2 perspective, however, diffuse and unintentional sources of change are more salient. This is an open-system perspective that explicitly links cultural change to other sources and types of change. Due to the prevalence of subcultural differentiation, such cultural changes will be more localized, rather than organization-wide, and more incremental, rather than revolutionary. Thus, paradigm 2 discussions of cultural change emphasize fluctuations in the content and composition of subcultures, variations in the structural and interpersonal relations among subcultures, and changes in the connections between subcultures and the dominant culture. Such localized changes may be loosely coupled to changes occurring within a dominant culture (Weick 1976).

[. . .]

Paradigm 2 views of cultural change emphasize environmental (or external) catalysts for change that have localized impact on many facets of organizational functioning. [. . .] The next section of this chapter focuses on recent work in two traditional non-cultural domains, differentiation and loose coupling, and explores the relevance of these ideas for a paradigm 2 view of change.

Differentiation channels attention so that a single organizational subunit enacts and responds to a small portion of an organization's overall environment. Channelling attention in this manner links subunits more tightly to their immediate environments, yet perhaps more loosely to each other (March and Simon 1958; March and Olsen 1976). Thus, subcultures in differentiated organizations are often loosely coupled to each other. Loose coupling can buffer the effects of subunits' responses, encouraging localized adaptation and experimentation (Weick 1976). Loose coupling dampens the flow of information within an organization across subunits. Subunits can experiment and respond to turbulent environments knowing the effects of actions and interpretations will be localized and the organization, as a whole, will be buffered from the repercussions of their actions. For example, subunits at an organization's periphery may be loosely coupled to subunits as its technical core (Thompson 1967; Weick 1976; Meyer and Rowan 1977; Scott 1981). Or, subunits that reflect an organization's dominant ideology may be loosely coupled to subunits that reflect dissent or deviance.

By localizing subunit responses (including behaviours, beliefs, and interpretations), and allowing inconsistencies to persist, loose coupling provides local havens for deviance and change. Indeed, loose coupling may provide the psychological safety that, according to Schein, is necessary to induce change. A paradigm 1 view of cultural change is traumatic because it entails an organization-wide collapse of a world view. In contrast, a paradigm 2 model of cultural change is incremental and localized; abrupt jolts that are caused by subcultures' adaptive responses, experiments, and idiosyncratic actions are dampened by loose coupling.

Although loose coupling has some beneficial effects, such as permitting deviance, providing safety for experimentation, and encouraging localized responses, it may also cause problems. For example, loose coupling may inhibit organization-wide changes. Top down organization-wide planned change efforts would have to cope with loosely coupled information channels and subunits' differential responses to information. Localized responses to environmental contingencies, and lessons from such responses, may not ripple beyond an acting subunit. A loosely coupled organization may not be equipped with the structures or processes which would enable it to transmit and retain the lessons from incremental, localized responses (Weick 1979).

Change from a paradigm 2 perspective, then, is localized, incremental, and often environmentally stimulated (if not controlled). Those studying or enacting change from a paradigm 2 perspective, but desiring an organization-wide impact, would therefore face a difficult predicament. Because locally based changes are often diffuse and loosely coupled to each other, their organization-wide repercussions are difficult to predict and problematic to control.

Paradigm 2's focus on locally based change is quite different from paradigm 1's concern with global patterns of change. When viewing an organization through a paradigm 2 lens, cultural members and researchers may not even be able to recognize changes in organization-wide patterns of consistency and consensus. A shared, integrating vision or common language is often unrecognized from this perspective. Moreover, paradigm 2 channels ambiguity. So, in addition to missing these paradigm 1 sources of clarity and integration, members and researchers with a paradigm 2 perspective also miss some evidence of people's perceptions of ambiguity.

Paradigm 3: Ambiguity

[. . .]
There is a third reaction to ambiguity that results in such a different concept of culture (and cultural change) that we have called it paradigm 3. Rather than denying or channelling it, ambiguity could be accepted. Complexity and lack of clarity could be legitimated and even made the focus of attention; from a paradigm 3 perspective, irreconcilable interpretations are simultaneously entertained; paradoxes are embraced. A culture viewed from a paradigm 3 vantage point would have no shared, integrated set of values, save one: an awareness of ambiguity itself.

Unlike paradigm 1, in paradigm 3 awareness of ambiguity is not experienced as a temporary stage in the process of attaining a new vision of clarity. From a paradigm 3 perspective, ambiguity is thought of as the way things are, as the 'truth', not as a temporary state awaiting the discovery of 'truth'. From this perspective, the clarity of paradigm 1 is viewed as over-simplification. Consistency and consensus are considered abstract illusions created by management (Siehl 1984) for the purposes of control.

In paradigm 3, cultural manifestations are not clearly consistent or inconsistent with each other. Instead, the relationships among manifestations are characterized by a lack of clarity from ignorance or complexity. Differences in meaning, values, and behavioural norms are seen as incommensurable and irreconcilable. Paradigm 2's attempts to achieve reconciliation by channelling attention (and thus differences) to discrete subunits (March and Simon 1958), or even attempts to resolve differences through sequential attention (Cyert and March 1963), would be seen as inevitably unsuccessful efforts to mask enduring difficulties. Similarly, organizational processes designed to resolve irreconcilable conflict are seen as temporary and superficial smoke screens. From a paradigm 3 perspective, researchers and cultural members see (and even look for) confusion, paradox, and perhaps even hypocrisy – that which is not clear. Rather than being 'a small clearing of lucidity in a formless, dark, always ominous jungle', a paradigm 3 enacted culture is the jungle itself.

A paradigm 3 portrayal of culture cannot be characterized as generally harmonious or full of conflict. Instead, individuals share some viewpoints, disagree about some, and are ignorant of or indifferent to others. Consensus, dissensus, and confusion coexist, making it difficult to draw cultural and subcultural boundaries. Certainly those boundaries would not coincide with structural divisions or permanent linking roles, as an absence of stability and clarity would weaken the impact of these integrating and differentiating mechanisms. Even the boundary around the organization would be amorphous and permeable, as various 'feeder' cultures from the surrounding environment fade in and out of attention.

Paradigm 3 resembles some non-cultural streams of organizational research. The first stream is exemplified by the work of March and his colleagues in their characterization of some organizations – particularly large public sector bureaucracies and educational institutions – as 'organized anarchies' (e.g. March and Olsen 1976; Sproull, Weiner and Wolf 1978; Starbuck 1983; Brunsson 1985; March and Cohen 1986). New or unusually innovative organizations are often viewed from a paradigm 3 perspective. Subcultures may also be havens from a paradigm 3 perspective. For example, members of research and development laboratories, and independent business units working within a larger corporate framework often seem to retain an unusual degree of comfort with ambiguity, and may even thrive on it. That kind of comfort is also evident among members of some occupational subcultures, such as academic research, book publishing, social work, and international business development. Finally, personality research indicates that some individuals develop unusually high tolerances for ambiguity (e.g. Rokeach 1960; Kahn *et al.* 1964; Van Sell, Brief and Schuler 1981). Thus, the acceptance of ambiguity, characteristic of paradigm 3, can surface at various levels of analysis.

One metaphor for a paradigm 3 enacted culture is a web. Individuals are nodes in the web, temporarily connected by shared concerns to some but not all the surrounding nodes. When a particular issue becomes salient, one pattern of connections becomes relevant. That pattern would include a unique array of agreements, disagreements, pockets of ignorance, and hypocrisy. A different issue would draw attention to a different pattern of connections. But from a paradigm 3 perspective, patterns of attention are transient and several issues and interpretations – some of which are irreconcilable – may become salient simultaneously. Thus, at the risk of mixing metaphors, the web itself is a momentary and blurred image, merely a single frame in a high speed motion picture: 'from this standpoint, culture is as much a dynamic, evolving way of thinking and doing as it is a stable set of thoughts and actions' (Van Maanen and Barley 1984: 307).

[. . .]

A paradigm 3 view of cultural change

What does change mean within this context? If culture is enacted or perceived in terms of a 'web' culture, in terms of transient patterns of attention that loosely link an amorphous set of individuals, then culture must be continually changing. Any change among and between individuals, among the patterns of connections and interpretations, is cultural change (at the organizational or sub-organizational level). Whereas paradigm 2 focuses our attention on environmental sources of subcultural change, paradigm 3 stresses individual adjustment to environmental fluctuations, including patterns of attention and interpretation.

[. . .]

Although cultural change is continual in a paradigm 3 enacted culture, it may go unnoticed. To be salient, change requires a backdrop of clarity. For a change in organizational patterns to be recognized, relatively stable patterns must have been acknowledged. For a subculture to be considered different in some way, members must be aware of their past subcultural connections. For a change in role relationships to be acknowledged, roles had to have been understood. A paradigm 3 portrayal of cultural change is paradoxical: it is continual and obscure. Whereas ambiguity tends to be invisible from the perspectives of paradigms 1 and 2, changes, as well as patterns of stability, become invisible from a paradigm 3 viewpoint. Not surprisingly, cultural change, conceived from such a dynamic and open-system perspective is virtually uncontrollable. Table 4.2 summarizes the three paradigms' views of cultural change.

Table 4.2   Contrasting the approaches to cultural change

Characteristics of cultural change	Paradigm 1	Paradigm 2	Paradigm 3
Nature of process	Revolutionary	Incremental	Continual
Scope	Organization-wide	Localized and loosely coupled	Issue-specific changes among individuals
Source	Often leader-centred	External and internal catalysts	Individual adjustments attention interpretation
Implications for managing process	If superficial, then controllable; if deeper, then difficult but possible, to control	Predictable and unpredictable sources and consequences of change	Relatively uncontrollable due to continual change

Paradigm 3 offers an approach to psychological safety that is radically different from that of the other two paradigms. That approach to safety has important implications for cultural change. In paradigm 1 psychological safety is provided by a solid foundation of clarity. In paradigm 2 psychological safety is provided by loose coupling between the locus of change – the subculture – and the rest of the organization. In paradigm 3 psychological safety is provided by a heightened awareness and acceptance of ambiguity. Expectations and evaluation criteria are not clear. Means and ends are perceived as connected loosely, if at all. Because it is difficult to connect actions to outcomes, individuals are less at risk when they experiment. Negative consequences of their actions are hard to detect. To the extent that a locus of control exists, it lies within the individual. Thus, a paradigm 3 perspective gives individuals a heightened sense of autonomy, and that autonomy brings safety.

Acceptance of ambiguity allows individuals greater freedom to act, to play, and to experiment (Rogers 1961; March and Olsen 1976; Weick 1979). With this freedom, preferences and interpretations can be allowed to emerge from actions, rather than prospectively guide behaviours (March and Olsen 1976; March 1981; Starbuck 1983; Brunsson 1985; Weick 1979, 1985). For these reasons, a paradigm 3 perspective should be most likely to be adopted in settings where creativity and constant experimentation are valued (classrooms, research laboratories, innovative industries, etc.); in contexts where ambiguity is unavoidably salient (large public bureaucracies and political organizations); in occupations where technology is unclear (social work and book publishing); and in work where ideological and cognitive openness is required (such as cross-cultural business and inter-organizational negotiations). In these situations, change is constant; indeed, change is the business of many of these kinds of organizations and occupations. Ironically then, paradigm 3's acceptance of ambiguity simultaneously fosters and obscures continual change – the very prevalence of that change makes it difficult to control.

Conclusion

[. . .]

These three paradigmatic views have quite different implications for those who wish to manage the cultural change process. Paradigm 1 carries the hope, and often the promise, that organization-wide cultural changes can be successfully initiated and controlled by those who hold leadership positions. It is of little surprise, then, that researchers and practitioners who write about the possibility and pragmatics of managing cultural change, usually do so from a paradigm 1 view. Paradigm 2 offers a more constricted view, suggesting that efforts to manage cultural change have localized impact – both intentional and unintentional – but that predictable, organization-wide control will be unlikely. Paradigm 3 suggests that all cultural members, not just leaders, inevitably and constantly change and are changed by the cultures they live in. Thus, beliefs about cultural control are determined and reflected by a person's choice or paradigmatic viewpoints.

The predicament of would-be 'value engineers' is further complicated if we are correct in our belief that, at any given time, a culture can be described and enacted from any and all three paradigms. To varying degrees, the processes of change suggested by each paradigm may be simultaneously occurring within a single organization. Thus, it is crucially important, for full understanding, to view any one organizational setting from all three paradigmatic viewpoints. This three-paradigm perspective draws attention to those aspects of cultural change that are, and more importantly perhaps, are not amenable to managerial control.

However, since paradigms serve as blinders for researchers and organizational members, it is likely that any one individual will find it easiest to view culture from only one paradigmatic perspective. This causes blind spots. If cultural change is perceived and enacted from only one paradigmatic perspective, then other sources and types of change may not be considered. If researchers and members focus on 'top-down' organizational-level processes, they will miss 'bottom-up' sources of change. If they attend only to locally based changes, they will miss global patterns and masked ambiguities. And, if ambiguities are ignored or hidden, experimentation and 'playfulness' may be inhibited. But by maintaining a constant awareness of ambiguity, individuals may not be able to notice change. Or, if their acknowledgement of ambiguity is sudden, they risk trauma and action paralysis.

An awareness of all three paradigms simultaneously would avoid the usual blind spots associated with any single perspective. However, a paradigm comprises a set of assumptions about culture, and thus, about organization. It determines the cultural 'reality' that members and researchers socially construct. As such, holding all three paradigms simultaneously – enacting multiple realities (and understanding their dynamic inter-relationships) – is extremely difficult. Yet to develop a better understanding of how organizations change, we must consider the complex dynamics of culture as well as those inter-related change processes from such a multi-paradigm approach.

Notes

1 The authors wish to thank Dan Denison, David Jemison, Peter Robertson, Edgar Schein, and Sim Sitkin for their helpful comments on an earlier draft. Portions of this article were presented at the meetings of the International Conference on Organizational Culture and Symbolism, Montreal, Canada, 1986, and the Annual meeting of the Academy of Management, Chicago, 1986.
2 Unlike many researchers who take a cognitive approach to culture (e.g. Geertz, 1973), we believe behaviours, as reflected in informal and formal organizational practices, must be included as part of culture. Because practices reflect specific, material conditions of existence that often are not reflected in the world of beliefs or ideas, it is essential that the study of culture includes these structural, economic, and social realities.
3 Paradigms are viewpoints, not objective attributes of a culture. Thus, both researchers and cultural members may or may not adopt the same paradigmatic perspective on a specific cultural context.

References

Barley, S. (1983) Semiotics and the study of occupational and organizational cultures. *Administrative Science Quarterly*, 28: 393–413.
Barnard, C. (1938) *Functions of the Executive*. Cambridge: Harvard University Press.
Bennis, W. (1983) The artform of leadership, in S. Srivastva and associates (eds) *The Executive Mind*. San Francisco: Jossey Bass.
Berger, P. and Luckmann, T. (1966) *The Social Construction of Reality*. New York: Doubleday.

Beyer, J. B. (1981) Ideologies, values, and decision-making in organizations, in P. Nystrom and W. Starbuck (eds) *Handbook of Organizational Design*, pp. 166–201. New York: Oxford University Press.

Brunnson, N. (1985) *The Irrational Organization*. New York: Wiley.

Christensen, S. and Kreiner, K. (1984) *On the Origin of Organizational Cultures*. Paper prepared for the First International Conference on Organizational Symbolism and Corporate Culture. Lund, Sweden.

Clark, B. (1970) *The Distinctive College: Antioch, Reed and Swarthmore*. Chicago: Aldine.

Clark, B. (1972) The organizational saga in higher education. *Administrative Science Quarterly* 17: 178–84.

Cyert, R. and March, J. (1963) *A Behavioral Theory of the Firm*. Englewood Cliffs, NJ: Prentice-Hall.

Deal, T. and Kennedy, A. (1982) *Corporate Cultures: The Rites and Rituals of Corporate Life*. Reading, MA: Addison-Wesley.

Geertz, C. (1973) *The Interpretation of Culture*. New York: Basic Books.

Golding, D. (1980) Establishing blissful clarity in organizational life: Managers. *Sociological Review*, 28: 763–82.

Gregory, K. (1983) Native view paradigms: multiple cultures and culture conflicts in organizations. *Administrative Sciences Quarterly*, 28: 359–76.

Hackman, R. (1984) The Transition that Hasn't Happened. Unpublished manuscript, Yale University, New Haven.

Jamison, M. (1985) The joys of gardening: collectivist and bureaucratic cultures in conflict. *The Sociological Quarterly*, 26: 473–90.

Kahn, R., Wolfe, D., Quinn, R. and Snoek, J. D. (1964) *Organizational Stress: Studies in the Role Conflict and Ambiguity*. New York: Wiley.

Kuhn, T. (1962) *The Structure of Scientific Revolutions*. Chicago: University of Chicago Press.

Lawrence, P. and Lorsch, J. (1967) Differentiation and integration in complex organizations. *Administrative Science Quarterly*, 12: 1–47.

Louis, M. (1983) Organizations as culture bearing milieux, in L. Pondy, P. Frost, G. Morgan and T. Dandridge (eds) *Organizational Symbolism*, pp. 39–54. Greenwich, CT: JAI Press.

March, J. G. (1981) Footnotes to organizational change. *Administrative Science Quarterly*, 26: 563–77.

March, J. G. and Cohen, M. D. (1986) *Leadership and Ambiguity*, 2nd edn. Boston: Harvard Business School Press.

March, J. G. and Olsen, J. P. (1976) Organizational choice under ambiguity, in J. G. March and J. P. Olsen (eds) *Ambiguity and Choice in Organizations*, pp. 10–23. Bergen, Norway: Universitetsforlaget.

March, J. G. and Simon, H. A. (1958) *Organizations*. New York: Wiley.

Martin, J. (1982) Stories and scripts in organizational settings, in A. Hastorf and A. Isen (eds) *Cognitive Social Psychology*, pp. 255–305. New York: Elsevier–North Holland.

Martin, J. (1986) Homogeneity, diversity, and ambiguity in organizational cultures. Invited address presented to Division 8 at the American Psychological Association, Washington DC.

Martin, J. and Siehl, C. (1983) Organizational cultures and counter-culture: an uneasy symbiosis. *Organizational Dynamics*, 52–64.

Martin, J., Sitkin, S. and Boehm, M. (1985) Founders and the elusiveness of a cultural legacy, in P. Frost, L. Moore, M. Louis, C. Lundberg and J. Martin (eds) *Organizational Culture: the Meaning of Life in the Workplace*. Beverly Hills: Sage.

Meyer, J. and Rowan, B. (1977) Institutionalized organizations: formal structure as myth and ceremony. *American Journal of Sociology*, 83: 340–63.

Morgan, G., Frost, J. and Pondy, L. (1983) Organizational symbolism, in L. Pondy, P. Frost, G. Morgan and T. Dandridge (eds) *Organizational Symbolism*, pp. 55–65. Greenwich, CT: JAI Press.

Nord, W. (1985) Can organizational culture be managed?, in P. Frost, L. Moore, M. Louis, C. Lundberg and J. Martin (eds) *Organizational Culture: The Meaning of Life in the Workplace*. Beverly Hills: Sage.

Ouchi, W. (1981) *Theory Z*. Reading, MA: Addison-Wesley.

Pascale, R. and Athos, A. (1981) *The Art of Japanese Management*. New York: Warner.

Peters, T. and Waterman, B. (1982) *In Search of Excellence*. New York: Harper and Row.

Pettigrew, A. (1979) On studying organizational cultures. *Administrative Science Quarterly*, 24: 570–81.

Pettigrew, A. (1985) *The Awakening Giant: Continuity and Change in ICI*. Oxford: Blackwell.

Pfeffer, J. (1981) Management as symbolic action: the creation and maintenance of organizational paradigms, in B. Staw and L. Cummings (eds) *Research in Organizational Behavior*, 3: 1–52. Greenwich, CT: JAI Press.

Rogers, C. (1961) *On Becoming a Person: a Therapist's View of Psychotherapy*. Boston: Houghton Mifflin.

Rokeach, M. (1960) *The Open and Closed Mind*. New York: Basic Books.

Sathay, V. (1985) *Culture or Related Corporate Realities*. New York: Irwin.

Schall, M. (1983) A communication-rules approach to organizational culture. *Administrative Science Quarterly*, 28: 557–81.

Schein, E. (1968) Organizational socialization and the profession of management. *Indusrtrial Management Review*, 191–201.

Schein, E. (1983) The role of the founder in creating organizational culture. *Organizational Dynamics*. Summer, 13–28.

Schein, E. (1985) *Organizational Culture and Leadership*. San Francisco: Jossey Bass.

Scott, W. R. (1981) *Organizations: Rational, Natural and Open Systems*. Englewood Cliffs, NJ: Prentice-Hall.

Selznick, P. (1957) *Leadership in Administration*. Evanston: Row Peterson.

Siehl, C. (1984) *Cultural Sleight-of-Hand: the Illusion of Consistency*. Unpublished doctoral dissertation, Stanford University, Stanford.

Smircich, L. (1983a) Concepts of culture and organizational analysis. *Administrative Science Quarterly*, 28: 339–59.

Smircich, L. (1983b) Organizations as shared meanings, in L. Pondy, P. Frost, G. Morgan and T. Dandridge (eds) *Organizational Symbolism*, pp. 55–65. Greenwich, CT: JAI Press.

Smith, K. and Simmons, V. (1983) A Rumpelstiltskin organization: metaphors on metaphors in field research. *Administrative Science Quarterly*, 28: 377–92.

Sproull, L., Weiner, S. and Wolf, D. (1978) *Organizing an Anarchy*. Chicago: University of Chicago Press.

Starbuck, W. (1983) Organizations as action generators. *American Sociological Review*, 48: 91–102.

Thompson, J. (1967) *Organizations in Action*. New York: McGraw-Hill.

Trice, H. and Beyer, J. (1984) Studying organizational cultures through rites and ceremonials. *Academy of Management Review*. 9: 653–69.

Van Maanen, J. and Barley, S. (1984) Occupational communities: culture and control in organizations, in B. Staw and L. Cummings (eds) *Research on Organizational Behaviour*, 6. Greenwich, CT: JAI Press.

Van Sell, M., Brief, A. and Schuler, R. (1981) Role conflict and role ambiguity: integration of the literature and directions for future research. *Human Relations*, 34: 43–71.

Webster (1985) *The American Heritage Dictionary*. New York: Dell Publishing.

Weick, K. (1976) Educational organizations as loosely coupled systems. *Administrative Science Quarterly*, 21: 1–19.

Weick, K. (1979) *The Social Psychology of Organizing* (2nd edn.). Reading, MA: Addison-Wesley.

Weick, K. (1985) Sources of order in underorganized systems: themes in recent organizational theory, in Y. Lincoln (ed.) *Organizational Theory and Inquiry: the Paradigm Revolution*, pp. 106–36. Beverly Hills: Sage.

Wilkins, A. (1983) Organizational stories as symbols which control the organization. In L. Pondy, P. Frost, G. Morgan and T. Dandridge (eds), *Organizational Symbolism*. Greenwich, CT: JAI Press.

Zucker, L. (1977) The role of institutionalization in cultural persistence. *American Sociological Review*, 42: 726–43.

5 | Ideas, action and cultures of schooling*

NIGEL BENNETT

Management literature often distinguishes between subjective values and objective behaviour. Young (1981) suggests instead that our thoughts and actions are indissolubly interconnected. How we act is shaped by what he calls our 'assumptive world', which is not a static set of ideas, but something we construct actively by taking 'facts', ascribing values to them, and trying to make sense out of them so that we can establish an understanding of how we relate to the world around us. Out of this process comes a fourth dimension, which impels us to act directly in relation to the world as we perceive it. Thus we might take a range of facts and opinions, including information which we cannot verify but are prepared to accept as true, and identify some as more important than others in the light of our existing beliefs. This creates a sense of what is right and good for a particular setting, and so allows us to decide whether we need to act, and if so, how. Young suggests that this active process of construction and reconstruction produces a hierarchical structure of values and beliefs. Low-level beliefs or precepts – for example, that in response to seeing two children fighting in the playground I should go and stop the fight – draw their validity from an appeal to what he calls 'middle range' constructs, which we use to manage the world as we have currently constructed it. These 'middle range' constructs are themselves drawn from symbolic, generalised, taken-for-granted fundamental values, often assertions, that suffuse our everyday actions and experience. Middle range constructs can be revisited quite frequently and amended, but the symbolic values are only revisited in extreme circumstances (Young 1981: 42). Thus we have a subjective understanding of the situation. If we fuse this together with the action we take in that situation, we have, says Young, a better understanding of how we deal with the world around us, by defining a 'life space' or 'action space' in which to operate.

* This material has been edited and originally appeared as part of 'Schools and management: ideas and action', Chapter 5 from *Managing Professional Teachers: Middle Management in Primary and Secondary Schools*.

A rather different but related idea comes from Argyris and Schon (1978). They suggest that in any situation it is possible to identify two sets of guiding principles influencing individual action. There will be the publicly stated 'espoused theory', through which the individual lines up what is going to be done with official policies or widely shared and acknowledged cultural norms. There will also be the private 'theory in use', which will be the real guiding principles behind what actions are actually taken. These may be identical, but it is equally possible for them to be at odds with each other: a teacher might 'espouse' publicly the school's formally stated philosophy of child-centred discovery learning but operate in the classroom on traditional, didactic lines. Young's 'assumptive world' allows for this: in a public setting this teacher might feel obliged to declare support for certain principles but find it impossible to carry them out in the classroom. Various actions will then flow from the perceived need to justify or conceal the discrepancy.

In what follows, we look at three important aspects of our work as teachers which have a significant influence on how we approach our managerial role. It is argued that just as issues such as school size, location, intake and age of pupils create differences between schools, so there are differences in the way we think about teaching, about the knowledge base of our teaching which creates our authority in the classroom, and in our perception of what is proper behaviour in our teaching and school life, which affect our stance towards our colleagues and our view of what is likely to be acceptable and effective managerial action.

Cultures of schooling 1: Our view of teaching

Although teachers share a common accountability to parents and governors, and through their governors to central government, for discharging their teaching duties, this commonality does not last long once we start exploring how they think about their actions to meet that accountability. In the first place, teachers of young children see their work differently from teachers of older pupils. The classic distinction between the answers to the question, 'What do you do?' is still common: primary school teachers are likely to answer 'I am a junior/infant teacher', while secondary teachers are more likely to answer, 'I teach history/physics', or 'I am a head of house'. This indicates a clear difference between their perception of what their job involves, and what they are responsible for. It is not a difference between being specialists and generalists, although primary teachers have to be competent in a range of subject areas, whereas secondary school subject specialists do not. The work of a primary teacher, handling thirty children of a particular age and embracing a particular range of developmental achievement, is just as much specialist work as that of a subject specialist, teaching a subject to a wide range of ages and abilities throughout the secondary and maybe the post-sixteen sector.

When we look at the work involved in being a primary teacher or teacher of a secondary school subject, we find more differences within each category. A reception class teacher faces different demands from those faced by a year six teacher in the same school, and teaching a year seven class creates different demands from teaching year ten GCSE students. Large groups require different approaches from small groups, classes consisting substantially of children for whom English is a second language have different needs from those of a class consisting entirely of mother-tongue children, and so on.

Not only do individual classes place different demands on their teachers, but the ways teachers respond to them are different. Wise *et al.* (1984) have suggested that we can view the work involved in teaching children in four ways: as *labour*, as *craft*, as *profession*, or as *art*. Each creates different sets of demands for the teachers to meet and their managers to attend to, and affects the nature of the relationship between them.

If teaching is seen as *labour*, it involves following set plans and procedures. Course programmes are established, the exercises and tasks required of the children identified, and all the assessment arrangements predetermined. Teachers will cover the exercises in a specified way, using laid-down teaching strategies, and sticking to a clear schedule. Their job is not to innovate or adapt the scheme, but to deliver it: the business of writing the scheme or syllabus and deciding what is to be taught and how, is not part of the teacher's responsibilities. Further, they will be supervised closely in carrying out the work. Teaching as labour sees the teacher as a production line worker in a traditional, machine-based factory, and assumes that effective practice which will produce the desired results if adhered to can be concretely determined and specified.

Labourer-teachers, according to Wise *et al.*, have to be *supervised*. That is to say, they must be monitored and observed closely in action, and assessed by reference to predefined standards of both practice and outcome. The management functions emphasised in this view of teaching are those of planning and control.

By comparison, teaching as a *craft* involves acquiring a range of specialist techniques, and learning general rules about how and when they should be employed. Teachers work without close supervision once they have been given their assignment, because it is assumed they are competent, but they do not have any say in what that assignment should be. They still work to clearly laid-down expectations of what they will teach, what will be learnt, and what forms of assessment will be employed. Teaching viewed as a craft, then, is a repertoire of skills and techniques which make teachers basically competent to operate independently on predetermined tasks. It assumes that general rules can be developed and that knowledge of these and of the techniques will produce the required results.

Craft-teachers are *managed*. That is, they are held accountable for results, but not for the methods employed unless the results are unsatisfactory. They are only subjected to close supervision if they fail to meet the standards required. Key management functions in this perspective are planning, organising and co-ordinating the work.

Teaching as a *profession* requires the teacher to go beyond the exercise of craft skills to diagnose problems, evaluate possible responses and adopt a chosen course of action. Wise *et al.* argue that being able to exercise such judgement depends on the possession of sound theoretical knowledge as well as technical skills, and that it must be supported by agreed standards of understanding and competence which can be justified by reference to theory. Enforcement of those standards will produce the required results.

Such professional teachers are not subject to management, but are supported by *administration*. Administrators ensure that adequate resources are provided, and discharge the management functions of organisation, coordination and budget. Evaluation of performance is carried out by professional peers, and a head of department, say, can only assess colleagues' work by virtue of her/his professional qualifications and status. Such a co-professional could also exercise Adair's (1983) management function of setting an example.

Teaching as an *art* is essentially a personalised view of teaching. It does not deny the importance of techniques nor of standards of practice, but because teaching rests on individual, personal understanding of what is needed for a particular setting, those techniques may be deployed in novel and unconventional ways. Rules and procedures give way to intuition, creativity, improvisation and expressiveness. The teacher as artist, then, has to rely on personal insight as well as theoretically grounded knowledge, and therefore requires considerable autonomy and discretion in order to function effectively.

The artist-teacher is not managed at all, but is led and encouraged. Once again, the results are all that are assessed. The only management function acknowledged, if any, is that of budget.

The characteristics of each perspective are set out in Table 5.1

Clearly, the relationship between the individual teacher as class teacher and the colleague as head of department, curriculum co-ordinator, or other 'middle manager' will be affected by the view of the teacher which each side takes. Only if both sides agree about the view of teaching which should underpin their practice is the relationship likely to be smooth. Nor should it be assumed that problems are only likely to arise if the 'manager' sees teaching work as requiring more supervision than the teacher. It is obvious that a teacher who sees her work as requiring the discretion to exercise her professional judgement while her manager sees it as a classroom craft which assumes

Table 5.1   Wise *et al.*'s (1984) four perspectives on teaching

Perspective	Key elements	Management relations	Management functions acknowledged
Labour	Follow set plans and procedures exactly	Close *supervision* of practice as well as outcomes	Planning Control
Craft	Possesses specialist skills and techniques Follows general rules of practice Works to clearly laid-down expectations of what will be taught	*Management* by results Procedures and techniques employed will be checked if results unsatisfactory	Planning Organising Co-ordinating
Profession	Possesses specialist skills and techniques Able to diagnose problems and identify solutions Strong theoretical grounding for work	*Administration* provides support and resources Evaluation of performance by peer professionals	Organising Co-ordinating Budget (Setting an example)
Art	Techniques deployed in novel and individualistic ways Judgement of appropriate practice both individualistic and unique	*Leaders* encourage the artist to perform Evaluation by results or outcomes	Budget

the application of general rules, will find the supervision exercised over her work repressive and constraining. But a teacher who sees his work as a craft while his manager sees it as an art will also be unhappy because the leadership she offers will not give him the guidance and direction he feels he should receive.

Public statements by the Department for Education and Employment and the Chief Inspector for Schools (e.g. Woodhead 1995) indicate a move by central government in England and Wales towards the clear specification of acceptable teaching methods. This suggests that teaching is being seen more as a craft or even as labour, with consequent changes in the kinds of supervision and control which will be required of teachers' classroom work. Government initiatives to create school-based schemes of initial teacher training – not, be it noted, education – give further support to this view, as did the articled and licensed teacher schemes. All these initiatives systematically play down the place of theoretical knowledge in the training process, making professional status that much harder to justify.

Against this, the rhetoric of teacher unions, teacher trainers and teacher staff-room conversations is a rhetoric of teachers as professionals. Ribbins (1992) comments that it may be seen as a 'folk term', an aspiration to a vaguely understood status attributed to other groups who may be regarded as professionals and who are seen to be more respected socially – and better rewarded – than ourselves. In this 'folk' language, 'professionals' such as doctors and lawyers are ascribed high social esteem and incomes because they possess esoteric knowledge barred to outsiders, regulate their own recruitment, training and standards of conduct, and can refuse the right to practise to those who fail to meet them (Becker 1962). They are also believed to work as autonomous individuals not subject to direct supervision (Ribbins 1992). Although few professions come anywhere near this ideal in practice it is understandable that teachers, faced with increasing restrictions on their autonomy, consumerist pressures from central government and a sustained public attack on their competence, should aspire to such status.

It is clear, then, that we can find a variety of perceptions of the work of a teacher, depending on the kinds of children being taught, the responsibilities held, and the fundamental concept of teaching. How this set of perceptions comes together will influence an individual teacher's attitude towards the children taught, the teaching colleagues who share the staffroom, and the parents and wider community who have dealings with the school. It will affect how they see these others, how they respond to actions, and how they act to take initiatives. It will affect what they see as a legitimate action in a particular setting – what an individual's obligations to others are – and in particular, when they see it as acceptable to take an initiative.

Our perception of teaching, then, forms a key dimension of our assumptive world by influencing what we will regard as acceptable and unacceptable actions on our own part and behaviour by others. It affects both our espoused theory and our theory in use. It is therefore a key determinant of the school's culture, in that it will influence the norms which shape informally what we do. But the difference between individual perceptions and organisational culture is that the culture is shared. This discussion has shown that it is likely that there can be disagreements between members of staff of any school about fundamental expectations, and this will have an impact on the degree of unity and coherence of the school's culture. This suggests that cultures of differentiation may be more common in schools than cultures of integration: we may have to identify subcultural forms.

Cultures of schooling 2: The knowledge base of our thinking

As well as our view of teaching, the type of knowledge which underpins our view of the world is also important in shaping the nature of our organisation's culture. Different perceptions of the world can create quite different expectations. Sackmann (1992) has suggested that it is possible to distinguish between four types of knowledge at the core of organisational cultures, each of which tends to generate different organisational forms. She identifies *dictionary* knowledge, or knowledge of *what* is to be done; *directory* knowledge, which is knowledge of *how* it is to be done; *recipe* knowledge, identifying how things *should* be done; and *axiomatic* knowledge, which states *why* things are to be done in the way that they are. These forms of knowledge bear a relationship to the typology of teaching put forward by Wise *et al.* (1984). Directory knowledge – a coherent and agreed view of how things must be done – relates clearly to the labour or craft views of teaching. Sackmann found that clear rules and procedures tended to create integrated cultures and hierarchical, 'rational' management styles. Recipe knowledge allied to dictionary knowledge relate to teaching as a profession, and are likely to create differentiated or even fragmented cultures, or, put another way, a multiplicity of subcultures. Axiomatic knowledge tended to be the basis of strong senior management groupings in organisations, along with a clear idea of who were 'the right kind of people' for the company. Sackmann suggested that this tended to fuse together dictionary and directory knowledge. Once again, it is likely to generate strong rules and requirements – a role culture (Handy 1993) or professional bureaucracy (Mintzberg 1979) – unless the consequence of strong axiomatic knowledge exercised over a long period of time creates a uniform recipe knowledge as well as directory knowledge.

If we link the idea of different kinds of knowledge, emphasising different aspects of our understanding, with our earlier discussion of assumptive worlds, it becomes possible to see the management task as trying to create a consensus around the kinds of knowledge which underpin an organisation. Axiomatic knowledge – the 'why' of practice – which fuses together in its sense of 'right' people's knowledge of 'what' is to be done and 'how', is likely to be [found in] the most easily directed organisation.

This can be very helpful in distinguishing between teachers' views on the academic content of their work and what they regard as acceptable methods of teaching it, although the two are linked. Researching secondary schools to examine the impact of external curriculum policies immediately prior to the establishment of the national curriculum in England and Wales (Bennett 1991), I found a clear culture of the autonomous, independent teacher. It was not appropriate to talk about problems of teaching or classroom discipline in the staffroom except to a small group of personal friends whom you trusted – as one teacher put it, it was unwise to be too open, and impossible to be too quiet. Although senior staff could admit to bad lessons and disasters, this example was not followed by others. In terms of directory knowledge – how to teach classes and maintain control – there was a clear culture of autonomy.

By comparison, there was no such unanimity in thinking about *what* teachers should teach. Here it was possible to find an epistemological distinction between teachers who saw themselves as *specialists* and those who saw themselves as *experts*. Specialist teachers saw themselves as subject teachers, with a narrowly defined set of responsibilities. They tended to come from mathematics and science backgrounds, and were able to define the measures of satisfactory teaching in largely quantitative terms – numbers of children passing tests. The pedagogy tended to be directive, as children were seen as having to master a set body of knowledge. As specialists, they knew that there would be occasions when they would have to teach subjects which were not their specialism, and when this occurred they were happy to accept – sometimes, indeed, actively sought – direction from the specialists in that field, concerning both content and method. Equally, as specialists they expected to be able to direct non-specialists [who] were teaching in their specialist area.

By comparison, expert teachers did not recognise the authority of others to direct them in their classroom practice. Instead of being specialist physicists, or chemists who taught children for a living, they were teachers of children whose academic background was in a particular subject. This view was especially common among the English teachers interviewed. While they could recognise that colleagues within the department might have greater knowledge of a particular author, or be especially talented at teaching poetry, they would not acknowledge – and rarely claimed – any authority to *direct* another teacher. What did exist among the most open departments was a willingness to ask for *advice* which could then be considered, accepted or rejected. The stimulus for this had been the introduction of GCSE some two years before, which had placed all teachers together into a position in which none had expertise to offer. It was therefore legitimate to ask for advice, since all that could be offered were suggestions. The consequence was a greater sense of openness.

This point serves to demonstrate a key argument of Schein (1983), that cultures are the means by which individuals cope collectively with uncertainty. Teachers rejected the idea of discussing problems in the staffroom, because to do so was a sign of failure. Failure had to be hidden, and the way to do this was to claim autonomy and discretion. Where teachers could rest their claim to success on specialist knowledge, or acknowledge together that they were facing a totally unknown situation in which everyone's ideas might be helpful, some collaboration, sharing or direction became acceptable. Thus the nature of the knowledge upon which the culture or subculture was built was important for defining the informal norms of acceptable behaviour.

Cultures of schooling 3: Openness or privacy?

The last paragraph has raised another crucial dimension to consider when thinking about school culture. Alongside the views which can be identified of the character of the teaching task, and the knowledge base upon which it is established, we have also to consider the assumptions which underpin the relationship which teachers have with their children and with one another.

Nias (1992) has suggested that teachers live a continuous paradox. Their primary concern is to establish and retain control which implies a strong sense of autonomy and discretion to do what they think is correct. However, many teachers are also very authority-dependent, happy to be told what to do and to get on with it. This willingness she identifies to get on with what they are told to do may be more apparent than real. In Scotland, Bell and Sigsworth (1990) found evidence that conformity to policy requirements was more a question of lip service than practical activity: in the classroom, teachers got on with doing things their way. Lieberman and Miller (1984) commented that this was common in the USA, both at primary and at secondary levels. The two quotations from teachers talking which they used most tellingly to make this point were the statements,

It is safer to be private. There is some safety in the tradition, even though it keeps you lonely.

and

I made a personal decision. I know a lot of teachers have done the same thing. You seal off the room and you deal with the students. You say, 'you and me and let's see what we can do alone.'

(Lieberman and Miller 1984: 9)

Bennett (1981) suggested that this privacy created a particular way of operating when taking decisions about the curriculum and teaching. Teachers would bring to any discussion a set of personal goals or wishes which they would seek to achieve, and another, equally important set which they were not prepared to concede. They would also bring a set of what he called, echoing sixteenth-century Anglican clerics, *adiaphora* – 'things indifferent', which could be conceded or sought depending on how the discussion went: negotiating points, if you like. A decision which did not achieve the desired changes would be accepted, with the mental reservation that the battle would be fought again another day, while one which challenged the reserved ground would be marginalised or ignored. It should be noted that this analysis was offered long before the national curriculum and DfEE pronouncements on required teaching approaches were part of the teachers' world in England and Wales, but Scotland and the USA both have long traditions of mandated curriculum policies which teachers still appear to resist in the privacy of their classroom practice.

A widely cited reason for this emphasis on privacy, as suggested above, is that teachers are worried about appearing to be failures. Fullan and Hargreaves (1992) suggest that it is the main reason why teachers are unenthusiastic about collaborative approaches to teaching and innovation, while Smylie (1990) argues that it generates not only methodological conservatism but also another aspect of school cultures: a lack of ambition among many teachers. Bennett (1991) suggests that the fear of failure is created by the fact that most teachers are themselves successes within the educational system they staff: that success gives them legitimacy within it. For the same reason, many teachers are more willing than academics and administrators to accept the high priority placed upon GCSE performance when judging schools: it is their own academic success which gives them legitimacy in their jobs, and to deny the importance of academic success is to deny the foundation of their own position.

References

Adair, J. (1983) *Effective Leadership*. Aldershot: Gower.

Argyris, C. and Schön, D. (1978) *Organizational Learning in Action: a Theory in Action Perspective*. Boston: Addison-Wesley.

Becker, H. S. (1962) The nature of a profession, in *Education for the Professions*, 61st yearbook of the National Society for the Study of Education.

Bell, A. and Sigsworth, A. (1990) Teacher isolation and school organisation in the small rural school, in G. Southworth and B. Lofthouse (eds) *The Study of Primary Education, A Sourcebook, Vol. 3: School Organisation and Management*. Lewes: Falmer.

Bennett, N. (1981) Who takes curriculum decisions? Paper to ARMC/Schools Council Programme 1 Seminar. Mimeo.

Bennett, N. D. (1991) Continuity and change in school practice: a study of the influences affecting secondary school teachers' work and of the role of local and national policies within them. Unpublished Ph.D. thesis, Brunel University Department of Government.

Fullan, M. and Hargreaves, A. (1992) *What's Worth Fighting For in Your School?* Buckingham: Open University Press.

Handy, C. (1993) *Understanding Organisations*, 4th edn. London: Penguin.

Lieberman, A. and Miller, L. (1984) *Teachers, Their World and Their Work*. Alexandria, VA: Association for Supervision and Curriculum Development.

Mintzberg, H. (1979) *The Structuring of Organizations: A Synthesis of the Research*. Englewood Cliffs, NJ: Prentice-Hall.

Nias, J. (1992) Introduction, in C. Biott and J. Nias (eds) *Working and Learning Together for Change*. Buckingham: Open University Press.

Ribbins, P. (1992) What professionalism means to teachers. Paper presented to the 1992 BEMAS Research Conference.

Sackmann, S. A. (1992) Culture and subcultures: an analysis of organizational knowledge. *Administrative Science Quarterly*, 37: 140–61.

Schein, E. J. (1983) *Organisational Culture: A Dynamic Model*, MIT/Sloan School of Management Working Paper no. 1412–83. Cambridge, MA: Massachusetts Institute of Technology.

Smylie, M. A. (1990) Teacher efficacy at work, in P. Reyes (ed.) *Teachers and Their Workplace: Commitment, Performance and Productivity*. Newbury Park, CA: Sage.

Wise, A. E., Darling-Hammond, L., McLaughlin, M. W. and Bernstein, H. T. (1984) *Teacher Evaluation: A Study of Effective Practices*. Santa Monica, CA: Rand.

Woodhead, C. (1995) *Education: The Elusive Engagement and the Continuing Frustration*, First Chief Inspector's Annual Lecture. London: Ofsted.

Young, K. (1981) Discretion as an implementation problem: a framework for interpretation, in M. Adler and S. Asquith (eds) *Discretion and Welfare*. London: Heinemann.

6 | Organizational structure and organizational effectiveness

BRIAN FIDLER

Introduction

In any undertaking employing more than one person, some form of organizational structure is required. Each person needs to know their own task within the organization and that of others with whom they come into contact. *In toto*, the individual tasks have to accomplish the organization's mission. There have to be ways of controlling and coordinating the activities of different individuals and dealing with unusual events. Thus all organizations have some form of structure which is more or less explicit.

The basic structure allocates people and resources to the tasks which have to be done and provides mechanisms for coordinating their work (Child 1984). It consists of organization charts, job descriptions and the constitution of policymaking, advisory and other groups. It provides basic working rules. The final element of the organizational structure is the individual job description for each employee. This needs to be written in a form which is helpful to the employee in knowing what is expected of him or her and forms the starting point for appraising staff. Thus when major organizational change is planned, organizational structure, and how it should be changed as part of the process, is a key consideration.

This chapter provides an overview of approaches to structuring organizations and discusses the components of organizational structure. Some bases for grouping staff are reviewed before a generic structure for educational organizations, the professional bureaucracy, is described. The issue of staff who work for more than one manager is discussed and a matrix structure suggested as a possible solution. The final element of an organizational structure, a job description is briefly described. Finally, the relationship between organizational structure and organizational change is considered.

Effectiveness

To be effective, an organization should be 'doing the right things' (Drucker 1977) or, more prosaically, achieving outcomes which are consistent with its expectations (Hoy and Miskel 1991). This demands:

1 An appropriate means of deciding what these 'things' should be and periodically reviewing such choices.
2 A means of allocating accountabilities to ensure that its decisions are carried out, the 'right things' are done and that the quality of outcomes matches expectations.

An organizational structure contributes to organizational effectiveness by facilitating these two requirements. This involves it in harmonizing individual motivations, group norms and institutional expectations (Hoy and Miskel 1991). In particular, the effectiveness of the structure requires a consistency among the design parameters and an appropriateness to its situation (Mintzberg 1979).

Similar organizations may have different structures. They depend on each organization's function, size and particular culture and history (Galbraith 1973). The structure provides continuity and predictability both for those inside and outside the organization. Thus it cannot be changed too frequently without creating confusion and uncertainty (Watson 1994). However, new tasks tend to be 'tacked on' to existing structures, e.g. work experience, and General National Vocational Qualifications (GNVQs), and there comes a point when a re-appraisal is worthwhile to determine whether a major revision to the organizational structure would help the school or college function more effectively.

There is no single organizational structure which is most effective for a given situation. All are compromises. The two principal competing requirements are coordination and control. Usually one is achieved at the expense of the other. The more there is tight control, the longer becomes the chain of command by which coordination between workers from different sections of the organization can be achieved. Conversely, the more individuals are permitted to respond to requests to coordinate their work from others, the less tight the control which is exercised over them and the less clear are their responsibilities.

The acid test of any structure is how it works in practice after people have had time to become accustomed to it. Any evaluation may be quite hard because individuals generally try to accommodate inadequacies in the structure and work round them. One sure sign of this is when the 'structure in use' is not the same as that which has been formally adopted. As proponents of Deming's approach to total quality management emphasize, individuals compensating for an inadequate structure can be a cause of further problems and provide a basic limitation on organizational effectiveness (Greenwood and Gaunt 1994).

Two basic approaches to structure

The two basic approaches to structure are:

1 Some form of bureaucratic hierarchy, i.e. authority based on position with formal rules of operation.

2 A collegial structure, i.e. decision-making among equals with substantial individual discretion about working practices.

Collegiality is discussed by Tony Bush in Chapter 7.

Bureaucratic hierarchy

Max Weber enumerated the following characteristics of an ideal bureaucracy (Hoy and Miskel 1991):

* Division of labour and specialization of expertise.
* Impersonal orientation, i.e. treating everyone equally and on the basis of facts not feelings.
* Hierarchy of authority for control and decision-making.
* Rules and regulations on the conduct of work.
* Career structure to progress up the hierarchy.

Mintzberg (1983) calls this a machine bureaucracy to differentiate it from other structures based on a bureaucracy. Weber claimed that such a structure can operate with a high degree of efficiency. Others have argued that its effectiveness, on the other hand, may be dependent on stable external conditions in which to operate.

Many organizational structures, including most schools, show some evidence of each of these characteristics though they are unlikely to be followed in pure form. Whilst organizations have a formal structure, they also have modes of working not covered by the formal procedures – the 'informal organization' – such as individuals reciprocating favours not sanctioned by the formal rules.

Hierarchy

In a hierarchy, each office-holder in the organization is accountable to a superior and the authority of office-holders is based on position or level in the hierarchy. Those at lower levels have power and authority delegated to them in accordance with their function. Thus power is shared, albeit unequally. More senior staff are responsible for the work done by those lower in the hierarchy and make decisions which are greater in scope and breadth. Appointment to a position in the hierarchy is on the basis of merit.

A tall hierarchy has many levels relative to its size, whilst those with fewer are described as flat hierarchies (Child 1984). Organizations with up to about 100 employees typically have four levels in the hierarchy – chief executive, heads of departments, supervisors and workers. A recent trend, particularly in multinational companies, has been to reduce the number of levels in their hierarchy ('de-layering'). This may make sense in organizations with 15 or more levels in their hierarchy, but not in schools and colleges, unless they have clearly redundant levels according to the principles enunciated below. Hierarchical levels are not the same as salary levels. In a school context, the existence of five responsibility points as in the current salary framework in England and Wales does not imply that there should be five levels in the hierarchy below deputy headship.

Although it is fashionable to decry bureaucratic structures as being inflexible and unresponsive to change, Jaques (1990) argues that the alternatives offered so far do not adequately address the basic issue of accountability. He believes that bureaucratic structures contain the essential ingredients of success, and suggests three principles to guide the creation of layers in a hierarchy. Managers must:

1 Add value to the work of subordinates as well as being accountable for it, i.e. make a personal contribution to outcomes.
2 Sustain a group of subordinates capable of doing the work, i.e. motivate and develop staff.
3 Give direction which the group will follow enthusiastically, i.e. provide leadership.

Rowbottom and Billis (1987) identify seven levels of differentiated work from operator (Level One) to chief executive of a conglomerate (Level Seven). In their terms, a teacher or lecturer would be at Level Two (making individual judgements about how to perform), a head of department at Level Three (making judgements about an area of work in open-ended situations) and a headteacher or principal at Level Four (making judgements about all the areas of work in an organization). They also identify other sorts of relationships. These they classify in seven categories (italics added):

• Line-managerial: managing staff to achieve results.
• Supervisory: help and supervision of staff to carry out *tasks set by a manager*.
• Coordinating: planning, monitoring progress to devise ways of achieving *agreed objectives*.
• Monitoring: checking on progress, reporting and *advising* on appropriate action.
• Collateral: mutual dependence; on the same hierarchical level.
• Service: responding to the expressed needs of another.
• Prescribing: prescribing tasks to be achieved and checking on results but *without any right to manage the process* to carry out the task.

These provide a greater precision in setting up and communicating work relationships. Whilst there should be only one line manager on each level having a responsibility for any employee, there may be other relationships of a more limited nature on the same level. They suggest representing the relationships on an organizational chart so as to bring out the important differences, e.g. line-management relationships in continuous lines and monitoring and coordinating relationships in dotted lines.

Curriculum specialists in primary schools provide an interesting example to analyse. They have a full-time class teaching responsibility and a responsibility for a particular curriculum area. The responsibility is not a managerial one since it does not include a responsibility for staff. A consultant responsibility on this framework would be characterized as either a service (providing advice when needed) or a monitoring function. If planning the curriculum area (in consultation with each teacher) is included in the task, it is clear that the responsibility is a coordinating one and that this is the most appropriate designation to use.

Span of control

The number of subordinates that a superior is responsible for is called the 'span of control' (the term 'control' is misleading since it is really face-to-face interaction which is the limiting factor). For a given number of staff in the organization, the span of control determines the number of levels in the hierarchy. How large a span of control can be and still be effective depends on a number of factors, principally the degree of complexity of the work being done. Where the work is complex and the work of individuals is interrelated, the span of control should be low.

For educational organizations there are special factors. On the one hand, teachers have a professional training which Mintzberg (1983) identifies as a principal standardizing feature of their work. Thus they should require less supervision than workers without such training. On the other hand, most teachers with a management responsibility carry out such tasks in addition to their teaching rather than as their sole responsibility. Unless appropriate non-teaching time is allocated to such managers, spans of control should be kept low.

Unity of command

One of the most basic of principles of any control and management structure is that of 'unity of command'. This states that any employee should be accountable to only one superior, so ensuring that the employee does not receive conflicting instructions and that one superior has an overview of the entire work of each employee. A corollary of this is that one person is ultimately in charge of any area of work. This gives unambiguous and clear lines of accountability, hence the term 'line manager'. Further, there is a 'line of authority' which passes from the chief executive officer (headteacher or principal) to delegated positions in the structure. This is referred to as the 'scalar principle':

> The more clear the line of authority from the top manager in an enterprise to every subordinate position, the more effective will be the responsible decision making and the organization communication system.
>
> (Koontz and O'Donnell 1978: 285)

Professional-as-administrator

In organizations which are largely professionally staffed an accommodating technique which may be used is to appoint senior professionals to managerial positions within the organization – the professional-as-administrator (Hughes 1985: 282). Recent work on the symbolic aspects of leadership indicates the importance of leaders espousing and articulating a vision for an organization (Bolman and Deal 1991). This may be particularly important in organizations such as schools and colleges where there are many competing priorities to be addressed and where decisions on these are value-based. Since many decisions are intimately connected with professional educational issues concerning the education of children and young people, the presence of senior staff who represent the values to which the institution wishes to subscribe, may be especially significant to people both inside and outside the school or college.

It does not follow from this precept that all senior positions should be occupied by former teachers if they do not require judgements of a professional educator but it does imply that special considerations should apply (Gittins 1989). Thus in appointing a bursar, for example, to a senior position it is important that:

- The post does not involve oversight of curricular or teaching decisions or professional practice.
- Budgetary and major financial decisions involve the headteacher and educationists.
- The post-holder recognizes that the post involves providing a service to aid the work of teachers, rather than seeking to control them, and has appropriate attitudes and social skills.

Organizational design

Whilst educational organizations have the education of young people as their principal concern, they also have to discharge administrative functions both to continue to exist and to prosper in the future, for example, employing teachers and maintaining premises. Thus, the organizational structure has to include not only educational activities but also general administrative and managerial tasks.

The activities of an educational institution may therefore be categorized as:

1 Providing educational services.
2 Organizational administration and maintenance, e.g. personnel, finance, premises and plant maintenance.
3 Planning future strategy, e.g. strategic planning, marketing.

Grouping of tasks

In any complex organization, one major problem is how to arrange the tasks and how to allocate individuals to them. Staff can be grouped in a number of ways, for example by:

(a) Worker specialization.
(b) Product or service.
(c) Geographical area.
(d) Function.

In the case of a school or college (a) would group teaching staff by their teaching subject, (b) would group them by the class, year group or course that they taught on and (c) would group them by the site on which they did their teaching. Method (d) would group teaching and non-teaching staff separately and subdivide the non-teaching staff by their function – finance, personnel, caretaking, cleaning, etc. Each grouping has advantages and disadvantages. Not all are mutually incompatible and different types may be used in different parts of the same organization, but the only way in which (a) and (b) can be used simultaneously is through a matrix structure (see below).

More senior posts are concerned with:

• Coordination and control of units which are at the same lower level.
• Increasing strategic considerations at higher levels – long-term, whole organization and dealing with the external world.
• Increasing organizational management and less direct contribution to client service at higher levels.

In deciding how many levels are needed in the vertical structure, the

> . . . first step [. . .] is to bring out clearly which of any existing or proposed posts really are to be main line-management ones. The second is to define the exact authority, if any, to be exercised by all others in the status chain.
>
> (Rowbottom and Billis 1987: 17)

Some functions may be undertaken by specially appointed employees or others whose jobs can be redesigned to take them on, but most will be further additions to the work of members of the teaching staff. Where two or more people are responsible for different aspects of some work and are located in different sections, this will either need to be within a matrix structure or a coordinating function will be required.

A related problem is how to continuously coordinate their work in a dynamic working environment. The extent of coordination and individual decision-making can be reduced by creating policies which cover much routine decision-making (e.g. school rules) and enunciate the principles which underpin further individual decision-making (e.g. equal opportunities).

Hybrid structures

A bureaucratic hierarchy is an idealized type. In practice, organizational structures for professional staff in education are adaptations. We shall examine two of these: professional bureaucracy; and overlapping work and dual accountability.

Professional bureaucracy

Whilst a hierarchy may be the basis for the most appropriate form of organizational structure for a large school or college, some allowance must be made for the professional dimensions of the work carried out. Mintzberg (1983) has coined the term 'professional bureaucracy' for a structure which is basically hierarchical but has professional workers in managerial positions and a participative mode of operation.

Components of an organization

Mintzberg identifies five component groups of any organization. The main work is carried out by three groups arranged hierarchically – operating core, middle line of managers, strategic apex. There are two groups who assist – technostructure and support staff. The five groups are shown in Figure 6.1.

Strategic apex
This comprises those who lead the whole organization or directly assist them. It is responsible for ensuring that the organization delivers the product or service to clients and satisfies those who control the organization or have power over it.

Middle line
This comprises middle and senior managers who directly control the work of the operating core.

Operating core
This group – the largest – actually makes a product or delivers a direct service to clients.

Technostructure
These are analysts removed from the main work flow. They may plan work, change it, evaluate it or train people to do it.

Support staff
These provide indirect support. Rather than advice they provide a service, e.g. canteen, resources technician, finance officer.

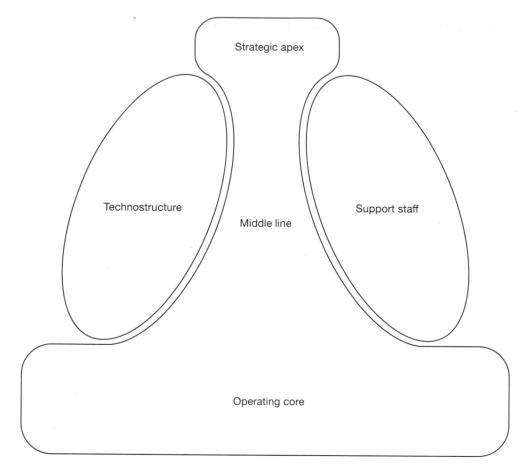

Figure 6.1   Mintzberg's five basic parts of an organization
Source: H. Mintzberg (1983) *Structure in Fives: Designing Effective Organizations*, Englewood Cliffs, NJ: Prentice-Hall, p. 11.

In different types of organization the five groups have different prominence. In the professional bureaucracy, the operating core (of teachers) is the mainstay of the organization. Typically the middle line are not very numerous as professionals achieve coordination by having similar training and skills rather than having to be supervised (Mintzberg 1983). Similarly there is little technostructure as professionals initiate change themselves. Generally there is a well-developed support staff. Their function is to serve the operating core who in turn provide the basic service of the organization to its clients.

Mintzberg (1979: 360) observed that professional bureaucracies often develop parallel administrative hierarchies: one democratic and bottom-up for the professionals, the other a top-down machine bureaucracy for the support staff. Whilst the two hierarchies are usually kept quite separate, they may be brought together in a functional unit, e.g. science staff and laboratory technicians. Either the two hierarchies meet at the head of science or coordination is achieved in the unit through a matrix structure.

Small organizations, such as a small primary school, can operate with a much simpler structure than a professional bureaucracy, as the head supervises and coordinates the work of other teachers directly. Clearly there comes a point in terms of size of school when such centralization of communication and decision-making becomes dysfunctional because the headteacher becomes overloaded, causing a log-jam in decision-making. Further, a lack of delegated authority prevents others from taking responsibility and gaining managerial experience.

Committee structure

In professional bureaucracies, in addition to posts of responsibility, a distinctive feature is the number of meetings of various kinds which involve most members of teaching staff in some way. There may be standing committees of functional positions like heads of department, and there may also be ad hoc and short-term working parties. Some research suggests that often the function of standing committees is not well defined: is their purpose to participate in decisions, to be consulted about decisions or to hear and discuss decisions which have already been made? How committees interrelate and who is responsible for expediting the decisions of committees are both often unclear (Hutchinson 1993). The extent and mode of involvement of staff in decision-making on different areas of work in a school or college needs to be planned (Fidler *et al.* 1991).

Ad hoc working parties often have a clearer mandate but a more varied membership than committees. Their members may be selected, volunteer or be democratically elected. If they are composed of members from different levels in an organization and operate in a non-hierarchical way, they may be well placed to consider future courses of action for the whole institution provided they have a clear but open mandate and are required to produce agreed recommendations within an agreed timescale (Stacey 1993). The combination of an orderly hierarchical structure and the more political mode of operation of an ad hoc strategic planning group can be an effective way of devising and implementing a future strategy in a chaotic environment. The hierarchical structure deals effectively with ongoing work and is also able to make and implement strategic decisions. A looser form of organization would have difficulty making a difficult strategic decision in an uncertain environment and also greater difficulty in trying to implement a controversial decision.

Overlapping work and dual accountability

In an ideal bureaucracy, any employee works on a single task and has a single superordinate. In practice, when much work is carried out in teams with members from different departments, this principle begins to break down. There are two ways of tackling this situation:

- rely on informal 'mutual adjustment', or
- modify the hierarchical structure.

Mutual adjustment

Mutual adjustment (Mintzberg 1983) occurs when individuals meet and discuss any problem and solve it together as a joint decision. Its weaknesses are that:

1 No one person is responsible for taking an initiative to solve a problem.
2 No one person is responsible for a solution.
3 If joint agreement is not possible, others higher up in the hierarchy have to notice and become involved.

Mutual adjustment is much used in organizations with a very simple structure where there are few formal responsibilities allocated and also, paradoxically, in organizations where the work is complex, unpredictable and pioneering. This is because no formal structure can be designed to give flexible responses to unforeseeable problems. Mutual adjustment is extremely effective between cooperative people of good will who are willing to broach and tackle problems but for those who prefer a quiet life and those of a less cooperative disposition, it can be ineffective. It can be very time-consuming and inefficient for dealing with routine and predictable problems.

Modification of the hierarchical structure

A variety of modifications of the hierarchical structure of increasing complexity can be made. The most straightforward is to make sure that teams have a clear and desig-nated team leader who is responsible for the success of the team. Any group with an executive function needs an executive leader however participative its mode of oper-ation.

In most cases, overlapping responsibilities prevent any obvious modification of the single-line structure. The root cause of the problem is the work of individuals which cannot be neatly pigeon-holed (Knight 1977). For short-term projects, a task group, working party or other group can be brought into existence. If this arrangement of dual accountability is formalized and made permanent, it is called a 'matrix structure'.

Matrix structures

An organizational structure in which large numbers of employees are in dual auth-ority relationships can be represented in a two-dimensional matrix. For example, lec-turers in a further education college may be based in divisions of subject specialists but contribute to multidisciplinary courses managed by a course leader. The course leader is responsible for the overall service to students – course structure, curriculum, provision of teaching, assessment arrangements – and for recruiting and counselling students. The head of a division is responsible for a particular subject area, its teach-ing, and the provision and development of its teaching expertise. Figure 6.2 shows a simple matrix structure. In it, staff are grouped by their specialism into departments A to E. Staff from departments contribute to interdisciplinary working groups (a) to (f). For example, staff member 1 from department A contributes to working group (b). The leaders of the working groups may be in departments or not and the heads of departments may be in working groups depending on their other commitments. In schools and colleges heads of departments would be in working groups and leaders of working groups would be in departments. If each member of staff were to contribute to more than one working group, a multidimensional matrix would be required to show the multiple relationships and responsibilities. This example in Figure 6.2 shows each arm of the matrix having equal precedence. The angle can be changed such that the most vertical arm has precedence, e.g. for appraisal (Wearne 1970).

Child (1984) identifies three variants of a matrix control structure:

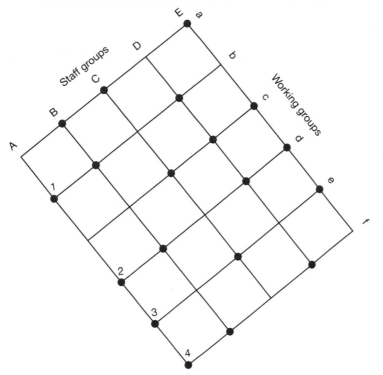

Figure 6.2   Simple matrix organizational structure
Source: Fidler, B. *Job Descriptions and Organizational Structure,* in Fidler, B. and Cooper, R. (eds) (1992) *Staff Management and Staff Appraisal in Schools & Colleges,* p. 211 (adapted).

- *Equal* – the two arms of the matrix are equally dominant.
- *Coordination* – the functional arm is dominant.
- *Secondment* – the project is dominant for the life of the project.

It is always essential to identify which of the two 'bosses' is responsible for which aspects of staff management. Failure to do so results in confusion, overlapping supervision and omission of important functions (Rowbottom and Billis 1987). The amount of detailed specification will be greatest where there is equal dominance.

A formal matrix structure offers flexibility and adaptability to change. It has open lines of communication and more diffuse managerial accountability giving greater responsibility to individual workers. However, there is evidence of conflict, lack of accountability, many meetings and paperwork particularly where the nature of the dual accountability has not been fully appreciated and allowed for. The principle of unity of command has been sacrificed in order to achieve greater horizontal communication.

In a college course, the course leader is responsible for course quality. He or she deals with students' problems and represents the course to the outside world. However, problems can only be solved by mutual adjustment with contributing lecturers or their heads of division. This is a relatively weak position for the course leader and so problems which cannot be resolved in this way have to be referred to higher levels than those involved in the matrix. One way to strengthen course leaders' powers is by placing resources in their hands. They would then commission course teaching from divisions or outside the institution. Divisions would need to 'earn' sufficient resources to continue to employ their staff complement. This illustrates a more general principle, viz. that control can either operate directly or indirectly through financial decisions.

Many situations in schools and colleges which involve a dual accountability relationship can be envisaged as matrices. For example, secondary teachers are often responsible both to one or more heads of departments for their subject teaching and also to a year or house head for their pastoral work, while primary school teachers may be responsible to both a head of a key stage and to subject coordinators. In both primary and secondary schools, classroom support staff and special needs assistants are often in dual accountability relationships where they are generally responsible to a senior member of staff, head of special needs or special needs coordinator but also work in the classrooms of individual teachers.

Job descriptions

Having devised an organizational structure, the final element is to create job descriptions for all staff. For existing staff these need to be negotiated initially and then periodically renegotiated as part of the appraisal process (Fidler and Cooper 1992). There is a good deal of misunderstanding about job descriptions.

> The objective of a job description is to record the facts about the job content. These should include the job title, reporting relationships upward and downward, the overall purpose of the job, a short description of the main activities, arranged in 'key result areas'.
>
> (Ungerson 1983: 1)

It should not be an extensive catalogue of all the minute tasks which are included within the job for this does not allow the job-holder to see 'the wood for the trees' nor to appreciate the relative importance of various aspects of the job.

Most jobs in educational organizations are likely to be a combination of:

- teaching;
- pastoral work; and
- management.

For different jobs, the relative importance and relative amount of time spent on each of these three facets will be different.

Tasks are likely to be a mixture of ongoing, short-term developments and rotating responsibilities. Associated with them will be a small number of targets requiring specific achievements over a fixed period of time. The targets may be:

- Remedial: bringing an aspect of the job back to an acceptable level of performance.
- Developmental: developing an aspect of the job.
- Problem-solving: finding a way of overcoming some problem aspect of the job.
- Personal development: identifying some temporary task which contributes to personal development but which may not be part of the enduring job description.

The targets can be expected to change regularly. Many will be completed in one year. An example of a school teacher's job description of this kind is given in Fidler *et al.* (1991) and Fidler and Cooper (1992).

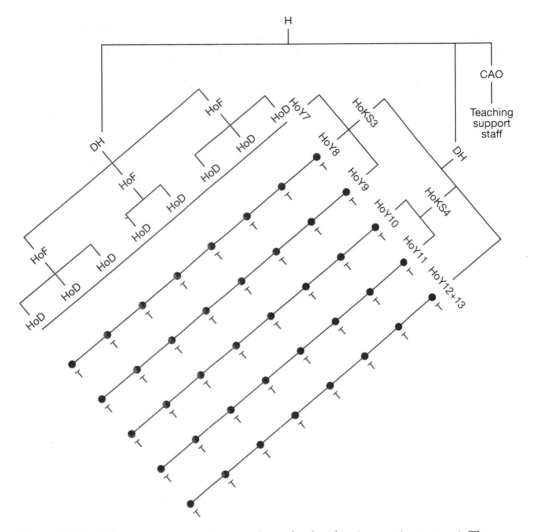

Figure 6.3 Possible senior structures in secondary schools (showing matrix structure). The senior management group might consist of head, deputy heads, chief administrative officer and heads of faculties. Key: CAO = chief administrative officer; DH = deputy head; HoD = head of department; HoF = head of faculty; HoKS = head of key stage; HoY = head of year.

Organizational change

As Glatter (1986) observed, there may be a tension between organizational maintenance and development. This can either be left implicit within the structure or made explicit by creating aspects of the structure which are specifically concerned with development. This is particularly important at the strategic level.

One place where this is visible is in the workings of school governing bodies in England and Wales. Most have separate committees to deal with a specific aspect of the school's activities – curriculum, staffing and finance, etc. – and have delegated powers to them for their area. However, issues of whole-school development require the full governing body because each committee has a limited remit. Generally, the full governing body is too large to be an effective strategy-forming body, being more suited to discuss and ratify recommendations made to it. One school has dealt with this problem by creating a strategy and development committee, consisting of the chair and vice-chair of governors and the chairs of the specialist committees as a way of combining expertise and ensuring two-way communication between the committees and whole-school developments.

At senior management level there are similar issues of group size, representativeness and two-way communication. A recent trend in secondary schools has been to reduce the number of deputy head posts, in some cases replacing one of them by a bursar post to head the non-teaching staff. Whilst cost pressures have been one spur to such changes, there may be advantages to widening the senior management group to a limited extent. Some whole-school functions have to be discharged by deputy heads but others, which have traditionally been done by deputies, can be delegated. A faculty structure, with a small number (three or four) of faculty heads becoming members of an enlarged senior management team, would both provide specialist subject expertise and provide a link to implement decisions in their faculties. Figure 6.3 gives an example of this.

Conclusion

This chapter has introduced some of the complexities of the study of organizational structures and the design of organizations. These provide the background knowledge required to make informed choices about how to structure educational organizations. Such a structure should be enabling, allowing a school or college to plan, implement and review changes to its strategy, to operate efficiently and effectively, and to review outcomes to ensure that they match expectations.

Structures are contingent on function, history and context, so the structure of each school or college will be different. However, each should aim to be functional as a whole and internally consistent in its parts. It should address and resolve such issues as: involvement and accountability; control and discretion; development and maintenance; and motivation and obligation. And, perhaps most important, any resolution of such tensions should be regarded as provisional rather than final and definitive (Pascale 1991). It needs to be fixed for the next few years and subject to review, for, ultimately, it is how any structure helps to achieve objectives which is paramount. As needs change, so should structures.

References

Bolman, L. G. and Deal, T. E. (1991) *Reframing Organizations: Artistry, Choice and Leadership*. San Francisco: Jossey Bass.

Child, J. (1984) *Organization: A Guide to Problems and Practice*, 2nd edn. London: Harper and Row.

Drucker, P. F. (1977) *Management*. New York: Harper's College Press.

Fidler, B. and Bowles, G. with Hart, J. (1991) *Planning Your School's Strategy. ELMS Workbook*. Harlow: Longman.

Fidler, B. and Cooper, R. (eds) (1992) *Staff Management and Staff Appraisal in Schools and Colleges: A Guide to Implementation*. Harlow: Longman.

Galbraith, J. (1973) *Designing Complex Organizations*. Reading, MA: Addison-Wesley.

Gittins, C. (1989) A bursar in a secondary school, in B. Fidler and G. Bowles (eds) *Effective Local Management of Schools: A Strategic Approach*. Harlow: Longman.

Glatter, R. (1986) The management of school improvement, in E. Hoyle and A. McMahon (eds) *The Management of Schools: World Yearbook of Education 1986*. London: Kogan Page.

Greenwood, M. S. and Gaunt, H. J. (1994) *Total Quality Management for Schools*. London: Cassell.

Hoy, W. K. and Miskel, C. G. (1991) *Educational Administration: Theory, Research and Practice*, 4th edn. New York: McGraw-Hill.

Hughes, M. (1985) Leadership in professionally staffed organizations, in M. Hughes, P. Ribbins and H. Thomas (eds) *Managing Education: The System and the Institution*. London: Cassell.

Hutchinson, P. (1993) 'The coupling of financial and curriculum decision making in two comprehensive schools', unpublished MSc dissertation, University of Reading.

Jaques, E. (1990) In praise of hierarchy. *Harvard Business Review*, 90(1): 127–33.

Knight, K. (ed.) (1977) *Matrix Management: A Cross-functional Approach to Organization*. Aldershot: Gower.

Koontz, H. and O'Donnell, C. (1978) *Essentials of Management*, 2nd edn. New York: McGraw-Hill.

Mintzberg, H. (1979) *The Structuring of Organizations*. Englewood Cliffs, NJ: Prentice-Hall.

Mintzberg, H. (1983) *Structure in Fives: Designing Effective Organizations*. Englewood Cliffs, NJ: Prentice-Hall.

Pascale, R. (1991) *Managing on the Edge: How Successful Companies use Conflict to Stay Ahead*. London: Penguin Books.

Rowbottom, R. and Billis, D. (1987) *Organizational Design: The Work-Levels Approach*. Aldershot: Gower.

Stacey, R. D. (1993) *Strategic Management and Organizational Dynamics*. London: Pitman.

Ungerson, B. (1983) *How to Write a Job Description*. London: Institute of Personnel Management.

Watson, T. (1994) *In Search of Management*. London: Routledge.

Wearne, S. H. (1970) Project and product responsibilities in industry. *Management Decision* Winter: 32–5.

7 | Collegial models*

TONY BUSH

Central features of collegial models

Collegial models include all those theories which emphasize that power and decision-making should be shared among some or all members of the organization. These approaches range from a 'restricted' collegiality where the leader shares power with a limited number of senior colleagues to a 'pure' collegiality where all members have an equal voice in determining policy. The definition suggested below captures the main features of these perspectives:

> Collegial models assume that organizations determine policy and make decisions through a process of discussion leading to consensus. Power is shared among some or all members of the organization who are thought to have a mutual understanding about the objectives of the institution.

The notion of collegiality has become enshrined in the folklore of management as the most appropriate way to run schools and colleges in the 1990s. It has become closely associated with school effectiveness and school improvement (Campbell and Southworth 1993) and is increasingly regarded as 'the official model of good practice' (Wallace 1989: 182). [. . .] Collegial models have the following major features:

1 They are strongly *normative* in orientation. [. . .] Their advocates believe that decision-making should be based on democratic principles but do not necessarily claim that these principles actually determine the nature of management in action. It is an idealistic model rather than one that is founded firmly in practice.
   [. . .]
2 Collegial models seem to be particularly appropriate for organizations such as schools and colleges that have significant numbers of professional staff. Teachers

* This material has been edited and originally appeared as Chapter 4 in *Theories of Educational Management*.

possess authority arising directly from their knowledge and skill. They have an *authority of expertise* that contrasts with the positional authority associated with formal models. Professional authority occurs where decisions are made on an individual basis rather than being standardized. Education necessarily demands a professional approach because pupils and students need personal attention. Teachers require a measure of autonomy in the classroom but also need to collaborate to ensure a coherent approach to teaching and learning. Collegial models assume that professionals also have a right to share in the wider decision-making process.

[. . .]

3 Collegial models assume a *common set of values* held by members of the organization. These may arise from the socialization which occurs during training and the early years of professional practice. These common values guide the managerial activities of the organization and in particular are thought to lead to shared educational objectives. Campbell and Southworth (1993: 66) refer to 'jointly held beliefs and values' in reporting their study of staff relationships in primary schools.

[. . .]

4 The *size* of decision-making groups is an important element in collegial management. They have to be sufficiently small to enable everyone to be heard. This may mean that collegiality works better in primary schools or in subunits than at the institutional level in secondary schools and colleges. Meetings of the whole staff may operate collegially in small schools but may be suitable only for information exchange in larger institutions.

The collegial model deals with this problem of scale by building-in the assumption that staff have *formal representation* within the various decision-making bodies. Significant areas of policy are determined within the official committee system rather than being a prerogative of individual leaders. The democratic element of formal representation rests on the allegiance owed by participants to their constituencies. A teacher representing the English department on a committee is accountable to colleagues who may have the right to nominate or elect another person if they are not happy about the way they are being represented.

Informal consultations with staff do not constitute collegiality. Where heads seek the advice of colleagues before making a decision the process is one of consultation whereas the essence of collegiality is participation in decision-making. Power is shared with staff in a democracy rather than remaining the preserve of the leader. Formal representation confers the right to participate in defined areas of policy while informal consultation is at the sole discretion of the leader who is under no obligation to act on the advice received.

5 Collegial models assume that decisions are reached by *consensus* rather than division or conflict. The belief that there are common values and shared objectives leads to the view that it is both desirable and possible to resolve problems by agreement. There may be differences of opinion but they can be overcome by the force of argument. The decision-making process may be elongated by the search for compromise but this is regarded as an acceptable price to pay to maintain the aura of shared values and beliefs. [. . .]

The case for consensual decision-making rests in part on the ethical dimension of collegiality. It is regarded as wholly appropriate to involve people in the decision which affect their professional lives. Imposing decisions on staff is considered morally repugnant and inconsistent with the notion of consent. [. . .]

Collegial models in higher education

Collegial approaches in British education originated within the colleges of Oxford and Cambridge universities (Becher and Kogan 1992: 72): 'Collegium designates a structure or structures in which members have equal authority to participate in decisions which are binding on each of them. It usually implies that individuals have discretion to perform their main operations in their own way, subject only to minimal collegial controls.'

The collegial model has been adopted by most universities. Authority of expertise is widespread within these institutions of scholarship and research. Glatter (1984: 23) describes universities as 'bottom-heavy institutions' and the nature of management should reflect this wide distribution of knowledge and competence. 'Any organisation which depends on high-level professional skills operates most efficiently if there is a substantial measure of collegiality in its management procedures' (Williams and Blackstone 1983: 94).

The collegial model is most evident within the extensive committee system. Decisions on a whole range of academic and resource allocation issues take place within a labyrinth of committees rather than being the prerogative of the vice-chancellor. Issues are generally resolved by agreement or compromise rather than by voting or dissent. In many universities democracy is compromised by a limited franchise. Certain institutions give full voting rights to all academic staff and some representation to students and perhaps also non-academic staff. Elsewhere membership of senate and the key committees is the preserve of senior staff.

[. . .]

There is a dichotomy in universities and colleges between academic policy, which is generally the responsibility of the collegial senate or academic board, and resource management which is usually the preserve of the vice-chancellor and heads of faculty. The committee system fits the collegial model while the powers accorded directly to senior managers suggest one of the formal models. Kogan (1984: 28) points to the risk of conflict between the democratic and hierarchical aspects of higher education management.

[. . .]

The rapid growth of higher education in the 1990s may have made it more difficult for the collegial aspects of universities to maintain their previous significance in the decision-making process. Middlehurst and Elton (1992: 261) argue that collegiality is threatened by the increased emphasis on competition.

[. . .]

Collegial models in secondary schools

The introduction of collegial approaches in secondary schools has been slower, less complete and more piecemeal than in higher education. The tradition of all powerful heads, with authority over staff and accountability to external bodies, has stifled several attempts to develop participative modes of management. The formal position is that heads alone are responsible for the organization and management of schools. This consideration has acted as a brake on some heads who wish to share their power and as a convenient justification for those reluctant to do so.

An early example of a collegial model in operation was seen at Countesthorpe college in Leicestershire in the 1970s. The main policy-making body was the 'moot' which was open to all staff and students. It met every six weeks and all other decision-making bodies were responsible to it. The main standing committee held office for one quarter of the year and comprised one quarter of the staff with student representation. All meetings were advertised and open. Proposals could emanate from any group or individual. The former principal, John Watts, outlines the main collegial features at Countesthorpe:

> The major policy decisions that have shaped the curriculum and discipline of the school have been made by the consensus of the staff. Increasingly, students have contributed to this consensus, and in some cases parents and governors have participated. I accepted the headship in 1972 because I found the policies and the means of determining them attractive.
>
> (Watts 1976: 130–1)

The Countesthorpe approach incorporated all the central elements of collegial models, including acknowledgement of teachers' authority of expertise and the emphasis on consensual decision-making by all the staff with student input. This example also illustrates the normative nature of collegiality because Watts regarded the approach as 'attractive'.

[. . .]

Collegial models in primary schools

Collegiality has become established during the 1980s and 1990s as the most appropriate way to manage primary schools. It is now the normative model of good practice in this phase of education. Its main features are probably the following:

- Staff working groups determine proposals for decision by the whole staff.
- The working groups are led by curriculum co-ordinators or consultants.
- The co-ordinators progressively acquire expertise in their specialist area, drawing on external expertise.
- The co-ordinators work alongside class teachers to demonstrate ideas in practice.
- The teachers operate in a climate in which constructive scrutiny of practice is expected.

(Campbell 1985: 152–3)

Little (1990: 177–80) describes how collegiality operates in practice and identifies the following elements of a collegial approach:

- Teachers talk about teaching.
- There is shared planning and preparation.
- The presence of observers in classrooms is common.
- There is mutual training and development.

The model outlined by Campbell (1985) and Little (1990) appears to depend on shared professional values leading to the development of trust and a willingness to give and receive criticism in order to enhance practice. It is a demanding approach that requires

commitment from staff if it is to become an effective vehicle for beneficial change. It is also an elusive model to operate even where staff are committed to the concept.
   [. . .]

Collegial models: goals, structure, environment and leadership

Goals

Collegial models assume that members of an organization agree on its *goals*. There is a belief that staff have a shared view of the purposes of the institution. Agreement on aims is perhaps the central element in all participative approaches to school and college management. Livingstone (1974: 22) outlines the functions of institutional objectives:

> First of all, goals provide a general guide to activity. A member of an organisation who is aware of the organisation's goal is better able to make his activities relevant to achieving it. Secondly, goals serve as a source of legitimacy. Activities can be justified if they can be shown to further achievement of the goals. Thirdly, they are a means of measuring success. . . . An organisation is effective if it achieves its objectives.

Campbell and Southworth (1993: 72) emphasize the need for staff to 'purpose the same' and quote from their research in primary schools: 'Teachers felt that it was important that they should have compatible ideals, agree the same aims and share the same purpose . . . "If you are aiming for a whole-school . . . then everybody has got to agree about aims and purposes".' The significance of agreed goals as a basis for school policies and activities is stressed by Watts (1976: 133–4) in his discussion of Countesthorpe college:

> the participatory system depends upon an initial agreement of aims . . . Countesthorpe was made possible by the first head's clear announcement of intention which enabled him to recruit a staff who wanted to work in that way. With head and staff agreed on basics, any conflicts can be resolved by open discussion with reference to them, provided all parties learn to tolerate conflict, use it to identify issues and make compromises in order to reach consensus.

There is a clear indication here that agreement on goals, central to the ethos of collegial models, is likely to be achieved only under certain conditions. One circumstance, identified by Watts (1976), is where staff have been chosen by the head and possess a common educational philosophy. [. . .] The acknowledgement of possible conflict over the goals of educational institutions threatens one of the central planks of collegial theory. The belief that staff can always reach agreement over institutional purposes and policies lies at the heart of all participative approaches. Recognition of goal conflict serves to limit the validity of collegial models.

Organizational structure

[. . .] Collegial models assume structures to be lateral or horizontal with participants having an equal right to determine policy and influence decisions.
   In education, collegial approaches are often manifested through systems of committees, which may be elaborate in the larger and more complex institutions. The decision-making process inside committees is thought to be egalitarian with influence dependent

more on specific expertise than an official position. The assumption is that decisions are reached by consensus or compromise rather than acquiescence to the views of the head or principal.

In schools, *ad hoc* working parties may be more effective than standing committees. At Wroxham [Primary School], there were several working parties that were regarded as effective in curriculum development, as the deputy head suggests: 'Staff meetings are not so good for curriculum development. It is more productive to promote informal discussion in the staff room. Smaller working parties work better with keen staff building up a document and presenting it to the whole staff' (Bush 1988: 40). The Pensnett comprehensive school in Dudley also developed a system of working parties that were charged with reviewing issues and preparing recommendations. Final decisions were taken by senior staff and governors. This is not really a collegial approach but it does represent a shift along the continuum towards collaborative working (Bush 1988: 38).

The external environment

There are several difficulties in assessing the nature of relationships between the organization and its *external environment*. Collegial models characterize decision-making as a participative process with all members of the institution having an equal opportunity to influence policy and action. However, where decisions emerge from an often complex committee system, it is no easy task to establish who is responsible for organizational policy. Noble and Pym (1970: 435–6) point to some of the elusive qualities of decision-making by committee:

> The most striking feature of the organisation to the newcomer or outsider seeking some response from it is the receding locus of power. In complex organisations in the spheres of education, industry, administration or commerce, this Kafkaesque experience is very common; wherever or at whatever level one applies to the organisation, the 'real' decisions always seem to be taken somewhere else.

The ambiguity of the decision-making process within collegial organizations creates a particular problem in terms of accountability to external bodies. The head or principal is invariably held responsible for the policies of the school or college. Leaders are thought to determine or strongly influence decisions and are accountable to external bodies for these policies.

Collegial models do not fit comfortably with these formal accountability assumptions. Are heads expected to justify school policies determined within a participatory framework even where they do not enjoy their personal support? Or is the reality that collegial policy-making is limited by the head's responsibility to external agencies? Heads must agree with, or at minimum acquiesce in, decisions made in committee if they are not to be placed in a very difficult position.

[. . .]

Collegial models tend to overlook the possibility of conflict between internal participative processes and external accountability. The often bland assumption that issues can be resolved by consensus leads to the comfortable conclusion that heads are always in agreement with decisions and experience no difficulty in explaining them to external bodies. In practice, it may be that the head's accountability leads to a substantially modified version of collegiality in most schools and colleges. There is also the risk of tension for the principal who is caught between the conflicting demands of participation and accountability.

[. . .]

Leadership

In collegial models the style of *leadership* both influences, and is influenced by, the nature of the decision-making process. [. . .] Collegial theorists tend to ascribe the following qualities to leaders in schools and colleges:

1 They are responsive to the needs and wishes of their professional colleagues. Heads and principals acknowledge the expertise and skill of the teachers and seek to harness these assets for the benefit of the pupils and students. Invariably they have been appointed to leadership posts after a long period as successful practitioners. Their experience makes them 'sensitive to the informal codes of professional practice which govern expectations for relations among teachers and between teachers and head' (Coulson 1985: 86).
2 Collegial heads seek to create formal and informal opportunities for the testing and elaboration of policy initiatives. This is done to encourage innovation and to maximize the acceptability of school decisions. As Brown (1983: 224) suggests in relation to primary schools: 'the headteacher who perceives his role as being that of a democrat . . . ensures that school organisation facilitates frequent staff discussion and co-ordination in order that decisions are made as a collective art'.
3 Collegial models emphasize the authority of expertise rather than official authority. It follows that authority in professional organizations such as schools or colleges resides as much with the staff as with the head. Instead of exerting authority over subordinates, the leader seeks to influence the decisions and actions of professional colleagues. The head also allows and encourages heads of department and curriculum co-ordinators to become co-leaders. [. . .]

In collegial models, then, the head or principal is typified as the facilitator of an essentially participative process. Their credibility with their colleagues depends on providing leadership to staff and external stakeholders while valuing the contributions of specialist teachers: 'The picture of a "good" headteacher which emerged from the teachers' comments on a "whole school" was of a person to whom they could talk and with whom they could discuss, who did not dictate, who was effectively a part of the staff group and whose philosophy was clear and shared by colleagues' (Campbell and Southworth 1993: 75). Heads and principals retain a pivotal role in the management of the institution and can exercise considerable influence over its direction as long as they retain the confidence and support of their professional colleagues. For Handy (1977: 186), this is the essential difference between formal approaches and collegial leadership, which depends on consent:

> The distinction between the organisation of consent and the traditional hierarchical organisation is that authority in the former is granted by those below whereas in the hierarchical state authority is conferred by those above. Your official role in the organisation of consent gives you little effective power – that is only won by the consent of those you seek to manage. Nor does this consent, once given, hold good for all time or for all circumstances. It needs constant ratification.

[. . .]

Collegiality and gender

The trend towards collegial management has been particularly noticeable in primary schools and most of the relevant literature refers to this sector. There may be several reasons for this disparity, including the fact that primary schools are generally small enough for 'whole-school' collegiality and have simple, unstratified structures. It may also be influenced by gender. Women invariably form the majority in primary schools and some have an all-female staff. There is also a much higher proportion of women leaders in primary schools than in secondary schools or colleges.

Al-Khalifa (1989: 89) claims that women adopt different management styles from men with a much greater emphasis on collaboration, co-operation and other 'feminine' behaviours. These styles, which are compatible with collegiality, are contrasted with 'masculine' aspects of management: 'Women managers pinpoint aspects of management practice which they find dysfunctional – namely aggressive competitive behaviours, an emphasis on control rather than negotiation and collaboration, and the pursuit of competition rather than shared problem-solving.'

Nias, Southworth and Yeomans (1989: 70–1) discuss the applicability of a gender perspective to the collegial culture prevalent in many primary schools but conclude on the basis of the research that this view is 'simplistic'. [. . .] They refer to examples of successful collaborative behaviour involving both women and men. However, Coleman (1994) presents evidence that women managers in education tend to be more democratic than men, demonstrating qualities of warmth, empathy and cooperation. This issue requires further research before conclusions can be drawn with confidence.

Limitations of collegial models

Collegial models have become increasingly popular in the literature on educational management and in official pronouncements about school development. Their advocates believe that participative approaches represent the most appropriate means of conducting affairs in educational institutions. However, critics of collegial models point to a number of flaws which serve to limit their validity in schools and colleges. There are eight significant weaknesses of collegial perspectives.

1 Collegial models are so strongly *normative* that they tend to obscure rather than portray reality. Precepts about the most appropriate ways of managing educational institutions mingle with descriptions of behaviour. While collegiality is increasingly advocated, the evidence of its presence in schools and colleges tends to be sketchy and incomplete. Baldridge *et al.* (1978: 33) present a powerful critique of collegial models in higher education which may also apply to schools:

> The collegial literature often confuses *descriptive* and *normative* enterprises. Are the writers saying that the university *is* a collegium or that it *ought* to be a collegium? Frequently, the discussions of collegium are more a lament for paradise lost than a description of present reality. Indeed, the collegial idea of round table decision making does not accurately reflect the actual processes in most institutions.

2 Collegial approaches to decision-making tend to be *slow and cumbersome*. When policy proposals require the approval of a series of committees, the process is often tortuous and time consuming. The participative ethic requires that a decision should be made by agreement where possible rather than by resorting to a voting process. The attempts to achieve consensus may lead to procedural delays such as a reference back to the sponsoring committee, or to consultation with other committees, individuals or external agencies. Participants may have to endure many lengthy meetings before issues are resolved. [. . .] The sheer length of the process may be a major factor in the relatively limited adoption of collegial approaches in schools. Most staff are engaged in classroom activities for much or all of the day. Meetings tend to be held after school when staff are tired and unprepared for a protracted attempt to achieve consensus on aspects of school policy.

3 A fundamental assumption of democratic models is that decisions are reached by *consensus*. It is believed that the outcome of debate should be agreement based on the shared values of participants. In practice, though, committee members have their own views and there is no guarantee of unanimity on outcomes. In addition, participants often represent constituencies within the school or college. Individuals may be members of committees as representatives of the English department or the science faculty. Inevitably these sectional interests have a significant influence on committees' processes. The participatory framework may become the focal point for disagreement between factions. Baldridge *et al.* (1978: 33–4) argue that democratic models greatly underestimate the significance of conflict within education.
     [. . .]

4 Collegial models have to be evaluated in relation to the special features of educational institutions. The participative aspects of decision-making exist alongside the structural and bureaucratic components of schools and colleges. Often there is tension between these rather different modes of management. The participative element rests on the authority of expertise possessed by professional staff but this rarely trumps the positional authority of official leaders. As Lortie (1969: 30) suggests, 'it seems unlikely that collegial ties play a major part in reducing the potency of hierarchical authority'.

5 Collegial approaches to school and college decision-making may be difficult to sustain in view of the requirement that heads and principals remain accountable to the governing body and to various external groups. Participation represents the internal dimension of democracy. *Accountability* may be thought of as the external aspect of democracy. Governors and external groups seek explanations of policy and invariably turn to the head or principal for answers to their questions. Heads may experience considerable difficulty in defending policies which have emerged from a collegial process but do not enjoy their personal support. [. . .]

6 The effectiveness of a collegial system depends in part on the attitudes of staff. If they actively support participation then it may succeed. If they display apathy or hostility, it seems certain to fail. Hellawell (1991: 334) refers to the experience of one primary head who sought to introduce collegial approaches

> I have worked very hard over the last few years, as the number of staff has grown, to build up a really collegial style of management with a lot of staff input into decisions that affect the school and they are saying that they don't like this. They would like an autocracy. They would like to be told what to do.

Campbell (1985) and Wallace (1989) argue that teachers may not welcome collegiality because they are disinclined to accept any authority intermediate between themselves and the head. This has serious implications for the role of the curriculum co-ordinator: 'Potential tension is . . . embedded in the relationship between the roles of curriculum consultant and class-teacher. Many teachers expect a high degree of autonomy over the delivery of the curriculum in their classrooms, yet their professional judgement may conflict with that of the consultant' (Wallace 1989: 187). [. . .]

7 Collegial processes in schools depend even more on the attitudes of heads than on the support of teachers. In colleges, the academic board provides a legitimate forum for the involvement of staff in decision-making and principals have to recognize and work with this alternative power source. In schools, participative machinery can be established only with the support of the head, who has the legal authority to manage the school. Wise heads take account of the views of their staff but this is a consultative process and not collegiality. Hoyle (1986: 91) concludes that its dependence on the head's support limits the validity of the collegiality model: 'Collegiality is not inherent in the system but is a function of leadership style whereby teachers are given the opportunity to participate in the decision-making process by benevolent heads rather than as of right.'

Contrived collegiality

Hargreaves (1994) makes a more fundamental criticism of collegiality, arguing that it is being espoused or 'contrived' by official groups in order to secure the implementation of national policy in England and Wales and elsewhere. He claims that genuine collegiality is spontaneous, voluntary, unpredictable, informal and geared to development. Contrived collegiality, in contrast, has the following contradictory features:

- Administratively regulated rather than spontaneous.
- Compulsory rather than discretionary.
- Geared to the implementation of the mandates of government or the headteacher.
- Fixed in time and place.
- Designed to have predictable outcomes.

(Hargreaves 1994: 195–6)

Within the post-Education Reform Act context in England and Wales, this analysis is persuasive. These dimensions of 'collegiality' support his analysis:

- Collegiality receives official support (Campbell 1985).
- The National Curriculum largely prescribes content and assessment.
- The concept of 'directed time' enables heads to prescribe participation in the decision-making process.

These elements do not necessarily eliminate the informal and spontaneous aspects of collegiality but they do lend support to Hargreaves' (1994) analysis.

Conclusion: is collegiality an unattainable ideal?

Collegial models are highly normative and idealistic. Their advocates believe that participative approaches represent the most appropriate means of managing educational institutions. Teachers exhibit that authority of expertise which justifies their involvement in the decision-making process. In addition, they are able to exercise sufficient discretion in the classroom to ensure that innovation depends on their co-operation. Collegial theorists argue that active support for change is more likely to be forthcoming where teachers have been able to contribute to the process of policy formulation.

Collegial models contribute several important concepts to the theory of educational management. Participative approaches are a necessary antidote to the rigid hierarchical assumptions of the formal models. However, collegial perspectives provide an incomplete portrayal of management in education. They underestimate the official authority of the head and present bland assumptions of consensus which often cannot be substantiated. Hoyle (1986: 100) argues that bureaucratic and political realities mean that collegiality does not exist in schools: 'In the absence of a true collegium, a situation which the existing law and external expectations preclude, the head either carries a fully-participating staff or fails to do so thus creating a situation of direct conflict.' This view may be too pessimistic but it remains true that those who aspire to collegiality often find that it cannot be implemented effectively. Little (1990: 187), following substantial research in the United States, concludes that collegiality 'turns out to be rare'.

A generation ago almost all schools and colleges could have been categorized as formal. In the 1990s, many are developing collegial frameworks. There is a discernible trend towards collegiality. It is uneven but it is tangible. Despite Hargreaves' (1994) justifiable criticisms of 'contrived collegiality', the advantages of participation in professional organizations remain persuasive. Collegiality is an elusive ideal but it is likely to become an increasingly significant model within the theory of educational management.

References

Al-Khalifa, E. (1989) Management by halves: women teachers and school management, in H. De Lyon and F. Migniuolo (eds) *Women Teachers: Issues and Experiences*. Milton Keynes: Open University Press.

Baldridge, J. V., Curtis, D. V., Ecker, G. and Riley, G. L. (1978) *Policy Making and Effective Leadership*. San Francisco: Jossey Bass.

Becher, T. and Kogan, M. (1992) *Process and Structure in Higher Education*. 2nd edn. London: Routledge.

Brown, C. M. (1983) Curriculum management in the junior school. *School Organisation*, 3(3): 221–8.

Bush, T. (1988) *Action and Theory in School Management, E325 Managing Schools*. Milton Keynes: The Open University.

Campbell, P. and Southworth, G. (1993) Rethinking collegiality: teachers' views, in N. Bennett, M. Crawford and C. Riches (eds) *Managing Change in Education: Individual and Organizational Perspectives*. London: Paul Chapman Publishing.

Campbell, R. J. (1985) *Developing the Primary Curriculum*. London: Holt, Rinehart and Winston.

Coleman, M. (1994) Women in educational management, in T. Bush and J. West-Burnham (eds) *The Principles of Educational Management*. Harlow: Longman.

Coulson, A. (1985) *The Managerial Behaviour of Primary School Heads*, Collected Original Resources in Education. Abingdon: Carfax Publishing Company.

Glatter, R. (1984) *Managing for Change, E324 Management in Post Compulsory Education, Block 6*. Milton Keynes: The Open University.

Handy, C. B. (1977) The organisations of consent, in D. W. Piper and R. Glatter (eds) *The Changing University*. Windsor: NFER-Nelson.

Hargreaves, A. (1994) *Changing Teachers, Changing Times: Teachers' Work and Culture in the Postmodern Age*. London: Cassell.

Hellawell, D. (1991) The changing role of the head in the primary school in England. *School Organisation*, 11(3): 321–37.

Hoyle, E. (1986) *The Politics of School Management*. Sevenoaks: Hodder and Stoughton.

Kogan, M. (1984) *Models and Structures, E324 Management in Post Compulsory Education*. Milton Keynes: The Open University.

Little, J. (1990) Teachers as colleagues, in A. Lieberman (ed.) *Schools as Collaborative Cultures: Creating the Future Now*. Basingstoke: Falmer Press.

Livingstone, H. (1974) *The University: An Organisational Analysis*. Glasgow: Blackie.

Lortie, D. C. (1969) The balance of control and autonomy in elementary school teaching, in A. Etzioni (ed.) *The Semi-Professions and Their Organisation*. New York: Free Press, a division of Macmillan Inc.

Middlehurst, R. and Elton, L. (1992) Leadership and management in higher education. *Studies in Higher Education*, 17(3): 251–64.

Nias, J., Southworth, G. and Yeomans, R. (1989) *Staff Relationships in the Primary School*. London: Cassell.

Noble, T. and Pym, B. (1970) Collegial authority and the receding locus of power. *British Journal of Sociology*, 21: 431–45.

Wallace, M. (1989) Towards a collegiate approach to curriculum management in primary and middle schools, in M. Preedy (ed.) *Approaches to Curriculum Management*. Milton Keynes: Open University Press.

Watts, J. (1976) Sharing it out: the role of the head in participatory government, in R. S. Peters (ed.) *The Role of the Head*. London: Routledge and Kegan Paul.

Williams, G. and Blackstone, T. (1983) *Response to Adversity*. Guildford: Society for Research into Higher Education.

8 | Models of co-ordination in educational organizations*

JAAP SCHEERENS

The two basic parameters of organizational analysis are the division of tasks and authority on the one hand and measures to interrelate these part-systems on the other. Mintzberg (1979: 2) describes these two processes, division and coordination, as 'two fundamental and opposing requirements' of every human activity.

Coordination within organizations can be achieved in two ways. First, the design of the organizational structure in terms of hierarchy, and lateral relationships between organizational sub-units, can be seen as the basis for coordination. Kickert (1979) calls this 'structural' coordination as opposed to 'procedural' coordination. The essential idea is that by means of changes in the structure of units and sub-units and the more permanent relationships between them, the pattern of adjustments and unifications is also changed. In this way, the classical organizational forms, such as the functional hierarchy, the product hierarchy or the matrix organization, are considered alternative ways of structural coordination.

Procedural coordination accepts the organizational structure as a given fact, and deals with purposeful adjustment between the sub-units of the organization. Mintzberg (1979: 3) mentions five 'coordinating mechanisms': mutual adjustment, direct supervision, standardization of work processes, standardization of work outputs and standardization of worker skills. He speaks of these coordinating measures as 'the glue that holds organizations together'. In mutual adjustment, coordination is achieved simply by means of informal communication. Direct supervision presupposes a hierarchical structure of authority; in its simplest form one individual takes responsibility for the work of others. The three types of standardization rely on the ability to preplan and specify processes and outputs. For instance, in standardization of worker skills, the kind of training required to perform the work is specified (Mintzberg 1979: 6).

The shape that coordination (structural and procedural) generally takes in educational organizations is important for two reasons. First, specifying the coordination

*This material has been edited and is from Chapter 2 of *Effective School: Research, Theory and Practice*.

structure and dominant coordination mechanisms exposes the essential features of a specific type of organization. Exposing these essential features of schools is the best method for describing the organizational context of specific effectiveness models. For instance, when one is attempting to apply some of the insights from public choice theory to enhance school effectiveness, it is quite important to consider to what extent such measures might upset traditional ways of coordination.

Second, there is a general belief that 'improving' coordination structures and mechanisms within schools is one of the keys to effectiveness. The general hypothesis is that more integrated rather than more segmented school organizations are more effective. This hypothesis has received some support in school effectiveness research literature.

Three models of cooperation within educational organization will be briefly discussed, the concept of 'organized anarchies', the notion of 'loose coupling' and the general typology of the school as a 'professional bureaucracy'. Attention will be placed on the potential each model has for understanding school effectiveness.

Organized anarchies

Cohen *et al.* (1972) describe organized anarchies as characterized by 'problematic preferences', 'unclear technology' and 'fluid participation'. With respect to problematic preferences, they state that the organization can 'better be described as a loose collection of ideas than as a coherent structure; it discovers preferences through action more than it acts on the basis of preferences'. Unclear technology means that the organization members do not understand the organization's production processes and that the organization operates on the basis of trial and error, 'the residue of learning from the accidents of the past' and 'pragmatic inventions of necessity'. When there is fluid participation, participants vary in the amount of time and effort they devote to different domains of decision-making (Cohen *et al.* 1972: 1).

According to Cohen *et al.*, decision-making in organized anarchies is more like rationalizing after the fact than rational, goal-oriented planning. 'From this point of view, an organization is a collection of choices looking for problems, issues and feelings looking for decision situations in which they might be aired, solutions looking for issues to which they might be the answer, and decision-makers looking for work' (Cohen *et al.* 1972: 2). They see educational organizations as likely candidates for this type of decision-making. In terms of coordination, organized anarchies have a fuzzy structure of authority and little capacity for standardization mechanisms.

Cohen *et al.* (1972) developed a computer simulation of garbage can decision-making. Generally speaking this model simulates the ways in which problems, decision-makers and solutions 'meet' as a function of the time of occurrence of choices, problems and solutions, as well as the energy participants can spend on a particular choice at a particular point in time and the energy that is required for a particular solution. The number of problems solved, and the total energy and time it takes to solve them, are then examined by comparing different structural arrangements. These are:

- The *decision structure*, the relationship between decision-makers and choices; e.g. there are hierarchical decisions when 'important', i.e. low numbered, choices must be made by important decision-makers, and specialized decisions when each decision-maker is associated with a single choice and each choice has a single decision-maker.

- Three arrangements with respect to *energy distribution*: one in which important people spend less energy, another in which unimportant people spend less energy, and a third in which all decision-makers spend equal energy.
- *Net energy load*, defined as the difference between the total energy required to solve all problems and the total effective energy available to the organization over all time periods.
- The *access* structure, or the relation between problems and choices. Three types are distinguished: unsegmented access (any active problem has access to any active choice), specialized access (each problem has access to only one choice) and hierarchical access (important problems are accessible only to important choices, and vice versa).

Some illustrative findings of this computer simulation are that 'decision-making by flight and oversight is a major feature of the process in general'. When the net energy load increases, 'problems are less likely to be solved and choices are likely to take longer.' Access hierarchy (important problems meet important decision-makers) leads to the resolution of important problems more than unimportant ones. Choice failures that occur (i.e. decisions that are not made) 'are concentrated among the most important and less important choices'. The authors interpret this last outcome as illustrating the fate of organizations that 'do not know what they are doing', that proceed by undertaking trivial activities to keep up appearances and avoiding 'extraordinary violence to the domains of participants or to their model of what an organization should be' (Cohen *et al.* 1972: 11).

Cohen *et al.*'s garbage can model is often treated as a provocative description of extremely poor decision-making. It should also be recognized, however, as [. . .] a substantive contribution to organizational theory. The garbage can model generates a lot of specific hypotheses amenable to empirical tests. The implicit message of the garbage can model with regard to the issue of school effectiveness is that schools could be run more efficiently if structural and procedural coordination were improved. [. . .]

Loosely coupled systems

The notion that organizational structures vary in the degree to which they need coordination is central in classical texts on organization theory. [. . .] Simon's (1964) concept of 'near decomposability' conveys the principle that complex systems will tend to decompose into sub-systems in such a way that interrelationships between sub-systems become minimized. In schools there are many instances of the least demanding form of interdependence, i.e. pooled coupling, when interdependence is limited to the sharing of common facilities. Although 'serial' interdependence is implied in the longitudinal planning of subject matter (for example, when pupils move from one grade to the next), the tightness of coupling varies according to the course subject and teacher habits.

Weick (1976) has used loosely coupled systems as a central construct to determine the specific nature of educational organizations. Weick uses loose coupling as a critique and a strong modification of the rational image of organizations (all-encompassing organizational goals, clear technology and a clearly formalized structure). Loose coupling expresses the notion that events or elements are somehow related, but at the same time separate or autonomous. Two broad classes of coupling mechanisms are those related to the functioning of the technical core of the organization on the one hand and those related to the authority of office on the other. In the latter case, the amount of discretionary power of teachers with respect to principals could be questioned. In the former case, a central question is whether the educational production function is explicitly determined; that is, whether or not established means–end relationships exist in the production of educational outcomes. Weick mentions the following elements of educational organizations, of which the tightness or looseness might be examined: intentions and actions, top and bottom, yesterday and tomorrow, administrators and teachers, means and ends ('frequently several different means lead to the same outcome'), teachers and materials, voters and school board, administrators and class-room, process and outcome, teacher–teacher, parent–teacher and teacher–pupil.

Weick is emphatic in stating that loose coupling has advantages and disadvantages and that it can be functional and dysfunctional, depending upon the particular context of specific organizations. Advantages of loose coupling are:

- Flexibility of response, in the sense that some portions of the organization can adapt to environmental changes, while others persist as they are (this feature becomes dysfunctional when archaic traditions are perpetuated).
- The provision of a sensitive sensing mechanism, in that loosely coupled systems contain many semi-independent elements that can be externally constrained (a negative interpretation of this characteristic being a certain vulnerability to producing faddish responses).
- The possibility of localized adaptation, which, in principle, affords a loosely coupled system a strong potential for change and innovation.
- A breakdown in one portion of a loosely coupled system need not affect other parts of the organization (the negative aspect of this feature is that it is probably difficult to repair the defective element).
- There is room for self-determination by the actors, which might have a favourable effect on their sense of efficacy (of course, self-determination could also have negative effects, for instance where individual teachers remain unaffected by a sensible initiative for innovation at the school level).
- Reduction of coordination costs in terms of money (overhead) and a reduction of conflicts; at the same time fund allocation (investment in coordination) will not be of much use as a means of change.

Weick's tentative answer to the question of what, given the loosely coupled character of educational organizations, keeps them together is that certification of teachers, a strict delineation of the recipients of education (i.e. the pupils) and inspection imply tighter coupling, while loose coupling is concentrated in the work processes. He further indicates that external conditions, such as competition for scarce resources, conflict and centralization in the national educational system, might force educational organization in the direction of tighter coupling.

An interesting implication of Weick's conception of loose coupling with respect to school effectiveness seems to be the realization that loose coupling has quite a few advantages for educational organizations. This means that the road to increased effectiveness does not simply run via more integrated educational organizations. Instead, more differentiated answers are needed to decide how much and in which part-systems of educational organization coordination is required.

Schools as professional bureaucracies

Certain aspects of loose coupling as described by Weick, particularly the alleged adaptability and flexibility of sub-systems, do not seem to coincide with experiences in the field of educational innovation. [. . .] The nature of the primary process in educational organizations as a conservative factor is somewhat underplayed in Weick's analysis. This aspect, the 'professional' nature of teachers' work, is the focus of another organizational image that sheds light upon the issue of coordination, namely, Mintzberg's (1979: 372) characterization of the school as a 'professional bureaucracy'.

The professional bureaucracy is depicted as a 'flat' structure, in which most of the power resides with the professionals in the operating core. Leadership in the professional bureaucracy is mostly to do with handling disturbance and performing maintenance and boundary-spanning tasks in order to 'buffer' the professional work. These buffering tasks are not supposed to be very spectacular since the environment is considered to be complex but stable. The major coordination mechanism within the professional bureaucracy is the standardization of skills acquired during a lengthy training period. Mintzberg (1979: 373) calls standardization of skills 'a loose coordinating mechanism at best, failing to cope with many of the needs that arise in the professional bureaucracy'. There is little room for interference of the leadership with the work of the professionals, nor is work-related interaction among the professionals common; they operate autonomously and resist rationalization of their skills. Consequently it is hard for educational administrators to control the work of the professionals even when cases of dysfunction are clear. Professionals oppose strict planning and external evaluation of their work.

The image of schools as professional bureaucracies explains the general resistance to change on the part of these organizations. Leadership, technological innovation and adaptation to environmental changes are not likely channels to make professionals alter their routines. The best approach to change, according to this organizational image, would be long-term alteration of the training programmes of teachers, with respect to teaching technologies and educational ideologies (for instance, when changing an orientation towards personal development into a more achievement-oriented attitude).

The professional bureaucracy explains why schools tend to be segmented organizations. When we are looking for organizational conditions that could help schooling to be more effective, the image of the professional bureaucracy can be seen as the null hypothesis. The message is that effective schools are those with a large percentage of effective teachers. Levers to enhance effectiveness should be sought by appealing to professional values and the mission of teaching, rather than through rationalization, technology or monetary incentives.

References

Cohen, M. D., March, J. G. and Olsen, J. P. (1972) A garbage can model of organizational choice. *Administrative Science Quarterly*, 17: 1–25.

Kickert, W. J. M. (1979) *Organization of Decision-Making: A Systems-Theoretical Approach.* Amsterdam: North-Holland Publishing Company.

Mintzberg, H. (1979) *The Structuring of Organizations.* Englewood Cliffs, NJ: Prentice-Hall.

Simon, H. A. (1964) *Administrative Behavior.* New York: Macmillan.

Weick, K. (1976) Educational organizations as loosely coupled systems. *Adminsitrative Science Quarterly*, 21: 1–19.

Towards a cultural and political perspective[*]

MIKE WALLACE AND VALERIE HALL

Combining metaphors: mixed or multiple?

Morgan (1986) suggests that any theoretical perspective on organisations constitutes a metaphor which directs attention to some features of phenomena under investigation, while ignoring other aspects. It is probably beyond human capacity to develop a single metaphor that provides an all-embracing explanation of social life. In recent years, an increasingly common approach to understanding organisations has been to mix metaphors by employing more than one perspective (Cuthbert 1984; Bush 1986; Bolman and Deal 1991).

[. . .]

A key issue in developing a conceptual framework encompassing two or more metaphors lies in whether we assume that two into one won't go: a dual perspective must then be handled as a mixed metaphor – interpretation of phenomena first from one perspective, then from another. We wish to test the opposite assumption: that two into one will go where phenomena may be addressed through a multiple metaphor – applying concepts from two or more perspectives to a phenomenon simultaneously.

There seems nothing sacred about the grouping of particular concepts to form a perspective. Different typologies of perspectives combine some concepts that others keep separate. The political perspective adopted by Bush, and Bolman and Deal, is divided by Morgan into the 'organization as political system' and the 'organization as instrument of domination'. It seems plausible to draw on the concepts of more than one perspective in developing multiple metaphors, rather than using one metaphor at a time as in the mixed metaphor approach.

[. . .]

[*]This material has been edited and originally appeared as Chapter 2 in *Inside the SMT: Teamwork in Secondary School Management*.

Limitations of single perspectives

[. . .]

Some organisational theorists and researchers into school management have adopted either a cultural perspective (e.g. Sergiovanni and Corbally 1984; Deal 1985; Nias, Southworth and Yeomans 1989; Nias, Southworth and Campbell 1992) or a political perspective (e.g. Ball 1987; Radnor 1990; Blase 1991). Both approaches offer valuable insights but, in focusing the research, each may be constrained by its emphasis on one set of concepts to the detriment of the other. This point may be illustrated by examining how exponents of the two perspectives interpret the way headteachers interact with other staff.

The analysis of primary school staff relationships carried out by Nias and her colleagues employs the notion of organisational culture to explain the pattern of interaction that they observed between staff. They portray how staff develop and sustain a shared set of beliefs and values about 'the way we do things here'. Concepts employed in their analysis are listed in Table 9.1. Conflicts between staff are interpreted as being addressed or avoided according to shared values about, say, the appropriateness of working towards compromise solutions. For Nias and her co-workers, conflicts give rise to the expression of underlying value consensus about how conflicts should be avoided or resolved: conflict on the surface masks consensus at a more implicit level.

Nevertheless, even in schools with a strong staff 'culture of collaboration', they accept that:

> . . . normative *control* was so pervasive that it is easy to lose sight of the fact that it too was the product of a *power differential*. Each school had a head with a strong 'mission' and well developed *political skills* who had been in post for at least ten

Table 9.1   Key concepts employed within different perspectives

Cultural (Nias et al. 1989)	Political (Ball 1987)	Cultural and political
Culture of collaboration	Power	Culture of teamwork
Beliefs	Control	Beliefs
Values	Goal diversity	Values
Understanding	Ideology	Norms
Attitudes	Conflict	Role
Meanings	Interests	Status
Norms		Rituals
Symbols		Consensus
Rituals		Power
Ceremonies		Resources
Negotiation		Hierarchy
Consensus		Interests
		Dialectic of control
		Authority
		Influence
		Conflict
		Contradiction
		Coalitions

years and to whom had accrued during that time a considerable amount of personal *authority*.

(Nias, Southworth and Yeomans 1989: 15; emphasis added)

The concepts we have highlighted are pushed into the background in the analysis, yet help us grasp how headteachers were in a uniquely strong position to persuade other staff to adopt their managerial values and so obtain value consensus through negotiation.

Conversely, Ball (1987) analyses interaction amongst staff in secondary schools in terms of conflict:

I take schools, in common with virtually all other organizations, to be *arenas of struggle*; to be riven with actual or potential conflict between members; to be poorly coordinated; to be ideologically diverse.

(Ball 1987: 19; original emphasis)

While Ball accepts that, overtly, much interaction is marked by apparent acceptance of a normative consensus amongst staff, he argues that implicit conflict lurks below:

interaction is centred upon the *routine*, mundane and, for the most part, uncontroversial running of the institution . . . routine organizational life is set within the *'negotiated order'* . . . a patterned construct of contrasts, *understandings, agreements and 'rules'* which provides the basis of concerted action . . . In this way conflicts may remain normally implicit and subterranean, only occasionally bursting into full view.

(Ball 1987: 20; emphasis added)

Key concepts employed in his analysis are listed in Table 9.1. Headteachers are interpreted as using various overt and covert strategies based upon their unique access to power to realise their interest in retaining control over other staff in the management of schools. Senior management teams (SMTs) are viewed as a means of supporting this interest, members other than heads being orientated towards them. Other staff, it is claimed, perceive the SMT as constituting 'the hierarchy': a group set apart from teachers who tend to exclude them from important aspects of decision making. The ability of the group to control the rest of the staff is reinforced by the 'norm of cabinet responsibility' whereby SMT members refrain from criticising SMT decisions in public.

The cultural concepts we have highlighted in the quotation above are underplayed in Ball's analysis but relate closely to that of Nias and her colleagues. In both analyses, concepts relating to the perspective that was *not* adopted are brought repeatedly into the account. The 'norm' of cabinet responsibility mentioned by Ball is essentially a cultural idea; the 'personal authority' of the head which features prominently in the analysis by Nias and her colleagues is a political notion. In order to explain the phenomena being studied, both analyses have actually used concepts from an alternative perspective in a subsidiary position within the dominant one. The way concepts from a second perspective creep in implies that the concepts of one perspective alone may not be up to capturing the range of phenomena encountered in the research to which this perspective was applied.

[. . .]

A complicating factor with significant methodological implications is the phenomenon that individuals may or may not behave according to their values, since in most situations they have some choice over whether to act (Giddens 1976). What passes for consensus on the surface may, as Ball contends, belie some form of hidden conflict. Gronn (1986) distinguishes several types of conflict along a continuum between action and inaction. In addition to conflict which is overt (and so readily observable), it may be covert where individuals refrain from dissenting activity; or latent where expression of dissent is interpreted as arising from personal problems. Inaction may follow from a perception of the greater power of others; it may even be due to lack of awareness of conflicting interests where individuals' perceptions are shaped in such a way that they accept their situations without question. [. . .]

A dual perspective: problems and potential

Given these constraints, is interaction best conceived, in common with Nias and her co-workers, as the rather cosy expression of shared values where conflict is bounded by underlying consensus on its resolution? Or is it, as Ball asserts, an often silent struggle between conflicting interests where apparent consensus masks suppressed conflict? We guess that interaction may be an expression of both the shared values of a culture and the differential use of power to realise particular interests. [. . .]

Our starting point is the assumption that individuals make different use of resources to achieve desired goals through interaction according to their beliefs and values, which they share to a greater or lesser extent with others, and of which they have only partial awareness. Values may be sustained or changed through interaction. This conception, where both culture and power are seen as integral components of interaction, follows Giddens's (1976) view: individuals communicate meaning within the context of normative sanctions and relationships of power. All three elements are intrinsic to interaction and are empirically inseparable although they may be distinguished analytically.

In order to tease out the main elements of this perspective, we will define the main concepts to be employed. Since the range of possible concepts is doubled in bringing together two perspectives, we have restricted our selection to those which gave most purchase in our research so as to aid conceptual digestion. We recognise that in so doing we lose distinctions between related concepts within either a cultural or a political orientation – a second drawback of a dual perspective.

Concepts drawn primarily from a cultural perspective

Meanings and norms may be subsumed within the notion of *culture*: a set of shared or complementary symbols, beliefs and values expressed in interaction. SMTs in our research developed a '*culture of teamwork*': shared beliefs and values about working together to manage the school. Beliefs and values include those relating to *norms*, or rules of behaviour. A norm common to the SMTs we studied was that decisions must be reached by achieving a working consensus, entailing the acknowledgement of any dissenting views. Where the meanings and norms held by one individual are shared with others, they belong to a common culture.

Some shared meanings take the form of *myths*: stories and rumours related to the organisation which are passed on between individuals and whose authenticity may be based upon impressionistic or hard evidence. Certain myths were connected with the institutional history: some members of each SMT had worked in the school for much of their professional lives. They had a rich store of anecdotes about people and events from years gone by, which were often a basis for interpreting the present. Rumours amongst staff in the different schools varied widely, including the perception that certain SMT members had more influence on decision making than their colleagues. This myth was based upon the impressions of individuals who were not party to the decision-making process as they did not attend SMT meetings, but who were made aware of decision outcomes.

Meanings which may or may not be shared by all parties to the interaction include those relating to the *role* of an individual or group. When individuals occupy a social position their actions are determined by what others expect of anyone in that position in terms of their responsibilities and individuals' idiosyncratic preferences. [. . .]

People may occupy many roles, giving rise to the possibility of *role conflict* where beliefs and values do not coincide. A few SMT members who were incentive-allowance holders had, in addition to their school-wide brief within the SMT, middle management responsibility for a faculty. They experienced some conflict between their beliefs and values as SMT members, where they were expected to serve the interests of the whole school, and those as middle managers where they were concerned to do the best for their own faculty.

A third area of shared meaning with significant implications for SMTs is *status*. This term refers to the relative position of a person on a socially defined scale or hierarchy of social worth. Common to all our research schools was a perception that the different grades of incentive allowance held by many teachers, generally awarded for increasing levels of management responsibility, represented a mark of their relative status. The management hierarchy extended further through deputies to heads.

[. . .]

Symbolic elements of culture are those whose patterns of action represent something else, typically a shared value. Such patterns include *rituals* – regularised and often habitual sequences of action (such as the seating arrangements for SMT meetings which demonstrated the value placed on everyone being able to contribute) – and, within this category, *ceremonies* which imply some form of celebration. Members of one SMT occasionally went out for a meal together. Hoyle (1986) suggests that much interaction amongst staff in schools is symbolic in that actions may have both an explicit managerial purpose and a part in signifying a shared value.

[. . .]

Concepts drawn primarily from a political perspective

Power refers to the capability of individuals to intervene in events so as to alter their course, and is defined by Giddens (1984) as a 'transformative capacity': the use of resources to secure desired outcomes. These *resources* vary widely, including sanctions, rewards, reference to norms of behaviour, attitudes and skills linked to individual personalities, and various kinds of knowledge. Individual personalities are expressed in interaction through preferences in the use of power according to particular beliefs and values. Aspects of individuals' personality are expressed through these preferences in a pattern of behaviour which may be summarised as their personal style as managers and teamworkers.

Sanctions within SMTs included the potential of heads to take disciplinary action while other SMT members could potentially withdraw their commitment to the SMT and act to undermine its work, say by leaking confidential information. [. . .]

Very diverse forms of knowledge may be used to alter the course of events in myriad ways. Contextual knowledge may be employed by individuals to judge when to give or withhold information. All SMT members used their knowledge of the school to contribute to SMT debates. Each member had expertise related to her or his individual management responsibility, and the more experienced members were frequently expert in colleagues' areas of work as a legacy of their past responsibilities. Some members of the SMTs kept in touch with the views of other staff and relayed their opinions to the team.

We found instances where heads withheld information from the SMT that they had been given in confidence by other staff concerning personal problems. Where heads were concerned about the performance of another SMT member, they generally addressed the issue with this person without divulging it to the full SMT. As we mentioned earlier, individuals had more or less extensive knowledge of the institutional history which influenced their current perceptions. Longer-serving SMT members referred, on occasion, to past experiences with a particular management strategy to support their argument in a current debate.

Power may be manifested in interaction yet, as we saw in the discussion of action and inaction, may also remain latent, since resources may still exist when they are not in use. Within interaction power may be regarded as a relationship, since action intended to secure particular outcomes involves the responses of others or their potential to act. [. . .]

For Giddens, power may or may not imply conflict. His conception contrasts with the 'zero-sum' formulation of Weber (1947) and Dahl (1957), the latter defining power as 'the ability to get someone to do something that he or she would not otherwise do'. Giddens' view of power allows for each protagonist within a conflict to use his or her transformative capacity in attempting to achieve interests that contradict those of others. It also suggests that, where there is consensus, individuals may have great capacity for working together to bring about change or to maintain the *status quo* both within and outside the SMT. Unanimous agreement among members in all SMTs on certain decisions led to a concerted effort to implement them. Within Giddens' conception, therefore, power does not disappear where individuals interact in attaining the same goal without resistance from inside or outside the group. Zero-sum conceptions of power, adopted by many conflict theorists, tend to define power out of existence where someone has the ability to get others to do something that they also want to do. Power exists in a zero-sum conception only where there is potential conflict, as opposed to potential synergy, and so fails to account for the ways in which people may use resources to achieve a shared goal.

Two types of power may be distinguished (Bacharach and Lawler 1980). *Authority* implies the use of resources to achieve desired ends in a way which is perceived by an individual as legitimate by beliefs and values associated with formal status. It includes the right to apply sanctions if necessary to secure compliance of others. Headteachers have extensive authority as managers which is enshrined in their conditions of service. Bacharach and Lawler regard authority as an all-or-nothing affair: people either have overall or delegated authority. [. . .]

The authority delegated to heads is itself part of a network of legally backed authority held by others inside and outside the school, including governing bodies,

which have representatives of teachers, parents, local government and the community.
[. . .]

Legislation tends to consist of general statements which often leave room for divergent interpretations about the relative degree of authority, delegated or otherwise, held by individuals and about the way in which this authority is or is not exercised. [. . .]

The exclusive amount of authority of headteachers to manage the school enables them to choose how much delegated authority to distribute within the team. Yet perceptions may differ within the SMT according to the beliefs and values of their members. In one school several members perceived that the head did not delegate enough for the team to operate effectively. The head was reticent to delegate further because of the risk of colleagues doing things of which she might not approve and yet for which she alone could ultimately be held externally accountable.

[. . .]

Up front or behind the scenes?

Influence, by comparison with authority, is the informal use of resources to achieve desired ends where individuals perceive there is no recourse to sanctions linked to the delegated authority accompanying status within the management hierarchy. A wide range of other sanctions may exist, such as refusal to contribute to SMT debate. The less delegated authority is held by individuals, the more influence is likely to be the main type of power. [. . .] A common example of the overt use of influence within SMTs was where individuals asked colleagues to do favours such as covering their teaching when they were particularly pressed.

A more covert use of influence in one SMT occurred when the deputies agreed to a decision during an SMT meeting, discovered afterwards in conversation that each deputy was uncomfortable with it, subsequently met to discuss this decision, and only then went to the head to ask if the decision could be altered. The theme of several organisational myths concerned assertions of covert use of influence either by the SMT (as where consultation exercises were held by other staff to be a sham) or individuals within it (as when one SMT member was claimed to be manipulating others without making his or her intentions explicit).

The term 'micropolitics' is often restricted to covert use of influence, following Hoyle's (1986) usage. Although he defines micropolitics as covering a continuum from conventional management procedures to 'almost a separate organizational world of illegitimate, self-interested manipulation', he confines description of micropolitical strategies largely to those which are covert. Bargaining is referred to as 'more micropolitical to the degree to which it is implicit rather than explicit, outside rather than inside formal structures and procedures, and draws upon informal resources of influence'. [. . .]

While accepting that there is a continuum between the two extremes of overt or covert use of resources within interaction to achieve particular ends, it is important to distinguish between them. We suggest that action (or refraining from acting) is *manipulative* either where it is a conscious attempt, covertly, to influence events through means or ends which are not made explicit; or where it is illegitimate, whether overt or not. The analysis of interaction is complicated by the fact that implicit or explicit means and ends may be regarded by either party to interaction as legitimate or illegitimate. [. . .] Depending on the perception of the actor or the person on the receiving end, an action may be:

- overt and legitimate;
- manipulative because it is covert, yet still legitimate;
- manipulative because it is illegitimate, whether overt or covert.

Within a team, legitimacy of action is defined according to the norms that make up the culture of teamwork. Several heads in our study attempted to create a climate which was conducive to collaboration, perhaps by offering food and drink at the beginning of an SMT meeting. Their aim was not made explicit to colleagues yet, for the heads, it was a legitimate element of their work as team leader.

Individuals attempt to realise their *interests*, seen as outcomes that facilitate the fulfilment of their wants. In other words, use of resources in action to realise interests reflects individuals' efforts to give expression to their values which, in turn, are framed by their beliefs.

Power as a relationship

Individuals in a relationship of power are each partly autonomous and partly dependent on the other, however asymmetrical the relationship. Each person is thus implicated in a multidirectional '*dialectic of control*' (Giddens 1984) manifested in interaction between individuals or groups. Interaction in schools is a complex network of interdependencies, depending upon the individuals involved at any point. Everyone has access to some resources. Conversely no individual has a monopoly on power: it is distributed throughout the organisation, albeit unequally. There is no sense in which heads, despite having exclusive authority in respect of colleagues' work, have exclusive control in practice over what their colleagues do.

Rather than assuming that some people have the power to determine the actions of others, we may instead conceive them as being able to *delimit* these actions. Heads may create conditions which open up the possibilities for SMT colleagues to take initiatives, yet at the same time attempt to keep these possibilities within boundaries that they define. The idea that control within interaction is dialectical implies a sequence of action and response where each party enables the other to choose what to do – but within limits. SMT members other than heads may also enable the latter to operate as team leader as long as the heads' actions lie within the bounds of acceptability to other members of the team. If a head was to step beyond the boundary, other members could potentially use their influence to persuade the head to step back, perhaps by indicating that they might withdraw their commitment to implementing a team decision.

[. . .]

The relationship between power and conflict is contingent upon individuals attempting to realise different and irreconcilable interests. *Conflict* refers to struggle between people expressed through their interaction. It does not necessarily arise when actions are taken to realise *contradictory interests* as long as action according to one interest is separated from action according to the contradictory interest (Wallace 1987, 1991). Mutual incompatibility between interests may be an enduring feature of social life and may not breed conflict where people are either unaware of their interests or the consequences of their actions, or are unwilling or unable to act on these interests. Where gender-related interests of women, for example, go unrecognised by women or are not acted upon, potential conflict with men within SMTs may be avoided.

[In SMTs,] actions reflecting the contradictory norms of contributing equally as team members to school management and a management hierarchy entailing the authority to direct the work of colleagues were kept separate in much interaction. While SMT members continued to adhere to both norms, usually only one was expressed at any time. When SMTs engaged in a debate, members generally acted according to the norm of contributing as equals. The opposing norm relating to a management hierarchy remained largely latent, though it may be expressed in the way heads chaired the meeting. If the heads were to use their authority to direct their SMT colleagues, the norm that there was a legitimate management hierarchy linked to status would be manifested, overriding the norm of equal contribution as team members. The norm of equal contribution would now recede into the background.

The potential for conflict would arise if some members acted according to their formal status while others acted as equal contributors within the same interaction, as might happen if other SMT members refused to accept heads' authority or act unilaterally within an area that they perceived to lie within the SMT's jurisdiction. The norm of a management hierarchy was potentially backed by sanctions linked to heads' authority, whereas the norm of equal contribution was not. Other SMT members could use influence by withdrawing their commitment to teamwork, on which heads depended. However, the participation of other members in teamwork was ultimately at the invitation of heads and conflict would be likely to result in reversion to a more hierarchical approach to management. In the rare instances where heads did act in this way, other members temporarily forsook the norm of contributing as equals by (equally temporarily) accepting the norm that the head held the overaching authority for decisions affecting the management of the school.

[. . .]

The gender dimension

The separate cultural and political perspectives which are the focus of our critique both fail to take adequate account of the different experiences of men and women as managers. The cultural perspective (Table 9.1) ignores the ways in which the distribution of power between women and men in wider society, as well as their different interests and goals, have an impact on how they behave in schools. The political concepts listed give insufficient emphasis to the culture of teamwork which has its roots in behavioural norms that cut across hierarchies based on male power and management structure and responsibilities based on gender differentiation. A challenge to our dual perspective combining culture and power is the extent to which it takes account of gender as a factor influencing teamwork in educational organisations. [. . .]

Other research in non-educational settings (e.g. Hearn *et al.* 1989; Coleman 1991) suggests that the experience of women in organisations is different from that of men and that the beliefs and values underpinning their behaviour may also be different. Our study of teams included both men and women who had made a commitment to teamwork. It emerged that they shared common professional values about collaboration, equity and collective responsibility that dominated their separate, private beliefs about men's and women's behaviour at work. We would be naïve to accept the almost total denial by most respondents (women and men) of the influence of gender on team behaviour as evidence that gender differentiation did not exist. On the other hand, the value that teamwork places on equal contribution appears to make it more likely that individuals will try to suppress or refrain from acting on values that subscribe to gender inequalities or differences in the workplace. The greatest threat to the value of equal contribution was an acceptance of the management hierarchy represented in our case study schools, by both women and men. What emerged was the potential that teamwork offers for a new model of leadership in which neither men nor women prescribe the dominant characteristics and to which both have equal access.

This possibility does not mean there were no instances in teamwork of gender-related behaviour. It was manifest at times in the type of language used to construct the meanings that frame teamwork. The three woman team leaders counted 'the need to protect against isolation' among their reasons for adopting a team approach. Men referred often to sports metaphors to highlight the value of teamwork. [. . .]

However, generally we found the discourse of teamwork to be supportive of it as a cooperative rather than competitive activity. Research into language and gender (Corson 1992) suggests women use talk for cooperative rather than competitive exchange more frequently and easily than men. In so far as teamwork reflects a commitment to collaboration with facilitative rather than directive team leadership, then we might expect the language of teamwork to be less 'masculine' than is common in male-dominated groups (which all six teams were numerically). On the other hand, we did not find significant differences in gender-related language between the three teams headed by men and the three headed by women. The decision to adopt a team approach seems to signify a shift in leadership style towards an 'androgynous' model which posits the possibility for leaders to exhibit the wide range of qualities which are present in both men and women.

We consider describing teamwork as androgynous more useful than aligning a team or collaborative way of working with either 'masculine' or 'feminine' approaches. We suggest that teamwork undercuts gender-based behaviour by proposing different norms and rules that make some behaviours legitimate, particularly those stressing collaboration, equity and consensual decision making. Some conflicts may have their origins in gender-influenced responses but are unlikely to be articulated in these terms. [. . .] Individual responsibilities and status were defined in terms of the management hierarchy and team membership rather than gender, as some earlier studies of school management hierarchies have shown (e.g. Richardson 1973).

There was little difference in participation by women and men in the rituals and ceremonies that helped affirm the values of their culture of teamwork. Both had allegiances based on faculty or departmental membership rather than gender affiliation. Politically, both men and women drew idiosyncratically upon resources associated with their personalities, skills and status. Although there were differences in delegation by individual headteachers, patterns were not gender specific. Nor were women any less likely than men to use power overtly or covertly in interaction.

References

Bacharach, S. and Lawler, E. (1980) *Power and Politics in Organizations*. San Francisco: Jossey Bass.
Ball, S. (1987) *The Micropolitics of the School*, London: Methuen.

Blase, J. (ed.) (1991) *The Politics of Life in Schools*, London: Sage.

Bolman, L. and Deal, T. (1991) *Reframing Organizations: Artistry, Choice and Leadership*. San Francisco: Jossey Bass.

Bush, T. (1986) *Theories of Educational Management*. London: Paul Chapman.

Coleman, G. (1991) *Investigating Organizations: A Feminist Approach*. Bristol: University of Bristol School of Advanced Urban Studies.

Corson, D. (1992) Language, gender and education: a critical review linking social justice and power. *Gender and Education*, 4(3): 229–54.

Cuthbert, R. (1984) *The Management Process, Block 3, Part 2, E324 Management in Post-Compulsory Education*, Milton Keynes: The Open University.

Dahl, R. (1957) The concept of power. *Behavioural Science*, 2: 201–15.

Deal, T. (1985) The symbolism of effective schools. *Elementary School Journal*, 85: 601–20.

Giddens, A. (1976) *New Rules of Sociological Method*. London: Hutchinson.

Giddens, A. (1984) *The Constitution of Society*, Cambridge: Polity Press.

Gronn, P. (1986) Politics, power and the management of schools, in E. Hoyle and A. McMahon (eds) *The Management of Schools*, London: Kogan Page.

Hearn, J., Sheppard, D., Tancred-Sheriff, P. and Burrell, G. (eds) (1989) *The Sexuality of Organization*, London: Sage.

Hoyle, E. (1986) *The Politics of School Management*, London: Hodder and Stoughton.

Morgan, G. (1986) *Images of Organization*. Newbury Park, CA: Sage.

Nias, J., Southworth, G. and Campbell, P. (1992) *Whole School Curriculum Development*, London: Falmer.

Nias, J., Southworth, G. and Yeomans, R. (1989) *Staff Relationships in the Primary School*. London: Cassell.

Radnor, H. (1990) Complexities and compromises: the new ERA at Parkview School. Paper presented at American Educational Research Association annual meeting, Boston.

Richardson, E. (1973) *The Teacher, the School, and the Task of Management*. London: Heinemann.

Sergiovanni, T. and Corbally, J. (eds) (1984) *Leadership and Organizational Culture*, Chicago: University of Illinois Press.

Wallace, M. (1987) Principals' centres: a transferable innovation? *School Organization*, 7(3): 287–95.

Wallace, M. (1991) Contradictory interests in policy implementation: the case of LEA development plans for schools, *Journal of Education Policy*, Vol. 6, no. 4, pp. 385–399.

Weber, M. (1947) *The Theory of Social and Economic Organizations*. London: Collier-Macmillan.

10 | Organizational effectiveness*

W. RICHARD SCOTT

Determining criteria of effectiveness

There are many possible bases for generating criteria of effectiveness, and as we would expect, many different constituencies have an interest in the effectiveness of any organization and will want to pursue criteria that reflect this interest.

Multiple criteria

[. . .]
Under a rational system model, since organizations are viewed as instruments for the attainment of goals, the criteria emphasized focus on the number and quality of outputs and the economies realized in transforming inputs into outputs. General criteria include measures of total output and of quality, productivity, and efficiency. More so than for the other two models, measures of effectiveness from a rational system perspective take the specific goals of the organization as the basis for generating effectiveness criteria.
[. . .]
The natural system model views organizations as collectivities that are capable of achieving specified goals but are engaged in other activities required to maintain themselves as a social unit. Thus, natural system analysts insist on adding a set of support goals to the output goals emphasized by the rational system model. Further, these support goals are expected to dominate output goals if the two do not coincide: organizations are governed by the overriding goal of survival. The criteria generated by this conception include measures of participant satisfaction and morale (indicators of whether the organization's inducements are sufficient to evoke contributions from participants adequate to ensure survival), the interpersonal skills of managers, and survival itself.

---

* This material has been edited and orginally appeared as Chapter 13 in *Organizations: Rational, Natural and Open Systems*.

The open systems perspective views organizations as being highly interdependent with their environments and engaged in system-elaborating as well as system-maintaining activities. Information acquisition and processing is viewed as an especially critical activity, since an organization's long-term well-being is dependent on its ability to detect and respond to subtle changes in its task environment. Yuchtman and Seashore specify one criterion that they argue is most appropriate for assessing the effectiveness of organizations from the open systems perspective: 'bargaining position, as reflected in the ability of the organization, in either absolute or relative terms, to exploit its environment in the acquisition of scarce and valued resources' (1967: 898). Criteria such as profitability, which may be viewed as the excess of returns over expenditures, are also emphasized by open systems analysts. And a great many theorists stress the importance of adaptability and flexibility as criteria of effectiveness. [. . .]

Analysts' diverse conceptions of organizations are not the only source of variation in effectiveness criteria. Other important bases of diversity include time perspective and level of analysis. Time considerations enter into the generation and application of effectiveness criteria in two senses. First, the criteria employed may vary depending on whether a relatively shorter or longer time frame is adopted. [. . .] Second, organizations are necessarily at different stages of their life cycles, and criteria appropriate for assessing effectiveness at one stage may be less so for another. [. . .] Cameron and Whetten (1981), in a study of eighteen simulated organizations, found that participants were more apt to stress the effectiveness of acquiring inputs at earlier stages in the history of their organization and the effectiveness of producing outputs at later stages.

Level of analysis is a critical factor in accounting for variations in effectiveness criteria. Our conclusions concerning the relative effectiveness of organizations will vary greatly depending on whether we emphasize their impact on individual participants, on the organization itself, or on broader, external societal systems. Cummings (1977: 60) argues for the first, social psychological–level criteria for assessing organizational effectiveness. He proposes that

> an effective organization is one in which the greatest percentage of participants perceive themselves as free to use the organization and its subsystems as instruments for their own ends.

Most analysts take the organization itself as the appropriate level of analysis for assessing effectiveness. Yuchtman and Seashore (1967: 896) explicitly adopt this posture, suggesting that a relevant view of effectiveness answers the question, how well is the organization doing for itself? Still other investigators adopt a more ecological framework and propose that organizations should be evaluated in terms of their contributions to other, more general systems. Parsons's (1960) approach to the study of organizations exemplifies this functionalist type of criteria.

Variations in theoretical perspectives on organizations, in time horizons and developmental stage, and in level of analysis – these help to account for the diversity of criteria proposed in analyzing effectiveness. Yet another source of diversity is to be found in the varying sets of participants and constituents associated with organizations.

Participants, constituents, and criteria

Whether organizations are viewed as rational, natural, or open systems, our conceptions of their goals, participants, and constituencies have become progressively more complex. We have been instructed by Simon (1957) to view even 'simple' output goals as complex and multi-faceted and we have learned from Etzioni (1964) and Perrow (1970) to add support or maintenance goals to output goals. This more complex conception of goals is reinforced by viewing organizations as collections of subgroups of participants who possess various social characteristics, are in different social locations, and exhibit divergent views and interests regarding what the organization is and what it should be doing. This conception of the organization as a political system can be expanded to include outside constituencies who hold goals 'for' the organization (Thompson 1967: 127), and who attempt to impose these goals on the organization.

It is important to emphasize that when we speak of goals in relation to ascertaining the effectiveness of organizations, we are focusing on the use of goals to supply evaluation criteria. Goals are used to evaluate organizational activities as well as to motivate and direct them. In a rational world, we would expect the criteria that are developed to direct organizational activities to be the same as those employed to evaluate them, but events in organizations are not always as rational and tightly coupled as some theorists would have us believe. Instead, we must be prepared to observe different criteria employed by those who assign tasks and those who evaluate performance. Discrepancies are more likely to occur when the control system becomes differentiated and these functions are assigned to different actors, but they can occur when the same persons or groups perform both directing and evaluating activities. An oft-cited problem in organizations develops when vague and broad criteria are used to direct task activities but very explicit criteria are employed to evaluate them, with the consequence that evaluation criteria deflect attention and effort from the original stated objectives to a different or narrower set of goals embodied in the evaluation system. Evaluation criteria often focus on the more easily measured task attributes and ignore others less readily assessed. Thus, social workers may be directed by their supervisors to provide therapeutic casework services but be evaluated primarily on the basis of the number and timeliness of their visits to clients and the correctness of their calculation of budgets. Such discrepancies are likely to result in a displacement of goals as participants come to realize what criteria are used to determine evaluations and to dispense rewards.

Varying goals – viewed both as directive and as evaluative criteria – will be held by different participant groups and constituencies in organizations. The managers of organizations may not speak with one voice but with many, since they may be composed of a shifting coalition of interests. Similarly, top managers' goals for directing and evaluating activities may not coincide with or be completely reflected in the criteria used by middle-level personnel such as supervisors or technical specialists. Performers vary in the extent to which their own conceptions of their work coincide with those of their superiors, and also in their capacity to enforce their preferences. Finally, many 'external' constituencies [. . .] have genuine interests in the functioning of an organization and may be expected to attempt to advocate and, if possible, impose their own effectiveness criteria on the organization. In general, the number of persons and groups who propose criteria for evaluating the performance of an organization will be much larger than the number who explicitly seek to direct its activities. According to this conception of organizations, we would expect little commonality in the criteria employed by the various parties who assess organizational effectiveness. This expectation is shared by Friedlander and Pickle (1968), who impute appropriate interests to such groups as owners, employees, creditors, suppliers, customers, governmental regulators, and the host community.

Another consideration complicating the examination of effectiveness is the recent challenges to the assumption that organizations necessarily exhibit a unified or consistent set of performances. The political models just reviewed allow for divergence and conflict of interests among participants but presume their resolution through negotiation and power processes. In the end, the organization is presumed to pursue a single program. Alternative models suggest the utility of viewing some organizations as 'organized anarchies' or as loosely coupled systems containing subunits that exhibit a high degree of autonomy and are capable of pursuing inconsistent objectives. This conception admits the possibility that, with respect to any specific criterion of effectiveness, an organization can be both effective and ineffective depending on what components are being evaluated!

Given the wide variety of participants, groups and constituencies that can attempt to set criteria for organizational effectiveness, what generalizations, if any, can be suggested to guide investigations in this area? We offer three predictions. First, the criteria proposed by each group will be self-interested ones. [. . .] We should not look for heroes or villains but for parties with varying interests. And all parties will evaluate the performance of the organization in terms of criteria that benefit themselves. Second, although no criteria are disinterested – each will benefit some groups more than others – all will be stated so as to appear universalistic and objective. This generalization receives support from Pfeffer and Salancik's (1974) study of the allocation of resources among university departments. They report that the stronger departments succeed in budget allocation contests not by imposing particularistic criteria on decisions but by ensuring that the universalistic criteria selected favor their own position. For example, strong departments that have larger graduate-student enrolments will favor this criterion in allocating resources while departments with larger numbers of undergraduate majors will seek to impose this criterion as a distribution rule. Third, given multiple sets of actors pursuing their own interests and a situation of scarce resources, we would expect little commonality or convergence and some conflicts in the criteria employed by the various parties to assess organizational effectiveness, a prediction supported by the study conducted by Friedlander and Pickle (1968).

One final constituency remains to be considered. Researchers who attempt to assess the effectiveness of organizations are not immune to these political processes. Which, and whose, criteria we choose to emphasize in our studies of organizations will depend on our own interests in undertaking the study. We must be willing to state clearly what criteria we propose to employ, recognizing that whatever they are and whoever espouses them, they are always normative conceptions, serving some interests more than others, and likely to be both limited and controversial.

Market and nonmarket organizations

The distinction between market-based and nonmarket organizations is especially salient when the question of effectiveness is raised. When properly functioning, the market provides a mechanism for linking the interests of organizational participants and external constituencies in such a manner that the former do not prosper unless they serve the interests of the latter. The effectiveness of market-controlled organizations is directly determined by their customers: if their interests are satisfied, then they will continue to supply the inputs required by the organization; if not, then they can withhold their contributions, causing the organization to suffer and perhaps ultimately to fail.

Under ideal market conditions an organization's output goals and system-maintenance goals are tightly linked. [. . .]

Other organizations, primarily government agencies, operate from the outset in non-market environments. As Downs (1967: 30) emphasizes, an important implication of this condition is that 'there is no direct relationship between the services a bureau provides and the income it receives for providing them.

Nonmarket organizations are particularly likely to lack clear output measures. When the goals are to provide for an adequate defence, to negotiate advantageous treaties with other countries, or to fight poverty, it is difficult to determine how effective performances are. Of course, other types of organizations also pursue goals that are vague and difficult to assess. Two problems are involved: how to select indicators – the evidence to employ in evaluating performances – and how to set standards – the criteria to be used in judging whether a given performance is good or poor. Issues of standard setting and indicator selection are discussed in the following section.

Assessing effectiveness

In order for an evaluation of a performance to occur, criteria must be selected, including the identification of properties or dimensions and the setting of standards; work must be sampled, with decisions made concerning the types of indicators to be employed and the nature of the sample to be drawn; and sampled values must be compared with the selected standards. In the current section, we discuss the setting of standards and the selection of indicators for assessing organization effectiveness and briefly comment on decisions regarding selection of the sample.

Setting standards

The setting of standards is a central component in establishing criteria for evaluating the effectiveness of an organization. By definition, standards are normative and not descriptive statements. The problem of how standards for assessing organizations are set is an interesting one but has received relatively little attention from social scientists. [. . .]

Thompson (1967: 84–7) proposes a model in which types of assessment are viewed as a function of a combination of two factors: (1) whether the standards of desirability are relatively clearly formulated or ambiguous, and (2) whether the beliefs about cause–effect relations are relatively complete or are incomplete. (This second factor is a measure of knowledge of the technology utilized during the throughput process; it is similar to the dimension of predictability.) He argues that when standards are clear and cause–effect relations are known, then *efficiency* tests are appropriate. Such tests assess not simply whether a desired effect was produced but whether it was done so efficiently – that is, with a minimum of inputs. If standards are clear but cause–effect relations are uncertain, then *instrumental* tests are suitable. These tests ascertain only whether the desired state was achieved and do not demand conservation of resources. When standards of desirability are themselves ambiguous, then the organization must resort to *social* tests. Social tests are those validated by consensus or by authority. Their validity depends on how many or on who endorses them. [. . .]

Thompson's typology is far from definitive, but it calls attention not only to the diversity of standards employed in assessing organizations but also to factors that help to account for these differences.

Selecting indicators

Among the most critical decisions to be made in attempting to assess organizational effectiveness is the choice of the measures or indicators to be employed. Three general types of indicators have been identified: those based on outcomes, those based on processes, and those based on structures. The advantages and disadvantages of each type will be reviewed.

Outcomes

Outcome indicators focus on specific characteristics of materials or objects on which the organization has performed some operation. Examples of outcome indicators are changes in the knowledge or attitudes of students in educational organizations, or changes in the health status of patients in medical institutions. Outcomes are often regarded as the quintessential indicators of effectiveness, but they also may present serious problems of interpretation. Outcomes are never pure indicators of quality of performance, since they reflect not only the care and accuracy with which work activities are carried out but also the current state of the technology and the characteristics of the organization's input and output environments. These matters are of little import when cause–effect knowledge is relatively complete and when organizations are able to exercise adequate controls over their input and output sectors – that is, when the organization is well buffered from its environment. In such situations, represented by the manufacture of standardized equipment in competitive markets, outcomes serve as safe indexes of quality and quantity of organizational performance. However, many types of organizations lack such controls over their work processes and task environments. [. . .]

In our view, the use of outcome measures presents difficult, but not unsolvable, problems in assessing effectiveness of organizations such as hospitals and schools. The problem of inadequate knowledge of cause–effect relations can be handled by the use of relative rather than absolute performance standards, so that the performance of an organization is compared against others carrying on similar work. This approach presumes that the organizations assessed can – or should – participate in the same cultural system and have access to the same general knowledge pool. A particular organization possessing more relevant knowledge – for example, having better-trained personnel – would be expected to perform better than one possessing less knowledge, but the use of relative standards ensure that an organization is not penalized for lacking knowledge that no one has.

The problem posed by the contribution of variations among input characteristics to variations in outcomes experienced is less easily resolved. Although we can safely assume that organizations have access to the same knowledge, we cannot assume that they have access to the same client pool or supply sources. Indeed, one of the principal ways in which organizations vary is in the amount and quality of inputs they are able to garner. The pattern of inputs characterizing various types of organizations is not as simple as might appear on superficial examination. For example, as might be expected, prestigious universities recruit highly intelligent students, as indicated by scores on standard entrance examinations or past performance in academic settings, whereas less highly regarded institutions accept higher proportions of less qualified students. By contrast, highly regarded teaching hospitals focus primarily on the care of the very sick or on those whose problems pose the greatest challenge to medical science. In these organizations, there is an inverse relation between presumed quality of institution and patient condition. We would expect organizations to seek to take credit for acquiring inputs that enhance their outcomes – a widely used indicator of quality for universities is the characteristics of the student body they are able to attract – but to resist being held accountable for inputs that negatively affect outcomes. Thus, teaching hospitals insist that if patient outcome measures are employed as indicators of performance quality, they be standardized to take account of differences in patient mix. Statistical techniques are available that allow analysts to adjust outcome measures to take into account differences in characteristics of inputs.

Outcome measures may also be affected by the characteristics of output environments. [. . .] As with inputs, we would expect organizations to prefer to take credit for conditions enhancing outcomes but insist that conditions having a negative effect be taken into account if outcomes are evaluated.

More generally, the decision as to how to treat input characteristics and output environments is not primarily a methodological but a theoretical issue. Do we wish to adjust for differences in student intelligence among universities in assessing student performance, or do we wish to regard student recruitment as an important aspect of a university's performance? [. . .] Answers to these and similar questions depend on whether we seek to concentrate simply on the organization's throughput processes – its technical-core activities – or to include in our assessment the performance of the organization's bridging units – its input and output components.

Still other issues are involved in the use of outcome measures to assess organizational effectiveness. Briefly, it is difficult to determine the appropriate timing of such measures. Some organizations insist that their full effects may not be apparent for a long period following their performance. For example, some educators claim that relevant academic outcomes can only be assessed long after the students have left school and have attempted to apply their knowledge in the 'real world'. And when is the appropriate time to assess a hospital's effect on a patient's health – immediately following a major therapeutic intervention such as surgery, at discharge, or following a post-hospitalization recovery period? Another problem in employing outcome indicators is the lack of relevant information. Many types of organizations have little or no data on outcomes achieved: they quickly lose contact with their 'products' – whether these be human graduates or manufactured commodities. The collection of relevant outcome data can become very costly indeed if it entails tracking down such products after they are distributed throughout the environment.

Partly because of these quite formidable difficulties in assessing and interpreting outcome measures, other types of indicators of organizational effectiveness are often preferred. These measures – of processes and structures – can be more briefly described.

Processes

Process measures focus on the quantity or quality of activities carried on by the organization. As Suchman (1967: 61) notes, this type of indicator

> represents an assessment of input or energy regardless of output. It is intended to answer the questions, 'What did you do?' and 'How well did you do it?'

Process measures assess effort rather than effect. Some process measures assess work quantity – for example, staying with our hospital illustration, we may ask how many laboratory tests were conducted during a given period or how many patients were seen in the emergency room. Others assess work quality – for example, hospitals might be rated by the frequency with which medication errors occur or by the proportion of healthy tissue removed from patients during surgery. Still other measures assess the extent of quality-control efforts – for instance, the autopsy rate in hospitals or the proportion of X-rays reviewed by radiologists.

In some respects, process measures are more valid measures of the characteristics of organizational performance. Rather than requiring inferences from outcomes to performance characteristics, process measures directly assess performance values. On the other hand, it is important to emphasize that all process measures evaluate efforts rather than achievements, and when the focus is on quality of performance rather than quantity, they assess conformity to a given standard but not the adequacy or correctness of the standards themselves. Process measures are based on the assumption that it is known what activities are required to ensure effectiveness. [. . .] Social critics such as Illich (1972, 1976) claim that the substitution of process for outcome is one of the great shell games perpetrated by modern institutions against individuals. Illich (1972: 1) argues that contemporary individuals are trained

> to confuse process and substance. Once these become blurred, a new logic is assumed: the more treatment there is, the better are the results; or, escalation leads to success. The pupil is thereby 'schooled' to confuse teaching with learning, grade advancement with education, a diploma with competence, and fluency with the ability to say something new. His imagination is 'schooled' to accept service in place of value. [. . .]

Recognizing that Illich's broad accusations have some merit, we would, however, express two sorts of reservations. Focusing on processes rather than outcomes represents a type of goal displacement. However, as noted earlier, goal displacement is a very widespread phenomenon and need not be regarded as pathological. Only when means and ends become disconnected is there cause for distress. Our second demurring relates to the case of organizations in institutionalized environments, in which, to a large extent, process *is* substance. In these organizations, conformity to ritually defined procedures produces a successful outcome, by definition. Ceremony is substance in many contemporary organizations, including religious bodies, legal firms, and many professionally staffed organizations.

Organizations are more likely to compile data on work processes than on outcomes. Performance quality and quantity are often regularly monitored. Gathering information on work processes, however, can still be problematic. Inspections based on observation of ongoing performances are both expensive and reactive – that is, likely to influence the behaviour observed. In most work situations there are numerous barriers to work visibility, and workers often resist attempts to directly observe their work in process. Many kinds of work occur under circumstances that render routine inspection impossible, and other kinds, such as those emphasizing mental activities, are by their nature difficult to observe. Because of such difficulties, organizations may rely on self-reports of activities performed. However, such data are likely to be both biased and incomplete representations of work processes (see Dornbusch and Scott 1975: 145–62). Because of these and related difficulties in obtaining process measures, many organizations rely on structural indicators of effectiveness.

Structures

Structural indicators assess the capacity of the organization for effective performance. Included within this category are all measures based on organizational features or participant characteristics presumed to have an impact on organizational effectiveness. [. . .] Schools are assessed by the qualities of their faculties measured in terms of types of degrees acquired, and by such features as the number of volumes in their libraries. These types of measures form the basis of accreditation reviews and organizational certification systems.

If process measures are once removed from outcomes, then structure indicators are twice remote, for these measures index not the work performed by structures but their *capacity* to perform work – not the activities carried out by organizational participants but their qualifications to perform the work. Structural indicators focus on organizational inputs as surrogate measures for outputs. [. . .]

As was the case with measures of organizational process, a number of observers have suggested that an emphasis on structural measures may have detrimental consequences for quality of outcomes. [. . .] Thus, we have the interesting situation in which some measures of organizational effectiveness based on the assessment of process or of structure are argued to adversely affect other measures of effectiveness based on outcomes.

Selecting samples

[. . .] A basic decision confronting the analyst who assesses the effectiveness of any organization is whether to focus on the actual work performed by the organization or instead to ask whether the organization is attending to the appropriate work. The first option takes as given the current program of the organization – its structures, processes, or outcomes – and seeks to ascertain its quality or effectiveness. The second option assumes a broader perspective, asking whether the organization is engaged in the right program. Never mind whether the organization is doing things right; is it doing the right things? Reinhardt (1973) labels the first criterion *microquality* and the second, *macroquality*. If this distinction were applied to a service organization, an assessment of microquality would focus on the quality of structures, processes, or outcomes actually experienced by clients who were the recipients of the organization's services. By contrast, an assessment of macroquality would seek to determine whether the appropriate services were being provided or, more critically, whether the proper clients were receiving services. [. . .]

Participants, constituents, and measures

Just as with evaluation criteria, we would expect differing participant and constituency groups to prefer some types of measures over others. Generally, we expect organizational managers to emphasize structural measures of effectiveness, in part because these reflect factors that are more under their control than other types of indicators. Thus, organizational administrators are likely to have considerable influence over the types of facilities provided or the standards used in hiring personnel. By contrast, we would expect performers or rank-and-file participants to emphasize process measures of effectiveness. Skilled and semiskilled workers, who have little or no discretion in the selection of their activities, will prefer to be evaluated on the basis of their conformity to their performance programs rather than on the basis of the efficacy of these programs. And professional personnel, who are granted discretion in their choice of activities, will also usually prefer to be evaluated on the basis of process measures – their conformity to 'standards of good practice' – since inadequacies in the knowledge base mean that they lack full control over outcomes.

Clients who use the products or receive the services are likely to focus primarily on outcome measures of effectiveness. They will evaluate the organization's product in terms of the extent to which it has met their own needs and expectations. [. . .] In circumstances where outcomes are difficult to evaluate, process measures will receive more weight from clients than outcome indicators. The most extreme cases involve institutionalized environments in which no outcomes at all can be demonstrated to occur regularly – although they are alleged to occur – so that both performers and recipients devote attention to evaluating conformity to established norms of practice.

All of the interest groups considered to this point – organizational managers, performers, and consumers – are likely to focus on microquality indicators of effectiveness. They will prefer to focus on the structures, processes, and outcomes associated with the work that the organization is actually performing. But another interest group consisting of the public at large, including some public regulatory bodies, will be more likely to emphasize measures of macroquality. Is the organization concentrating its attention and resources on the proper products or problems? Do eligible clients have access to its services? Is the community as a whole benefiting from its operation?

Our final constituency are the researchers dedicated to the objective, scientific analysis of organizational effectiveness. We would hope to find this group busily engaged in analyzing *all* types of indicators of effectiveness, exploring their interrelation, and employing criteria variously drawn from all of the interested parties. [. . .] It is our belief that organizational analysts are more likely to identify with organizational managers and professional performers than with client and public interests. Indeed, most of the research on organizations is conducted by persons who train future managers while consulting for present ones. Also, most of the data available to us for analysis are collected by the organizations for their own purposes or are based on information supplied by organizational managers. Organizations, as noted above, are much less likely to collect data on outcomes than data based on their structural features and processes. If we want data on outcomes – and especially on outcomes that represent measures of macroquality – we will have to collect them for ourselves, or persuade governmental agencies to collect them for us. We should not minimize the cost or the value of such data in correcting the bias that currently exists in indicators of organizational effectiveness.

References

Cameron, Kim S. and Whetten, D. A. (1981) Perceptions of organizational effectiveness over organizational life cycles. *Administrative Science Quarterly*, 26 (December): 525–44.

Cummings, L. L. (1977) Emergence of the instrumental organization, in P. S. Goodman and J. M. Pennings (eds) *New Perspectives on Organizational Effectiveness*, pp. 56–62. San Francisco: Jossey Bass.

Cummings, L. L. (1982) Organizational behavior. *Annual Review of Psychology*, 33: 541–79.

Dornbusch, S. M. and Scott, W. R. with the assistance of Buschino, B. C. and Laing, J. D. (1975) *Evaluation and the Exercise of Authority*. San Francisco: Jossey Bass.

Downs, A. (1967) *Inside Bureaucracy*. Boston: Little, Brown.

Etzioni, A. (1964) *Modern Organizations*. Englewood Cliffs, NJ: Prentice-Hall.

Friedlander, F. and Pickle, H. (1968) Components of effectiveness in small organizations. *Administrative Science Quarterly*, 13 (September): 289–304.

Illich, I. (1972) *Deschooling Society*. New York: Harper and Row, Harrow Books.

Illich, I. (1976) *Medical Nemesis*. New York: Random House.

Parsons, T. (1960) *Structure and Process in Modern Societies*. Glencoe, IL: Free Press.

Perrow, C. (1970) *Organizational Analysis: A Sociological View*. Belmont, CA: Wadsworth.

Pfeffer, J. and Salancik, G. R. (1974) Organizational decision making as a political process: the case of a university budget. *Administrative Science Quarterly*, 19 (June): 135–51.

Reinhardt, U. E. (1973) Proposed changes in the organization of health-care delivery: an overview and a critique. *Milbank Memorial Fund Quarterly*, 51 (Spring): 169–222.

Simon, H. A. (1957) *Administrative Behavior* (2nd edn.). New York: Macmillan (1st edn., 1945).

Suchman, E. A. (1967) *Evaluative Research*. New York: Russell Sage Foundation.

Thompson, J. D. (1967) *Organizations in Action*. New York: McGraw-Hill.

Yuchtman, E. and Seashore, S. E. (1967) A system resource approach to organizational effectiveness. *American Sociological Review*, 32 (December): 891–903.

PART 2

School and college effectiveness: theory, research and practice

11 | Towards a theory of educational effectiveness[*]

BERT CREEMERS

Introduction

[. . .]

Educational effectiveness is an important concept with the educational sciences. A comprehensive analysis of the effectiveness of education, taking the different levels of the educational system into account, can in a way be seen as the core of educational science and research. Educational research in this field is aimed at explaining the variance in educational outcomes, based on a theory about causes and effects in education. In this sense, a theory of educational effectiveness can be seen as an integral theory about education which takes into account the outcomes of education, the inputs, the processes and the contexts in which education takes place. In this sense, the concept of educational effectiveness is a welcome addition to educational research in general, and provides a programme for research. Such a programme has to address questions about outcomes and criteria for effectiveness, inputs, processes and contexts.

[. . .]

Outcomes of education: criteria, size and stability

In the past, research on school effectiveness was criticized for its criteria of effectiveness. Research took educational outcomes in the academic field as the only criterion. In addition, the measurement of this criterion was quite poor, involving, for example, the proportion of students going from primary to secondary education, or marks in school exams. At this moment, the best criterion for educational effectiveness is the value education adds to the initial attributes of students. Added value conceptions stress the point

*This material has been edited and is from *The Effective Classroom*.

that students have a background, an aptitude for learning, a home environment and a peer group, which have already contributed to the knowledge and skills they have acquired at the moment education starts. In examining educational effectiveness, we have to take into account the student's background as well as the student's initial attributes with respect to the specific subjects under study. This requires measurement of general attributes like intelligence and motivation as well as initial attributes with respect to the subjects under study, such as performance in mathematics, reading, etc.

Effectiveness is related to goals in education. Therefore, educational effectiveness is distinguished on the one hand from the study of educational effects, which also takes into account unexpected outcomes of education, such as the results of the hidden curriculum. On the other hand, it is distinguished from the concept of educational efficiency, which is concerned with the relationship between the effects of education and the inputs of education, most of the time in terms of finance.

Effectiveness stresses the point that factors at the different levels of the educational system contribute to educational outcomes: the student level, the classroom level, the school level and the contextual level. In research on educational effectiveness we have to specify the level under study, the factors at the various levels and the ways in which levels are supposed to contribute to the processes at other levels.

Educational effectiveness restricts the criteria for effectiveness to what can be achieved by schools and what schools are for. School effectiveness research was criticized because it took into account only a restricted set of outcomes, such as basic skills and knowledge. Therefore, 'multiple outcomes' are proposed as criteria for effectiveness. The following are some examples of these multiple outcomes:

- Traditional outcomes are *basic skills and knowledge*, such as reading, mathematics and language. Looking at the history of educational effectiveness, it is quite understandable that such a great deal of attention is given to basic skills and knowledge, because disadvantaged students did not succeed in these fields (Brookover *et al.* 1979; Edmonds 1979).
- An outcome frequently used in the past for educational effectiveness was *compensation* for initial attributes (equity). The idea of equity is connected with a belief in the school effectiveness movement that schools can to some extent compensate for initial differences. On the basis of educational research so far with respect to effectiveness, one can conclude that the compensatory powers of schools are quite small. Recent studies (Brandsma 1993) obtain almost the same results as evaluations of so-called compensatory programmes in the past, such as Head-Start, Follow-Through and, in the Netherlands, the Education and Social Environment Project (Scheerens 1987; Slavenburg and Peters 1989). Although equity is a longstanding aim in education, it turns out that schools do not contribute much to the reduction of pre-existing differences between students.
- *Social skills and attitudes*, for example towards school and towards different school subjects, were not systematically researched in the past. The idea behind these outcomes is that schools should be more than places for academic development, and that schools should develop not only academic and cognitive skills but also social and aesthetic skills, and, on top of that, should influence attitudes that are important in their own right but can also influence academic outcomes.
- *Higher-order skills*, such as problem solving, are useful criteria for educational effectiveness, especially in higher grades.

- The same holds for *meta-cognitive knowledge and skills*, which refer to learners' knowledge of and control over their cognitive processes by organizing, monitoring and modifying them, and includes strategies of how to learn.
- Finally, a broad range of 'new' educational goals are formulated in different fields, such as educational technology, creativity and moral behaviour.

Some research results can be interpreted as arguments against the immediate adoption of multiple outcomes within school effectiveness research. One of the most striking findings of school effectiveness research in the earlier years was the fact that schools which did not go for a broad range of educational goals but restricted themselves to a small set of academic outcomes had better results than schools with a broad range. This holds especially for low-SES schools (Teddlie and Stringfield 1993). The recommendation for educational practice of stealing time from other subjects for the basics can be seen as the practical implication of these empirical findings (Levine and Lezotte 1990) [. . .]

Several studies showed no relationship between the academic and the affective outcomes of education (Mortimore *et al.* 1988) or a negative relationship (Marsh *et al.* 1985). In recent publications, Knuver (1993) and Knuver and Brandsma (1993) present the results of research on the relationship between so-called affective outcomes and academic outcomes. In these Dutch studies, academic outcomes do have an effect on attitudes towards arithmetic, attitudes towards school and the well-being of students. This suggests that attitudes, and other affective outcomes, are the result of academic outcomes. The results of the research in this field seem to be quite inconsistent, but one can conclude that there is at least a relationship between affective and cognitive outcomes.

The foregoing deals with criticisms with respect to outcomes, especially the criticism that the criterion for effectiveness in educational research is not well chosen. There are several ways to define outcomes, and from a technical point of view it is no problem to develop instruments to measure them. For a theoretical perspective (what factors contribute to what kinds of outcomes), it is also important to have more measures for school and classroom effectiveness. On the basis of the above research results, however, we should be careful in the selection and definition of outcomes. But this is just one aspect of criticism.

Another point of criticism is that the effects of effective schools are insignificantly small. In fact, this is a more general problem concerning the influence of education as a whole, which has to do with the question of what education contributes to the educational career of students. We know that the largest part of the variation in school results between students is explained by aptitude and social background. Only a small proportion of variance can be explained by variables at the school and instructional levels (see, for instance, Walberg 1984). The proportion of variance that is left over after controlling for aptitude and SES is at most 20 per cent, although these proportions vary depending on the study (and its statistical procedures). Of this 20 per cent, only a small proportion is accounted for by factors we have studied so far in school effectiveness research (from less than 1 per cent up to at most 2–3 per cent of the total variance, although higher percentages may be presented when only the between-school variance is considered and the 20 per cent between-school variance is seen as the total vairiance).

When differences between effective and non-effective schools are phrased in terms of their effects on the careers of individual school students, it turns out that these differences (even if they are quite small in the Netherlands) mean that there is a difference for individual students between being referred or not being referred to special education, in grade retention or promotion, and in the choice of a higher level of secondary education. So, even when effects are quite small in a statistical sense, they can be very important for the individual careers of students (Bosker and Scheerens 1989).

A third point of criticism is that the effects of schools are quite unstable. The discrepancy between the results of different studies is quite large. Most of the time the correlations between school subjects within a grade are rather unstable in primary schools (between 0.55 and 0.80) as well as in secondary schools (between 0.45 and 0.75). Sometimes, this discrepancy is even larger. In primary education, correlations have been found between 0.10 and 0.65, and in secondary education between 0.25 and 0.90 (Bosker 1991).

To sum up, the first problem for the development of a theory about educational effectiveness has to do with the outcomes of education. Although some arguments are formulated against the use of all kinds of critieria, it is important to use more criteria than before in future research to determine effectiveness, especially in the areas of academic outcomes such as higher-order skills and meta-cognitive knowledge and skills. From a technical point of view multiple outcomes have a preference because they permit the analysis of different constellations of classroom and school factors against each outcome, and it is also possible to deal statistically with the multitude of data that come with them. We have to keep in mind that the educational effects at the classroom and school levels are quite small, but significant. The instability of grades may be improved by a greater cohesion and constancy within schools.

Educational processes: factors contributing to educational effectiveness

A theory of educational effectiveness is not concerned in the first place with the outcome effectiveness criteria or the effectiveness criteria alone, but in particular with the question of how these goals can be achieved.

Educational effectiveness deals with the question of why schools with initially comparable students differ in the extent to which they achieve their goals. In a system approach, a distinction is made between the input, context and processes (in addition to outcomes) of education. The input consists of all kinds of variables connected with financial or personnel resources, and the background of students. By context is meant the socioeconomic, political and educational context of schools; for example the guidelines for education and the national evaluation systems.

The most important factors concern the ongoing processes at the classroom and school levels. The question school effectiveness research deals with most of the time is what kind of factors within schools and classrooms make a difference between effective and less effective schools. In fact, this question was the background for the school effectiveness movement that started with the first studies in this field by Brookover et al. (1979) and Edmonds (1979). Their research proved that schools differ in the extent to which they can achieve results with comparable groups of students. Early school effectiveness research aimed to find the factors that caused the distinction between effective and less effective schools. In these so-called outlier studies, evidence was found that a small number of factors contribute to effectiveness. Most famous was the five-factor model of Edmonds (1979). Later, this model was criticized from a methodological and conceptual point of view (Scheerens and Creemers 1989), but in the early days of school effectiveness and school improvement the five-factor model (and later other models with slightly more factors) drew a great deal of attention from educational practice and policymaking. It seemed quite easy to change schools from non-effective to effective by just introducing programmes for the improvement of some factors, such as a programme for the evaluation of student progress in schools or in-service training for the improvement of the educational leadership of principals (Lezotte 1989).

Later it became clear that it is not easy to improve schools. Effective and non-effective schools differ on more than just a small amount of factors. This conclusion led to more research to distinguish between effective and non-effective schools. The earlier studies were mostly outlier studies but after criticism of the methodology of the outlier studies, more survey studies were carried out, enlarging the list of characteristics of effective education.

When the idea of effective education spread to countries other than the United States, replication studies were carried out to test whether or not the same characteristics of effective education could be found in other countries. The results of these studies did not confirm the lists of factors produced by research in the United States. Generally speaking, on the one hand the list of characteristics was enlarged and on the other hand replication studies could not find much empirical evidence for the initial 'factors' or characteristics. In addition, a conceptual approach was advocated, whereby a framework or theory should explain the differences between effective and non-effective education, which might be a point of departure for further research.

Recently, the results of these three types of studies (outlier studies, survey studies and theoretical studies) have been reviewed. Creemers and Knuver (1989), Creemers and Lugthart (1989), Reynolds (1989, 1991, 1992), Levine and Lezotte (1990), Scheerens (1990, 1992), Stringfield and Schaffer (1991), Creemers (1992a) and Levine (1992), sum up factors that make a difference between effective and non-effective education within schools and classrooms, each for their own country. The review of research provided by Levine and Lezotte in 1990 is of special interest. They produced a list of effective school correlates, based on 400 studies of school effectiveness in the United States:

- productive school climate and culture;
- focus on student acquisition of central learning skills;
- appropriate monitoring of student progress;
- practice-oriented staff development at the school site;
- outstanding leadership;
- salient parent involvement;
- effective instructional arrangements and implementation;
- high operationalized expectations and requirements for students;
- other possible correlates.

This general list, which contains almost everything that can be found in schools and is enlarged with 'other possible correlates', is broken down into other factors. For example, the correlates for effective instructional arrangements and implementation are:

- successful grouping and related organizational arrangements;
- appropriate pacing and alignment;
- active/enriched learning;
- effective teaching practices;

- emphasis on higher-order learning in assessing instructional outcomes;
- coordination in curriculum and instruction;
- easy availability of abundant, appropriate instructional materials;
- classroom adaptation;
- stealing time for reading, language and maths.

In total, hundreds of correlates of effectiveness are presented. In the correlational studies large numbers of schools and variables are involved, so in this way even small correlations can be significant. In the outlier studies, a few schools or classes but many factors are usually studied. There are always some, or even many, variables that seem to distinguish between these small numbers of schools. That is probably why in replication studies a number of factors do not reappear. The correlates gathered by Levine and Lezotte (1990) are more a result of research methods and techniques than a collection of genuine, clear and relevant concepts in a theory about effectiveness.

In a study in the United Kingdom by Mortimore *et al.* (1989), only twelve factors could be found:

- purposeful leadership of the staff by the headteacher;
- the involvement of the deputy head;
- the involvement of teachers;
- consistency among teachers;
- structured sessions;
- intellectually challenging teaching;
- a work-centred environment;
- limited focus within sessions;
- maximum communication between teachers and pupils;
- record keeping;
- parental involvement;
- a positive climate.

All these factors are comparable with the factors mentioned by Levine and Lezotte, but Mortimore *et al.* found fewer factors. Quite a few of the American factors did not prove to be related to effectiveness. In twelve Dutch studies even fewer factors could be found to distinguish between effective and non-effective schools, some of which provided evidence for the five factors originally distinguished by Edmonds (Scheerens 1992). Scheerens and Creemers (1989) conclude that an orderly climate, frequent evaluation, achievement orientation, high expectations and direct instruction seem to contribute to effectiveness in the Netherlands.

Many correlates for effectiveness are available, more or less supported by empirical research, but for the interpretation and understanding of educational effectiveness we need an overarching idea, a conceptual framework that will be developed in the next section.

Conceptual framework

The development of a conceptual framework is an important contribution to educational effectiveness research, because it can guide the design of research studies and the interpretation of the results at a later stage.

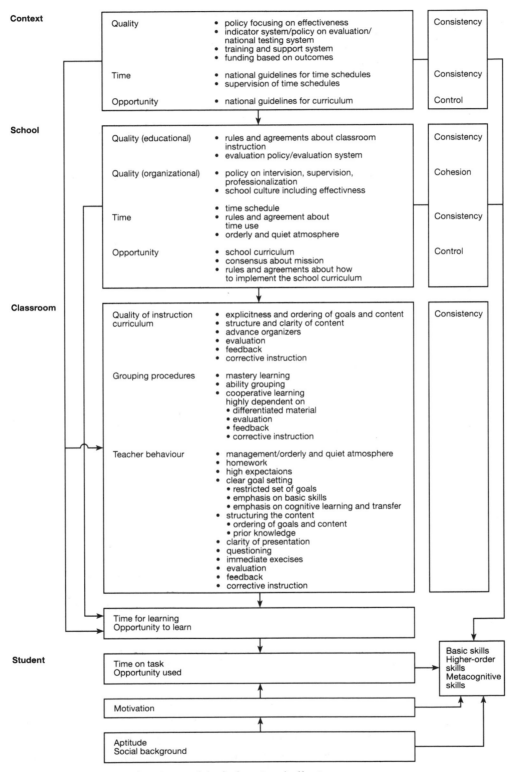

Figure 11.1   A comprehensive model of educational effectiveness

Based on theoretical notions and studies carried out so far, it is possible to make a list of 'promising' factors of educational effectiveness that have to be taken into account in developing a theory. It became evident that 'time on task' and the 'opportunity to learn' are important intermediating variables that can explain student outcomes. For the selection of 'explanatory' variables, lists of correlates, like the ones mentioned in the previous section, are available.

In recent years, several models for school effectiveness have been developed. The basic idea behind all models for school effectiveness is to distinguish between levels in education. All models include at least the individual student level, the classroom level and the school level, and the higher levels in the models provide the conditions for what happens at the levels below. Factors at the higher levels contribute to the outcomes or are conditional for what happens at the lower levels. This means that not just one level induces results, but a combination of levels.

Further elaborations of this basic multilevel model were provided by Creemers (1991), Scheerens (1991) and Stringfield and Slavin (1992). All these models are based to some extent on Carroll's model for school learning, in which the time needed for mastering the educational objectives is considered as a function of student characteristics, such as aptitude and motivation, and the quality of instruction. Most of the models developed so far are rather detailed at the classroom level.

At the school level, the selection of variables is not so clear. Based on ideas about how the school level can provide conditions for the instructional level, and also on insights from organizational theories, possible factors are discerned at the school level. In the QAIT-MACRO model (Stringfield and Slavin 1992) these factors are meaningful goals, attention to academic functions, coordination, recruitment and training, and organization. In the model provided by Scheerens (1990), achievement orientation, organization of the school in terms of educational leadership and consensus, quality of the school curricula in terms of content coverage, form and structure, and an orderly atmosphere are distinguished. But how these factors influence what goes on at the classroom level, between classes at the same grade level and between grade levels, remains unclear. The instructional model provided by Creemers (1991) again distinguishes between school curriculum variables and organizational variables. Connected with this idea of a formal relationship between what goes on in classrooms, between classrooms and between the class and the school level are the concepts of consistency, cohesion, constancy and control.

Basic variables, excepting students' aptitude and motivation, at the student level are the time and opportunity they need to master the goals. Education at the classroom level provides time and opportunity for learning. The quality of instruction also contributes to the effectiveness of education, but is mediated by time and opportunity, which are influenced by the quality of instruction. At the school and context levels above the classroom level, variables related to time, opportunity and quality are conditions for instructional effectiveness. In this way, all levels are put in line with each other, which can clarify the way they influence each other and ultimately contribute to students' achievement. The overall framework, which has been developed based on the review here, can be sketched as in Figure 11.1. In the following, some further explanation of the model will be given.

Student level

The students' backgrounds, motivation and aptitudes strongly determine their achievement. Time on task is the time students are willing to spend on school learning, and on educational tasks, but it is determined not only by the motivation of students, but also by the time provided by the school and by processes at the school and classroom levels. Time on task is the time in which students are really involved in learning, but this time has to be filled by opportunities to learn. These opportunities concern the supply of learning materials, experiences and exercises by which students can acquire knowledge and skills. In fact, learning opportunities are the instructional operationalization of the objectives of education, whereas tests are the evaluative operationalization of the same objectives. In this respect one can speak about the content coverage of the curriculum. Here again a distinction is made between opportunities offered in the instructional process and students' use of the offered experiences.

Classroom level

As well as time and opportunity, the quality of instruction determines the outcomes of education. Based on theoretical notions and empirical research, it is possible to select effective characteristics of the components of quality of classroom instruction: curriculum, grouping procedures and teacher behaviour. With respect to the curriculum these are the following:

- explicitness and ordering of goals and content;
- structure and clarity of content;
- advance organizers;
- material for evaluation of student outcomes, feedback and corrective instruction.

With respect to grouping procedures they are:

- mastery learning;
- ability grouping;
- cooperative learning; all of which are highly dependent on
  - differentiated material
  - material for evaluation, feedback and corrective instruction.

With respect to teacher behaviour they are:

- management, and orderly and quiet atmosphere;
- homework;
- high expectations;
- clear goal setting
  - restricted set of goals
  - emphasis on basic skills
  - emphasis on cognitive learning and transfer;
- structuring the content
  - ordering of goals and content
  - advance organizers
  - making use of prior knowledge of students;
- clarity of presentation;
- questioning;
- immediate exercise after presentation of new content;
- evaluation, feedback and corrective instruction.

It is obvious that teachers are the central component in instruction at the classroom level. They make use of curricular materials and they carry out grouping procedures in their classrooms. However, teachers need curricular materials, which should be consistent with the grouping procedure used.

In addition to these, more formal characteristics can be discerned (Creemers 1992). Consistency is a formal characteristic for effectiveness, pointing at the fact that at the classroom level the characteristics of the components should be in line with each other.

School level

From looking at the well-known lists of effective school factors (Levine and Lezotte 1990; Scheerens 1992; Reynolds 1993b), it becomes clear that most of the factors (such as an orderly climate in the school or evaluating student achievement at school level) are in fact reflections of the indicators of quality of instruction, time and opportunity to learn at classroom level. Because of a lack of research studies that analyse the school and classroom levels in one design, it is hard to say what the separate contribution of these factors might be in accounting for student-level variance when controlling for classroom-level factors. In any case, many school-level factors are rather meaningless when they are not clearly linked to classroom factors (Creemers 1992b). Even if they do have an independent effect on pupil achievement, it is still not clear how this effect comes about and how it should be interpreted.

In the model, all school-level factors are defined as conditions for classroom-level factors. This definition restricts the selection of school level factors to only those factors conditional for and directly related to quality of instruction, time or opportunity to learn. At the school level we can distinguish conditions for the *quality of instruction* with respect to the *educational* aspects:

- rules and agreements about all aspects of classroom instruction, especially curricular materials, grouping procedures and teacher behaviour, and the consistency between them;
- an evaluation policy and a system at school level to check pupil achievement, to prevent learning problems, or to correct problems at an early stage, including regular testing, remedial teaching, student counselling and homework assistance.

With respect to the *organizational* aspects of the school level, important conditions for *quality of instruction* are:

- a school policy on intervision and supervision of teachers, departmental heads and headteachers (educational leadership), and a school policy to correct and further to professionalize teachers who do not live up to the school standards;
- a school culture inducing and supporting effectiveness.

Conditions for *time* at the school level are:

- the development and provision of a time schedule for subjects and topics;
- rules and agreements about time use, including the school policy on homework, pupil absenteeism and cancellation of lessons;
- the maintenance of an orderly and quiet atmosphere in the school.

Conditions for the *opportunity to learn* at the school level are:

- development and availability of a curriculum, school working plan or activity plan;
- consensus about the 'mission' of the school;

- rules and agreements about how to proceed, how to follow the curriculum, especially with respect to transition from one class to another or from one grade to another (Creemers *et al.* 1992).

At the school level consistency between the components, which are in line with each other, is an important condition for instruction. All members of the school team should take care of that, thereby creating cohesion. Creemers (1991) points out the importance of continuity in all the conditions mentioned above, meaning that schools should not change rules and policies every other year. This implies the constancy principle, which, however, can only be found in a longitudinal setting, by comparing school level factors from year to year. The control principle refers not only to the fact that student achievement should be evaluated, but also the quiet atmosphere in the school. Control also refers to teachers holding themselves and others responsible for effectiveness.

Context level

The same components as mentioned before, quality, time and opportunity to learn, can be distinguished at the context level. Quality refers to the following conditions:

- a (national) policy that focuses on effectiveness of education;
- the availability of an indicator system and/or a national policy on evaluation or a national testing system;
- training and support systems promoting effective schools and instruction;
- funding of schools based on outcomes.

Time refers to national guidelines with respect to the time schedules of schools and the supervision of the maintenance of schedules. The opportunity to learn refers to national guidelines and rules with respect to the development of the curriculum, the school working plan and the activity plan at the school level, for example, by a national curriculum.

It is clear that at the different levels, certainly at the context level, resources are also important, but resources should be defined as in this model: availability of materials, teachers and other components supporting education in schools and classrooms. At the context level, consistency, constancy and control are again important formal characteristics, emphasizing the importance of the same material characteristics over time and of mechanisms to ensure effectiveness.

Research in educational effectiveness

[. . .]

The next phase – and this is a phase that accompanies all theory development – is that of looking for empirical evidence. For that purpose, we need well-designed large survey studies as well as case studies, with an emphasis on the measurement of multiple outcomes and on processes at the classroom level and at the school level. A first step could be a secondary analysis of available large datasets to test the model. Topics in the area of educational effectiveness research are, for example:

- the combination of effective characteristics of the components of instruction in such a way that effective arrangements become available;
- the relationship between the levels with respect to time, opportunity and especially the quality of education;

- the relationship between the organizational and educational system at the school level with respect to effectiveness;
- the variance in effectiveness within schools (related to their effectiveness at classroom level), which implies analysis and research of the formal characteristics of effectiveness.

Recent developments in the area of data analysis techniques will make it possible to combine regression and multilevel techniques at short notice. The topics mentioned earlier refer to fundamental research with respect to the concepts of educational effectiveness and the development of techniques to measure them. Of special importance are international comparative studies, like the IEA and ISERP, which can provide information on factors and variables that are stable between countries, and on the influences of the context on educational effectiveness (Mortimore 1992). Effectiveness levels themselves are not stable. For the purpose of school improvement, but also for the development of a theory on the question of what induces effective education, we need studies about schools in transition (Freiberg *et al.* 1990; Chrispeels 1992; Teddlie and Stringfield 1993). This implies research on the development of schools as educational organizations, and especially the measures schools take to initiate novice teachers in their organization.

Finally, we need research on and evaluation of school improvement projects based on the results of school effectiveness research (Reynolds 1993a). This creates a starting point for future theory development and research to increase our body of knowledge about instructional, school and educational effectiveness.

The future of effective instruction: theory into practice

[. . .]

Central in educational effectiveness, as has been made clear, are the teaching and learning processes going on at the classroom level. It turns out that, especially at the classroom level, the characteristics of components that explain variation in student behaviour can be found. They explain differences in learning processes and in the outcomes of learning processes. The components at the classroom level and their effective characteristics are important for improvements in student learning. We found different components at the classroom level, such as teacher behaviour, the curriculum and grouping procedures, and we looked for characteristics of these components that contribute to the effectiveness of the instructional processes. In particular, we were looking for empirical evidence for these effectiveness characteristics. The components and their effective characteristics are interrelated and can be supported by factors at the school level and the contextual level. The characteristics of the components and the interrelationships between them emphasize the importance of teachers in this respect. Teachers create and maintain an environment in their classes in which learning can take place and learning outcomes can be achieved.

[. . .]

It is sometimes suggested that the pursuit of, for example, affective outcomes might need different characteristics of the components from the pursuit of cognitive outcomes. I would like to stress the point that, theoretically, effective instruction does not refer to a small restricted set of outcomes, like knowledge and skills, but to learning outcomes in a broad area, from cognitive knowledge and skills to values, moral education and character education. Brooks and Kann (1993) and Leming (1993) advocate effective instruction in this respect. As yet, there is no convincing empirical evidence to support the hypothesis that teachers should behave differently when they are aiming at different educational goals. Effective instruction can therefore be implemented to enhance student achievement in numerous educational domains. Effective instruction will exert not only direct positive influences on achievement in these domains, but also indirect: if cognitive achievement is promoted, achievement in other areas is also stimulated.

However, I would like to emphasize that in areas such as social and aesthetic outcomes, and values, moral education and character education, there is not a very close relationship between the knowledge provided by schools and the behaviour of students (Lockwood 1993). In general, cognitive outcomes are determined by school and teacher factors to a much higher extent than are outcomes in other educational domains. This again means an emphasis on the crucial role of teachers in education in general and more specifically in the determination of classroom level processes. Teachers can combine the effective characteristics of the curriculum and grouping procedures with their own instructional behaviour.

Perhaps a lot of teachers are already familiar, through their own experiences, with the characteristics of effective instruction outlined in this study. The characteristics do not involve sophisticated and trendy tricks and they reflect only elements of everyday teaching. They all concern decisions teachers have to make day by day in their classrooms. Moreover, all the linkages described in this book are supported by empirical evidence. Even when teachers are acquainted with the knowledge base for effective instruction, they often experience problems when they try to put their knowledge into practice. Teachers are often aware of the importance of effective learning time and opportunity to learn, but many of them show behaviour that does not increase learning time or the opportunity to learn and sometimes even reduces it. Even when they succeed, the long-term effects of their instructional practices can be reduced when the next teacher in line shows different and less effective behaviour. Therefore, the factors mentioned at the school and contextual levels that can promote and foster effective education are also vitally important.

The future of effective instruction is situated in the hands of the teaching profession even more than it lies in theory development and empirical research. Teachers have to take the responsibility for learning processes and the outcomes of their students.

References

Bosker, R. J. (1991) 'De consistentie van schooleffecten in het basisonderwijs' (The consistency of school effects in primary education). *Tijdschrift voor Onderwijsresearch*, 16(4): 206–18.

Bosker, R. J. and Scheerens, J. (1989) Issues in the interpretation of the results of school effectiveness research. *International Journal of Educational Research*, 13(7): 741–51.

Brandsma, H. P. and Knuver, J. W. M. (1989a) Organisational differences between Dutch primary schools and their effect on pupil achievement, in D. Reynolds, B. P. M. Creemers and T. Peters (eds) *School Effectiveness and Improvement. Proceedings of the First International Congress, London*, pp. 199–212. Groningen/Cardiff: RION/University of Wales.

Brandsma, H. P. and Knuver, J. W. M. (1989b) Effects of school and classroom characteristics on pupil progress in language and arithmetic. *International Journal of Educational Research*, 13(7): 777–88.

Brookover, W. B., Beady, C., Flood, P. and Schweitzer, J. (1979) *School Systems and Student Achievement: Schools Make a Difference*. New York: Praeger.

Brooks, B. D. and Kann, M. E. (1993) What makes character education programs work? *Educational Leadership*, 51(3): 19–21.

Chrispeels, J. (1992) *Purposeful Restructuring: Creating a Culture for Learning and Achievement in Elementary Schools*. London: Falmer Press.

Creemers, B. P. M. (1991) *Effectieve instructie: een empirische bijdrage aan de verbetering van het onderwijs in de klas* (Effective instruction: an empirical contribution to improvement of education in the classroom). The Hague: SVO.

Creemers, B. P. M. (1992a) School effectiveness, effective instruction and school improvement in the Netherlands, in D. Reynolds and P. Cuttance (eds) *School Effectiveness: Research, Policy and Practice*, pp. 48–70. London: Cassell.

Creemers, B. P. M. (1992b) School effectiveness and effective instruction: the need for a further relationship, in J. Bashi and Z. Sass (eds) *School Effectiveness and Improvement. Proceedings of the Third International Congress, Jerusalem*, pp. 105–32. Jerusalem: The Magnes Press.

Creemers, B. P. M. and Knuver, A. W. M. (1989) The Netherlands, in B. P. M. Creemers, T. Peters and D. Reynolds (eds) *School Effectiveness and School Improvement. Proceedings of the Second International Congress, Rotterdam*, pp. 79–82. Lisse: Swets and Zeitlinger.

Creemers, B. P. M. and Lugthart, E. (1989) School effectiveness and improvement in the Netherlands, in D. Reynolds, B. P. M. Creemers and T. Peters (eds) *School Effectiveness and Improvement. Proceedings of the First International Congress, London*, pp. 89–103. Groningen/Cardiff: RION/University of Wales.

Edmonds, R. R. (1979) Effective schools for the urban poor. *Educational Leadership*, 37(1): 15–27.

Freiberg, H. J., Prokosch, N., Treister, E. S. and Stein, T. (1990) Turning around five at-risk elementary schools. *School Effectiveness and School Improvement*, 1(1): 5–25.

Knuver, J. W. M. (1993) *De relatie tussen klas- en schoolkenmerken en het affectief functioneren van leerlingen* (The relationship between class and school characteristics and the affective functioning of pupils). Groningen: RION.

Knuver, A. W. M. and Brandsma, H. P. (1993) Cognitive and affective outcomes in school effectiveness research. *School Effectiveness and School Improvement*, 4(3): 189–204.

Leming, J. S. (1993) In search of effective character education. *Educational Leadership*, 51(3): 63–71.

Levine, D. U. (1992) An interpretive review of US research and practice dealing with unusually effective schools, in D. Reynolds and P. Cuttance (eds) *School Effectiveness: Research, Policy and Practice*, pp. 25–47. London: Cassell.

Levine, D. U. and Lezotte, L. W. (1990) *Unusually Effective Schools: A Review and Analysis of Research and Practice*. Madison, WI: National Center for Effective Schools Research and Development.

Lezotte, L. W. (1989) School improvement based on the effective schools research. *International Journal of Educational Research*, 13(7): 815–23.

Lockwood, A. L. (1993) A letter to character educators. *Educational Leadership*, 51(3): 72–5.

Marsh, H. W., Smith, I. D. and Barnes, J. (1985) Multi-dimensional self-concepts: relations with sex and academic achievement. *Journal of Educational Psychology*, 77(5): 581–96.

Mortimore, P. (1991) School effectiveness research: which way at the crossroads? *School Effectiveness and School Improvement*, 2(3): 213–29.

Mortimore, P. (1992) Issues in school effectiveness. In D. Reynolds and P. Cuttance (eds) *School Effectiveness: Research, Policy and Practice*, pp. 154–63. London: Cassell.

Mortimore, P., Sammons, P., Stoll, L., Lewis, D. and Ecob, R. (1988) *School Matters: The Junior Years*. Wells: Open Books.

Mortimore, P., Sammons, P., Stoll, L., Lewis, D. and Ecob, R. (1989) A study of effective junior schools. *International Journal of Educational Research*, 13(7): 753–68.

Reynolds, D. (1993a) Linking school effectiveness knowledge and school improvement practice, in C. Dimmock (ed.) *School-Based Management and School Effectiveness*, pp. 185–200. London: Routledge.

Reynolds, D. (1993b) Conceptualising and measuring the school level. Paper presented at the Annual Meeting of the American Educational Research Association, Atlanta.

Scheerens, J. (1987) *Enhancing Educational Opportunities for Disadvantaged Learners*. Amsterdam: North-Holland.

Scheerens, J. (1990) School effectiveness research and the development of process indicators of school functioning. *School Effectiveness and School Improvement*, 1(1): 61–80.

Scheerens, J. (1991) Foundational and fundamental studies in school effectiveness: a research agenda. Unpublished paper commissioned by the Institute for Educational Research (SVO) in the Netherlands.

Scheerens, J. (1992) *Effective Schooling: Research, Theory and Practice*. London: Cassell.

Scheerens, J. and Creemers, B. P. M. (1989) Conceptualizing school effectiveness. *International Journal of Educational Research*, 13(7): 691–706.

Slavenburg, J. H. and Peters, T. A. (eds) (1989) *Het project Onderwijs en Sociaal Milieu: Een Eindbalans* (The Education and Social Environment Project: a final evaluation). Rotterdam: Rotterdamse School Advies Dienst.

Stringfield, S. C. and Schaffer, G. (1991) 'Results of school effectiveness studies in the United States of America', in B. P. M. Creemers, D. Reynolds, G. Schaffer, S. Stringfield and C. Teddlie (eds) *International School Effects Research Workshop*, pp. 139–56. Kaohsiung: College of Education, National Kaohsiung Normal University.

Stringfield, S. C. and Slavin, R. E. (1992) A hierarchical longitudinal model for elementary school effects, in B. P. M. Creemers and G. J. Reezigt (eds) *Evaluation of Educational Effectiveness*, pp. 35–69. Groningen: ICO.

Teddlie, C. and Stringfield, S. (1993) *Schools Make a Difference: Lessons Learned from a 10-year Study of School Effects*. New York: Teachers College Press.

Walberg, H. J. (1984) Improving the productivity of America's schools. *Educational Leadership*, 41(8): 19–27.

12 | School effectiveness and school improvement in the United Kingdom*

DAVID REYNOLDS, PAMELA SAMMONS, LOUISE STOLL, MICHAEL BARBER AND JOSH HILLMAN

Introduction

School effectiveness research in the United Kingdom has had a somewhat difficult infancy. The traditional hegemony of British educational research, which was orientated to psychological perspectives and their emphasis upon individuals and families as determinants of educational outcomes, created a professional educational research climate somewhat unfriendly to school effectiveness research, as shown by the initially very hostile British reactions to the Rutter *et al.* (1979) study *Fifteen Thousand Hours* (e.g. Goldstein 1980). Other factors that hindered development were:

1 The problems of gaining access to schools for research purposes, in a situation where the educational system was customarily used to considerable autonomy from direct state control, and in a situation where individual schools had considerable autonomy from their local educational authorities (or districts), and where individual teachers had considerable autonomy within schools.
2 The absence of reliable and valid measures of school institutional climate (a marked contrast to the situation in the United States for example).
3 The incomplete development of British sociology of education's understanding of the school as a determinant of adolescent careers, where pioneering work by Hargreaves (1967) and Lacey (1970), was de-emphasized by the arrival of Marxist perspectives that stressed the need to work at the relationship between school and society (e.g. Bowles and Gintis 1976).
4 The demolition of Bernstein's (1977) attempted conceptualization of school curricular arrangements which used the variables of 'classification' and 'framing', as undertaken in the work of King (1983). The failure of Bernstein's dimensions to relate

*This edited and revised material is based on an ICSESI conference paper.

together in predicted directions, or even to relate together at all, created an intellectual cul-de-sac for many of the people who had been interested in schools as organizations.

More recently, however, there has existed in the British educational research community, a climate much more favourable to the endeavours of the school effectiveness community, a function in part of the greatly increased attention given to school functioning within the political sphere.

[. . .]

The school effectiveness research base: 1967 to 1996

1967 to 1989

Early work in this field came mostly from a medical and medico-social environment, with Power (1967) and Power et al. (1972) showing differences in delinquency rates between schools and Gath (1977) showing differences in child guidance referral rates.

Early work by Reynolds and associates (1976, 1982) into the characteristics of the learning environments of apparently differently effective secondary schools, using group-based cross-sectional data on intakes and outcomes, was followed by work by Rutter et al. (1979) on differences between schools measured on the outcomes of academic achievement, delinquency, attendance and levels of behavioural problems, utilizing this time a cohort design that involved the matching of individual pupil data at intake to school and at age 16 years.

Subsequent work in the 1980s included:

1 'Value-added' comparisons or educational authorities on their academic outcomes (Department of Education and Science 1983, 1984; Gray et al. 1984; Gray and Jesson 1987; Willms 1987; Woodhouse and Goldstein 1988).
2 Comparisons of 'selective' school systems with comprehensive or 'all ability' systems (Steadman 1980, 1983; Gray et al. 1983; Reynolds et al. 1987).
3 Work into the scientific properties of school effects, such as size (Gray 1981, 1982; Gray et al. 1986), the differential effectiveness of different academic subunits or departments (Fitz-Gibbon 1985; Willms and Cuttance 1985; Fitz-Gibbon et al. 1989), contextual or 'balance' effects (Willms 1985, 1986, 1987) and differential effectiveness of schools upon pupils of different characteristics (Aitken and Longford 1986; Nuttall et al. 1989).
4 'One-off', small-scale studies that focused upon usually one outcome and attempted to relate this to various within-school processes. This was particularly interesting in the cases of disruptive behaviour (Galloway 1983) and disciplinary problems (McManus 1987; McLean 1987; Maxwell 1987).

Towards the end of the 1980s, two landmark studies appeared concerning school effectiveness in primary schools (Mortimore et al. 1988) and in secondary schools (Smith and Tomlinson 1989). The Mortimore study was notable for the wide range of outcomes on which schools were assessed (including mathematics, reading, writing, attendance, behaviour and attitudes to school), for the collection of a wide range of data upon school processes and, for the first time in British school effectiveness research, a focus upon classroom processes.

The Smith and Tomlinson (1989) study is notable for the large differences shown in academic effectiveness between schools, with for certain groups of pupils the variation in examination results between similar individuals in different schools amounting to up to one-quarter of the total variation in examination results. The study is also notable for the substantial variation that it reported in results in different school subjects, reflecting the influence of different school departments – out of 18 schools, the school that was positioned 'first' on mathematics attainment, for example, was 'fifteenth' in English achievement (after allowance had been made for intake quality).

1990 to the present

Ongoing work in the United Kingdom remains partially situated within the same intellectual traditions and at the same intellectual cutting edges as in the 1980s, notably in the areas of:

1 Stability over time of school effects (Goldstein *et al.* 1993; Gray *et al.* 1995; Thomas *et al.* 1995).
2 Consistency of school effects on different outcomes – for example, in terms of different subjects or different outcome domains such as cognitive/affective (Goldstein *et al.* 1993; Sammons *et al.* 1993, Thomas *et al.* 1995).
3 Differential effects of schools for different groups of students (for example, of different ethnic or socio-economic backgrounds) or with different levels of prior attainment (Jesson and Gray 1991; Goldstein *et al.* 1993; Sammons *et al.* 1993).
4 The relative continuity of school sectors over time (Goldstein 1995; Sammons *et al.* 1995).
5 The existence or size of school effects (Gray *et al.* 1990; Daly 1991; Thomas and Mortimore 1994), where in most studies 8 to 12 per cent of the total variance in pupil achievement is attributable to educational influences, a figure very close to that being generated within the Dutch educational research community (Creemers 1992). There are strong suggestions that the size of primary school effects may be greater than those of secondary schools (Sammons *et al.* 1993, 1995).
6 Departmental differences in educational effectiveness (Fitz-Gibbon 1991, 1992). [The ALIS (A-Level Information System) method of performance monitoring of Fitz-Gibbon and colleagues has recently been expanded to include public examinations at age 16, a scheme known as YELLIS (Year Eleven Information System) and has been also expanded into the primary school sector with PIPS (Performance Indicators in Primary Schools).]

School effectiveness: the balance of strengths and weaknesses

Overall, the British effectiveness knowledge base would seem to have four positive features:

1 High levels of methodological sophistication, in which the utilization of a cohort design, matched data on individuals at intake and outcome and multiple level methodologies are now widely agreed as best practice. Britain has also been in the forefront of the development of multilevel statistical modelling (Goldstein 1995).

2 The use of multiple measures of pupil outcomes, which have included in British work those such as locus of control, attendance, delinquency, behavioural problems, attitudes to school, self-esteem and attitudes to school subjects as well as academic outcomes (see for examples Reynolds *et al.* 1978; Mortimore *et al.* 1988).

3 The use of multiple measures of pupil intakes into school, utilizing prior achievement as well as factors such as age, gender, parental socio-economic status, parental education and parental ethnicity or racial background. Cutting edge research from other countries (e.g. Teddlie and Stringfield 1993) often utilizes *either* achievement measures *or* detailed socio-economic data upon background, but rarely both, as in British best practice. The effect of controlling for one or other on the estimates of schools' effects has been explored in Sammons *et al.* (1994).

4 The development of advanced conceptualizations and findings about the role of the school level in potentiating or hindering adolescent development, where the early findings within the sociology of education have been usefully built on by the case studies of Reynolds, Rutter and Mortimore. Recent work by Hargreaves (1995) shows the continued sophistication of British thinking in this area.

If there are any intellectual 'downsides' to the British tradition, they would seem to lie in the following areas:

1 The majority of British studies that have collected data upon school and classroom processes have sampled only within socio-economic contexts that are disadvantaged and deprived (e.g. Rutter in a London borough with high levels of social deprivation, and Reynolds in the Welsh mining valleys). This has resulted in an inability within the British research community to further investigate the variation in 'what works' by context that is such an exciting and potentially productive feature of the American school effectiveness research tradition (e.g. Hallinger and Murphy 1986; Wimpelberg *et al.* 1989; Teddlie and Stringfield 1993).

It is also possible that the near exclusion within British sampling frames of very advantaged catchment areas, of independent schools with intakes from very affluent backgrounds, and of religiously administered schools with intakes of probably above-average achievement might have both constrained variance in organizational practices at the school level, and might have also resulted in the generation of accounts of organizational functioning that are not necessarily applicable to all school types.

2 The absence of more than rudimentary attempts to discern those classroom or instructional processes that might be related to outcomes, reflecting the absence within a British context of the focus upon classroom learning environments that is evident within the American research traditions of learning environment research (Good 1983) and within the Dutch tradition of learning and instruction (Creemers 1994).

3 The historic lack of any 'interface' between school effectiveness research and school improvement practice, reflecting the very different intellectual ancestries of the two 'paradigms' (see Reynolds *et al.* 1993; Stoll 1996). Whilst this situation has begun to change considerably in recent years as we note below, historically there has been little of the take up of effectiveness knowledge into British improvement programmes that has been so evident in the United States (e.g. McCormack-Larkin 1985). Neither in the United Kingdom has there been more than partial take up of the insights from school improvement programmes into school effectiveness research designs, in spite

of the evident utility of some of the improvement variables, such as 'collegiality', 'development planning' and 'school culture' to potentially explain variation in schools' outcomes.

Great Britain has been notable for the direct application of school effectiveness knowledge to schools *without* much influence from the school improvement community, as in the attempt to translate the findings of the *Fifteen Thousand Hours* study (Rutter *et al.* 1979) into some of the participating schools (Maughan *et al.* 1990; Ouston and Maughan 1991) and the Reynolds *et al.* (1989) 'Change Agents' material in which effectiveness knowledge was cascaded through schools by specially trained school personnel. The failure of those projects to generate more than marginal change in outcomes probably reflects again the historically isolated intellectual nature of the British effectiveness community.

4 The absence of more than rudimentary attempts at theory generation, although the reviewing of the field (e.g. Mortimore, 1991; Reynolds *et al.* 1994) and the related attempted causal ordering of some of the school effectiveness variables does suggest the beginnings of attempts to move beyond the simple description of relationships to more sophisticated analyses. In no way, though, do these British attempts appear as advanced as the cross level model of Stringfield and Slavin (1991) or as creative as Scheerens' (1992) attempt to improve the explanatory power of school effectiveness factors by relating them to 'meta theories' like contingency theory and public choice theory.

What factors make some British schools effective?

Accepting that United Kingdom effectiveness research has its balance of strengths and weaknesses, the knowledge base about 'effective' school and classroom level processes generated from the wide variety of studies noted above seems to distil into nine key factors:

1 *Professional leadership*
   Gray (1990) notes that the importance of the headteacher's leadership is one of the clearest of the messages from school effectiveness research. Three characteristics have been found to be associated with successful leadership:
   (a) Strength of purpose, involving proactive management, an emphasis upon recruitment of persons who 'fit' the school and the generation of consistency and purpose within the school's management team (Sammons *et al.* 1994).
   (b) Sharing of leadership positions, as noted in the Mortimore *et al.* (1988) finding of the involvement of the deputy headteacher in decision-making and by findings from the same study related both to the involvement of teachers in school management and curriculum planning and to consultation with teachers about spending and other policy decisions.
   (c) A headteacher's role as the 'leading professional', implying involvement in and knowledge about what goes on in the classroom, including the curriculum, teaching strategies and the monitoring of pupil progress (Rutter *et al.* 1979; Mortimore *et al.* 1988).

2 *Shared vision and goals*
   Schools are clearly more effective when staff build consensus on the aims and values

of the school and where they put this into practice through consistent and collaborative ways of working. This is seen in:

(a) Unity of purpose, involving a consensus on values (Rutter *et al.* 1979).

(b) Consistency of practice, in which adopting a particular approach to school curriculum guidelines (Mortimore *et al.* 1988) and to discipline (Reynolds 1976; Rutter *et al.* 1979) has a positive impact on the progress of pupils.

(c) Collaboration, as shown by the collegiality found in the Rutter *et al.* (1979) study and teacher involvement in decision-making found in the effective schools of the Mortimore *et al.* (1988) study.

3 *A learning environment*

The ethos of a school is partly determined by the vision, values and goals of the staff as noted above, and also by the climate in which pupils work. Two key aspects of this latter factor are:

(a) An orderly atmosphere (Rutter *et al.* 1979; Mortimore *et al.* 1988).

(b) An attractive working environment (Rutter 1983; Mortimore *et al.* 1988).

4 *High-quality teaching and learning*

This is generated by:

(a) Maximization of learning time, including the proportion of the day given to academic subjects (Bennett 1978), the proportion of time in lessons devoted to learning (Rutter *et al.* 1979) or to interaction with pupils (Mortimore *et al.* 1988; Alexander 1992), the proportion of time spent on work matters rather than on administrative/maintenance activities (Galton and Simon 1982; Alexander 1992) and the existence of well-managed lesson transitions.

(b) An academic emphasis, as noted by Smith and Tomlinson (1989) in relation to entry of a high proportion of pupils in public examinations, and by Rutter *et al.* (1979) in relation to senior staff checking that homework had been done.

(c) Curriculum coverage, in which more effective schools give pupils higher OTL (opportunity to learn). Bennett (1992) has demonstrated wide variation in curriculum coverage both for pupils within the same class and in different schools. The work of Tizard *et al.* (1988) in infant schools pointed out that 'it is clear that attainment and progress depend crucially on whether children are given particular learning experiences' (1988: 172).

5 *High expectations*

Crucial factors seem to be that high expectations are implicated in generating a more active role for teachers in helping pupils (Sammons *et al.* 1994), the communication and reinforcement of expectations as noted in Mortimore *et al.* (1988) and the provision of intellectual challenge, as noted in the Tizard *et al.* (1988) study, where teachers' expectations of both individual pupils and classes as a whole had a strong influence on the content of lessons, and to a large extent explained differences in curriculum between classes with similar intakes.

6 *Positive reinforcement*

This involves clear and fair discipline (Clegg and Megson 1968; Reynolds and Murgatroyd 1977; Heal 1978; Rutter *et al.* 1979; Mortimore *et al.* 1988) and direct and positive feedback such as praise and appreciation (Rutter *et al.* 1979).

7 *Monitoring pupil progress*

Well-established mechanisms for monitoring the performance and progress of pupils, classes, the school as whole and the efficacy of improvement programmes are important features of effective schools. These are detailed as:

(a) Monitoring pupil performance/achievement, as in the sound record keeping noted within the Mortimore *et al.* (1988) study.
(b) Evaluating school performance, as in the notions of programme evaluation within effective school improvement of the Hargreaves and Hopkins' (1991) model of cyclical school improvement.

8 *Pupil rights and responsibilities*
These can affect the self-esteem of pupils positively, as in the good staff/pupil relations found in the Rutter *et al.* (1979) effective schools, and as found in schools where there existed shared out of school activities between teachers and pupils (Rutter *et al.* 1979; Smith and Tomlinson 1989).

Also important may be the positive effects of having high proportions of pupils with positions of responsibility within the school, thus conveying trust in pupils and setting standards of mature behaviour (Ainsworth and Batten 1974; Reynolds 1976; Rutter *et al.* 1979).

9 *Purposeful teaching*
This is likely to be related both to efficient organization as in the Rutter *et al.* (1979) study, which found positive effects of preparing the lesson in advance, and to structured lessons, as in the Mortimore *et al.* (1988) findings of a positive effect of efficient organization of classroom work, a limited focus in sessions and a well-defined framework within which a degree of pupil independence and responsibility for managing their own work could be encouraged.

From school effectiveness to school improvement?

As we noted above, the lack of any close links or 'synergy' between British school effectiveness research and British school improvement practice is one of our notable historical legacies. The school improvement enterprise within the United Kingdom began to emerge within the 'teacher as researcher' movement (e.g. Elliott 1980, 1981), later encompassed school self-evaluation and review (e.g. Clift and Nuttall 1987), and then later still tried to develop an integrated, holistic process that linked the review/diagnosis of organizational health with subsequent work on the organization and culture of schools as evidenced in the Hargreaves Report (1984) on *Improving Secondary Schools*, the Guidelines for Review and Institutional Development in Schools of McMahon *et al.* (1984) and the British activities of the International School Improvement Project (ISIP) of Hopkins (1987).

In general, the improvement paradigm of the 1980s that those various British movements reflected celebrated a 'bottom-up' approach to school improvement, in which the improvement attempts were to be 'owned' by those at the school level, although outside school consultants or experts could put their knowledge forward for possible utilization. This approach tended to celebrate the 'folk-lore' or practical knowledge of practitioners rather than the knowledge base of researchers, and focused on changes to educational processes rather than to school management. It wanted the outcomes or goals of school improvement programmes to be debated and discussed, rather than accepted as given. Those working within this paradigm also tended to operate at the level of the practitioner rather than at the level of the school, with a qualitative and naturalistically orientated evaluation of the enterprise being preferred to quantitative measurement (Stoll 1996).

The school effectiveness research paradigm has, of course, a very different intellectual history and has exhibited a very different set of core beliefs by comparison with the changing approaches of the school improvers. It has been strongly committed to the use of quantitative methods, since British researchers were concerned to refute the 'schools make no difference' hypothesis advanced by Coleman *et al.* (1966) and Jencks *et al.* (1971) by utilizing the same conventional methods of empirical research as their perceived opponents had utilized. Many researchers had also believed that British teachers would pay more attention to work conducted within the quantitative paradigm.

School effectiveness researchers have also been primarily concerned with pupil academic and social outcomes, which is not surprising given the political history of school effectiveness research, which has built on the beliefs of Ron Edmonds and his associates that 'all children can learn'. Processes within schools only have an importance within the school effectiveness paradigm to the extent that they affect outcomes – indeed, one 'back maps' with the paradigm from outcomes to process. The school effectiveness paradigm furthermore regards pupil and school outcomes as fundamentally given. School effectiveness researchers indeed often talk of a 'good' or 'excellent' school as if the definition of these were unproblematic.

Lastly, the British school effectiveness paradigm is organizationally rather than process based in terms of its analytic and descriptive orientation, preferring to restrict itself to the more easily quantifiable or measurable. As an example, Fullan's (1985) process factors such as 'a feel for the process of leadership' or 'a guiding value system', or 'intense interaction and communication' are largely eschewed in favour of organizationally and behaviourally orientated process variables such as 'clear goals and high expectations' and/or 'parental involvement and support'.

From the outline of the history of the two paradigms in Britain above, it can be seen that the disciplines of school effectiveness and school improvement have been 'coming from' very different places intellectually, methodologically and theoretically. A crude characterization that contrasts both approaches can be seen in Table 12.1.

Table 12.1   The separate traditions of British school effectiveness and school improvement (after Reynolds *et al.* 1993)

School effectiveness	School improvement
Focus on schools	Focus on individual teachers or groups of teachers
Focus on school organization	Focus on school processes
Data driven, with emphasis on outcomes	Rare empirical evaluation of effects of changes
Quantitative in orientation	Qualitative in orientation
Lack of knowledge about how to implement change strategies	Concerned with change in schools exclusively
More concerned with change in pupil outcomes	More concerned with journey of school improvement than its destination
More concerned with schools at a point in time	More concerned with schools as changing
Based on research knowledge	Focus on practitioner knowledge

Merging school effectiveness and school improvement in Britain

The unhealthy separation of the two communities in Britain has been frequently remarked upon (Mortimore 1991; Stoll and Fink 1992; Reynolds *et al*. 1993; Hopkins *et al*. 1994; Stoll and Fink 1996). Recently, there are signs of *rapprochement*, synergy and interaction between the communities, a development which was given considerable momentum by the British Economic and Social Research Council funding a symposium series for over 30 key individuals in the field to meet and take stock of achievements and challenges (the proceedings have been edited by Gray *et al*. 1996). Further 'confluence' of perspectives is in evidence in many of the school improvement/development programmes now in operation in Britain. Programmes and examples are available in Reynolds *et al*. (1996).
  [. . .]

Conclusions

We have outlined in this chapter the historical origins of research and practice in the fields of British school effectiveness and school improvement. Whilst it is clear that there have been major advances in the quality and quantity of research, it is also clear that historically we have had problems in relating together the two 'paradigms'. It is, therefore, immensely reassuring to note the systematic evidence that recent school improvement practice is drawing on the school effectiveness paradigm in very many productive ways. We all sincerely hope that this confluence of perspectives, amounting in fact to a new school effectiveness and school improvement paradigm, will continue in the late 1990s.

It is also worth noting that the interface between school effectiveness, school improvement and educational policymaking is again proving to be a productive one. There are increasing signs of convergence in the interests of British policy bodies, such as OFSTED and the Department for Education and Employment, and the practice and findings of school effectiveness researchers. Both sides can only benefit from this, with policymakers becoming more aware of the complexities of judging school effectiveness and initiating change in schools as they appreciate the insights of the effectiveness knowledge base, and with researchers appreciating the contingencies of a policymaking perspective.

In the research community, a number of areas seem to be beginning to generate creative work at the research/policy interface:

- The 'site' of ineffective schools, the exploration of their characteristics and the policy implications that flow from this (Barber 1995; Reynolds 1996).
- The possibility of routinely assessing the 'value-added' of schools using already available data (Fitz-Gibbon and Tymms 1996), rather than by utilization of specially collected data.
- The characteristics of 'improving' schools and those factors that are associated with successful change over time, especially important at the policy level since existing school effectiveness research gives only the characteristics of schools that have *become* effective (this work is being undertaken by Gray, Hopkins and Reynolds).
- The description of the characteristics of effective Departments (Harris *et al*. 1995; Sammons *et al*. in press).

- The application of school effectiveness techniques to sectors of education where the absence of intake and outcome measures has made research difficult, as in the interesting foray into the early years of schooling of Tymms *et al.* (1995), in which the effects of being in the reception year prior to compulsory schooling were dramatic (an effect amounting to two standard deviations) and where the school effects on pupils in this year were also very large (approximately 40 per cent of variation accounted for).
- The analysis of 'context specificity' through study of those factors which 'travel' internationally in explaining variation and those which do not (Reynolds *et al.* 1994), together with the potential utility of factors and policies derived from outside of the United Kingdom in improving British Schools (Reynolds and Farrell 1996; Bierhoff 1996).

Research is still continuing in the areas of:

- Differential effectiveness.
- Stability and change in schools over time.
- The long-term impact of schools.
- The generation of more sophisticated explanations of, and models of, school processes.

Overall, although the field is still limited by shortages of research funds and trained researchers, the prospects in the United Kingdom seem more promising than at any time-to-date.

References

Ainsworth, M. and Batten, E. (1974) *The Effects of Environmental Factors on Secondary Educational Attainment in Manchester: A Plowden Follow Up*. London: Macmillan.

Aitken, M. and Longford, N. (1986) Statistical modelling issues in school effectiveness studies. *Journal of the Royal Statistical Society, Series A*, 149(1): 1–43.

Alexander, R. (1992) *Policy and Practice in Primary Education*. London: Routledge.

Barber, M. (1995) Shedding light on the dark side of the moor. *Times Educational Supplement*, 12 May.

Bennett, N. (1978) Recent research on teaching: a dream, a belief and a model. *British Journal of Educational Psychology*, 48: 127–47.

Bennett, N. (1992) *Managing Learning in the Primary Classroom*. Stoke: Trentham Books for the ASPE.

Bernstein, B. (1977) Aspects of the relations between education and production, in B. Bernstein (ed.) *Class, Codes and Control*. London: Routledge and Kegan Paul.

Bierhoff, H. (1996) *Laying the Foundations of Numeracy: A Comparison of Primary School Textbooks in Britain, Germany and Switzerland*. London: National Institute for Economic and Social Research.

Bowles, S. and Gintis, H. (1976) *Schooling in Capitalist America*. London: Routledge and Kegan Paul.

Clegg, A. and Megson, B. (1968) *Children in Distress*. Harmondsworth: Penguin.

Clift, P. and Nuttall, D. (eds) (1987) *Studies in School Self Evaluation*. Lewes: Falmer Press.

Coleman, J. *et al.* (1966) *Equality of Educational Opportunity*. Washington, DC: US Government Printing Office.

Creemers, B. (1992) School effectiveness and effective instruction – the need for a further relationship, in J. Bashi and Z. Sass (eds), *School Effectiveness and Improvement*. Jerusalem: Hebrew University Press.

Creemers, B. (1994) *The Effective Classroom*. London: Cassell.

Daly, P. (1991) How large are secondary school effects in Northern Ireland? *School Effectiveness and School Improvement*, 2(4): 305–23.

Department of Education and Science (1983) *School Standards and Spending: Statistical Analysis*. London: DES.

Department of Education and Science (1984) *School Standards and Spending: Statistical Analysis. A Further Appreciation*. London: DES.

Elliott, J. (1980) Implications of classroom research for professional development, in E. Hoyle and J. Megarry (eds) *World Yearbook of Education 1980*. London: Kogan Page.

Elliott, J. (1981) *School Accountability*. London: Grant McIntyre.

Fitz-Gibbon, C. T. (1985) A-level results in comprehensive schools: the COMBSE project year 1. *Oxford Review of Education*, 11(1): 43–58.

Fitz-Gibbon, C. T. (1991) Multilevel modelling in an indicator system, in S. Raudenbush and J. D. Willms (eds) *Schools, Classrooms and Pupils*. San Diego: Academic Press.

Fitz-Gibbon, C. T. (1992) School effects at A-level – genesis of an information system, in D. Reynolds and P. Cuttance (eds) *School Effectiveness: Research, Policy and Practice*. London: Cassell.

Fitz-Gibbon, C. T. and Tymms, P. B. (1996) *The Value Added National Project: First Report*. London: School Curriculum and Assessment Authority.

Fitz-Gibbon, C. T., Tymms, P. B. and Hazelwood, R. D. (1989) Performance indicators and information systems, in D. Reynolds, B. P. M. Creemers and T. Peters (eds) *School Effectiveness and Improvement*. Groningen: RION.

Fullan, M. (1985) Change processes and strategies at the local level. *Elementary School Journal* 85(13): 391–421.

Galloway, D. (1983) Disruptive pupils and effective pastoral care. *School Organisation*, 13: 245–54.

Galton, M. and Simon, B. (1982) *Inside the Primary Classroom*. London: Routledge and Kegan Paul.

Gath, D. (1977) *Child Guidance and Delinquency in a London Borough*. London: Oxford University Press.

Goldstein, H. (1980) Critical notice – *Fifteen Thousand Hours* by Rutter *et al. Journal of Child Psychology and Psychiatry*, 21(4): 364–6.

Goldstein, H. (1995) *Multilevel Models in Educational and Social Research: A Revised Edition*. London: Edward Arnold.

Goldstein, H., Rasbash, J., Yang, M., Woodhouse, G., Pan, H., Nuttall, D. and Thomas, S. (1993) A multilevel analysis of school examination results. *Oxford Review of Education* 19(4): 425–33.

Good, T. (1983) Classroom research: a decade of progress. *Educational Psychologist*, 18: 127–44.

Gray, J. (1981) A competitive edge: examination results and the probable limits of secondary school effectiveness. *Educational Review*, 33(1): 25–35.

Gray, J. (1982) Towards effective schools: problems and progress in British research. *British Educational Research Journal*, 7(1): 59–69.

Gray, J. (1990) The quality of schooling – frameworks for judgement. *British Journal of Educational Studies*, 38(3): 204–33.

Gray, J. and Jesson, D. (1987) Exam results and local authority legaue tables, in A. Harrison and J. Gretton (eds) *Education and Training UK, 1987*, pp. 33–41.

Gray, J., McPherson, A. and Raffe, D. (1983) *Reconstructions of Secondary Education*. London: Routledge and Kegan Paul.

Gray, J., Jesson, D. and Jones, B. (1984) Predicting differences in examination results between local educational authorities: does school organisation matter? *Oxford Review of Education*, 10(1): 45–68.

Gray, J., Jesson, D. and Jones, B. (1986) The search for a fairer way of comparing schools' examination results. *Research Papers in Education*, 1(2): 91–122.

Gray, J., Jesson, D. and Sime, N. (1990) Estimating differences in the examination performance of secondary schools in six LEAs – A multilevel approach to school effectiveness. *Oxford Review of Education*, 16(2): 137–58.

Gray, J., Goldstein, H., Jesson, D., Hedger, K. and Rasbash, J. (1995) A multilevel analysis of school improvement: changes in schools' performance over time. *School Effectiveness and School Improvement*, 6(2): 97–114.

Gray, J., Reynolds, D., Fitz-Gibbon, C. and Jesson, D. (1996) *Merging Traditions: The Future of Research on School Effectiveness and School Improvement*. London: Cassell.

Hallinger, P. and Murphy, J. (1986) *The Social Context of Effective Schools. American Journal of Education*, 94: 328–55.

Hargreaves, D. (1995) School culture, school effectiveness and school improvement. *School Effectiveness and School Improvement*, 6(1): 23–46.

Hargreaves, D. H. (1967) *Social Relations in a Secondary School*. London: Routledge and Kegan Paul.

Hargreaves, D. H. (1984) *Improving Secondary Schools. Report of the Committee on the Curriculum and Organisation of Secondary Schools*. London: ILEA.

Hargreaves, D. H. and Hopkins, D. (1991) *The Empowered School*. London: Cassell.

Harris, A., Jamieson, I. and Russ, J. (1995) A study of effective departments in secondary schools. *School Organisation*, 15: 3.

Heal, K. (1978) Misbehaviour among schoolchildren: the role of the school in strategies for prevention. *Policy and Politics*, 6: 321–33.

Hopkins, D. (1987) *Improving the Quality of Schooling*. Lewes: Falmer Press.

Hopkins, D., Ainscow, M. and West, M. (1994) *School Improvement in an Era of Change*. London: Cassell.

Jencks, C. *et al.* (1971) *Inequality*. London: Allen Lane.

Jesson, D. and Gray, J. (1991) Slants on slopes: using multilevel models to investigate differential school effectiveness and its impact on pupils' examination results. *School Effectiveness and School Improvement*, 2(3): 230–51.

King, R. (1983) *The Sociology of School Organisation*. London: Methuen.

Lacey, C. (1970) *Hightown Grammar*. Manchester: Manchester University Press.

Maughan, B., Ouston, J., Pickles, A. and Rutter, M. (1990) Can schools change?: outcomes at six London secondary schools. *School Effectiveness and Improvement*, 1(3): 188–210.

Maxwell, W. S. (1987) Teachers' attitudes towards disruptive behaviour in secondary schools. *Educational Review*, 39(3): 203–16.

McCormack-Larkin (1985) Ingredients of a successful school effectiveness project. *Educational Leadership*, March: 31–7.

McLean, A. (1987) After the belt: school processes in low exclusion schools. *School Organisation*, 7(3): 303–10.

McMahon, A., Bolam, R., Abbott, R. and Holly, P. (1984) *Guidelines for Review and Development in Schools (Primary and Secondary Handbooks)*. York: Longman/Schools Council.

McManus, M. (1987) Suspension and exclusion from high school: the association with catchment and school variables. *School Organisation*, 7(3): 261–71.

Mortimore, P. (1991) School effectiveness research: which way at the crossroads? *School Effectiveness and School Improvement*, 2(3): 213–29.

Mortimore, P., Sammons, P., Stoll, L., Lewis, D. and Ecob, R. (1988) *School Matters: The Junior Years*. Salisbury: Open Books.

Nuttall, D., Goldstein, H., Prosser, R. and Rasbash, J. (1989) Differential school effectiveness. *International Journal of Educational Research*, 13(7): 769–76.

Ouston, J. and Maughan, B. (1991) Can schools change? *School Effectiveness and School Improvement*, 2(1): 3–13.

Power, M. J. *et al.* (1967) Delinquent schools? *New Society*, 10: 542–3.

Power, M. J., Benn, R. T. and Morris, J. N. (1972) Neighbourhood, school and juveniles before the courts. *British Journal of Criminology*, 12: 111–32.

Reynolds, D. (1976) The delinquent school, in P. Woods (ed.) *The Process of Schooling*. London: Routledge and Kegan Paul.

Reynolds, D. (1982) The search for effective schools. *School Organisation*, 2(3): 215–37.

Reynolds, D. (1996) Turning around ineffective schools: some evidence and some speculations, in J. Gray, D. Reynolds, C. Fitz-Gibbon and D. Jesson (eds) *Merging Traditions: The Future of Research on School Effectiveness and School Improvement*. London: Cassell.

Reynolds, D. and Murgatroyd, S. J. (1977) The sociology of schooling and the absent pupil, in H. C. M. Carroll (ed.) *Absenteeism in South Wales*. Swansea: Faculty of Education.

Reynolds, D. and Farrell, S. (1996) *Worlds Apart? A Review of International Surveys of Educational Achievement Involving England*. London: HMSO for the Office of Standards in Education.

Reynolds, D., Sullivan, M. and Murgatroyd, S. J. (1987) *The Comprehensive Experiment*. Lewes: Falmer Press.

Reynolds, D., Davie, R. and Phillips, D. (1989) The Cardiff programme – an effective school improvement programme based on school effectiveness research. *Developments in School Effectiveness Research* (special issue of the *International Journal of Educational Research*), 13(7): 800–14.

Reynolds, D., Hopkins, D. and Stoll, L. (1993) Linking school effectiveness knowledge and school improvement practice: towards a synergy. *School Effectiveness and School Improvement*, 4(1): 37–58.

Reynolds, D., Creemers, B. P. M., Stringfield, S., Teddlie, C., Schaffer, E. and Nesselrodt, P. (1994) *Advances in School Effectiveness Research and Practice*. Oxford: Pergamon Press.

Rutter, M. (1983) School effects on pupil progress – findings and policy implications. *Child Development*, 54(1): 1–29.

Rutter, M., Maughan, B., Mortimore, P. and Ouston, J. (1979) *Fifteen Thousand Hours: Secondary Schools and their Effects on Children*. London: Open Books.

Sammons, P., Nuttall, D. and Cuttance, P. (1993) Differential school effectiveness: Results from a re-analysis of the Inner London Education Authority's Junior School Project Data. *British Educational Research Journal*, 19(4): 381–405.

Sammons, P., Hillman, J. and Mortimore, P. (1995) *Key Characteristics of Effective Schools: A Review of School Effectiveness Research*. London: OFSTED.

Sammons, P., Thomas, S., Mortimore, P., Owen, C. and Pennell, H. (1994) *Assessing School Effectiveness: Developing Measures to put School Performance in Context*. London: OFSTED.

Sammons, P., Thomas, S., Mortimore, P., Cairns, R., Bausor, J. and Walker, A. (1996) Understanding school and departmental differences in academic effectiveness, in *School Effectiveness and School Improvement*.

Scheerens, J. (1992) *Effective Schooling*. London: Cassell.

Smith, D. and Tomlinson, S. (1989) *The School Effect: A Study of Multiracial Comprehensives*. London: Policy Studies Institute.

Steedman, J. (1980) *Progress in Secondary Schools*. London: National Children's Bureau.

Steedman, J. (1983) *Examination Results in Selective and Non-Selective Schools*. London: National Children's Bureau.

Stoll, L. (1996) Linking school effectiveness and school improvement: issues and possibilities, in J. Gray and D. Reynolds (eds) *Merging Traditions: The Future of School Effectiveness and School Improvement Research*. London: Cassell.

Stoll, L. and Fink, D. (1992) Effecting school change: the Halton Approach. *School Effectiveness and School Improvement*, 3(1): 19–41.

Stoll, L. and Fink, D. (1996) *Changing Our Schools: Linking School Effectiveness and School Improvement*. Buckingham: Open University Press.

Stringfield, S. and Slavin, R. (1991) 'Raising societal demands: high reliability organisations, school effectiveness, success for all and a set of modest proposals'. Paper presented at Interuniversitair Centrum Voor Onderwijsevaluatie, Twente, October.

Teddlie, C. and Stringfield, S. (1993) *Schools make a Difference: Lessons Learned from a Ten Year Study of School Effects*. New York: Teachers' College Press.

Thomas, S. and Mortimore, P. (1994) *Report on Value Added Analysis of the 1993 GCSE Examination Results in Lancashire*. London: Institute of Education.

Thomas, S., Sammons, P. and Mortimore, P. (1994) 'Stability in secondary schools. Effects on students' GCSE outcomes'. Paper presented at the Annual Conference of the British Educational Research Association, Oxford.

Tizard, B., Blatchford, P., Burke, P., Farquhar, C. and Plewis, I. (1988) *Young Children at School in the Inner City*. Hove: Lawrence Erlbaum.

Willms, D. (1985) The balance thesis: contextual effects of ability on pupils' 'O' grade examination results. *Oxford Review of Education*, 11(1): 33–41.

Willms, D. (1986) Social class segregation and its relationship to pupils' examination results in Scotland. *American Sociological Review*: 51.

Willms, D. (1987) Differences between Scottish Education Authorities in their examination attainments. *Oxford Review of Education*, 13: 211–37.

Willms, D. and Cuttance, P. (1985) School effects in Scottish secondary schools. *British Journal of Sociology of Education*, 6(3): 289–305.

Wimpelberg, R., Teddlie, C. and Stringfield, S. (1989) Sensitivity to context: the past and future of effective schools research. *Educational Administration Quarterly*, 25: 82–107.

Woodhouse, G. and Goldstein, H. (1988) Educational performance indicators and LEA league tables. *Oxford Review of Education*, 14: 301–20.

13 | School effectiveness research: the policy makers' tool for school improvement?*

SALLY BROWN, JILL DUFFIELD AND SHEILA RIDDELL

[. . .]

The rapid progress to centre stage made by school effectiveness research is not confined to the United Kingdom. Other European countries, especially the Netherlands (e.g. Creemers and Sheerens 1989; Creemers 1992; Scheerens 1992), have been very active in this kind of work. The combination of an emphasis on measuring the performance of schools and the promise of this research appears to hold for school improvement has been seductive. This is not to suggest that everything is plain sailing; like any field of research, this one has had its critics (e.g. Sirotnik 1985; Angus 1993), but the battle has engaged only at a distance. The more pressing concern for school effectiveness researchers has been that of how to close the gap that divides them from those who work on school improvement. In particular, there is something of a chasm between, on the one hand, the large scale quantitative work that purports to identify the characteristics of effective schools and, on the other hand, studies such as those in Belgium that see the distinctive culture of the individual school as central to the implementation of innovations for improvement (e.g. Vandenberghe et al. 1993; Staessens and Vandeberghe 1994).

A major aim of this chapter is to take a critical look at research into school effectiveness, especially its potential to lead to improvements in schools. [. . .]

Policy makers' interest and expectations

School effectiveness research offers policy makers the engaging prospect of being able to identify the charcteristics of effective schools and then make use of these findings to bring about improvements in less effective institutions. One problem with this, however, is that the promise of such remedies has attracted a mixed bag of followers.

*This material has been edited and originally appeared in the *European Education Research Association Bulletin*.

Politicians of a right wing persuasion have been able to use the climate of opinion that has been partially created by us [school effectiveness researchers] both to attack school standards generally and to propose the improvement of those standards by use of what are clearly non rational methods . . . We are also talking about what to do about the large number of intellectual cowboys, and some cowgirls, who are purporting to use the school effectiveness paradigm in their consulting, a particularly unwelcome occurrence in those cases where the effectiveness consultants are former headteachers who were prematurely retired because of ineffectiveness.

(Reynolds 1994: 6–7)

Notwithstanding such misuse, it seems reasonable to expect that responsible policy makers will heed a body of research that claims to describe and explain how schools make a difference to pupils' achievements, and to be able to 'back map' the educational processes that lead to positive achievements.

[. . .]

This body of research is seen, therefore, through ambitious eyes as having the potential to resolve the big problems of education. If multilevel modelling can explore schools' differential effectiveness, stability of effectiveness, relationships between subject department and institutional effectiveness, or those between the primary and secondary sectors, then there is a tacit assumption that this will lead to an understanding of these phenomena and so to the means for improving schools.

A bold vision of this kind for the future does not imply insensitivity to the shortcomings of current research and its (so far) limited impact on practice. Indeed, following Reynolds *et al.* (1993: 153) the SOED commented

that school effectiveness studies are very deficient at the level of processes rather than factors; that they customarily show a 'snap-shot' of a school at one point in time rather than an evolutionary picture through time; that they are rarely 'fine-grained enough' for the purposes of school improvement; that their definition of attainment might be too narrow to form a valid measure of the performance of a school; and that there is an assumption that effectiveness factors identified for effective schools can simply be 'back mapped' onto ineffective schools.

Interestingly, however, the important criticisms that have been made concerning the lack of theoretical underpinning for most school effectiveness research (Angus 1993; Reynolds 1993) seem not to be salient features for the SOED. Although there is an awareness that correlational studies are inadequate for providing an understanding of why and how schools establish and maintain (or not) effectiveness, the idea that such understanding will require the development of better theory is not discussed. The answer is seen to rest in a pragmatic challenge to researchers to integrate aspects of methodology, qualitative and quantitative, in order (Reynolds *et al.* 1993: 156)

to define attainment . . . find ways of measuring it . . . provide estimates of improved school effectiveness with school-based activities studies . . . make clear the processes within schools which flow from the selected activities, and demonstrate how these processes impinge on the wider school community.

There are, of course, other examples of explorations of collaboration between school effectiveness and school improvement researchers. For instance, the South Bristol Value Added Task Group has brought together complementary initiatives from the National

Foundation for Educational Research (NFER) QUASE project and the Centre for School Improvement (CSI) at the University of Bath (Harris *et al.* 1995).
   [. . .]

The prevalence of the top-down management model

A top-down way of construing school effectiveness has the effect of placing the primary emphasis on formal organisational variables with the assumption that matters of teaching, learning, socialisation and curriculum will follow. The same way of thinking is a feature of much of the work on school improvement where schools' development planning is central. From such plans there are seen to emerge, for example,

> a series of priorities which ideally are supported by action plans. These are working documents for teachers. In them the priority is subdivided into *targets and tasks*, responsibilities are allocated, a time frame established and evaluation or progress checks are identified.
>
> (Hopkins 1994: 5)

Yet the classroom is where the crucial decision making occurs, and the questions at school level should be concerned with whether school practices encourage and support or inhibit the strategies that result in effective learning. There is, indeed, increasing evidence (e.g. Fitz-Gibbon 1991), especially from studies using new statistical techniques, that the greater part of the variance among pupils' achievements can be accounted for by differences at classroom rather than school level. The recent study at the University of Bath of 'accelerating' subject departments (i.e. those adding significant value to pupil progress measures) concluded that these departments were characterised

> as being either working with or neutralising external influences. The schools they worked in were broadly supportive, but this was not a major factor in their success. They were largely successful because of their own efforts.
>
> (Harris *et al.* 1995)

Despite such findings, it is still the school on which the focus is invariably placed.

   There are, however, some school effectiveness researchers for whom these findings have tempered the dominance of the top-down model that depends heavily on quantitative school level data. Gray and Wilcox (1994: 14) have argued that insiders' (teachers') views need to be treated as seriously as those of external reviewers, and a range of studies (including the current International School Effectiveness Programme – ISERP, undated) have collected qualitative data from individual teachers and even pupils.

   In our view this is not enough. If the crux of school effectiveness is the quality of teaching and learning, then it is the classroom to which school improvers have to turn to achieve change. It has been argued elsewhere (Brown and McIntyre 1993: 15–16) that any serious attempt to innovate in classrooms has to start from where teachers are and how they construe their own teaching, their pupils and what they are trying to achieve. An approach which simply supplements quantitative data collection with qualitative does not achieve this. The strategy that many school effectiveness studies adopt collects the qualitative data, usually through semi-structured interviews or questionnaires, within frameworks that reflect the *researchers'* constructs. These are based on findings from earlier work which typically included variables that researchers' or policy makers' hunches suggested might be important. They reveal nothing about how the teachers make sense of their educational world, nor about which variables are most salient in their thinking. Such revelations require much more detailed and phenomenological studies of classrooms, and these are rare in the school effectiveness and school improvement repertoires.

Our argument is that adherence to a top–down management model will not facilitate and, indeed, can be expected to impede the success of strategies to improve schools. The problem will be deepened if, in addition, the conceptualisation of the field is too simple.

Challenges to simple concepts

Like many other policy makers, those in the Scottish Office, despite their caveats, are clearly attracted to the simple notion of using findings, which purport to explain both what schools are like and what they do to be effective, as the basis for showing other schools how to improve. In fact, the notion is simple-minded rather than simple and it has several characteristics that demonstrate this.

In the first place, it fails to address the issue of how the findings are to be integrated into the thinking and practice of those who are seen as needing to improve. The involvement and commitment of teachers, with a sense of ownership and responsibility for decision-making, is an essential element for innovation. In those circumstances, it cannot be assumed that teachers will be ready to accept the findings as an agenda handed down from on high; such resistance was found, indeed, at an early stage in the well known Effective Schools' Project of the Halton Board of Education, Ontario, Canada.

This neglect of the conditions necessary for change to occur arises from a paucity of theory in both school effectiveness and school improvement work. We have argued elsewhere (Brown, Riddell and Duffield, 1996) that attempts to develop and test models of school effectiveness have been based heavily on researchers' and policy makers' hunches about what works, supported and developed by large scale correlational studies, and for the most part resting on behaviourist assumptions. The effectiveness correlates have taken little account of the variables that are most salient for those in schools and classroom who have the responsibility for making the schools effective and whose implicit theories (no matter how misguided they may appear) will provide the basis for understanding why things turn out the way they do.

On the school improvement side, Hopkins (1994) has observed

> Even the best of school improvement work has failed to elaborate *theories of school development* or begun in any sustained way to develop and evaluate a range of *models of school improvement intervention.*

In the same paper, he has attempted to initiate debate on theories and models of this kind with the intention of helping to unify the effectiveness and improvement fields and prevent them from remaining moribund. This is no small task, not least because much school effectiveness research has aspired to measure relatively stable characteristics of schools and so nail them to an effectiveness scale (in the UK this is seen as particularly important in facilitating parents' choice of schools), while school improvement rests on the assumption that characteristics of schools can be changed.

The assumption about stability, however, is just one of the factors that distinguish the two paradigms. The large scale, correlational, quantitative, effectiveness studies focus on outcomes that are readily measurable (especially on basic skills, examination grades and attendance) and on generalizable findings. These studies contrast with school improvers' work where the concerns are the individual institution with its distinctive processes and multiple goals, and the development of an understanding of the specific aspects of change that lead to greater success in the particular school. Perhaps the most striking aspect of the contrast is that between the criteria for effectiveness and those for improvement. The former reflect an essentially norm-referenced system where any school's performance will always be assessed in relation to that of others on generalised measures across schools. No positive change in effectiveness will be recognised unless a school overtakes its competitors; absolute growth is of no consequence unless there is relative growth. In school improvement, however, the important question is whether the school's performance is in some sense 'better' than its own previous performance, and performance can refer to any kinds of goals, whether general across schools or idiosyncratic to the institution.

Policy makers may, of course, regard all this as simply a pedantic diversion on the part of researchers, and no good reason to abandon notions of making use of clear-cut effectiveness findings for improvement purposes. The trouble is that the findings are not clear-cut; they display the complexities and uncertainties that are characteristic of real schools. A school's overall performance can change significantly over two or three years; its effects can be different for children of different ethnic or social backgrounds, gender or abilities; academic effectiveness may not be associated with social effectiveness; and, as we have already mentioned, it appears that much (if not most) of the variation in performance results from effects at classroom rather than school level. Add to these the fact that education seems to account for, at best, 10 to 15 per cent of the variance in pupils' performance (substantially less than family and community background variables) and one gets a sense of what 'not clear-cut' means.

Quite apart from these uncertainties, however, there is a major 'gap' in the work on school effectiveness to which researchers are anxious to give their attention. Indeed, it is an area that has to be of central concern to policy makers if they are to address the issue of how to improve schools that are currently regarded as failing young people. It is to this 'gap' we now turn.

The problem of ineffectiveness

One of the limitations often cited for this body of research is its concentration on effective contexts. Reynolds (1994: 19–24) makes a forceful case for the study of *ineffective* schools. He argues that researchers in both school effectiveness and school improvement traditions have limited the interest to the understanding of success and have neglected explanations of failure. This reflects a long standing and widespread scepticism (e.g. Purkey and Smith, 1983) about the assumption that less effective schools should try to emulate the characteristics and strategies of more effective schools if they are to improve.

How an 'ineffective' school improves may well differ from ways in which more effective schools maintain their effectiveness.

(Gray and Wilcox 1994: 2)

Some writers (Gray *et al.* 1993; Stoll 1993) have also pointed to the potential gains in looking at effective schools that are deteriorating and ineffective schools that are improving.

The general point is important within as well as across schools. The University of Bath Study, for example, used only accelerating departments in schools. As they point out, it is possible that other departments in the same schools might display the same characteristics without performing particularly well. While a variety of commonalities (at both school and departmental levels) were observed in relation to accelerating departments across different schools, there is no information about which of these features (any or all?) also applied to static or deteriorating departments.

There are dangers, however, in characterising schools according to an effective/ineffective dichotomy. While Reynolds (1994) was clearly thinking of schools that he would expect virtually everyone to regard as disaster areas with no more than a very few effective features (what Louis and Miles 1990, refer to as 'depressed schools'), it may be the case that not many schools actually fall into that category. Our own experience suggests that few Scottish schools are clear 'outliers', and distinctions between schools usually have to be made on the basis of the proportion of subject departments for which performance on effectiveness measures is significantly above or below those of other schools in the same local authority.

Furthermore, Gray and Wilcox (1994) in searching for studies that did provide evidence on how to improve ineffective schools found very few from which they could generalise and identify 'common messages'. They concluded (1994: 15):

Most [studies] are not specifically about how 'ineffective' schools improve but about the more general processes of improvement *per se.* We still suspect there are problems and barriers to change which are specific to 'ineffective' schools but which research has not teased out as yet . . . [However] As Andy Hargreaves [1994: 54] has noted: '*faith* in generalised and scientifically known principles of school effectiveness has begun to be superseded by commitments to more ongoing, provisional and contextually sensitive processes of school improvement'.

These authors were cautious about how (if at all) it is possible to use existing knowledge to turn around ineffective schools. They argued that a necessary prerequisite is to capture teachers' enthusiasm for, and commitment to, change; pressures for improvement which have no perceived rewards for teachers have little chance of success. Unless everyone in the school has a shared appreciation of a common problem to be resolved, and a sense of ownership of the strategies to be used in pursuing that resolution, teachers will be unconvinced that effort should be expended to bring about change. As Staessons (1993: 127) has put it

the norms and values that underlie the internal functioning of schools, and that determine the thinking and working of teachers, also determine what is possible and what is unthinkable with respect to improvement.

Reynolds (1994) takes a different tack. He is one of the very few authors who has documented work that failed to turn around an ineffective school (Reynolds 1992: 178–82).

Although he has been careful not to be absolutely definite about the features that are common to ineffective schools, he has listed the possibilities in strong terms and offered a powerful agenda for engineering such schools into ways of working that he sees as providing high quality education. The first, short-term stage of his strategy sets the scene.

> we would need to be directive with them, and would need to directly tell them what to do, independent of whether they agree or not. There is little point in attempting to use principles of 'ownership' or 'collegiality' in our early help attempts – people who have collectively permitted a school to hit educational rocks are unlikely to be those who steer it off them.
>
> (Reynolds 1994: 22)

This approach is not, of course, consistent with our earlier assertion of the priority for teachers to have a sense of ownership and responsibility for decision making as a pre-requisite for successful innovation. Our view is that Reynolds' coercive/paternalistic approach would have a low chance of success in Scotland, but there is a further ethical/practical concern. Explicit identification of a school as 'ineffective' is unlikely to promote co-operative strategies for improvement. Realistically, to get a research foot in the door it is probably necessary to fudge the issue of why one is choosing to work in that school, and the ethics of that are questionable. If the intention is also to work in effective schools that are deteriorating, a similar problem is likely to be faced.
[. . .]

In conclusion

David Reynolds has made clear his position on how knowledge from school effective-ness should be used in the preparation of teachers and, by implication, further afield.

> some say that it is unethical to impose prior definitions of what are 'effective' prac-tices upon trainees as taken for granted educational knowledge. For myself, if we do have valid knowledge as to what helps children develop, then I would regard it as unethical *not* to give it. Others say that giving knowledge of effective prac-tices prevents trainees from discovering what is their own effective practice, even though I would argue that the effectiveness knowledge base would facilitate this.
>
> (Reynolds 1994: 5)

Reynolds' position is one with which we believe our 'responsible policy makers' would concur and, to a large extent, so would we. The danger, however, lies in associating this with ideas that there is some accepted package that forms the 'effectiveness knowledge base', that it can be transferred down to the minds of teachers and student teachers in a straightforward way to effect school improvement, and that the measured effective-ness of schools is the most important set of variables in determining their decisions for action. In this paper, we have looked at some of the factors that impinge on this attract-ive but flawed notion (*not* promoted by Reynolds) that the findings of school effec-tiveness research can feed directly into school improvement.

One of the more important of these factors is the conceptualisation of education, shared by many policy makers and much of the research, as a top-down management process. This has had the effect of placing the initial emphasis at the top of the school and on the formal organisational variables. The idea (but by no means always the execution) is to move down from the locus of central development planning to the classroom where, as everyone agrees, change has to take place if improvement is to be effected. We have argued that the chances of success of this strategy are limited because it takes little account of how those who have to implement the change (the teachers) make sense of their work in classrooms.

The hazards are increased if the complexities of schools and the uncertainties of the research findings are not recognised. As a field that is deficient in theory, it starts at a disadvantage and suffers from the juxtaposition of distinctively different paradigms in the two traditions of school effectiveness and school improvement. The idea that sets of characteristics of effective schools and of general strategies for improvement can be established with confidence should be undermined by such things as the difficulty of replicating research findings, the uncertain stability of schools' performances and the lack of uniformity of effects across various kinds of goals, subject departments or different groups of pupils.

Rather than these various cautions, however, some researchers would argue that the major problem with the existing knowledge base is the paucity of understanding of ineffective schools and how they might improve. We have discussed some of the difficulties associated with progress in this aspect of the research field. Disagreement on appropriate strategies, the identification of ineffectiveness (improving or not) and the ethics of labelling schools in this way all present hurdles to be faced.

[. . .]

A clear achievement of research on school effectiveness has been that it has captured the attention of policy makers and engaged them in a dialogue about the meaning of research findings and their application to policy and practice. However, its further responsibility is to explicate, and persuade policy makers to appreciate, the complexities and limitations of the field and to divert them from the early, seductive, simpleminded models. Such models were fortified by what Reynolds (1994: 10) referred to as 'the frankly grubby empiricism of purely statistical approaches' and, in our view, by naive expectations that knowledge can be 'delivered' to teachers for use in the same way that coal can be delivered to households for burning.

References

Angus, L. (1993) The sociology of school effectiveness. *British Journal of Sociology of Education* 14(3): 333–45.

Brown, S. and McIntyre, D. (1993) *Making Sense of Teaching*. Milton Keynes: Open University Press.

Brown, S., Riddell, S. and Duffield, J. (1996) Possibilities and problems of small-scale studies to unpack the findings of large-scale school effectiveness, in J. Gray, D. Reynolds, C. Fitz-Gibbon and D. Jesson (eds) *Merging Traditions: The Future of Research on School Effectiveness and School Improvement*. London: Cassell.

Creemers, B. (1992) School effectiveness and effective instruction – the need for a further relationship, in J. Bashi and Z. Sass (eds) *School Effectiveness and Improvement*. Jerusalem: Hebrew University Press.

Creemers, B. and Scheerens, J. (eds) (1989) Developments in school effectiveness research, a special issue of *International Journal of Educational Research* 13(7): 685–825.

Fitz-Gibbon, C. T. (1991) Multilevel modelling in an indicator system, in S. W. Raudenbush and J. D. Willms (eds) *Schools, Classrooms and Pupils: International Studies of Schooling from a Multilevel Perspective*. San Diego: Academic Press.

Gray, J., Jesson, D., Goldstein, H. and Hedger, K. (1993) *The Statistics of School Improvement: Establishing the Agenda*. Paper presented to the ESRC Seminar Series on School Effectiveness and School Improvement, Sheffield University, July 1993.

Gray, J. and Wilcox, B. (1994) *The Challenge Turning Round Ineffective Schools*. Paper presented to ESRC Seminar Series on School Effectiveness and School Improvement, University of Newcastle Upon Tyne, October 1994.

Hargreaves, A. (1994) *Changing Teaching: Changing Times*. London: Cassell.

Harris, A., Jamieson, I. and Russ, J. (1995) *A Study of Effective Departments in Secondary Schools. School Organisation*, 15(3).

Hopkins, D. (1994) *Towards a Theory for School Improvement*. Paper presented to the ESRC Seminar Series on School Effectiveness and School Improvement, University of Newcastle Upon Tyne, October 1994.

ISERP (undated) *The International School Effectiveness Research Programme: An Outline*. Paper distributed at the ISERP symposium organised by D. Reynolds at the annual conference of the British Educational Research Association. Oxford, September 1994.

Louis, K. S. and Miles, M. B. (1990) *Improving an Urban High School: What Works and What Fails*. London: Cassell.

MacBeath, J. and Mortimore, P. (1994) *Improving School Effectiveness: a Scottish Approach*. Paper presented to the Annual Conference of the British Educational Research Association, Oxford University, September 1994.

Purkey, S. C. and Smith, M. S. (1983) Effective Schools: a review. *Elementary School Journal*, 84: 427–452.

Reynolds, D. (1992) School effectiveness and school improvement in the 1990s, Chapter 10, in D. Reynolds and P. Cultance (eds) *School Effectiveness: Research, Policy and Practice*. London: Cassell.

Reynolds, D. (1993) *School Effectiveness: The International Perspective*. Paper presented to ESRC Seminar Series on School Effectiveness and School Improvement, Sheffield University, October 1993.

Reynolds, D. (1994) *Inaugural Lecture* given on 19 October 1994 at the University of Newcastle Upon Tyne (in mimeo).

Reynolds, D., Hopkins, D. and Stoll, L. (1993) Linking school effectiveness and school improvement. *School Effectiveness and School Improvement*, 4(1): 37–58.

Riddell and Brown (eds) (1991) *School Effectiveness Research: Its Messages for School Improvement*. Edinburgh: HMSO.

Scheerens, J. (1992) *Effective Schooling: Research, Theory and Practice*. London: Cassell.

Scottish Office Education Department (SOED) (1990) *The Role of School Development Planning in School Effectiveness*. Edinburgh: HMSO.

Sirotnik, K. A. (1985) School effectiveness: a bandwagon in search of a time. *Education Administration Quarterly*, 21(2): 135–40.

Staessons, K. (1993) Identification and description of professional culture in innovating schools. *Qualitative Studies in Education*, 6(2): 111–28.

Staessons, K. and Vandenberghe, R. (1994) Vision as a core component in school culture. *Journal of Curriculum Studies*, 26(2): 187–200.

Stoll, L. (1993) *Linking School Effectiveness and School Improvement: Issues and Possibilities*. Paper presented to the ESRC Seminar Series on School Effectiveness and School Improvement, Sheffield University, October 1993.

Tibbitt, J., Spencer, E. and Hutchinson, C. (1994) Improving school effectiveness: policy and research in Scotland, *Scottish Educational Review*, 26(2): 151–57.

Vandenberghe, R., D'hertefelt, M. and De Wever, H. (1993) Schools as implementers of an externally proposed improvement programme, in F. Kieviet and R. Vanderberghe (eds) *School Culture, School Improvement and Teacher Development*. Leiden: DSWO Press.

14 | A study of 'effective' departments in secondary schools*

ALMA HARRIS, IAN JAMIESON AND JEN RUSS

Introduction

This study reports empirical work with a small sample of schools in a West-Country city. For some years the School of Education at the University of Bath had worked with a consortium of schools in the southern part of the city as part of the evaluation of the local education authority (LEA) Technical and Vocational Education Initiative (TVEI) project. In the last two years interest from both sides has focused on 'improving and proving' the performance of the schools, drawing on the work of the school-effectiveness and school-improvement movements.

In 1994 a variety of factors came together which made this study possible. The southern part of the city was chosen as one of the areas for the piloting of the National Foundation for Educational Research (NFER)'s quantitative analysis for self evaluation [QUASE] project. This initiative allowed the completion of multi-level data at both the departmental and the school level for the schools. At the same time the School of Education won a research grant from the Department of Employment's Training Enterprise and Education Division (TEED) unit for a study of the characteristics of 'improving schools' which involved schools in the consortium (Harris and Russ 1994). Finally, the School of Education decided that it would make school improvement a major thrust of its work and consequently, it founded a Centre for School Improvement.

Within the consortia, a planning group known as the value-added task group was set up to coordinate work on raising levels of achievement. Various initiatives were brought together which had both a research and an action orientation. Central to this work was the multi-level data provided by the NFER's QUASE Project. This project assessed the progress schools made with their pupils between joining the school and taking GCSE examinations. It took into account key factors which have been shown to affect outcomes, such as the pupils' prior attainment (measured by intake measures)

*This material has been edited and originally appeared in *School Organisation*.

together with features of the school's background, or context. Basic information concerning the school's context was collected via a simple pro forma, and a detailed analysis of the pupils' attendance and post-16 destinations was carried out. Moreover, there was an option for questionnaire surveys of year 11 pupils and their parents to be conducted on various aspects of the schools and of school life.

From this range of data, QUASE profiles were produced for each of the participating schools using six academic-performance indicators. These performance indicators were based on the GCSE attainment and they provided an analysis of individual subject areas (see the Appendix). The information collected allowed QUASE to produce a 'value-added analysis' for individual schools and individual subject areas. This data made it possible to observe that within schools which were considered either relatively effective, neutral or relatively ineffective individual departments had different performances. This finding duplicated that of Nuttall *et al.* (1989), and more recently, that of Thomas *et al.* (1994).

On the basis of this finding, the value-added task group decided that it would be useful for Bath's Centre for School Improvement to undertake a study of departmental effectiveness. [. . .] The research was to concentrate on a small number of departments which were effective in the sense that their GCSE results, computed by NFER on a value-added basis, indicated that the students studying these subjects were progressing further than might be expected from consideration of their intake (cf. Mortimore 1991). It was further agreed that the study should be a qualitative one relying primarily on interview data from the senior management team, the departmental members and pupils.

Methodology

A literature search revealed how little work has been undertaken on departmental effectiveness. There was, of course, the usual collection of guide books on effective departments written by successful practitioners, for example, by Marland and Hill (1981), although the evidence base for these works was rarely made clear beyond personal experience. The various reports of Her Majesty's Inspectorate (HMI) on individual schools and their overview reports, for example, *Ten Good Schools* (Her Majesty's Inspectorate [HMI], 1977) provide clues to effectiveness as judged by the inspectorate, but most of this material is at the whole-school level. Similarly, the Office for Standards in Education (OFSTED) *Handbook for the Inspection of Schools* offers criteria which, by implication, can be applied at the level of the department.

The research literature, while wide ranging on the topic of whole-school effectiveness and whole-school improvement (cf. Rutter *et al.* 1979; Reynolds 1985; Mortimore *et al.* 1988; Levine and Lezotte 1990; Fullan 1992), has been relatively silent on departmental effectiveness. Only recently has research highlighted the importance of this area. For example, several research studies have shown that a substantial proportion of the variation in effectiveness among schools is due to variation among classrooms and departments within schools (Creemers 1992; Scheerens 1992). Furthermore, other studies have demonstrated the importance of comparing subject, or departmental-level effectiveness when considering individual school effectiveness (Raudenbush 1989; Willms and Raudenbush 1989; Fitz-Gibbon 1991; Luyten 1994; Thomas *et al.* 1994).

Prior to these studies few research projects have concentrated specifically upon departmental effectiveness. Of these projects, the NFER's study of effective heads of department is possibly the most notable (Earley and Fletcher-Campbell 1989). This research project concentrated upon the management of effective departments and the focus was primarily on the components of effective management practice. In contrast, other research studies, such as those by Smith & Tomlinson (1989) and Fitz-Gibbon (1991), have concentrated largely upon subject-level issues without much consideration of departmental organisation or management.

The central aim of our study was to explore effective departments from the perspectives of *participants* using semi-structured interviewing (Brown *et al.* 1995). In order to construct an interview schedule, however, the research team had to rely heavily on the more general material on *school effectiveness* and then deduce *departmental-level* questions. The research-literature surveys provided, for example, by Levine (1992), Reynolds (1992), Scheerens (1992) and Mortimore (1993), were scrutinised. Two sets of interview questions were subsequently produced, one for members of the senior-management team (which focused on school-level matters and their perception of the relevant department), the other for departmental members (which focused on the organisation and activities of the department itself). Finally, a set of questions for pupils was developed which began with some general questions about teaching and learning in the school and then progressively focused on the key department. A total of six 'effective' departments were selected for study representing a range of subjects (English, mathematics, science and humanities).

From the data, the research team were able to isolate some key features or characteristics of effective departments. These were grouped under the separate headings of effective management and effective teaching and learning. Before describing these characteristics, however, the relationship between whole-school management and effective departmental management will be considered.

Whole-school management and departments adding significant value

Many research studies have shown that the style of management adopted within a school is of central importance to the perceived and realised effectiveness of the whole school (Bolam *et al.* 1993). It is a commonplace observation in the effective schooling literature to state that for departments to be really effective they need to be 'nested' inside schools which are themselves managed effectively. As a direct consequence of this observation we explored whether there were any consistent relationships between the school's management policy and the effective departments.

[. . .]

We found that there were several aspects of whole-school policy that our departments were actively building upon. The first was a stress on the importance of the pupils that clearly went beyond the usual professional rhetoric. The schools in our study were characterised by systematic developments aimed at providing a caring environment for pupils, and every effort was made to involve them fully in the life of the school. The leadership of these institutions acknowledged that they were trying to raise the expectations of both pupils *and* staff. This manifested itself in themes for assemblies as well as in more concrete strategies like systematic attempts to give young people more ownership and a voice in the running of the school. Significantly all the schools we visited with departments had school councils which, to a greater or lesser extent, were attempting to include pupils in genuine decision making. This was viewed positively by the pupils, who considered it to be an indication of their importance in the life of the school.

The emphasis on pupils could also be seen in the whole-school strategies concerned with pupil behaviour and rewards. By and large, these schools were noticeable for policies which emphasised the importance of rewarding positive behaviour and a wide range of achievements (not just the academic). Using rewards rather than punishments to change behaviour was considered by staff to be important in raising motivation. This whole-school policy provided an important backdrop to departmental policy on rewards and punishments. Most of the departments replicated the emphasis on reward, and they had adopted ways of working which reinforced the whole-school policy.

The other whole-school aspect which encouraged departments to become more effective was the stress which heads and senior management teams were beginning to place on the scrutiny of examination and test results at a departmental level. We found that the involvement of the SMT in working with departments to use examination results in a formative way was an important contributor to effectiveness. Heads of department in these schools knew that they were being held accountable for the results in their subjects, but in the accelerating departments this was not viewed as a threat. Instead, the heads of department felt that this was a process which was both a necessary and justifiable route to further departmental improvement.

Notwithstanding these observations, in general the effective departments did *not* feel that they were operating in structures and cultures that were particularly supportive of their specialist endeavours. Despite working in different schools they nearly all believed that the senior management of their institution was not sufficiently collegiate. While to some extent this response is rather predictable given the well-known tensions that exist between the SMT and other members of staff, it is somewhat surprising. Our findings showed that there was some congruence between the general school ethos and the management style and departmental working. It is possible that this is a relationship which would benefit from further scrutiny and consideration by the SMT in each institution. In particular, in some cases we found that the management style of the SMT appeared to be in stark contrast to the style chosen by the successful heads of department.

Managing effective departments

Climate for change

In looking at the management styles and structures of the departments there were some interesting similarities in the way in which they were managed. Interestingly, three of our departmental heads were relatively new and had inherited less than satisfactory situations in their departments. In these schools there was a view that 'something needed to be done' and so the incoming head of department had inherited a situation where innovation and change were expected. When this factor is coupled with poor departmental performance, it is clear that these heads of department inherited a situation which was likely to be more favourably disposed towards new methods of working. Clearly, the climate for change is an important factor in becoming more effective and a new head of department has the advantage of being able to create this climate more readily.

Vision

All of these departments were marked by a clear and shared sense of vision that largely emanated from, and was propagated by, the head of department. This vision embraced the nature of the subject and how it should be organised for teaching purposes. One of the most striking findings of this study was the great emphasis on collegiate styles of management adopted by the head of department. By and large, these were 'talking departments', that is, departments that were marked by a constant interchange of professional information at both a formal and an informal level. Departmental meetings tended to be frequent, often in addition to those scheduled for all the departments in the school, and with clear purposes. One department systematically used some of these meetings for the professional development of staff.

Collegiality

One mark of collegiality, which was present in many of the departments, was the amount of delegation of tasks. The heads of department exhibited trust in their colleagues, and most teachers in the department were allocated particular responsibilities for which they took the lead on behalf of the whole department.

The collegiate model of management was led in slightly different ways by different heads of department depending on their personal style. All of them could probably be described as 'leading professionals' in the sense that their own mode of practice was regarded as the model to follow, particularly in teaching. Although none of these departments was marked by much prescription about teaching styles or strategies, there were shared characteristics such as enthusiasm for the subject and for pupils' learning which underpinned their work together. Being a 'leading professional' did not mean that these heads of department were advocates of all the latest innovations in their subjects; indeed, in some cases the heads of department were most cautious about 'innovation for innovation sake'. This meant that they safeguarded their colleagues from inappropriate developments and unnecessary additional work by carefully scrutinising the latest developments. Although they were knowledgeable about new developments in their subject areas, and they were certainly receptive to new ideas, their main strategy was to embed their version of good practice in their departments without too many 'innovation distractions'. Their strong vision of what good teaching looked like in their field largely determined whether an innovation was considered and subsequently adopted.

The leadership style of these heads of successful departments also varied within the more general collegiate model. The variation was a function of personal style and the context within which they worked. One head of department, who had inherited a department in serious difficulties, was very much a leader whose role was to persuade the rest of the department about the wisdom of new ways of working. Other heads of department were more inclined to see themselves as coordinators of other professionals. All of these heads of departments seemed very skilled at managing interpersonal relationships within their departments. The degree of trust and confidence in their abilities enabled them to bring everybody along with difficult decisions.

Organisation and resource management

In managerial terms the real success of these departments lay in their ability to organise key elements of the teaching and learning process in an effective way. All of these departments had detailed and agreed schemes of work that had been collectively approved. Sometimes these schemes had been worked on by the whole department; sometimes a system of division of labour had been evolved whereby particular members of staff worked on areas of their own expertise. These schemes of work generally had the following features: they were consistent with the general vision of the subject in the department; they were very detailed, with clear guidance; they were regarded as important documents, and they were easily accessible in the department; and they had been agreed by all the department after a discussion.

If the schemes of work were indicators of good organisation in the departments, then so was the management of resources and their deployment. With one exception these were not particularly well-resourced departments, but the resources they had were particularly well deployed. For example, in an accelerating science department money had been spent on making sure that a large amount of good-quality equipment was available, particularly glassware, so that pupils would never be short of the material to undertake the majority of experiments. This allocation decision was made instead of the purchase of more sophisticated equipment that would have been used by a few able pupils. For most of the accelerating departments the bottom line was the enhancement of teaching and learning for *all* pupils. This was achieved through the optimum allocation of material and human resources.

[. . .]

Monitoring and evaluation

Another aspect of good management that was a noticeable feature of these departments was their stress on pupil-record keeping. Each of these departments could produce, almost instantly, a detailed profile of each of the pupils taking the subject, which recorded their progress, very often including detailed assessments of their strengths and weaknesses in the subject. Very often such records were systematically shared with pupils so that they too knew exactly how they were doing in the subject and on what aspects they needed to work harder.

A consistent feature of the departments was the systematic monitoring and evaluation of pupils' learning outcomes within class groups. In these departments, mechanisms for monitoring pupil progress and for self-evaluation were found to be tightly in place and reinforced throughout the department. Information about the progress of individual students was seen to be collected through a variety of means, on a regular basis, and it was shared within and across departments/faculties. The recording and reviewing procedures in place in the 'accelerating' departments were also found to be important in the early identification of potential underachievement. Where this was the case we found that the departments had specific strategies for offsetting this trend and addressing the problem.

If one considers record keeping as one aspect of review, then these departments also showed themselves to be good at reviewing their own progress as a department. Particular aspects of the work of the department were regularly selected for systematic review. While this was often led by the head of department, the other members of staff also had the opportunity to raise issues which were concerning them. As mentioned earlier, the accelerating departments tended to work cooperatively, hence any discussion and subsequent policy making involved the whole department.

Teachers

When considering the effectiveness of departments it is difficult to ignore the effectiveness of individual teachers. There is a view in teaching that equates good results directly with the abilities of individual teachers. So, was it possible that these departments were effective simply because they comprised particularly able teachers? Of course we have no direct evidence of whether this was the case or not. But neither the heads of department themselves nor the members of the SMTs we interviewed believed that was true; indeed the SMTs thought that part of the skill of the heads of department had been in creating an effective department out of a traditional mix of teachers.

We consider this analysis to be broadly correct; a significant part of the success of these departments lay in their ability to channel some of the energies and skills of their staff to maximum effect with their pupils. This is why good resource allocation, agreed schemes of work, record keeping and systematic reviews proved to be so important. With such support mechanisms in place, all departmental members could comfortably work to their individual capacities and strengths. Without such support mechanisms there was a greater danger that the department would suffer from a greater amount of idiosyncratic teaching.

Staff turnover

There was one final element which looked distinctive in these effective departments, and that was low staff turnover (albeit in schools which were generally marked by low staff turnover). The effective-schools literature has also shown that low staff turnover is an important feature of effective schooling. It would seem that for departments, like schools, a consistency of approach with pupils is an advantage.

Effective teaching and learning

Structure and feedback

At the heart of effective departments must be the effective organisation of teaching and learning. It was noticeable that the pupils we interviewed identified, by and large, these departments as being different from most of the other departments in the school. The pupils were able to comment on characteristics of the teaching and learning in the department which they identified themselves as being good practice. For example, one group of pupils' comments included:

> X is really good because you get varied but structured lessons. We do lots of different things but they all relate to the topic. Then at the end of the lesson we pack up early and just sit and go over what we've done. We talk about it and then the teacher explains how it fits into the next lesson's work. The course is like a jigsaw and the teacher puts the bits together for us.

> I think Y is good because you know where you are. You are told how you are doing most lessons and what you need to do in order to get better. It's like the teacher is mapping out things for you and you're not on your own.

What became clear from these comments and others of a similar type made by the pupils interviewed was the importance of structuring and feedback. The structuring of lessons so that they formed part of a coherent whole to pupils was clearly important. Similarly, the opportunity to receive regular feedback on progress was considered useful and in most cases highly reassuring for pupils.

Syllabus matching

We found that the departments under study took a great deal of time and effort in the selection of what to teach their pupils. The key element here was finding the content, and ways of teaching it, which matched the capacities and interests of the pupils. The most notable example of this was the time that was spent in selecting the right syllabus for GCSE. The head of geography put it clearly:

> If you're looking at exam results the key thing is the syllabus . . . I think people spend far too little time thinking about that. There are 15/16 different syllabuses just for geography and they all have different characteristics, all of which are going to be better for some pupils than others.

A head of science made a very similar point. He had chosen a syllabus which matched his detailed view of the characteristics of his pupils: they had relatively low literacy skills, a dislike of writing, an interest in real-world problems, and they liked lots of practical work. The head of department saw his job as trying to find a syllabus that would match these characteristics and which would also allow his staff to practice 'real science' with the pupils. The end result of this cognitive-matching process tends to be greater opportunities for success for larger numbers of pupils.

The process did not stop at syllabus selection, however, another distinctive feature of these effective departments was the care taken to translate these syllabi into schemes of work. There were several features of these schemes of work which are worthy of comment. First, these tended to be schemes which the whole department had worked on and had agreed. Secondly, they were very detailed and were regarded as the lynch-pin of the department's work. Thirdly, they were constantly modified in the light of the experience of teaching them.

Nearly all the Key Stage 4 schemes of work, and most of the rest, reflected the strong influence of modularisation, that is, of the systematic sub-dividing of work into small units. This resulted in pupils being given relatively small units of work in which to achieve. Most of the heads of department argued that short-term target setting was important for their pupils since this gave them achievable goals and the experience of success at regular intervals.

Assessment

This modularisation was reinforced by the assessment system – each module was assessed. In general terms it was argued that this served two important functions. First, the pupils found it motivating to work for short-term targets; secondly, the teacher believed that it was a very useful tool in diagnosing pupil strengths and weaknesses.

In general, another distinctive feature of these departments was the care and attention paid to the process of assessment. The assessment system tended to have the following features. First, there was excellent, detailed and up-to-date record keeping – one example included a sophisticated spreadsheet of student marks. Secondly, great stress was placed on trying to make marking *consistent* within the department. Thirdly, efforts were made to try and give the pupils, particularly the older ones, a stake in the assessment. They were often invited to mark each other's and their own work and discuss their marks with their teacher in order to try and understand the strengths and weaknesses of their own efforts. Fourthly, the assessment system was used as the vehicle for frequent feedback to the pupils, feedback that tended to be more criterion than norm referenced. Finally, as mentioned earlier, most of these effective departments made a great deal of use of the merit system to reward performance, actively seeking out occasions to give rewards. These assessment-linked activities tended to provide the pupils with a clear sense of progression, which assisted motivation. In particular, it allowed them to highlight some of their own weaknesses on which they could concentrate.

Of course a significant amount of assessment was related to homework. The departments in our study had consistent, and consistently applied, homework policies. This resulted in a clear routine for the setting and marking of homework. Such homework often involved, or had the potential to involve, parents. Homework tended to be returned quickly, and good work was celebrated and displayed, thus reinforcing the pupils' homework behaviour. Our interviews with pupils appeared to indicate that they tended to undertake more homework in the subjects of effective departments.

Routines

The general picture which we built up of these accelerating departments was that they had managed to establish routines and ways of working with children which the pupils appeared to accept, even enjoy, and which were productive. A small part of the secret of achieving this appeared to lie in the way in which these departments inducted the children when they first entered in year 7. An immediate attempt was made to establish what was different and special about the subject. For example, in one English department where there was particular concern about reading abilities on entry:

> We decided to invent a reading experience. As soon as the kids came into school they're challenged to do seven or eight activities, to keep a diary of their reading, to read several books, do some research in the library and they have to have all of this authenticated by different people, the librarian, English teacher, parent, etc., and when they bring a full authentication to the teacher then they'll get a commendation and a reading plaque or something like that.

In science, the special nature of laboratories was emphasised; the thrill of doing experiments, and finding out how things worked was stressed alongside the fact that laboratories were dangerous places. The importance of establishing a routine was reinforced by the head of department.

The point of these distinctive beginnings is partly to establish at an early point the special nature of the subject, its discourse (that is, its distinctive language) and way of working. It can be argued that studying an academic subject is ultimately about acquiring its special way of seeing the world. Most, but not all, of the departments were wedded to varieties of constructivism, that is, getting young people to construct their own view of how things were in their subject. This was often translated as trying to get students to behave as geographers, scientists, writers, etc., by using the language and tools of the discipline. All this was enacted with a keen eye on the demands of the GCSE examiner. One head of department said,

> I tend to make glossaries of the key words and phrases from the actual past papers ... and make sure that the kids are used to the language that's being used in the questions. That's a key thing, a key problem with low ability students; it is not that they cannot answer a lot of the questions they face, but that they cannot interpret the question to realise that they do know the answer.

Teaching and learning

More generally, we built up a picture of these departments as places where the syllabus and the special ways of working which were required to be successful were shared with the pupils. Pupils were encouraged to construct their own view of the world as seen through the focusing lenses of the discipline, and this view was carefully refocused if necessary to ensure examination success. A degree of personal autonomy was encouraged – the coursework folders were for *their* benefit; adequate notes should be taken because they were to be used for *their* revision. Our cross-section of pupil interviews did seem to indicate that this message had been largely successful.

The picture we received of teaching and learning in the departments under scrutiny was of a set of reasonably consistent practices which were concerned with the infrastructure of teaching and learning, for example, assessment and monitoring of pupil performance. When it came to teaching style then, in general, a degree of autonomy ruled; within the infrastructure each teacher was allowed to go her or his own way. There were tendencies in the direction of constructivist modes of teaching, and there was a certain commitment to student-centred, active modes of learning, but it would be wrong to characterise whole departments in this manner. One head of department argued that the pressures to move from didactic modes were strong:

> Our kids don't have very good concentration spans, which means that more than ten minutes of talking to them is actually quite redundant, which in itself ironically promotes good learning because you have to think of other ways of promoting learning rather than trying to pass over information from the front.

From the pupils we picked up messages about different styles and ways of working by different teachers within the same department. Another head of department was quite clear about the need to choose the method which best fitted the task, from a repertoire of teaching styles.

> I'm perfectly prepared to do some dictation or write on the board and get them to copy it if I feel those notes are crucial.

Although he later went on to emphasise the importance of having:

> a variety of teaching and learning styles.

By contrast, the accelerating mathematics department characterised itself using traditional methods. The head of department said:

> They're not really what you'd call modern type of methods. I'm not [modern]. I'm very traditional. Everyone sits facing the front. There's no group work to my lessons.

Another facet of departmental activity we examined for distinctive ways of working was the issue of differentiation. Were these departments effective because they were particularly good at handling a wide range of pupils? Without a comparison with other departments it is not technically possible to answer this question, but none of these departments felt that they had evolved particularly satisfactory ways of differentiating between pupils of very different ability. Practices certainly varied; whilst all but one English department used setting for years 10 and 11, practices varied before that, with some departments using mixed-ability approaches. There seemed to be a majority view that mixed-ability teaching was likely to get better results in years 7 to 9, although some departments did not use it because of the general school policy.

All the departments made use of the schools' special-needs departments, although the actual practice varied from department to department, for example, withdrawal or in-class support. Despite this variation in practice, all these effective departments were very clear about the role of special-needs teachers in supporting their subject, and this clarity was probably beneficial. Support was obviously targeted at the lower achieving pupils, and there was a consistent use of withdrawal and/or smaller classes/groups for these children. Overall, we judged that there was a greater stress on getting these children to achieve than in supporting the most able to achieve the highest grades.

To summarise, at the individual classroom level, the research finding was that effective teaching and learning was stimulated and strengthened when there was: first, an attempt to involve all pupils in the learning process by providing a variety of tasks which dealt with individual small-group and large-group situations; second, where teachers encouraged cooperative learning with pupils working together as part of a team sharing experiences, being given different roles and developing their own self-esteem; thirdly, where pupils were actively involved in review and reflection of the learning process and where they were given the opportunity of engaging in some form of action-planning process which contributed to their learning; fourthly, where teachers developed meaningful, formative, developmental and motivational forms of assessment which reinforced and built confidence.

The research showed that teachers felt they were most successful and effective in the classroom when they were able to activate and manage the learning process in these ways. In addition, the finding concerning group management in the classroom suggested the importance of preparing lessons in advance, of keeping the attention of the whole class, of unobtrusive discipline, of a focus on rewarding good behaviour and of swift action to deal with disruption. The accelerating departments tended to make good use of homework, to set clear academic goals and to have confidence in students' capacity to learn and achieve.

External influences

Most of the factors which we have discussed in connection with the accelerating departments relate to influences which are internal to the schools. The effective-schools research also indicates that successful schools are ones which, in general, manage to harness external factors for their own ends – swimming with the tide.

By and large, the departments we studied seemed to be able to either turn these external factors to their advantage or to ignore or neutralise them so that they did not have any detrimental effect on their work. A good example is the National Curriculum.

It may be of some significance that most of our departments are in the core subjects which were the first to be reformed. This simply means that these departments, English, maths and science, have had a longer period in which to come to terms with the twists and turns of the reforms. As we have already noted, one of the common characteristics of these departments was their comprehensive and settled schemes of work. English, maths and science departments have, by and large, found the National Curriculum helpful, or at least have found that it allows them to do what they want to do. This was not the case with geography/humanities departments. Here the National Curriculum was regarded as muddle headed and as an impediment to teaching 'real geography'. The departmental solution was to not take too much notice of it; they pay lip service to those elements where this is deemed to be necessary, say for an inspection.

Two of the schools visited had had OFSTED inspections, and the prospect of an inspection hung over the rest. In general, the effects seemed beneficial. It made the departments think more clearly about their policies and strategies and made them go through the discipline of committing their policies to paper – usually a helpful and clarifying exercise. Another helpful aspect of the reforms was the emphasis on testing and examination results. There was clear evidence in all the schools that this aspect of performance, despite its obvious technical limitations, was given high priority. The departments certainly scrutinised their results carefully and seemed able to engage in a constructive, reflective dialogue about improvement. Clearly, this was assisted by the fact that the results in these departments were good!

The final external element that is worth noting is the effect of the catchment area and parental involvement. All the schools we visited were in a south-west city, and they had a pupil population that underrepresented, to a greater or lesser extent, middle-class, potentially high-achieving young people. Most, but not all, of our effective departments could point to successful strategies for involving parents more fully in their work. In geography this involved the setting of investigative six-week homework projects which many parents clearly became involved in. In English it involved a reading partnership between home and school. As we have already noted, all of the departments were good at keeping comprehensive records of pupil achievement: in addition this information was used to keep parents particularly well informed about how their children were performing. Finally, these successful departments were good at winning the interest of children by imaginative programmes of teaching and learning. As a result of this, positive messages are likely to be carried home and the subject, and parents are more likely to be supportive.

Conclusions

In this investigation of effective departments within south-west city schools, our strategy was to look for similarities in the work of the departments which seems likely to translate into effective teaching and learning. Looking back on our evidence we are convinced that these departments do present a reasonably consistent profile which is consistent with high performance. In presenting our findings we have concentrated on the similarities between the departments rather than the differences, and in so doing we have perhaps run the danger of suggesting that there is a recipe of an effective department. Our view, in fact, is that there are some fundamental problems connected with the organisation of teaching and learning which all departments have to solve, but that there are various ways of solving these problems. A good example from this study is that some departments tended to get consistent behaviour from their teachers by binding them tightly into the culture and values of the department; other departments, whilst not eschewing culture, placed a much greater emphasis on structural and organisational solutions to the same problem. The end result was as important as the methods of achieving it.

If we briefly summarise the major features of our effective departments, we would characterise them as being good at either working with or neutralising external influences. The schools they worked in were broadly supportive, but this was not a major factor in their success. They were largely successful because of their own efforts, and the major features of their success included:

- a collegiate management style;
- a strong vision of the subject effectively translated down to the level of the classroom;
- good organisation in terms of assessment, record keeping, homework, etc.;
- good resource management;
- an effective system for monitoring and evaluating;
- structured lessons and regular feedback;
- clear routines and practices within lessons;
- a syllabus matching the needs and abilities of pupils;
- a strong pupil-centred ethos that systematically rewards pupils;
- opportunities for autonomous pupil learning;
- a central focus on teaching and learning.

[. . .]

To date, most school-effectiveness research studies have been large scale and directed at the level of the whole school. In a sense this is odd because these studies stress the importance of an emphasis on teaching and learning in the school, yet it is departmental rather than whole-school management which is closest to this core function. Brown *et al.* (1995) have suggested that traditional forms of school-effectiveness research should be complemented by smaller-scale studies which draw upon ethnographic and phenomenological approaches. We believe that this study is a *complementary approach* which demonstrates the potential of school-effectiveness studies located at the departmental or classroom level.

References

Birchenough, M., Abbot, R. and Steadman, S. (1989) *Reviewing School Departments*. Harlow: Longman.

Bolam, R., McMahon, A., Pocklington, K. and Weindling, D. (1993) *Effective Management in Schools*. A report for the DfE via the School Management Task Force Professional Working Party. London: HMSO.

Brown, S., Ridell, S. and Duffield, S. (1995) Possibilities and problems of small-scale studies to unpack the findings of large scale school effectiveness, in J. Gray, D. Reynolds, C. Fitz-Gibbon and D. Jesson (eds) *Merging Traditions: the Future of Research on School Effectiveness and School Improvement.* London: Cassell.

Creemers, B. (1992) School effectiveness and effective instruction – the need for a further relationship, in J. Bashi and Z. Sass (eds) *School Effectiveness and Improvement.* Jerusalem: Hebrew University Press.

Earley, P. and Fletcher-Campbell, F. (1989) *The Time to Manage?* Windsor: NFER-Nelson.

Fitz-Gibbon, C. T. (1991) Multilevel modelling in an indicator system, in S. Raudenbush and J. D. Willms (eds) *Schools, Classrooms and Pupils.* San Diego: Academic Press.

Fullan, M. G. (1992) *Successful School Improvement.* Buckingham: Open University Press.

Harris, A. and Russ, J. (1994) *Pathways to School Improvement.* Sheffield: TEED, Dept of Employment.

Her Majesty's Inspectorate (HMI) (1977) *Ten Good Schools.* London: HMSO.

Levine, D. U. (1992) An interpretative review of US research and practice dealing with unusually effective schools, in D. Reynolds and P. Cuttance (eds) *School Effectiveness Research: Policy and Practice.* London: Cassell.

Levine, D. U. and Lezotte, L. W. (1990) Unusually effective schools: a review and analysis of research and practice. *International Journal of Educational Research,* 13: 815–25.

Luyten, H. (1994) Stability of school effects in secondary education: the impact of variance across subjects and years, paper presented at the *Annual Meeting of the American Educational Research Association,* 4–8 April, New Orleans.

Marland, M. and Hill, G. (eds) (1981) *Departmental Management.* London: Heinemann.

Mortimore, P. (1991) Effective schools from a British perspective: research and practice, in J. R. Bliss, W. A. Firestone and H. E. Richards (eds) *Rethinking Effective Schools: Research and Practice.* Englewood Cliffs, NJ: Prentice-Hall.

Mortimore, P. (1993) School effectiveness and the management of effective learning and teaching. *School Effectiveness and School Improvement,* 4: 290–310.

Mortimore, P., Sammons, P., Stoll, L., Lewis, D. and Ecob, R. (1988) *School Matters: The Junior Years.* Wells, Somerset: Open Books.

Nuttall, D., Goldstein, H., Prosser, R. and Rashash, J. (1989) Differential school effectiveness. *International Journal of Education Research,* 13: 769–76.

Raudenbush, R. (1989) The analysis of longitudinal multilevel data international. *Journal of Educational Research,* ch. 3 of the special issue Developments in school effectiveness research, 13: 712–40.

Reynolds, D. (ed.) (1985) *Studying School Effectiveness.* Basingstoke: Falmer Press.

Reynolds, D. (1992) School effectiveness and school improvement, an updated review of the British literature, in D. Reynolds and P. Cuttance (eds) *School Effectiveness: Research, Policy and Practice.* London: Cassell.

Rutter, M., Maughan, B., Mortimer, P. and Ouston, J. (1979) *Fifteen Thousand Hours.* London: Open Books.

Scheerens, J. (1992) *Effective Schooling Research: Theory and Practice.* London: Cassell.

Smith, D. J. and Tomlinson, S. (1989) *The School Effect: a Study of Multi-racial Comprehensives.* London: Policy Studies Institute.

Thomas, S., Sammons, P. and Mortimore, P. (1994) Stability in secondary schools: effects on students, GCSE outcomes, paper presented at the *BERA Annual Conference,* Oxford, September.

Willms, J. D. and Raudenbush, S. W. (1989) A longitudinal hierarchical linear model for estimating school effects and their stability. *Journal of Educational Measurement,* 26: 210–232.

Appendix

Quantitative analyses for self evaluation (QUASE): six performance indicators:

- total GCSE score;
- average GCSE score;
- maths GCSE score;
- English GCSE score;
- number of A–C grades achieved;
- number of A–G grades achieved.

(Source: NFER QUASE Project.)

15 | Quality management in education*

ANDREW TAYLOR AND FRANCES HILL

Introduction

Market forces are now having a much greater impact on education than ever before. Consequently the operating environment is becoming more complex and uncertain and the organizational structures in educational institutions are having to adapt and change at an even greater pace than in the past. Competitiveness, and perhaps even future survival in this context, will depend to a large extent on the ways in which change and improvement are managed. One model for such adaptation is total quality management (TQM), which has been used already in other industrial and commercial sectors. [. . .]

What is TQM?

Total quality management has many definitions. Essentially it is concerned with customer-focused organizational improvement, achieved through the activities of groupings of employees at various levels in the structure. The employees identify problems and opportunities for improvement and engage in endeavours which determine root causes of these problems, generate and choose solutions and implement improvements. These activities are usually supported by the development of teams and a focus on corporate goals. The teams primarily identify with matters of specific relevance to their own functions in order to engender a sense of involvement in organizational affairs. TQM proposes that all employees can make an impact on the quality of goods and services provided, thus the organization's systems and processes are regarded as highly as its products and outputs.

*This material has been edited and originally appeared in *Quality Assurance in Education*.

According to the tenets of TQM, the only meaningful definition of quality is the customers' perceptions of quality. Thus educational institutions must have mechanisms in place, which regularly establish these customer needs and perceptions. Furthermore they must be able to respond to this information in an appropriate time-frame. In TQM the concept of a customer has been extended to include internal as well as external customers. Moreover, everyone in the organization is not only a supplier but also a customer of someone else. [. . .]

Apart from being customer-centred, TQM also promotes the importance of internal employee relations, since employee morale, commitment and motivation are ultimately determinants of external customer relations. Finally, TQM implies a focus on the cost of quality or, more correctly, on the cost of not having quality, i.e. the price of non-conformance (Crosby 1979).

TQM and quality assurance

There can sometimes be confusion as to the relationship between TQM and quality assurance. On the one hand, they are viewed as complementary, sometimes even synonymous; others would argue that their very philosophies are in opposition. Consideration of the criteria to be used for evaluation of organizational performance (see Figure 15.1) might provide further illumination. These criteria are commonly summarized as:

- *Goal attainment*, i.e. how well the organization achieves its strategic objectives.
- *Resource utilization*, i.e. how well the organization makes use of its available resources.
- *Adaptability*, i.e. the capacity of the organization to review its performance and match the changing requirements of its environment (Nadler and Tushman 1980).

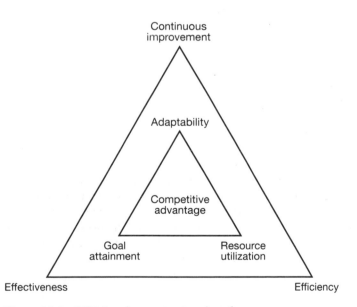

Figure 15.1   TQM and organizational performance

The first two criteria are primarily concerned with effectiveness and efficiency respectively, while the third addresses issues of change and improvement. Quality assurance involves supplying evidence to external agencies about an organization's potential effectiveness. It is the intention that 'third-party assessment' of a quality assurance system will remove the need for several second-party assessments. Quality assurance systems have often originated from safety-critical industries such as aerospace, nuclear power and defence. Their most recent embodiment is BS 5750:1987 (British Standards Institution, 1987) or its international equivalent, ISO 9000 (International Standards Organisation 1987). This approach places great emphasis on written evidence, documented systems and procedures. However, it does not require any focus on either cost-effectiveness or continuous improvement *per se*.

By contrast, TQM has 'improvement' as its main goal. Unlike ISO 9000 there is no minimum standard which one may attain. The process of TQM is thus described as a never-ending journey, owing to the changing demands of the environment and the relentless search for improvement opportunities. TQM embraces all the three critiera mentioned above, at the same time giving recognition to the impact on quality of the whole organization, whereas ISO 9000 is mainly confined to the purchasing, sales and production functions, or their equivalents.

It would be incorrect to say that quality assurance does not encourage improvement. The process of documenting (agreed) systems and procedures brings discipline and greater consensus to that which previously was informal and perhaps ambiguous. Nonetheless, beyond that initial rigour, quality assurance tends to preserve the status quo.

Main elements of TQM

The essential elements of TQM may be summarized as follows:

- Quality is conceptualized as customers' perceptions.
- A customer is defined as anyone who receives a product or service, whether inside or outside the organization.
- The aim is to identify and meet the customer requirement through the design, development and management of processes which are error-free, i.e. by concentrating on prevention to eliminate waste and reduce costs.
- By utilizing the internal customer concept, the result of each process is viewed as a product; consequently evaluation takes place immediately, possibly by the immediate customer but preferably by the processor.
- Central to TQM theory is the idea of continuous self-improvement; therefore TQM organizations are essentially learning systems.
- TQM requires the involvement and commitment all organizational members in quality matters and continuous improvement.
- TQM requires superior quality information systems to provide timely measures of and feedback on performance.

With regard to this last point, a subtle distinction is made, however, between the measurement of individuals' performance and that of the processes within which they work. TQM would therefore distance itself from a preoccupation with performance indicators which focus on individuals (Starcher 1992). Many of the performances and results are the ultimate responsibility of management who work 'on the systems' rather than of the individuals who work 'within the systems'. To concentrate on the measurement of individuals undermines a team ethos and counters the acceptance of shared corporate goals.

Total Quality Management treats quality – of performance and outputs – as a strategic issue, fundamental to organizational effectiveness. The theory has already been shown to be effective in many types of organization. In general terms it would also seem to be appropriate for the education sector. Nevertheless it would be inadvisable to import such concepts without fully evaluating the need for modification. Indeed, in an earlier phase of the TQM movement, there was resistance from many service organizations, which resented the application of concepts which were largely perceived as having a manufacturing origin. These criticisms have now been rebutted, as service sector exemplars have emerged. The same pattern may be repeated in the education sphere.

Quality in education

Educational establishments may be described as open systems (see Figure 15.2), since they possess most of the attributes originally identified by Katz and Kahn (1966) as characterizing such systems, namely:

> . . . the importation of energy from the environment, the throughput or transformation of the imported energy into some product form which is characteristic of the system, the exporting of that product into the environment, and the re-energising of the system from sources in the environment.

Educational institutions are also currently in a market environment where the whole basis of competition has changed and has become more complex. Some now believe that TQM may prove the key success factor for individual institutions, i.e. TQM may be a necessary and sufficient means of improving customer service and customer

Inputs		Outputs	Outcomes
Capital	Transformation process	Graduates	
Labour		Research	
'Managers' Academics Administrators Support staff	Supplier/customer chains	Services	Benefits to society in general
Raw materials		Products	
Student Other			
Information		Knowledge	

Figure 15.2   An open systems model of higher education

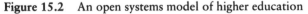

satisfaction. Along with this intra-system competition for resources there is also a marked increase in the influence of powerful supplier and customer groupings, which are demanding higher quality and better service. For example, the influence of the academic audit unit (AAU), Government policies and suggestions about student choices through a variety of mechanisms such as 'voucher systems' and the like, lobbying from industry and commerce for research which is closer to the market, and the increased emphasis on research and teaching quality.

Education bodies as service organizations

While much of the current thinking on quality has emerged from manufacturing contexts, it is probably more appropriate to compare educational institutions with service sector organizations.

In general the provision of a service is characterized by the:

- extent to which the customer is involved in the delivery process itself, i.e. the production and consumption of the service are temporally inseparable to a greater degree than in a manufacturing context;
- potentially more variable nature of the delivered service, compared with a manufactured product, because it is more reliant on the personality and mood of the individuals involved;
- impermanence of the quality of the service, i.e. the customer can refer only to his/her memory for future review of the experience.

Research has revealed that the processes of delivery of services are often of as much importance to the customer as the content of the services themselves, e.g. the cuisine in a high-class restaurant is taken for granted by the customer; what matters to him/her is how the food is served, presentation style, environment, speed of delivery and courtesy of staff, etc.

Given this view of services, TQM in education must apply to all involved in the delivery of those services, before, during and after:

> Total Quality Management is an approach to improving the effectiveness and flexibility of businesses as a whole. It is essentially a way of organising and involving the whole organisation; every department, every activity, every single person at every level. For an organisation to be truly effective, each part of it must work properly together, recognising that every person and every activity affects, and in turn is affected by, others.
>
> (Oakland 1989)

The internal supplier/customer relationship

[. . .]

TQM should not be confined to teaching and academic matters. Many customer-related activities require considerable interaction between administrative and academic staff during the processes of delivery of services to students (see Figure 15.3), whether for teaching or research – for example, schools liaison, student enrolment and admission, examining procedures, careers advice and counselling.

Moreover, many of the high-profile interfaces with students involve administrative functions such as student records, examinations office, careers office, accommodation

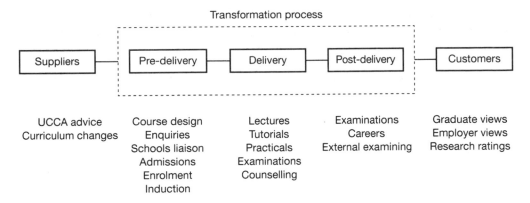

Figure 15.3   The 'team' ethos of TQM in higher education

and catering. Thus the students' perceptions of the organization may be heavily influenced by non-academic staff. There is also some evidence to suggest that seemingly 'trivial' factors, such as how the gatekeeper deals with visitors when the car-park is full, or how the switchboard operator deals with callers, not only are significantly symptomatic of the organization's culture but also can make a major impact on the enquirer's perception of the organization's quality of service.

This internal supplier/customer concept needs to be more fully developed in education. Certainly it suggests the need for a greater realization by various groupings in educational establishments that they share a common purpose, namely the provision of an appropriate and enriching learning experience for every student. [. . .]

TQM would point to a greater preoccupation with the learning process than with curriculum content. Furthermore it would lead to a focus on systematic curriculum review as well as the bureaucratic and sometimes unhealthy concern for course regulations alone.

Strategic quality management

As regards the relative merits and the relationship between quality assurance and TQM, the debate is far from resolved (Ribbins and Whale 1991; Walsh 1991). This issue is not merely of academic interest; it also has far-reaching implications for the implementation of quality activities in any organization. It is difficult to understand the subtle differences inherent in these two approaches. One difference is that TQM implies a truly strategic approach to the alignment of the organization with its environment, whereas quality assurance can often be a delegated, operational issue. Educational institutions have traditionally been described in organizational terms as 'professional bureaucracies' (Mintzberg 1983), located in an operating environment which is complex but stable. The professional bureaucracy is a modified form of bureaucratic structure, which gives a greater degree of autonomy to the professionals, who need to exercise discretion and judgement to be effective. This organizational structure tends to be common in education, hospitals and organizations where the core skills of the professionals are central to the organization's continued existence.

The stability and standardization in the structures of the professional bureaucracy are congruent with the requirements of quality assurance systems, which emphasize written procedures and formalized methods.

However, today's environment in education has moved to a new position of complexity and relative instability. In response, structures are also evolving to facilitate a more organic, less formalized arrangement, which can react more quickly and even anticipate changes in its environment. In organizational terms, a structure akin to an 'adhocracy' may be more suitable. Adhocracy, fully described by Mintzberg (1983), is an organizational form which suits complex environments, where the tasks are complex and uncertain.

In such circumstances, quality assurance may not be a benefit, being likely to retard the speed of response to an unacceptable degree. Conversely, TQM, with its greater emphasis on problem ownership and decentralized decision making, would appear to be quite different in approach. It could be described as a process more supportive of a self-evaluating organization and one which is more likely to encourage sustained long-term improvement. TQM does not imply a complete absence of systems; it is a question of emphasis, wherein the decision makers feel either hindered or aided by the degree of formalization.

Indeed, rather than sustain a debate about whether or not TQM is 'better' than quality assurance, it might be more helpful to suggest that the approach to quality which an organization adopts should be contingent on other organizational factors, in addition to the nature of its environment. In particular, TQM should not be contemplated until an organization has basic management systems and procedures in place, i.e. until it is effectively organized. To attempt to implement TQM without such effective frameworks would be counter-productive. Thus one cannot pronounce that TQM or quality assurance is more appropriate for education. It is necessary to recognize the differences between educational institutions and to develop quality practices which are congruent with other factors.

Potential benefits of TQM in education

The benefits which are likely to accrue through the application of TQM are:

1 Continuous and sustained organizational improvement.
2 Increased levels of external customer satisfaction.
3 Tangible and significant cost savings of the order of 5–10 per cent of operating costs.
4 A focus on the importance of interdisciplinary teams with combinations of academic and administrative staff.
5 Improvements in employee morale, commitment and motivation.
6 A new way of managing the organization which promotes company-wide goal congruence, accountability and involvement.

Possible problems with TQM in education

Scholarship and excellence

One should be mindful that some of the traditions of education are different from those of industrial enterprises. For example, the importance of scholarship and excellence and the cultivation of creativity, innovation and genius are not yet valued to the same extent elsewhere. Moreover, the profit motive is not the prime reason for sustaining the organization but rather the traditional motive of disseminating and advancing knowledge.

Individuals in education are often driven by a desire to be the best possible scholars, as determined by their peers. This striving for excellence recognizes no trade-off with cost or time, so that analogies in the quality literature which describe a Rolls-Royce and a Mini as cars of potentially equal quality dependent on the customer's perception have little meaning.

It is also worth noting that the customer dimension in the quality literature has evolved too. Initially the (quality assurance) convention was to meet customer requirements. This evolved to a wider recognition of the need to achieve customer satisfaction. Currently the received wisdom is to anticipate and exceed customers' needs and expectations and 'delight' customers. So the goal is shifting from one of providing an acceptable level of quality at an economic cost, to one of exceeding the required levels in the belief that the extra cost is, in reality, an investment. In this dimension, education may have been in advance of industry and commerce.

Identifying 'customers'

There would also appear to be some confusion about who the external customers of an educational institution actually are, e.g. Government, research councils, accreditation bodies, students, academic peers, employers and society at large. Until the mission and objectives of the organization are clarified with regard to such matters, there will inevitably be a prevalent lack of common purpose. The same could be said for the idea of internal customers. To adopt this concept would require radical changes to organizational and administrative structures and, perhaps more importantly, to attitudes.

Some complexities are associated with the development of these ideas. For example, students are in one sense raw materials which become final products, yet in another sense they are customers themselves. Moreover, the extent of variability in these 'raw materials' is uncommon in manufacturing or service organizations generally. Others would argue that the product of education is the learning opportunity, i.e. the product is in effect the process. However, there is a danger in becoming so preoccupied with the limitations of the model that one misses the benefits to be gained from its appropriate application.

Furthermore, the industrially-based terminology of TQM may need to be modified to make it appropriate and acceptable to the academic community; for example, the notion of external customers, while valid in itself, may evoke some hostility owing to its commercial undertones.

'Right first time' thinking

Another term often quoted in the TQM context is 'right first time'. This may be misinterpreted within education as being counter to experimentation, research and innovation, although, when one understands that the phrase is intending to convey a shift from inspection-centred thinking towards prevention, there may be less resistance to the idea. 'Right first time' thinking applied to experimentation recognizes the possibility, and even desirability, of failure. Its thrust is not to stifle experimentation but rather to ensure that the objectives and methodology have been clearly thought through to minimize time-wasting and prevent unnecessary mistakes. Moreover, the most important aspect of 'right first time' is the ability to learn from mistakes by understanding what went wrong, to identify the causes of error, and to establish processes which ensure that the mistakes will not be repeated and that the learning is disseminated throughout the organization.

Quality and value added

In the wider education context, 'right first time' thinking suggests a greater emphasis on strategic planning, communication and feedback. Indeed feedback is one of the key aspects of TQM, since it requires timely measurement of performance and outcomes, and communication of those results back to the antecedents, including the schools and colleges as suppliers of the students (see Figure 15.4). Some feedback elements are weak within many educational institutions – in other cases it is not the lack of feedback but the lack of resultant action which is missing.

Appropriate feedback also presupposes measurements or 'performance indicators'. Performance indicators and quality measures for something as complex as the learning process are difficult objectives. Once again there are divided views on developing measurable indicators which focus on educational and not managerial issues. There is also considerable debate concerning the place of peer review and 'customer assessment', and on the feasibility of applying value-added measures to the learning process. If Figure 15.4 is a type of Value Chain, as described by Porter (1985), then it might be possible to explore the notion of value in the context of the learning process. To gain competitive advantage, an educational institution must perform its activities either at lower cost or better than its competition, thereby gaining product or service differentiation.

If the use of the value concept is legitimate, it is then possible to define quality as 'satisfying customers by meeting their informed needs and providing value'. On some occasions it is not simply a matter of giving customers what they want, but also of understanding what they need and helping them to reach that same understanding. This is especially true in professionally driven situations such as medicine, architecture or education. Assessing value in education is not merely a financial transaction, just as in a restaurant the value of a meal is much more than the cost of the ingredients and labour.

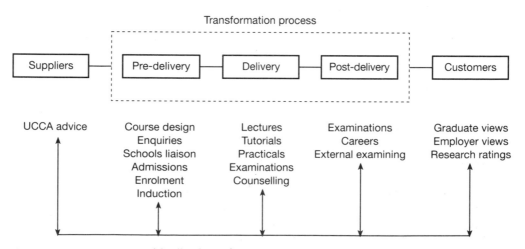

Figure 15.4   Importance of feedback mechanisms

Interdisciplinarity, individuality and the team ethos

The concept of interdisciplinarity is often narrowly interpreted as an academic matter. TQM would suggest that effective improvement and problem solving come from groups composed of all who have a bearing on the problem and preferably from 'teams' forged from those groups. The team ethos is not common in education, particularly in higher education, partly because of the nature of research, and the criteria for promotion. Individual knowledge is often perceived as the key to personal recognition and advancement within the system; consequently there is a natural tendency towards individualism. Undoubtedly teams have strengths over individuals, but it is also important to recognize the healthy Western tradition for individuality. Wholesale adoption of team-based improvement activities is an oversimplification of the TQM mindset, which fails to recognize the long tradition in education for committee-based consensus and collegiality.

Implications for education

Educational institutions are likely to reap significant benefits from an appropriate implementation of total quality management. However, implementation would require considerable planning and management commitment to cultural change. Part of this cultural change would involve an examination of the team concept and its potential contribution to work-group and cross-functional improvement. Educationists would need to have a much clearer focus of what quality means in this context and, more importantly, what it means to their customers.

Furthermore, these customers and their needs should be understood by the whole organization. Stronger feedback mechanisms would need to be developed in order to understand accurately and continuously the external environment. This in part will require measures of quality which are meaningful. Moreover, in view of the variability of students' abilities, closer relationships ought to be forged with schools and colleges. This will have a twofold benefit: the schools will have a greater commitment to the educational institution and will better understand its requirements; second, the educational institution will have less of a problem dovetailing its curriculum with that of the schools and it will also be likely to receive more applications for places.

Above all, it must be realized that TQM will not itself improve anything without the involvement and commitment of the vast majority of those in any organization. A realistic time-frame for implementation would be over a period of years, with significant benefits not likely to be manifested for at least the first 12 months – 'TQM demands a whole new perspective, a perspective of "five years hence" rather than this year's AGM' (PA Consulting Group 1990).

References

British Standards Institution (1987) BS 5750: Quality Systems. London: British Standards Institution.

Crosby, P. B. (1979) Quality is Free, The Art of Making Quality Certain. New York: McGraw-Hill.

International Standards Organisation (1987) ISO 9000: Specification for Design/Development, Production, Installation and Servicing. London: International Standards Organisation.

Katz, D. and Kahn, R. L. (1966) *The Social Psychology of Organisations.* New York: John Wiley.

Mintzburg, H. (1983) *Structure in Fives: Designing Effective Organizations*, pp. 189–213. New York: Prentice-Hall.

Nadler, D. A. and Tushman, M.L. (1980) A model for diagnosing organizational behaviour. *Organisational Dynamics*, 9 (Autumn): 9–14.

Oakland, J. S. (1989) *Total Quality Management,* London: Butterworth-Heinemann.

PA Consulting Group (1990) *The Total Quality Experience: A Guide for the Continuing Journey*, p. 39. London: PA.

Porter, M. E. (1985) *Competitive Advantage, Creating and Sustaining Superior Performance.* London: Free Press, Collier-Macmillan.

Ribbins, P. and Whale, E. (1991) Managing Quality. *Management in Education*, 5(2): 22–31.

Starcher, R. (1992) Mismatched management techniques. *Quality Progress*, December: 49–52.

Walsh, K. (1991) *Managing Colleges into the Next Century.* London: Further Education Staff College.

White Paper CM1541 *Higher Education: A New Framework.* London: HMSO.

16 | Current developments in value added

FURTHER EDUCATION DEVELOPMENT AGENCY

Introduction

There is now a great deal of interest in developing expertise in measuring value added. The publication of raw examination results has prompted many colleges to look to value-added measures to provide fairer indicators of their performance. In addition, institutions are increasingly recognising the part value-added analyses can play in helping them to improve quality. FEU's briefing note *Value Added: An Update* (1994) identified five ways in which value-added data might be used:

- to inform guidance and selection;
- to improve the identification of learning support needs;
- to help motivate students and inform reviews and target setting;
- to help teams manage for quality improvement; and
- to contribute toward promoting and marketing the college.

Despite this interest, there remain challenges to overcome if the powerful potential of value-added measures is to be realised. In particular:

- developing a methodology for measuring value added for vocational programmes and for adults;
- where a methodology already exists, for example for GCE A-levels, developing expertise to exploit the uses which can be made of value-added data for internal quality improvement purposes.

This publication:

- briefly describes FEDA's current investigation into the feasibility of developing a methodology for measuring value added in vocational areas and for adults;
- provides further guidance on the uses to which value-added data can be put within colleges; and
- outlines areas for development.

Developing the methodology

A number of methods of measuring value added for GCE A-level students are in use at the present time in colleges. These include:

- The A-level Information System (ALIS);
- The Audit Commission Model;
- the *Guardian* value-added tables; and
- those devised by colleges themselves (for example, at Greenhead College).

While there are significant variations between them, all compare achievements at entry (GCSE results translated into a points score) with those at exit (points score based on GCE A-level results). For example, Figure 16.1 from ALIS is based on average GCSE scores and GCE A-level point scores for individual subjects, while Figure 16.2, from the Audit Commission, is based on aggregated GCSE scores and total GCE A-level point scores.

While there is a significant overall statistical correlation between GCSE and GCE A-level scores, the correlation between levels of success at GCSE and in advanced vocational programmes is much weaker. Attempts to apply to vocational programmes the method used for measuring value added on GCE A-level programmes produce results of much less statistical significance. Such approaches often use output data scores based on the 'equivalences' between vocational qualification and GCE A-levels. The weak correlation between such input and output data means that any conclusions drawn from value-added calculations of this kind must be treated with caution. Certainly action should not be taken on the basis of these conclusions without supporting evidence.

Comparable difficulties arise in relation to adults on GCE A-level programmes. Many took GCSEs or O-levels many years ago, and/or have had life experiences which mean

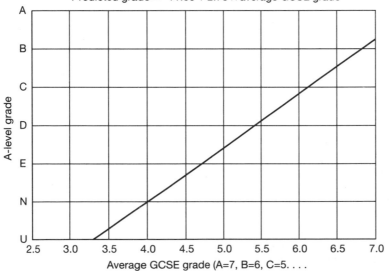

Figure 16.1   A-level economics ALIS 1994

their current achievement level is not accurately reflected in examination results achieved in quite different circumstances. Some may have no academic qualifications at all and yet have high achievement levels. Again, traditional approaches to measuring value added, with input data based on GCSE scores, will not be very helpful for these learners.

As a consequence of these technical difficulties, FEDA is investigating the feasibility of developing alternative or, more probably, additional input data. The focus is on two groups:

- students embarking on a number of specified Advanced GNVQ programmes 1994–96;
- adult students on GCE A-level programmes.

Ten colleges were selected to take part in the feasibility study. They are collecting a wide range of data from their students, from which, it is hoped, a more limited range of significant input data may be identified.

Decisions about the various types of data to be collected were made on the basis of a review of the literature and advice from technical experts. They include:

- previous qualifications;
- socio-economic data, e.g. gender, postcode;
- attitudinal data (from questionnaires);
- the results of psychometric tests of general ability;
- the results of literacy and numeracy tests;
- tutors' predictions.

While some of these data could be gathered via centralised college student records, separate arrangements were made to collect most of the data required.

Now that the data has been collected, it will be collated and analysed by the technical consultants for the project, and in due course compared with the output data based on students' achievements at exit. The investigation will, it is hoped, enable the alternative input data to be analysed and the most feasible and valid to be selected for more widescale trials.

Using value-added measures

Colleges which have been undertaking the systematic collection of value-added data for several years have recognised that such data can be used effectively only within the context of well-developed and constructive procedures for student support and quality management. Value-added data supplement, and often confirm, other data. However, the mathematical procedures on which it is based are relatively complex, and the statistical and technical limitations need to be understood and acknowledged.

Most ways of measuring value added, whether for individual subjects or using total GCE A-level scores, are undertaken centrally within the college or, in the case of ALIS, externally to it. As illustrated in the Figures 16.1 and 16.2, typically the data is presented with GCE A-level points score on the vertical axis and GCSE points score on the horizontal axis. Individual performances can then be shown and a regression line

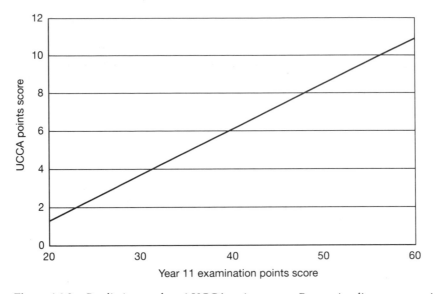

Figure 16.2 Predicting students' UCCA points score. Regression lines can provide a benchmark for a student's UCCA points scores based on the year 11 examination score
Source: YCS 1987 cohort

calculated, which shows the general relationship between specified levels of achievement on entry and at exit.

Such regression analysis can be carried out with larger sets of data, covering, for example: college performance over a period of years, groups of colleges (such as those participating in ALIS), or a nationwide sample such as the value-added data drawn up by Welsh Joint Education Committee (WJEC) for all Welsh colleges.

Once value-added data has been analysed, it needs to be studied and any emerging patterns identified. The reasons for patterns need to be considered and hypotheses about them generated. Recommendations to do things differently might then be made if appropriate.

Another way of identifying patterns is to consider how college norms differ from national ones. For example, some colleges find they generally add more value to students with lower GCSE scores than those with higher scores. Someone then needs to make decisions about what action, if any, should be taken; decide how to evaluate it; and ensure action is carried out and evaluated.

Who should be given these responsibilities will be determined in part by the aspects of college provision which appear to need development and in part by the expertise of staff available. Nevertheless, even if cross-college patterns are initially identified, action should, as far as possible, be taken at team level.

Where individuals or staff teams have been involved in pattern recognition and instrumental in deciding what to do, they are less likely to perceive value-added data as a threat or personal criticism. It is important therefore that briefings and staff development about using value-added data should be presented within the context of continuous improvement and should encourage a sense of ownership in the process.

Guidance

FEDA is working with ten colleges developing guidance on how to use value-added data within colleges for quality improvement. What follows is emerging guidance on how value-added measures and analyses may be used to help improve provision. Value-added measurement is, however, most effective when it is used in conjunction with other performance indicators, and incorporated into existing systems and practices.

1 In guidance and selection

In many colleges, there is a tension between maximising access and setting people up to fail. This is reflected in the funding methodology which requires meeting growth targets while not losing achievement units.

It will be important for colleges to consider their position on this and develop admission/access policies in the light of their missions and the needs of their local communities. Value-added data, however, might also help them to:

- Develop more sophisticated selection criteria. For example, most colleges state that GCE A-level students should normally have four or five GCSEs at grade C or above. However, college and/or national value-added data might well provide some useful evidence on which to base advice about choice of individual subjects, especially if a particular progression route, such as to higher education, is desired.
- Help marginal students make realistic choices.

Two specific ways of presenting data may help. The first is chances charts, which have been developed by ALIS. Particularly at the minimum entry level, they can be used to help students assess their own chances of success. Chances charts show the percentage of students with a given GCSE score who achieve various GCE A-level grades for a subject. Figure 16.3 illustrates this for Physics.

Figure 16.3b shows that while most students coming in with an average GCSE score of between 4.75 and 5.5 achieve D or E grades, a small percentage do achieve A and B grades. Individuals can then assess their chances of success and make choices accordingly. For example, a student whose results were far worse than expected because of a family trauma at the time of GCSE examinations, might conclude that while average chances of a high grade might be low, theirs is likely to be higher and worth trying; whereas a student whose GCSE results were better than predicted might conclude it is unlikely they will gain a high grade in physics.

An alternative way of presenting data is in best ever charts. These show, for each GCE A-level subject, the best ever result achieved by a student in the college with a given GCSE score. These can encourage students to have higher expectations and can motivate those who are disappointed with GCSE results, but who nonetheless have reasonably good ones. On the other hand, best ever charts may also help students to realise that their expectations are unrealistically high and enable them to consider alternatives, such as GNVQs or different combinations of subjects. This does not, of course, mean that they should be used to justify the exclusion of students who meet minimum entry requirements.

Project colleges are currently exploring the introduction of such data into existing systems for interviewing and guiding students. The potential use is probably greater after GCSE results have been received and students are concerned with choosing their GCE A-level subjects or are considering alternative programmes.

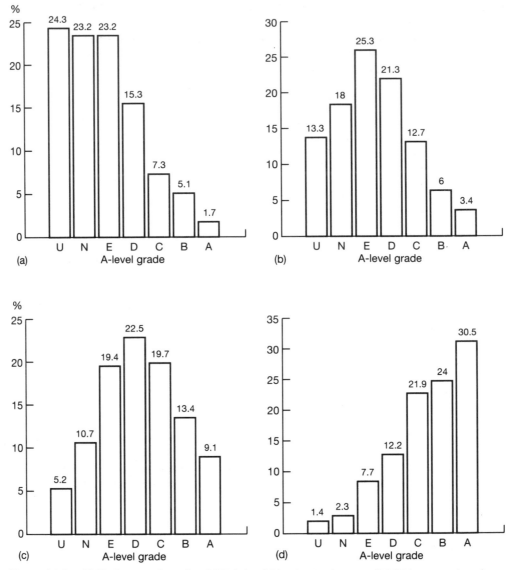

Figure 16.3   ALIS chances chart for GCE A-level Physics (a) Average GCSE between 4 and 4.75 (b) Average GCSE between 4.75 and 5.5 (c) Average GCSE between 5.5 and 6.25 (d) Average GCSE between 6.25 and 7

Consideration needs to be given to which staff should be involved, for example guidance staff and/or subject teachers. Such staff will then need briefing on how to use such data effectively with students.

2 In helping identify learning support needs

Staff in project colleges have found that analysis of value-added data can help identify patterns of under-achievement which indicate a need for additional learning support.

Learning support in this sense may range from additional tuition support to help in writing essays, as well as more general study skills.

A brief analysis of GCE A-level value-added data may be undertaken at cross-college level, but the search for patterns is more likely to be successful at subject level. Staff will need to:

- examine value-added data for their subject within the college over a period of several years;
- focus particularly on those students below the regression line and compare with national norms if available and/or previous years' norms within the college;
- look for patterns, for example, ways in which students below the line are different from those above it;
- if any clear patterns emerge, consider whether the provision of extra learning support may help, such as study skills, numeracy, literacy, enhanced tutorial support, independent learning skills.

> For example, one college discovered from such an analysis that students with poor writing skills were more likely to be below the regression line than above it for any level of GCSE score at entry. As a consequence, they negotiated with partner schools the provision of some joint support for year 11 pupils before they came to the college.

- test the hypothesis on a trial basis by providing the learning support identified;
- compare the results with those achieved before to evaluate the success of the trial;
- decide whether to continue, extend or abandon the trial on the basis of the results.

The ideas outlined above were originally drawn up on the basis of value-added analyses undertaken retrospectively using the actual GCE A-level results of students who had completed their courses.

Project colleges are increasingly finding that such an approach is also helpful on-programme, for example, using predicted results or mock examination results. Thus, the performance of individual students can be plotted and compared with norms based on previous years' results. Students falling significantly below the line can be identified and offered additional tutorial or workshop support as appropriate. In this respect the use of value-added data to identify learning support needs merges with its use in reviewing and motivating students.

3 Helping to motivate and review progress

Once enrolled on a GCE A-level programme, students can be helped to review their progress and be motivated to achieve more by the use of value-added analysis. Some colleges use such data on entry to set challenging but realistic targets for students and have formal systems of reviewing progress using assignment grades and mock examination results termly or twice termly. Students' achievements on the course are plotted against their 'expected' grades given their entry qualifications. This is shared with the students during tutorials and used to negotiate and set new targets and motivate them further.

Other project colleges are more wary of sharing value-added data with students, especially early on, but use it to inform debate among the staff who, in turn, use the insights to inform their contact with students, whether in the classroom or in tutorials.

If someone was doing significantly better than expected this might take the form of general praise and encouragement for example. Only if students were faring significantly worse than might be expected, would staff consider sharing value-added graphs with students and using the difference between expected and actual performance to explore any difficulties and perhaps set new targets.

The wariness some colleges feel seems to stem from a desire to avoid labelling students on entry. One of the positive aspects of college post-16 provision is that it provides some students with an opportunity to make a new start. Some colleges are loath to interfere with this by establishing targets based on previous performance and possibly thus creating self-fulfilling prophecies. Care needs to be taken to raise expectations of staff and students as far as possible and to use value-added data to provide additional encouragement. Best ever tables are another way of doing this.

Some colleges may wish to nominate a member of staff to identify under-achievers at specified points in the academic year. In a sixth-form college with a large GCE A-level programme this might be the vice-principal. In a larger more diverse general FE college it might be done by groups of GCE A-level tutors or their co-ordinator. The advantages of this being done beyond the subject level might include:

- a more coherent approach across different sections of the college;
- more options for intervention;
- someone to ensure the needs of the large numbers of students in the middle band are considered and not left out simply because they are not at the extremes.

Again, staff at subject and college levels may need staff development in order to use value-added data effectively. Staff need to recognise that the purpose is to encourage and motivate students to do as well as they can. They may need support in exploring how to do this (and how not to do it). It is likely that discussions with students on a one-to-one basis in tutorials will be most effective, perhaps as part of the recording achievement and action planning process. It may be, however, that the same approach will not be equally motivating for all students. In short, sensitivity and judgement are required.

4 Helping to manage for quality improvement

FEU's briefing note *Value Added: an Update* (1994) states: 'The most effective practice FEU has encountered has been where course or subject teams have been able to make practical use of the data, even though the collection and analysis of data may have been undertaken centrally at college or multi-institutional level. In these cases, value added has been calculated for a subject and given to the staff team which has then had responsibility to:

- receive and discuss the data;
- identify any patterns, for example, over time value added has increased/decreased; value is added more to weaker students than to stronger; to girls more than boys, etc.;
- consider reasons for the patterns, for example, changes in selection criteria, changes in teaching and learning strategies;
- recommend what, if anything, to do differently;
- report on action to be taken;
- decide how to evaluate action.

Sometimes such practices are seen as part of normal monitoring, review and evaluation procedures. When this is the case, any difficulties can often be identified and rectified at team level and value-added measurement can be seen as a helpful tool to aid continual improvement.'

The experience of project colleges has supported this view, but in addition there needs to be a management framework around the team's activities. Before the team undertakes its analysis, it needs to understand how college policies may affect the data, for example, whether the college filters students who underachieve out of taking examinations. In other words, value-added data should not be looked at in isolation, but in the context of college policies.

After its value-added review has been done and recommendations for action made, the team will need to report to senior managers, who subsequently may wish to respond by:

- Accepting the recommendations for action put forward.
- Suggesting others.
- Making decisions about whether to continue with the programme. For example, some colleges have decided not to continue with a GCSE resit programme because the value added has been so limited. This is a decision that can only be made at a senior college level in the light of the mission of the college and the overall curriculum portfolio.
- Identifying any cross-college issues and deciding what action should be taken.

Senior managers will also need to consider any staff development implications.

Another very constructive use of value-added data in managing for quality improvement is in identifying and celebrating excellence. Once success is identified, the factors underlying it often become apparent and can be transferred elsewhere.

5 Promoting and marketing the college

The college may wish to use evidence from its value-added analyses to help promote and market the college. Value-added data should be seen alongside data the college has to publish, and judgements made accordingly.

Until some form of national system of measuring value added is introduced, it is unlikely that a college would wish to publish its value-added results in full. In addition, findings based on small numbers over a short period of time can be very unreliable. As a matter of good marketing practice, colleges would be unwise to make claims based on such unstable results. Nonetheless, it may be possible to identify positive messages about the college from the systematic analysis of value-added results over a number of years which can be used for promotional purposes.

The process could be as in the following sections:

Analysis of data

Someone at college level will need to analyse the value-added data to look for patterns. For example:

- Does the college add more value to weaker or stronger students on entry?
- Does the full range of students taking a particular subject achieve consistently good results in terms of value added?

- Does the college do particularly well for specified groups of students, such as girls in physics?

The role of this person will depend to some extent on the structure of the college. It might, for example, be the quality manager. This would mean that any patterns identified could also inform the annual quality review.

Identification of strengths and positive messages

Once the value-added patterns are identified it should be possible to identify the positive messages within them. For example, the college value added for girls in Physics may be consistently higher than the national average. This is a finding which appropriate members of college staff may wish to mention when visiting girls' schools.

Ensure positive messages are given to appropriate staff for marketing purposes

Having identified positive messages from the patterns in the data, it will be necessary to ensure the right people know about them in order to use them appropriately. An obvious person who needs to know is the marketing manager who will incorporate them in the communication mechanisms and schedules which tie in with the publication of college publicity materials. Others too may find such messages useful. For example:

- Members of the senior management team going to talk to local schools about progression opportunities at the college.
- Admissions staff about subject specific messages. For example, if the college was particularly good at adding value for students with weaker GCSE scores at GCE A-level French.

It may be advisable to communicate such positive messages to all staff so they have them available to use whenever they are appropriate. Mechanisms for communicating the messages and guidance on how to use them would need to be considered and set up. It is important to think widely about how to use such messages for promotional purposes. For example, potential audiences might include:

prospective students
careers staff in schools
parents
employers
the press
local radio
governors

The messages may need to be different for different audiences.

Review and evaluation

It will be important to review and evaluate the process. For example:

- Are positive messages being identified from the patterns in the data?
- Are the messages communicated to appropriate staff?

- Are staff using them appropriately and creatively with a variety of audiences?
- Could more be done?

Summary and conclusion

The various uses to which value-added data can be put within colleges are still being trialled and developed by the project colleges among others. New developments and refinements are emerging all the time.

Common issues seem to be:

- The need for sensitivity in relation both to staff and students.
- Identifying how value-added measures can be used within existing systems and procedures.
- The need for staff development.
- Identifying what can be done centrally and what needs doing at subject level.
- Creating a culture of continuous improvement/ownership of the data and suggested improvements.
- The importance of seeing value-added measures as a useful additional tool rather than the complete answer to quality improvement.

17 | Measuring added value in schools*

ANDREW McPHERSON

The publication of examination and test results, resulting in 'league tables' and calls for calculations of the contribution schools make to pupils' progress – the 'added value' they offer – raise a number of difficult questions. This first National Commission on Education (NCE) Briefing describes the complex factors, values, and interests that should be taken into account when attempting to measure schools' performance.

This chapter draws on developments in research on school effectiveness to address questions about the value of information on schools' examination and test results. It identifies pitfalls and advocates certain methods. It argues that there is no single solution that can be recommended on technical grounds alone: even the best techniques have limitations. Value judgements will always be involved as well as issues of accountability and cost.

British schools have been required to publish their public examination results for over a decade. Many people are affected by these requirements: parents, pupils and teachers; school governors, school boards and education authorities; indirectly the employers, colleges and universities who select school leavers, and central government.

But does such information enable us to say with reasonable assurance that one school is better than another, or better or worse than it used to be? How can the information be used, and not abused? And how can we ensure that it will meet the needs of the wide range of interested parties? This briefing focuses on test and examination results at the secondary stage, but the main arguments can be generalised to other stages of education, and other measurable outcomes.

1 By themselves, examination results do not show a school's added value

Test and examination results differ from one school to the next. This is undisputed, and is one of the main reasons given by government for its concern with standards.

*This material has been edited and originally appeared in *National Commission on Education*, Briefing No. 1.

But schools also differ from each other in their pupil intakes. This, too, is undisputed. The type of school influences the gender and denominational composition of the pupil intake. The location of the school influences the ethnic and social mix. Type and location both affect pupils' levels of attainment on entry, as do many other factors.

A school's 'added value' is the boost that it gives to a child's previous level of attainment. 'Raw' outcome scores do not measure this boost. Test and examination results provide misleading indicators of added value if they are not adjusted for differences between schools in the attainment of their pupils on entry.

2 Nevertheless, unadjusted results are informative

Raw outcome measures are informative because they reflect actual attainment and activity. They tell one, for example, that a particular syllabus is being studied to a certain standard. But they convey information only when properly presented. They should be based on entire year groups of pupils and should identify any special cases or exclusions from the year-group base, such as pupils with special educational needs and transferred pupils.

Information about attainment on a subject-by-subject basis is often useful. But when one is looking at an individual pupil's attainment, whether overall or in specified areas of the curriculum, it must be aggregated, and this will entail value judgements. For example, it must be decided whether each grade level, or subject or type of examination, should be equally weighted or not.

Single outcome measures may not serve all users equally well and may thereby give one set of users priority over another. For example, summary measures of attainment may be too general to meet class teachers' or parents' diagnostic requirements for individual pupils. Similarly, judgements of value and priority are also implicit in the choice of a statistic to summarise outcomes: in the use of a mean or median, for example, rather than a distribution.

3 Unadjusted outcome information should be accompanied by information on the school's contribution to pupil progress

Parents need information on the value added by a school. School managers need information on the quality of the teaching input in a school. To meet such needs, one must take account both of the level of a pupil's 'prior attainment' before entry to the school or stage in question, and of other factors that might influence progress.

This cannot be done infallibly because there is no information available at present about methods through which schools boost attainment that can safely be assumed to apply to all schools in the future.

For example, studies typically find that about half of the variation among pupils in attainment in public examinations can be predicted from, or statistically 'explained' by, pupils' attainment on entry to secondary school. But such correlations do not necessarily tell us what caused the variations, or whether and how the pupils' prior attainment contributed to their later attainment.

If the cause lay solely with the pupil, then the school's boost, or added value, is the difference between the earlier and the later attainment. This is because the school was not responsible for the earlier level of attainment and its influence on later attainment.

On the other hand, the cause of the correlation between earlier and later attainment might lie partly with teachers. For example, teachers might wrongly expect from their pupils only levels of later attainment commensurate with their earlier attainment; and these teacher expectations might themselves then influence later attainment. If so, not all of a pupil's prior attainment should be subtracted when estimating a school's success in adding value.

The point is that the adjustment of outcome scores must always have a proper theoretical justification. Even the most 'commonsense' of adjustments is based on theory. Theories are not infallible, and therefore the particulars of any adjustment *may* be open to improvement and *must* be open to inspection and argument.

What is not open to argument, however, is that it should always be possible to adjust outcome scores for prior attainment. This is logically entailed in the idea of a pupil's 'progress'. Progress *is*, so to speak, an adjusted outcome score, the *difference* between an earlier and a later attainment. Schools are there to help pupils to make progress, so there can be no argument against the principle of adjustment if one wishes to know the added value of a school.

Nor can one dismiss the practice of adjusting outcome scores solely on the grounds that parents could never understand such adjustments. This would imply that parents could not understand the concept of pupil progress. Were this true, all attempts to inform parents would fail. A similar argument applies to adjustments for factors other than prior attainment, for example family background.

4 Pupil progress is correlated with various non-teacher factors

Pupil progress may be correlated with *factors within the school for which teachers are not responsible*. The history and religious denomination, if any, of the school may be associated with pupil progress as well.

Also correlated with progress are the characteristics of a pupil's *household*. These include: household size and adult composition; the educational level of the parent or parents; and the parents' occupations. Other factors associated with progress include the level of material and social (dis)advantage in the immediate *neighbourhood* of the home, and aspects of the wider *opportunity structure*, including the level and character of local employment opportunities, and the opportunities for further progress in education and training.

5 The assessment of the effects on pupil progress of schools and other agents should be based on an explicit theory of good standing

There is substantial agreement amongst researchers, based on solid evidence, about a number of desirable features of any such theory. The first is that schooling is *longitudinal*. It takes place over time as pupils make progress and as schools maintain their effectiveness, improve or deteriorate. Any pupil can have a bad day, any school a bad year. Sensible judgements will therefore be based, not on snapshots, but on repeated measures of pupils and schools.

A second feature is that schooling is *multilevel*: pupils are grouped within classes, classes within schools, and schools within larger administrative and other types of grouping.

Both features are self-evident and should inform the way in which outcome scores are adjusted and used. Where they do not, adjusted scores will fail to inform the full range of users of the information; they may misinform them (see 7 and 8 below); and the statistical robustness of effects will be wrongly estimated.

A third requirement of a good theory is that it must be *multivariate* and *comprehensive* taking account of all factors involved. It is not sufficient to adjust outcome scores only for pupils' prior attainment. Outcome scores must be open to adjustment for other non-school factors that boost or retard progress.

The case for adjusting for non-school factors is not self-evident. But it cannot be dismissed by anyone who believes that a pupil's progress will benefit from the informed involvement of parents, or by anyone who believes that successful education is the product of a partnership between teachers and others. Adjustments are required if we are to avoid misinforming all parties to the partnership about the effectiveness of their several contributions.

6 A single statistic may not be an adequate summary of a school's effect on pupil progress

There are two reasons for this. The first is that theories are always capable of improvement. Different theories entail different adjustments to outcome scores. This is already argued in section (3) in relation to adjustments for prior attainment. A similar argument applies to other adjustments, for example for family background. Whether or not an adjustment for family background, or any other factor, is invidious, depends on the theory underlying the adjustment.

The second reason is that, even when the theory or account of schooling is agreed, different users of the information may reasonably require different adjustments to be made. Two illustrations are given, one in each of the following two sections.

7 A school may boost the progress of different types of pupils at different rates

One school may give a special boost to pupils who are already doing well or, alternatively, to pupils who previously have struggled. Another may succeed in spreading learning gains more evenly over all its pupils. A third may succeed in boosting the science attainments of girls in particular, whilst a fourth may give a particular boost to the language-related attainments of pupils from homes where the first language is not English.

All four schools could, nevertheless, achieve the same average attainment level and the same average amount of added value. In these cases, the averages would obscure as much about the school as they revealed. They would be of little help to a parent who wanted to make an informed choice for a particular son or daughter having a particular level of attainment and with a particular language capability.

Average pupil attainment in six schools unadjusted for pupil intake, and with four adjustments

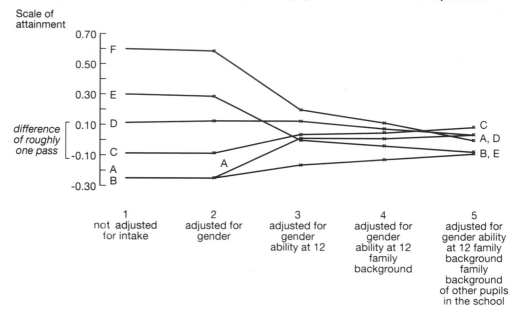

Figure 17.1   The chart shows the effects of four statistical adjustments for pupil intake on estimates of the quality of six secondary schools (schools A to F). The six schools are chosen from an education authority in which all schools are all-through comprehensives (showing more schools would clutter the illustration). Individual attainment is measured here by the number of passes in public examinations taken at sixteen, seventeen or eighteen years by pupils who were in their final compulsory year in 1983–84. The scaling of attainment is such that a difference of 0.2 corresponds roughly to one pass.

In other words, a school may add different aspects and levels of value for different types of pupils. A method which can produce only one summary statistic for a school always runs the risk of misrepresenting that school's successes and failures and of misleading parents.

One advantage of a multilevel approach is that, subject to data availability, it allows one to test whether a single-statistic summary is adequate, or whether separate summaries are required for separate types of pupils. Multiple summaries may seem complex. But any complexity is simply a reflection of the respect that good statistics must have for the individuality of the pupils and schools involved.

8   The interests of parents and the interests of teachers may dictate mutually conflicting but equally valid adjustments to outcome scores

A pupil's attendance at a particular school may confer advantages which have little or nothing to do with the action of teachers. Some studies have found that the characteristics of the pupil body as a whole are correlated with individual pupils' progress. In such studies, a pupil of, let us say, average prior attainment has tended to make more progress in a school where the prior attainment of all pupils was above average, than in a school where the prior attainment of all pupils was below average. Similar effects are sometimes observed for measures of family background.

Let us suppose that such correlations are wholly owing to peer-group effects outside the classroom: that is, to pupils learning from each other or preventing each other from learning in ways that a teacher could not reasonably be expected to influence. In summarising the effectiveness or added value attributable to teachers in a school, we would want to discount that part of a pupil's progress that was owing to such peer-group effects. This gives us a first added-value statistic for the school.

Parents, by contrast, will be interested in all of the advantages that will accrue to their child by virtue of their attendance at the school, whether these advantages arise from classroom teaching, from peer-group effects, or from anything else. It is not in parents' interest to discount peer-group effects when assessing the value of a school for their child. This gives us a second added-value statistic for the school.

Thus, a single-statistic summary cannot be presumed in advance to serve teachers and parents alike or, by extension, to serve education authorities and other interested parties. What is required is a multilevel capability – in this example a representation of pupils having certain individual characteristics, themselves grouped within schools so as to have certain collective or 'school-level' characteristics, namely the overall composition of the pupil body.

Again, there is a seeming complexity. We have two estimates of added value for the one school. But the complexity is simply an honest reflection of the different interests of two of the parties to the partnership of schooling. It is not a gratuitous imposition of the method.

9 Features of a good indicator system

A good indicator system must allow for the differences that characterise individual pupils and schools, for different explanations of these differences, and for the different interests of the range of parties to whom schools are accountable.

It is the job of statistics to produce the simplest and most economical summary of a school's value that is consistent with this variety and with the purpose or purposes of the indicator. The resultant summary might be simple or it might be complex. But complexity is not in itself an argument against aiming for the best possible indicator system.

Any attempt to improve schooling by means of informing choice presupposes that parents are capable of understanding at least the complexity of an adjusted outcome score. To reject that possibility is to reject the possibility of informing parents.

Nor is the cost of a good indicator system a decisive objection. We do not know the cost of the mistaken judgements, needless anxieties and fruitless 'further investigations' that are triggered by false signals from poor indicator systems. Misplaced complacency is costly too. In industry poor systems of quality control result in poor products and contribute to the very economic difficulties that better schools are expected to address.

A good indicator system will therefore aim to improve its own validity. It will not be content merely to 'indicate'. It will endeavour to describe outcomes and processes directly, to be valid in itself.

Whilst it is unrealistic to expect to build research enquiry into each and every application of an indicator system, the capability for testing its assumptions and improving its procedures should exist somewhere and should be available to everyone with an interest in better schooling. It will take quality to recognise quality.

Conclusions

1 Schools' test and examination results are informative, but 'raw' results are misleading indicators of the added value of a school if they are not also adjusted for intake differences.
2 'Raw' results should therefore be accompanied by an assessment of the contribution a school makes to its pupils' progress. The assessment should take account of each pupil's prior level of attainment and of other factors inside and outside of the school that may have influenced progress.
3 The basis of the assessment must be made clear, including any assumptions about the responsibility of teachers or others for the factors affecting progress; and the assessment must have solid theoretical backing.
4 A single statistic may not adequately summarise progress. Different types of pupils may progress at different rates. Parents and teachers may legitimately wish to know about different things. What is needed is a good indicator system.
5 A bad indicator system will hinder progress towards better schools and carry hidden costs.
6 A good indicator system will:

   • take account of different needs and uses;
   • be as simple as possible, while recognising the individuality of pupils, families and schools;
   • prefer measures of stability and change in performance to single 'snapshots'; and have built into it the means of monitoring and improving its own validity.

18 | Value-added principles, practice and ethical considerations

LESLEY SAUNDERS

Introduction

This chapter discusses the role of 'value-added' measures of schools' performance in the school effectiveness and improvement debates. It considers what the key issues are for educators and educationists wishing to make use of value-added analyses in such a context; the major challenge is to see how far it is possible to enlist detailed (and often complex) school effectiveness data in the service of schools and their supporting bodies, such as local education authorities (LEAs) and government departments and agencies, such as the Office for Standards in Education (OFSTED) or the Schools Curriculum and Assessment Authority (SCAA). This, as is increasingly evident, is by no means a straightforward matter. it means, amongst other things, taking due account of the following:

- The context in which value-added analyses has been developed.
- The purposes to which value-added data may be put.
- The methodological principles underlying value-added measurements.
- What value-added measurements reveal.
- What the key issues are for schools as diverse, complex organizations.
- What the key issues are for educationists and educational policymakers more generally, in terms of an explicit ethical agenda.

This chapter discusses each of these areas in turn, in order to help clarify the limits, as well as the benefits, of value-added measurements of school performance. In doing so, it draws heavily on the work currently being undertaken at the National Foundation for Educational Research (NFER) for secondary schools and LEAs. But the broad principles apply equally to institutions in the primary, special and tertiary sectors.

Underpinning the chapter is the belief that the only defensible rationale for introducing value-added measurement of performance into an already crowded agenda of educational initiatives is in order to assist with school improvement and the raising of pupils' levels of attainment. The chapter accordingly concludes with a series of summary points related to that aim.

The context for value-added

There are several distinct traces in the development of value-added measurement of institutional performance; these traces have to do with the evolving study of school effectiveness, developments in the measurement of performance, and changes in educational ideology respectively.

As the famous study *Fifteen Thousand Hours*[1] succeeded in demonstrating in the late 1970s, some schools are measurably more effective than others in terms of increasing children's life chances. This piece of research, together with the ensuing programme of research on school effectiveness to which it gave rise, has arguably contributed to the shift of focus of concern about the UK's education system away from national monitoring of aggregate statistics towards a scrutiny of the performance of individual schools. [. . .]

It was inevitable, and desirable, that this new emphasis on performance (as distinct, say, from other legitimate concerns like curricular process or learning experience) should have concentrated attention on how best to *measure* performance or 'achievement outcomes' in Mortimore and Stone's phrase, [2] which would show how far schools had actually contributed to the achievements of their pupils. It is now ten years since the publication of 'The search for a fairer way of comparing schools' examination results'[3] and the intervening years have seen an impressive development in solving problems of statistical methodology so as to enable both individual pupil and school academic achievements to be more rigorously analysed. [. . .]

From the early 1990s onwards, the debate about 'value-added' measures of performance i.e. measures of performance which would reveal the 'increment on performance of each individual child that goes to [the school]' became vociferous and many-facted. A simple index of bibliographical references shows that twice as much literature was published on the topic of value-added in 1995 as in 1990.

Perhaps the paradox is that, on the one hand, value-added measures of performance have certainly taken the debate about standards and quality in a new and helpful direction, but that, on the other, it is also arguable that the educational profession as a whole would not now be exploring this more sophisticated form of evidence with such interest had not the government been so concerned with public accountability and published tables of individual school performance.

The purposes of value-added

[. . .]
Value-added analyses are currently being used to:

- '*compare like with like*' in terms of schools' background and context;
- represent pupils' *progress* rather than raw achievement;
- identify which institutions are doing *better/worse than one would predict*;
- provide similar information about *individual departments/year groups*; and
- identify which pupils are *performing above or below expectations*.

Value-added analyses have received most attention when they appear in the public domain as an antidote to, or modification of the Department for Education and Employment (DfEE) league tables of academic performance. Another, rather different, use is for providing confidential feedback to schools and/or LEAs to assist with school improvement. There are elements of summative, evaluative, formative and informative purposes in the kinds of value-added analyses now being developed, at NFER and elsewhere [. . .]

The NFER's current work focuses on school improvement (largely at the request of schools and LEAs). In the process of developing this work, not only have the statistical and methodological techniques become refined, but much has been learnt about the effective uses of value-added data in schools and LEAs.

Methodological principles

The NFER has been engaged for several years in developing value-added measures of performance, including analyses of reading tests, of GCSE results, of Key Stage 1 SATs data and of post-16 vocational qualifications. From 1993, NFER has used this expertise to offer a confidential service to schools and LEAs. QUASE (Quantitative Analysis for Self-Evaluation)[4] and ERIC (Examination Results in Context)[5] are funded separately, but provide similar services: a series of data tables is compiled, on an annual basis, on different aspects of school performance, including several GCSE-related performance indicators and analyses for individual subject areas, in order to give institutions detailed information on their relative strengths and weaknesses. The analysis takes into account external factors which have been empirically shown to be associated with outcomes, such as pupils' prior attainment, together with features of each school's background or context. Data on pupils is mainly that which schools/LEAs already collect, such as sex, ethnic group, scores on intake tests, eligibility for free school meals, and so forth.

The NFER's work conforms to the following five criteria of good practice in undertaking value-added analyses, according to Gray (1995)[6]:

Individual pupils

Data is needed on individual pupils (rather than aggregated to school level).

Outcome measures

Outcome measure(s) for each pupil are needed, reflecting all levels of pupil performance, rather than, say, a criterion of five or more higher grade GCSEs.

It needs to be pointed out that there is no single aggregated outcome measure – even for a limited indicator like pupils' GCSE grades – which can definitively represent a school's academic performance. Different measures produce different results. Depending on whether one uses total GCSE score, average GCSE score, scores in any of the three core subject areas, number of grades A–C, or number of grades A–G (each of which is a valid measure in itself), a different picture is likely to result, and consequently a different rank ordering in any league table. NFER's work consequently uses a range of up to seven outcome measures – all related to GCSE examination results – in reporting back results to schools. Often a difference between results using total and those using average GCSE scores can say something about how effective a school's general entry policy on GCSEs has been. Alternatively, by looking at the difference between number of A–C grades and of A–G grades, it is possible to identify any bias in favour of lower or of higher achievers.

Prior attainment

Prior attainment measure(s) for each pupil (preferably individual scores, not broad groupings) are needed, plus some items of information about the pupil's background.

As far as secondary schools are concerned, NFER uses the kind of diagnostic tests schools have traditionally employed for their intake year, such as cognitive ability, verbal and non-verbal reasoning, maths and reading tests. Obviously, there is a very wide range of such tests in use and a 'composite intake measure' from the twenty or so most reliable and valid tests in use has been derived. Among the criteria for such tests is the requirement that pupils' attainment is presented as an individual standardized score. Ideally, tests which are to be used as baseline assessments in this way would be 'low stake', i.e. do not represent public judgements on the outcomes from a previous institution's provision.

Pupil background

If prior attainment is not available, several items of information about pupil's background (including a measure of social advantage as well as social disadvantage, according to Gray) should be used. As well as prior attainment data, NFER uses sex, ethnic group, level of any special educational need, eligibility for free school meals and date of birth at the pupil level, and additionally builds in information about the overall school context or background.

Multilevel modelling

Multilevel modelling should be used to analyse the data. Multilevel modelling is essentially an extension of regression analysis, and allows data to be analysed hierarchically. That is to say, it facilitates the *simultaneous* examination of various factors operating at pupil, at cohort and at school level which help to explain differences between schools' performance. The outcomes of this kind of analysis for individual schools can be represented by a bar chart (Figure 18.1) which shows the school's results at the three stages of analysis – based on raw scores, on allowance for pupil factors and on allowance for pupil and school factors respectively. What the bar chart does not show – but accompanying numerical tables should aways show, as in Table 18.1 – is the confidence limits which need to be assigned to each value. These represent the level of certainty with which we can say that a value is positive or negative, and by how much.

Between them, these five criteria for doing value-added analyses enable an accurate picture to be compiled of the progress different pupils make in different schools, given their different starting points.

The price to be paid for this depth and rigour is, however, as has been stated, an unavoidable degree of complexity in the analyses and their interpretation, especially for the statistical layperson. NFER therefore provides a detailed commentary, customized

Table 18.1   QUASE performance indicators data. Unadjusted and adjusted differences between school's results and expected performance on six performance indicators

	Type of performance indicator					
	Total GCSE score	Average GCSE score	Maths GCSE score	English GCSE score	Number of grades A to C	Number of grades A to G
Unadjusted – average	−9.58	−1.23	−1.43	−.82	−2.03	−.57
Lower limit	−13.58	−1.75	−2.00	−1.39	−2.81	−1.14
Upper limit	−5.58	−.70	−.85	−.25	−1.25	.00
Adjusted (1) – average	−6.56	−.89	−.96	−.47	−1.41	−.29
Lower limit	−9.23	−1.22	−1.42	−.92	−2.00	−.71
Upper limit	−3.89	−.56	−.50	−.02	−.82	.12
Adjusted (2) – average	6.46	.07	.00	.39	.63	1.81
Lower limit	3.80	−.25	−.43	−.01	.05	1.40
Upper limit	9.11	.39	.44	.80	1.21	2.22

Adjusted (1): with pupil data taken into account.
Adjusted (2): with pupil data and school context taken into account.

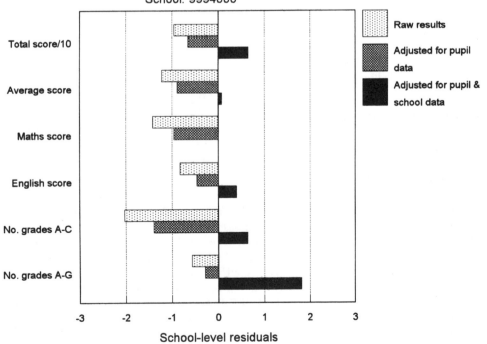

Figure 18.1   QUASE performance indicators data

for each school, to assist senior managers not only in interpretation but also in generating action points. [. . .]

It is worth making a brief response at this stage to the point of principle which Goldstein and Spiegelhalter (1996)[7] make about the provision of confidential data like QUASE. They allege that the 'inherent secrecy [of schemes like ALIS, the A-level information system established a decade ago by Professor Fitz-Gibbon at the University of Newcastle upon Tyne] would seem to lend itself to manipulation by institutions, e.g. by ignoring the existence of wide uncertainty intervals or by the selective quotation of results'. Goldstein has been a major contributor to the ethical debate surrounding value-added by continuing to insist on, amongst other matters, the intractable difficulties of using such data in the public domain to judge schools as good or bad. But to propose, as he does, that providing confidential data to schools is vitiated in principle would surely be true only if:

- quantitative data is allowed to predominate over every other kind of evidence *and*
- schools use the data in a judgmental rather than a heuristic way *and*
- the data filters into the public domain rather than being used internally as a basis for dialogue and reflection within the institution.

On the contrary, it could be argued that, due in part to commentators like Goldstein, the emphasis in the value-added debate has shifted in favour of a concern with finding out what is going well and why, and what needs to be put right, than with proving something in the marketplace – though of course no-one would pretend that the latter preoccupation has vanished.

What value-added measurements reveal

Feedback to individual schools and LEAs, although it is the central purpose of services like those provided by NFER, is not the whole story, however. The data analysis carried out to fulfil this has yielded a valuable database of information on secondary schools and their pupils which provides useful insights into the factors which affect performance in the secondary sector as a whole, both at the pupil and at the school level.

NFER's data gathered from both QUASE and ERIC (see above) in recent years confirms much other research in this field and in particular demonstrates the following:

- *Schools can and do make a difference*, despite there being factors over which schools have little or no control. In fact, between 80 and 90 per cent of the variance between schools in GCSE performance is explained by a combination of pupil- and school-level factors. For example, QUASE results in 1994 showed that, for *average GCSE score*, the amount of variance between schools which could be explained by pupil-level factors was 77 per cent, and by a combination of pupil and school-level factors was 88 per cent. The implication of this is that the vast bulk of apparent differences between schools' performance at GCSE can be accounted for in terms of identifiable factors, most of which are beyond schools' direct or immediate control. The remaining variance which cannot be accounted for in terms of known factors could thus be said to reflect the real differences between schools' performance, and these are the result of the cumulative impact of decisions, at policy as well as at classroom level, made by the school staff in their professional capacity. This can be seen in Figures

18.2 and 18.3, which give outcomes based on *total* GCSE score and on *average* GCSE score, respectively. The apparent range of performance of schools – the distance between best and worst – progressively decreases as more factors are taken into account. Schools can change their relative rank order, depending on whether one looks at raw or adjusted scores. Nonetheless, there is still an apparently irreducible difference between schools which cannot be explained by any of these factors.

- There is a strong positive relationship between intake measures (such as the London Reading Test or the Cognitive Abilities Test) and performance in GCSE examinations at age 16. *The best single predictor of attainment is a pupil's level of attainment in the past.*
- Socio-economic disadvantage – as measured by the proportion of pupils eligible for free school meals – has a very strong negative correlation with all performance outcomes.
- Furthermore, pupils in schools where there is a high proportion of pupils with special educational needs or who are eligible for free school meals tend to have lower scores than pupils in other schools, *whether or not they are themselves so affected*. This is an empirical finding. 'Allowing for' this factor in the aggregate analyses should not be confused with 'making allowances for' individual pupils (who may always, of course, confound teachers', parents' and psychologists' expectations of them *as individuals*).
- Girls outperform boys on most adjusted performance indicators, except for mathematics, in which boys still marginally outperform girls.
- Pupils of Chinese, Indian, Pakistani and Bangladeshi ethnic origin tend to outperform white pupils on adjusted performance indicators. Pupils of Afro-Caribbean ethnic origin have a slight tendency to underperform relative to white pupils.
- Pupils staying in the same school for the whole of Key Stage 4 do better than those who change schools during this period.
- There is considerable departmental variation within the same school in terms of how well boys do compared with girls, and/or how far above or below predictions pupils in different academic ability groups perform.
- Attendance is significantly related to GCSE performance in terms of both numbers and grades achieved, even when prior attainment is taken into account.

Each of these findings is interesting and important in itself and tells policymakers as well as researchers and teachers where extra effort and/or resources may need to be put in. What emerges overall is that, although many schools are doing no worse and no better than would be expected, there is a proportion of schools which perform relatively badly on raw scores but better than expected when pupil or pupil-and-school factors are taken into account, as Figure 18.4 shows. These are the schools in the upper left-hand quadrant. Conversely, there are some apparently successful schools which may not in fact be doing justice to all their pupils – the schools in the lower right-hand quadrant. Schools which appear in the lower left-hand quadrant are those which appear to do badly on both raw and adjusted scores, and for whom some radical overhaul of management and classroom practice may be needed. Judgements based on adjusted scores about which schools are effective and which are not may therefore contradict judgements based on raw scores. Integrity demands that, where judgements are being made in the public domain, they have an explicit basis which explains how they have been arrived at and what their limitations are.

[. . .]

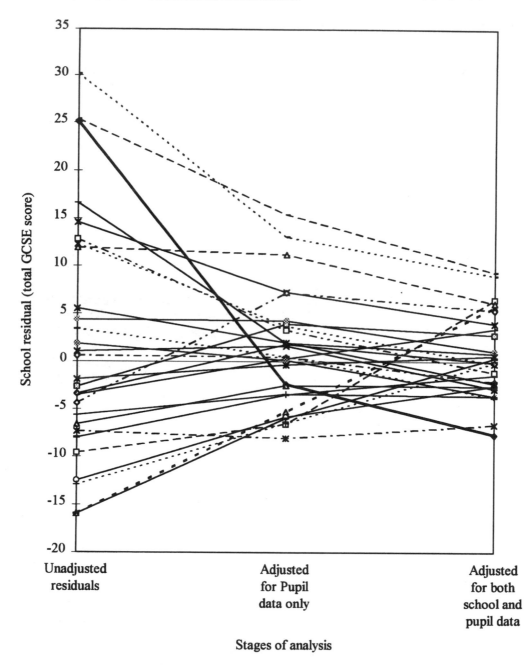

Figure 18.2   QUASE 93/94: School residuals at different analysis stages (total GCSE score). The various symbols represent different schools

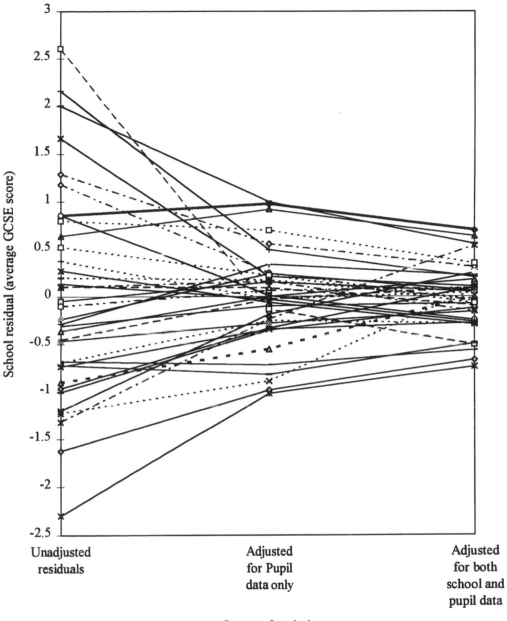

Figure 18.3   QUASE 93/94: School residuals at different analysis stages (average GCSE score). The various symbols represent different schools

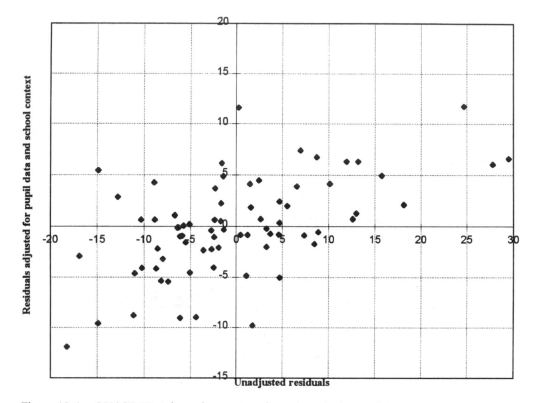

Figure 18.4   QUASE 95: Adjusted versus unadjusted residuals (total GCSE score)

Key issues for educators and educationists

The technical expertise in the study and creation of added value data which has been developed by researchers in the UK is now formidable and impressive – though naturally we may expect refinements to continue to be made to the detail. What many of us are now discovering is that this is only the beginning. We are certainly at the point where it is possible to say that good practice in *providing* value-added analyses should include:

- stringent *quality assurance and quality control*, procedures;
- *robust statistical methods*, which should be 'transparent' and open to scrutiny;
- use of *more than one outcome indicator*;
- use of outcome indicators which reflect *the whole spectrum of performance*;
- scrutiny of both *school-level and departmental-level* performance;
- presentation of *information in different forms*, e.g. tabular, verbal and graphic, which also make statistical confidence limits explicit;
- *interpretation and commentary*; plus suggestions for *action points* for the individual school;
- incorporation of *feedback* from users/clients.

So far as the *users* of value-added measurements are concerned, the following criteria probably ought to apply:

- the use of such data should be an integral part of the school's planned cycle of *review over time* (three years' worth of data is the minimum needed to show trends);
- the system should be *efficiently organized, cost-effective, with clear purposes and responsibilities*;
- the data should be used by senior management to generate *action points*;
- the central focus of all this activity should be the *pupils and their individual progress*.

It should be clear, however, that these points constitute a necessary but not yet sufficient basis for using value-added data for school improvement. As yet more sophisticated methods for measuring value-added are developed, they will need to be closely accompanied by clear answers – or at least the possibility of clear answers – to the following kinds of question:

- *What tensions are there in the implementation of value-added measurement?* Whose agendas are being served, and for what purposes? Who is funding the research?
- Who is in control of *how the results will be used*? Is the project a research exercise, an accountability exercise or a service, or some combination of all three?
- Is the effort worthwhile? *Do value-added approaches help to improve education in practice?* This is obviously the crucial question, to which there are as yet no clear-cut answers. 'The picture that emerged [from schools using value-added data] was of a very peripheral level of awareness, a tendency not to attend meetings, to read reports sparingly and to take no action on reports once read.[8] This may not be surprising, according to Brown *et al.* (1995)[9] who argue that the notion of a top-down, management-oriented approach to school improvement based on school effectiveness data is 'simple-minded', because it fails to address the question of how the findings are to be integrated into the thinking and practice of those who are seen as needing to improve, and because such findings are in any case based on policymakers' and/or researchers' own constructs. They take the view that much better theories of school development need to be elaborated, including a firmer grasp of what constitutes 'ineffectiveness'.

This means that the conceptual, ethical and political frameworks within which value-added approaches ought to be situated will need to be constantly negotiated. Different groups have interdependent roles to play in this: researchers and the media have responsibilities as much as teachers, managers and policymakers for ensuring that 'the complexities of schools and the uncertainties of the research'[9] are fully recognised.

References

1 Rutter, M., Maughan, B., Mortimore, P., Ouston, J., with Smith, A. (1979) *Fifteen Thousand Hours*. London: Open Books.
2 Mortimore, P. and Stone, S. (1990) Measuring educational quality. *British Journal of Educational Studies*, 39(1): 69–82.
3 Gray, J., Jesson, D. and Jones, B. (1986) The search for a fairer way of comparing schools' examination results. *Research Papers in Education*, 1(2): 91–122.
4 Schagen, I. (1995) *Quantitative Analysis for Self-Evaluation. Technical Report of Analysis 1995*. Slough: NFER.

5 Kendall, L. (1995) *Examination Results in Context: Report on the Analysis of 1994 Examination Results*. London: AMA.
6 Gray, J. (1995) Developing value-added approaches: the experiences of three LEAs, in J. Gray and B. Wilcox *Good School, Bad School: Evaluating Performance and Encouraging Improvement*. Buckingham: Open University Press.
7 Goldstein, H. and Spiegelhalter, D. J. (1996) League tables and their limitations: statistical issues in comparisons of institutional performance. *Journal of the Royal Statistical Society*, 159: 3.
8 Williamson, J. and Fitz-Gibbon, C. T. (1990) On the lack of impact of information. *Educational Management and Administration*, 18(1): 37–45.
9 Brown, S., Duffield, J. and Riddell, S. (1995) School effectiveness research: the policy-makers' tool for school improvement? *European Educational Research Association Bulletin*, 1(1): 6–15.

PART 3

Managing change for school and college improvement

19 | Planning, doing, and coping with change*

MICHAEL G. FULLAN

For the growing number of people who have attempted to bring about educational change, 'intractability' is becoming a household word. Being ungovernable, however, is not the same as being impervious to influence. And the inability to change *all* situations we would ideally like to reform does not lead to the conclusion that *no* situation can be changed. (To complicate matters even further, to conclude that a situation can be changed in a certain way does not mean that it should be.)

[. . .]

Why planning fails

Understanding why most attempts at educational reform fail goes far beyond the identification of specific technical problems such as lack of good materials, ineffective in-service training, or minimal administrative support. In more fundamental terms, educational change fails partly because of the assumptions of planners and partly because some 'problems' are inherently unsolvable. These two issues are explored in the next two subsections.

Faulty assumptions and ways of thinking about change

In a word, the assumptions of policy-makers are frequently *hyperrational* (Wise 1977, 1979, 1988). One of the initial sources of the problem is the commitment of reformers to see a particular desired change implemented. Commitment to *what should be changed* often varies inversely with knowledge about *how to work through a process of change*. In fact, as I shall claim later, strong commitment to a particular change may be a barrier to setting up an effective process of change, and in any case they are two quite distinct aspects of social change. The adage 'Where there's a will there's a way'

*This material has been edited and originally appeared in *The New Meaning of Educational Change*.

is not always an apt one for the planning of educational change. There is an abundance of wills, but they are *in* the way rather than pointing the way. [. . .] a certain amount of vision is required to provide the clarity and energy for promoting specific changes, but vision by itself may get in the way if it results in impatience, failure to listen, etc. Stated in a more balanced way, promoters of change need to be committed and skilled in the *change process* as well as in the change itself.

[. . .] Lighthall (1973) states [. . .] that educational change is a process of coming to grips with the *multiple* realities of people, who are the main participants in implementing change. The leader who presupposes what the change should be and acts in ways that preclude others' realities is bound to fail. [. . .] Innovators who are unable to alter their realities of change through exchange with would-be implementers can be as authoritarian as the staunchest defenders of the status quo. This is not to say that innovators should not have deep convictions about the need for reform or should be prepared to abandon their ideas at the first sign of opposition. It is to say that [. . .] innovators need to be open to the realities of others: sometimes because the ideas of others will lead to alterations for the better in the direction of change, and sometimes because the others' realities will expose the problems of implementation that must be addressed and at the very least will indicate where one should start.

[. . .] In short, one of the basic reasons why planning fails is that planners or decision-makers of change are unaware of the situations that potential implementers are facing. They introduce changes without providing a means to identify and confront the situational constraints and without attempting to understand the values, ideas, and experiences of those who are essential for implementing any changes.

But what is wrong with having a strong belief that a certain aspect of schooling should be changed? Is it not appropriately rational to know that a given change is necessary, and to make it policy, if one is in a position to do so? Aside from the fact that many new programs do not arise from sound considerations [. . .], there are other more serious problems. The first problem is that there are many competing versions of what should be done, with each set of proponents equally convinced that their version is the right one. Forceful argument and even the power to make decisions do not at all address questions related to the process of implementation. The fallacy of rationalism is the assumption that the social world can be altered by seemingly logical argument. The problem, as George Bernard Shaw observed, is that 'reformers have the idea that change can be achieved by brute sanity'.

Wise (1977: 45) also describes several examples of excessive rationalization, as when educational outcomes are thoroughly prescribed (e.g. in competency-based education) without any feasible plan of how to achieve them. Wise characterizes the behavior of some policy-makers as wishful thinking: 'When policy makers require by law that schools achieve a goal which in the past they have not achieved, they may be engaged in wishful thinking. Here policy makers behave as though their desires concerning what a school system should accomplish, will, in fact, be accomplished if the policy makers simply decree it'. Wise goes on to argue that even if rational theories of education were better developed – with goals clearly stated, means of implementation set out, evaluation procedures stated – they would not have much of an impact, because schools, like any social organization, do not operate in a rational vacuum. Some may say that they should, but Wise's point is that they do not, and wishing them to do so shows a misunderstanding of the existing culture of the school (see Lortie 1975; Sarason 1982).

In fact it might be more useful to accept the nonrational quality of social systems and move on from there. Patterson, Purkey, and Parker (1986) suggest that organizations in today's society do not follow an orderly logic, but a complex one that is often para- doxical and contradictory, but still understandable and amenable to influence. They contrast the assumptions of the rational conception with those of a nonrational con- ception on five dimensions. *First*, goals: School systems are necessarily guided by mul- tiple and sometimes competing goals [. . .]. *Second*, power: In school systems, power is distributed throughout the organization. *Third*, decision making: This is inevitably a bargaining process to arrive at solutions that satisfy a number of constituencies. *Fourth*, external environment: The public influences school systems in major ways that are unpredictable. *Fifth*, teaching process: There are a variety of situationally appro- priate ways to teach that are effective.

For Patterson and his colleagues the central difference between rational and nonra- tional models lies in their interpretation of reality: Proponents of the rational model believe that a change in 'procedures' will lead to improvement. When their 'if–then' procedures don't work, they become 'if–only' procedures, tightening up rules to influ- ence what is seen as a deficiency in response. Proponents of nonrational models recog- nize that organizations do not behave in a logical, predictable manner, and try to work this to their advantage. Wishing for, waiting for, and urging the system to become more rational is in itself irrational – it won't happen.

Another faulty assumption, ironically, is the problem of how to implement the implementation plan. Many people have responded to the research of the 1970s, which documented implementation problems, by developing elaborate implementation plans designed to take into account factors known to affect success. Designed to help, but actually adding insult to injury, complex implementation plans themselves become another source of confusion and burden on those carrying out change. Levine and Leibert (1987) identify this very problem in their discussion of how to improve improvement plans at the school and district levels. They observe that 'comprehensive or semicomprehensive planning requirements often have the unintended effect of over- loading teachers and administrators' (1987: 398) and provide excuses at the school level by directing blame toward the plan. Among other guidelines, Levine and Leibert suggest: 'Do not overload schools or allow them to overload themselves as part of a futile bureaucratic attempt to "demonstrate" that they are doing everything possible to improve achievement' (1987: 406); and 'assistance from the central office must be fur- nished primarily through technical support from persons, not forms to fill out and dead- lines to meet on paper' (1987: 407). I will discuss specific guidelines for better implementation planning later in this chapter.

In short, implementation planning is itself a process of innovation. Planners, whether a teacher in a coaching project or a leader of a large-scale reform effort, have to combine expertise and knowledge about the direction and nature of the change they are pursuing, with an understanding of and an ability to deal with the factors and strat- egies inherent in the process of change.

Unsolvable problems

More disturbing is the conclusion reached by several people who have attempted to understand or combine theory and practice in their daily work: that some problems are so complex that in the final analysis and final action they are simply not amenable to solution [. . .]. That is not to say that our efforts to solve them cannot be improved. But let us admit the hypothetical possibility that some social problems in a complex diverse society contain innumerable interacting 'causes' that cannot be fully understood. Nor can we necessarily change those factors that we do understand as causes. Further, there is such an overload of problems that it is not possible to solve very many of them with the time, energy, and resources at our disposal.

Wise (1977: 48) refers to the ways in which statements of goals for education frequently ignore this more basic question of whether the goals can be attained: 'To create goals for education is to will that something occur. But goals, in the absence of a theory of how to achieve them, are mere wishful thinking. If there is no reason to believe a goal is attainable – as perhaps evidenced by the fact that it has never been attained – then a rational planning model may not result in goal attainment'.

In solving educational problems, it is not just the number of factors to be understood but the reality that these factors sometimes change during the process; for example, people's attitudes change. [. . .]

There are two issues [here]. The first is that with complex social problems the total number of variables (and their interactive, changing nature) is so large that it is logistically infeasible to obtain all the necessary information, and cognitively impossible for individuals to comprehend the total picture even if the information is available (see Schön 1971: 215). The second is that even if some experts were able to comprehend the total picture themselves, our theories and experiences with meaning and implementation suggest that they would have a devil of a time getting others to act on their knowledge – partly because others will not easily understand the complex knowledge, and partly because the process of implementation contains so many barriers that have nothing to do with the quality of knowledge available.

In sum, to return to the opening paragraph of this section, planning fails partly because of the assumptions of planners and partly because the problems may not be solvable. The hubris of the change agent becomes the nemesis of implementers and others affected by new programs. The first form of hubris occurs when policy-makers assume that the solutions that they have come to adopt are unquestionably the right ones. We have seen that those solutions are bound to be questioned on grounds of competing values or technical soundness.

The second and related form of hubris, which compounds the problem, occurs when planners of change introduce new programs in ways that ignore the factors associated with the process of implementation – factors that are only partly controllable, but that are guaranteed to be out of control if ignored. The more the planners are committed to a particular change, the *less* effective they will be in getting others to implement it if their commitment represents an unyielding or impatient stance in the face of ineluctable problems of implementation. Commitment to a particular program makes it less likely that the planners will set up the necessary time-consuming procedures for implementation, and less likely that they will be open to the transformation of their cherished program and tolerant of the delays that will inevitably occur when other people begin to work with it. If we react to delays and transformations by assuming that they arise from the incompetence or bullheadedness of those implementing the program, we will add one more major barrier to the considerable number already operating. The solution is not to be less committed to what we perceive as needed reforms, but to be more sensitive to the possibility that our version of the change may not be the fully correct one, and to recognize that having good ideas may be less than half the battle compared with establishing a process that will allow us to use the ideas and discover additional ones along the way.

[. . .]

Planning and coping

[. . .]

We have come to the most difficult problem of all. When all is said, what can we actually do to plan for and to cope with educational change? This section contains an overview of the assumptions, elements, and guidelines for action. [. . .] First, I introduce the topic by indicating some of the basic issues and by noting that advice will have to vary according to the different situations in which we find ourselves. Second, I provide some advice for those who find that they are forced to respond to and cope with change introduced by others. Third, the bulk of the section is addressed to the question of how to plan and implement change more effectively.

Change is full of paradoxes. Being deeply committed to a particular change in itself provides no guidelines for attaining the change, and may blind us to the realities of others that would be necessary for transforming and implementing the change effectively. Having no vision at all is what makes for educational bandwagons. In the final analysis, either we have to give up and admit that effective educational change is impossible, or we have to take our best knowledge and attempt to improve our efforts. We possess much knowledge that could make improvement possible. Whether this knowledge gets used is itself a problem of change, part of the infinite regression that, once we have gained some knowledge of the process of change, leads us to ask how we get that knowledge – of the process of change – used or implemented.

[. . .] I do not think that a detailed technical treatment on how to plan for change is the most profitable route to take, although such a treatment may have some benefit. The most beneficial approach consists in our being able to understand the process of change, locate our place in it, and act by influencing those factors that are changeable and by minimizing the power of those that are not. All of this requires a way of thinking about educational change that has not been characteristic of either planners or victims of past change efforts.

In general, there are four logical types of change situations we could face as individuals. These are depicted in Figure 19.1. There are many different specific roles even within a single cell, which cannot be delineated here, but people generally find themselves in one of the four situations depending on whether they are initiating/promoting a change or are on the receiving end, and whether or not they are in authority positions. I start with coping, or being on the receiving end of change (cells III and IV), because this is the most prevalent situation.

Coping with change

Those in situations of having to respond to a particular change should assume neither that it is beneficial nor that it is useless; that much is clear from the previous analysis. The major initial stance should involve *critical assessment* of whether the change is desirable in relation to certain goals and whether it is 'implementable' – in brief, whether it is worth the effort, because it will be an effort if it is at all worthwhile.

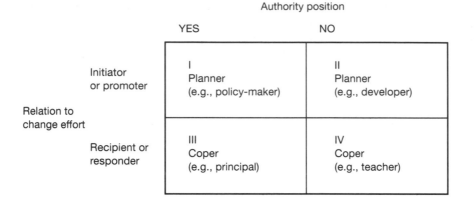

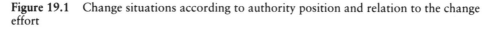

Figure 19.1   Change situations according to authority position and relation to the change effort

Several criteria would be applied: Does the change address an unmet need? Is it a priority in relation to other unmet needs? Is it informed by some desirable sense of vision? Are there adequate (not to say optimal) resources committed to support implementation (technical assistance, leadership support, etc.)? If the conditions are reasonably favorable, knowledge of the change process [. . .] could be used to advantage; for example, pushing for technical assistance, opportunities for interaction among teachers, and so on. If the conditions are not favorable or cannot be made favorable, the best coping strategy consists of knowing enough about the process of change so that we can understand why it doesn't work, and therefore not blame ourselves; we can also gain solace by realizing that most other people are in the same situation of non-implementation. In addition, we can realize that implementation, in any case, cannot be easily monitored; for most educational changes it is quite sufficient to *appear* to be implementing the change, such as by using some of the materials. In sum, the problem is one of developing enough meaning vis-à-vis the change so that we are in a position to implement it effectively or reject it, as the case may be.

Those who are confronted with unwanted change and are in authority positions (cell III) will have to develop different coping mechanisms from those in nonauthority positions (cell IV). For the reader who thinks that resisting change represents irresponsible obstinacy, it is worth repeating that nonimplementable programs and reforms probably do more harm than good when they are attempted. The most responsible action may be to reject innovations that are bound to fail and to work earnestly at those that have a chance to succeed. Besides, in some situations resistance may be the only way to maintain sanity and avoid complete cynicism. In the search for meaning in a particular imposed change situation, we may conclude that there is no meaning, or that the problem being addressed is only one (and not the most important or strategic) of many problems that should be confronted. The basic guideline is to work at fewer innovations, but do them better – because it is probably not desirable, and certainly not humanly possible, to implement all changes expected, given what we know about the time and energy required for effective implementation.

We should feel especially sorry for those in authority positions (middle management in district offices, principals, intermediate government personnel in provincial and state regional offices) who are responsible for leading or seeing to implementation but do not want or do not understand the change – either because it has not been sufficiently developed (and is literally not understandable) or because they themselves have not been involved in deciding on the change or have not received adequate orientation or training. The psychiatrist Ronald Laing captures this situation in what he refers to as a 'knot'.

> There is something I don't know
>   that I am supposed to know.
> I don't know what it is I don't know,
>   and yet am supposed to know,
> And I feel I look stupid
>   if I seem both not to know it
>   and not know *what* it is I don't know.
> Therefore, I pretend I know it.
>   This is nerve-wracking since I don't
>   know what I must pretend to know.
> Therefore, I pretend I know everything.
>   R. D. Laing, *Knots* (1970)

A ridiculous stance to be sure, as painful as it is unsuccessful. It can, of course, be successful in the sense of maintaining the status quo. Depending on one's capacity for self-deception, it can be more or less painful as well. In any case, teachers know when a change is being introduced by or supported by someone who does not believe in it or understand it. Yet this is the position in which many intermediate managers find themselves, or allow themselves to be. Those in authority have a need for meaning too, if for no other reason than the change will be unsuccessful if they cannot convey their meaning of it to others.

Planning and implementing change

The implications for those interested in planning and implementing educational change (cells I and II) are very important, because we would all be better off if changes were introduced more effectively. It is useful to consider these implications according to two interrelated sets of issues: What *assumptions* about change should we note? How can we plan and implement change more effectively?

Assumptions about change

The assumptions we make about change are powerful and frequently subconscious sources of actions. When we begin to understand what change is as people experience it, we begin also to see clearly that assumptions made by planners of change are extremely important determinants of whether the realities of implementation get confronted or ignored. The analysis of change carried out so far leads me to identify 10 'do' and 'don't' assumptions as basic to a successful approach to educational change.

1 Do not assume that your version of what the change should be is the one that should or could be implemented. On the contrary, assume that one of the main purposes of the process of implementation is to *exchange your reality* of what should be

through interaction with implementers and others concerned. Stated another way, assume that successful implementation consists of some transformation or continual development of initial ideas. [. . .]

2 Assume that any significant innovation, if it is to result in change, requires individual implementers to work out their own meaning. Significant change involves a certain amount of ambiguity, ambivalence, and uncertainty for the individual about the meaning of the change. Thus, effective implementation is a *process of clarification*. It is also important not to spend too much time in the early stages on needs assessment, program development, and problem definition activities – school staff have limited time. Clarification is likely to come in large part through *practice* [. . .].

3 Assume that conflict and disagreement are not only inevitable but fundamental to successful change. Since any group of people possess multiple realities, any collective change attempt will necessarily involve conflict. Assumptions 2 and 3 combine to suggest that all successful efforts of significance, no matter how well planned, will experience an implementation dip in the early stages. Smooth implementation is often a sign that not much is really changing [. . .].

4 Assume that people need pressure to change (even in directions that they desire), but it will be effective only under conditions that allow them to react, to form their own position, to interact with other implementers, to obtain technical assistance, etc. Unless people are going to be replaced with others who have different desired characteristics, relearning is at the heart of change.

5 Assume that effective change takes time. It is a process of 'development in use'. Unrealistic or undefined time lines fail to recognize that implementation occurs developmentally. Significant change in the form of implementing specific innovations can be expected to take a minimum of two or three years; bringing about institutional reforms can take five or more years. Persistence is a critical attribute of successful change.

6 Do not assume that the reason for lack of implementation is outright rejection of the values embodied in the change, or hard-core resistance to all change. Assume that there are a number of possible reasons: value rejection, inadequate resources to support implementation, insufficient time elapsed.

7 Do not expect all or even most people or groups to change. The complexity of change is such that it is impossible to bring about widespread reform in any large social system. Progress occurs when we take steps (e.g. by following the assumptions listed here) that *increase* the number of people affected. Our reach should exceed our grasp, but not by such a margin that we fall flat on our face. Instead of being discouraged by all that remains to be done, be encouraged by what has been accomplished by way of improvement resulting from your actions.

8 Assume that you will need a *plan* that is based on the above assumptions and that addresses the factors known to affect implementation (see the section below on guidelines for action). Evolutionary planning and problem-coping models based on knowledge of the change process are essential (Louis and Miles 1990).

9 Assume that no amount of knowledge will ever make it totally clear what action should be taken. Action decisions are a combination of valid knowledge, political considerations, on-the-spot decisions, and intuition. Better knowledge of the change process will improve the mix of resources on which we draw, but it will never and should never represent the sole basis for decision.

10 Assume that changing the culture of institutions is the real agenda, not implementing single innovations. Put another way, when implementing particular innovations, we should always pay attention to whether the institution is developing or not.

Effective planning

Assumptions, whether consciously or unconsciously held, constitute our philosophy of change. The purpose of this section is to make this philosophy more explicit in the forms of the conceptions and skills that underpin successful planning, that is, planning that results in improvement in practice.

In order to engage in successful change, we need to develop a way of thinking about change based on a thorough understanding of the processes [involved]. Such knowledge, once obtained, is far more powerful as a resource than a memorized list of specific steps that we should follow. The fundamental goal for planners is to achieve a feel for the change process and the people in it, which entails a blend of research and experiential knowledge. As Cohen (1987: 485) says, we should 'use research findings to supplement . . . professional experience and wisdom, not to supplant it'. Lindblom and Cohen (1979) make a more complete argument for the necessity of combining knowledge from 'professional inquiry' with what they call 'ordinary knowledge'. Both types of knowledge are necessary for solving problems.

In other words, change is not a fully predictable process. The answer is found not by seeking ready-made guidelines, but by struggling to understand and modify events and processes that are intrinsically complicated, difficult to pin down, and ever changing. Sarason (1971: 217) explains that change agents do not confront their own conceptions of how to go about change and thus do not learn to improve their approaches: 'I confess that I find it somewhat amusing to observe how much thought is given to developing vehicles for changing target groups and how little thought is given to vehicles that protect the agent of change from not changing in his [her] understanding of and approach to that particular instance of change'.

Concentrating on a way of thinking about planning is far from an abstract exercise in theorizing. It helps us identify which factors need to be addressed. It helps us recognize that concentrating on one or two sets of factors while neglecting others is self-defeating. It provides ideas for formulating a 'plan' designed to address and review how these factors are operating in a given instance. I have frequently stated that good ideas, while necessary, are not sufficient for influencing others to change. To the extent that good ideas or visions of change are not combined with equally good conceptualizations of the process of change, the ideas will be wasted. Just as meaning about the substance of change is necessary, so is the development of a sense of meaning and competence about how best to approach it.

Rational planning models, as we have seen, do not work. Patterson, Purkey, and Parker (1986: 61) argue for strategic planning appropriate for the 'nonrational' world of school systems – planning that takes into account ever changing external factors, integrates these with internal organizational conditions, is medium or short range rather than long range, and uses qualitative as well as quantitative data. In their words,

The goal of strategic planning is to produce a stream of wise decisions designed to achieve the mission of the organization. Emphasis shifts from product to process. Just as the planning process builds in flexibility for adaptation to changing conditions in and out of the organization, it also accepts the possibility that the final product may not resemble what was initially intended.

Louis and Miles (1990: 193) provide a clear analysis of this evolutionary planning process in action in their study of urban high schools. They first stress that a small number of themes are interrelated: vision-building, evolutionary planning, resource assistance, and problem-coping. In effective schools these themes feed on each other. The planning theme is the one of interest here.

The evolutionary perspective rests on the assumption that the environment both inside and outside organizations is often chaotic. No specific plan can last for very long, because it will either become outmoded due to changing external pressures, or because disagreement over priorities arises within the organization. Yet, there is no reason to assume that the best response is to plan passively, relying on incremental decisions. Instead, the organization can cycle back and forth between efforts to gain normative consensus about what it may become, to plan strategies for getting there, and to carry out decentralized incremental experimentation that harnesses the creativity of all members to the change effort.

This approach is evolutionary in the sense that, although the mission and image of the organization's ideal future may be based on a top-level analysis of the environment and its demands, strategies for achieving the mission are frequently reviewed and refined based on internal scanning for opportunities and successes. Strategy is viewed as a flexible tool, rather than a semi-permanent expansion of the mission.

Louis and Miles (1990) draw several key conclusions from the cases.

- Effective evolutionary planning must be built on the direct involvement of the principal or some other key leader in the school (1990: 199).
- Action precedes planning as much as follows it: 'In "depressed schools" one of the few ways of building commitment to a reform program is for successful action to occur that actualizes hope for genuine change. Effective action . . . often stimulates an interest in planning rather than vice versa' (1990: 204).
- Multiple themes often precede mission statements: 'The more successful of our schools had no *a priori* mission statements. Instead, multiple improvement efforts coalesced around a theme or set of themes only after the activity had begun' (1990: 206). In one school, for example, initial themes focused on improvements in facilities and climate; moved to serve the needs of the whole student, incorporating social service agencies; and shifted gradually to a general vision.
- It is best to start small, experiment, and expand the successful while contracting the less successful: 'The objective of evolutionary planning is to capitalize on the "low risk" quality of smaller scale innovation to increase certainty. This in turn increases motivation and the possibility of concerted, more 'tightly coupled' action across the school' (1990: 211). This approach also 'permits schools to take advantage of unanticipated opportunities' (1990: 210–11).
- Leadership-dominated early planning must shift to shared control with teachers and others. The control base expands as evolutionary planning unfolds (1990: 214).

While Louis and Miles' focus is at the school level, the principles of effective planning are being found and advocated in a wide range of organizations in business

(Morgan 1989; Peters 1987) and in school systems (Crandall *et al.* 1986; Patterson *et al.* 1986). Complex change means facing a paradox. On the one hand, the greater the complexity, the greater the need to address implementation planning; on the other hand, the greater the thoroughness of implementation planning, the more complex the change process becomes. People get better at the change process by continuously acting and reflecting on the principles of effective implementation planning.

[. . .]

References

Cohen, M. (1987) Improving school effectiveness, in V. Kochler (ed.) *Handbook of Research on Teaching.* New York: Longman.

Crandall, D., Eiseman, J. and Louis, K. (1986) Strategic planning issues that bear on the success of school improvement efforts. *Educational Administration Quarterly,* 22(3): 21–53.

Laing, R. D. (1970) *Knots.* London: Tavistock.

Levine, D. and Leibert, R. E. (1987) Improving school improvement plans. *The Elementary School Journal,* 87(4): 397–412.

Lighthall, F. (1973) Multiple realities and organisational nonsolutions. *School Review,* February: 255–87.

Lindblom, C. and Cohen, D. (1979) *Usable Knowledge.* New Haven, CT: Yale University Press.

Lortie, D. (1975) *School Teacher: a Sociological Study.* Chicago: University of Chicago Press.

Louis, K. and Miles, M. B. (1990) *Improving the Urban High School.* New York: Teachers College Press.

Morgan, G. (1989) *Riding the Waves of Change.* San Francisco: Jossey Bass.

Patterson, J., Purkey, S. and Parker, J. (1986) *Productive School Systems for a Non-rational World,* Alexandria, VA: Association for Supervision and Curriculum Development.

Peters, T. (1987) *Thriving on Chaos.* New York: A. Knopf.

Sarason, S. (1971) *The Culture of the School and the Problem of Change.* Boston: Allyn & Bacon.

Sarason, S. (1982) *The Creation of Settings and the Future Societies.* San Francisco: Jossey Bass.

Schön, D. (1971) *Beyond the Stable State.* New York: Norton.

Wise, A. (1977) Why education policies often fail: the hyper-rationalisation hypothesis. *Curriculum Studies,* 9(1): 43–57.

Wise, A. (1979) *Legislated Learning.* Berkeley, CA: University of California Press.

Wise, A. (1988) The two conflicting trends in school reform. *Phi Delta Kappan,* 69(5): 328–33.

20 | Perspectives on educational change*

GEVA M. BLENKIN, GWYN EDWARDS AND A. V. KELLY

[. . .]

It is doubtful whether any one typology can successfully encapsulate all the phenomena with which it is concerned but we suggest that attempts to promote, research and analyse educational change are most adequately represented within the following six perspectives: the technological; the cultural; the micropolitical; the biographical; the structural; the sociohistorical.

Each perspective has its own implicit assumptions concerning the nature of change, of schools as institutions and of human agency. It would be wrong to assume that any one perspective offers a privileged or more accurate interpretation of how change occurs, how change could be more effectively promoted or how change is explained in educational institutions; descriptively, prescriptively and analytically they all have their merits and limitations. Neither should the perspectives be treated as discrete entities. Although each offers a unique set of insights into the change process, they clearly overlap and interrelate. They function, primarily, not as descriptors of empirical reality but as important heuristic devices in seeking to understand the nature and process of educational change.

The technological perspective

The technological perspective emerged as the dominant means of conceptualizing and initiating change during the 1960s as the 'unplanned drift' of earlier years gave way to a more rational and systematic approach, . . . which assume[s] schools to be rational organizations that are 'readily manipulated and easily changed' (Lieberman and Rosenholtz 1987: 81). Teachers themselves are, at best, perceived as 'rational adopters' who

*This material has been edited and was originally published as Chapter 2, 'Educational change: a theoretical overview' in *Change and the Curriculum*.

will readily recognize the value of, and therefore implement, the proposals they are offered or, at worst, are treated as 'stoneage obstructionists' who have to be 'neutralized' through the use of teacher-proof materials (Ponder and Doyle: 1977).

Adherents to this perspective view the process of curriculum change as a form of instrumental action concerned with finding the most effective and efficient means of bringing about prestated intentions. Central to the perspective is the logic of technical rationality, an epistemology of practice derived from positivist philosophy which maintains that problems of practice are technical in character and that practitioners, therefore, are first and foremost instrumental problem solvers. Thus, in an educational context, professional practice is directed towards the resolution of well-formed instrumental problems through the systematic application of the theories and techniques of the empirical sciences (Schön 1983: 1987). Closely associated with technical rationality – if not synonymous – is its bureaucratic counterpart, defined by MacIntyre (1985) as 'the rationality of matching means to ends economically and efficiently' (op. cit.: 25).

[. . .]

In Western industrial societies so entrenched is technical rationality and so pervasive the discourse it generates that it becomes difficult to conceive, let alone actualize, alternative forms of social and institutional life. The consequence of this for educational practice is neatly summarized by Giroux. He states:

> The growing removal of curriculum development and analysis from the hands of teachers is related to the ways technocratic rationality is used to redefine teachers' work. This type of rationality increasingly takes place within a social division of labour in which thinking is removed from implementation and the model of the teacher becomes that of the technician or white-collar clerk. [. . .]
>
> (Giroux 1989: 180)

As well as its underpinning logic of technical rationality, the technological perspective has a number of other major deficiencies. First, it is assumed that innovators and classroom practitioners construe practice in the same way. Consequently, there is a failure to recognize and make allowance for the inevitable 'slippage' between the original conception of an innovation or policy initiative and the interpretation of it at the site of implementation. Second, the ideas of innovators or policy-makers are considered to be inherently superior to those of classroom practitioners. Teachers are perceived merely as 'cogs in the wheel' and their role is reduced to that of 'production line technocrats'. Third, important features of schools as organizations tend to be missed, obscured or downplayed. The established systems of meaning that exist in schools are invariably disregarded and any adverse reaction to innovation is typified, with negative connotations, as resistance to change. [. . .] Fourth, the technological perspective embodies a limited and, in our opinion, distorting view of the curriculum. The curriculum is seen as a tangible product that can be planned and constructed independent of its transactional context. It is therefore assumed that to effect change involves little more than a change of product. Indeed, this assumption was explicit in the early work of the Schools Council. [. . .] And, we would argue, similar simplistic assumptions are inherent in the thoughts and actions of those who support the imposition on schools of centrally prescribed curricula.

It might be implied from what we have said so far that from a technological perspective attempts to change schools are invariably through the initiatives of agencies external to the school. This is not necessarily the case. It is the logic which informs the procedures through which change is effected, rather than the locus of initiative, that characterizes the technological perspective. Thus, related to this perspective are those *internally* initiated approaches to change which emphasize the school as a functional organization which can be improved through the systematic application of prespecified procedures. Holt (1987) cites strategies such as organization development (OD) and Guidelines for Review and Institutional Development (GRIDS) as examples.

[. . .]

[Technological change] strategies have achieved limited success – at least in terms of take-up – in educational systems. A number of theories have been forwarded to account for this lack of success. [. . .]

Rosario provides a succinct summary of the alternative explanations that have been advanced to account for the phenomenon of resistance to [change in schools]

> [. . .] some look to individual psychology, pointing to such personality-maintain-ing factors as habit, selective perception, insecurity, and so on. Others argue that the reasons for resistance are more related to the nature of schools as formal organizations. For these, schools are complex social systems whose properties make them virtually impenetrable to change. Such properties include domestica-tion, role invisibility, situational imperatives and loose coupling, among others. Still others maintain that the problem of school resistance is traceable to cultural features of the school. Schools in this case are seen as cultural entities in them-selves, with norms, rules and behavioral regularities that function to inhibit change.
>
> (Rosario 1986: 39)

Resistance then can be explained, not as some generalized institutional characteristic or individual disposition, but as a consequence of a complex interplay of biographical, organizational or cultural factors. These perspectives will be examined [. . .] in the course of this chapter.

The cultural perspective

This perspective, in contrast to the technological, treats educational organizations as cultural entities, as 'complex social organizations held together by a symbolic webbing rather than a formal system driven by goals, official roles, commands and rules' (Deal 1990: 7). Whilst the technological perspective emphasizes the management of change, the cultural perspective is more concerned with its meaning (Rudduck 1986a). It locates and examines the process of change within the sociocultural milieu of educational prac-tice and one of its central concerns is 'the meaning of teaching to teachers and the origins of those meanings' (Feiman-Nemser and Floden 1986: 505). Its basic premise implies that 'innovation cannot be assimilated unless its meaning is shared' (Marris 1974: 113).

[. . .]

[S]chool culture is perceived as having both an interpretative and normative func-tion. It provides the contextual clues through which events and actions are interpreted by institutional members and, simultaneously, it regulates the way they are expected to behave. Culture gives meaning and purpose to human endeavour by providing a degree of stability, certainty and predictability (Deal 1987). And, as we will discuss later in this chapter, the norms, beliefs and values that constitute this culture provide the framework both within and through which teachers construct, legitimate and preserve their professional identities.

Words and terms used in defining culture – 'standard practices', 'shared expectations', 'core values', 'regularities', etc. – seem to imply that cultures are homogeneous entities, persistent over time and space. This is clearly not true of cultures in general nor of school cultures in particular. Admittedly, the nature of schooling is such that teachers do, to a significant extent, share a common occupational culture. But, as Feiman-Nemser and Floden (1986: 50) argue, 'the assumption of cultural uniformity is . . . untenable', for teachers, in terms of age, experience, sociocultural background, ethnicity, gender and personal circumstances, display diverse characteristics. Nor are the schools they occupy homogeneous. Among other things, they vary in size, situation, architecture, pupils' age range, and internal organization. Consequently [. . .] there are considerable variations both between and within schools in the uniformity of their cultures. Rather than homogeneous entities, schools are sites where a number of different cultures intersect and interact. [. . .] Moreover, cultures are, to varying degrees, dynamic. Schools have witnessed considerable change in their technologies and social relationships and, while substantive changes in the deeper meanings of schooling may be less apparent, the cultural perspective at least acknowledges the possibility of such transformations.

Nor are the norms, beliefs and values that constitute school cultures all of equal significance. Corbett et al. (1987) draw an important distinction between norms that are 'sacred' and those that are 'profane' [. . .]. The former are 'essentially immutable' (Rossman et al. 1988: 10): the teachers' bottom line. Changes that challenge these norms 'represent attacks on professional raison d'être, on the cornerstones of teachers' constructions of reality' (op. cit.: 12). Consequently such changes may be met initially with 'forthright resistance' (Corbett et al. 1987: 36) and, if the challenge persists, with 'the creation of a culture of opposition' (ibid.). By comparison, profane norms are less deeply embedded and, 'although occupying strategic positions in the day-to-day world' (Rossman et al. 1988: 11), are susceptible to change, some more so than others.

This distinction provides a useful basis for reconceptualizing a number of aspects of educational change, particularly the phenomenon of resistance. Resistance to change can now be explained as a lack of congruence between the existing school culture and the culture embedded in the change proposals. As Rudduck (1986b: 7) observes, 'in our efforts to change I think we have generally underestimated the power of the existing culture of the school and classroom to accommodate, absorb or expel innovations that are at odds with the dominant structures and values that hold habit in place'. The distinction [. . .] implies that the more congruent an innovation is with a school's prevailing culture – or, conversely, the less it challenges the sacred norms – the greater are its chances of being successfully implemented. [. . .]

A number of researchers focus more specifically on the occupational culture of teaching and attempt to assess the implications of their findings for curriculum change. Of particular significance is the work of Lortie (1975). He describes the occupational culture of teaching as individualistic, present-oriented and conservative. In summarizing Lortie's work, Hargreaves (1989: 54) claims that 'teachers avoid long term planning and collaboration with their colleagues and resist involvement in whole school policy-making in favour of gaining marginal improvements in time and resources to make their own individual classroom work easier'. Other research confirms Lortie's findings, indicating that teachers in most schools remain isolated from one another and rarely discuss their classroom practices or seek collegial solutions to classroom problems (Heckman 1987). This cult of privatism is reinforced by a work ethic that expects teachers to demonstrate a high degree of competency working in classrooms on their own. This expectation is hardly conducive to risk-taking, especially for those practitioners in the process of establishing their credibility in the profession. This syndrome reinforces itself. It has been shown that teachers are often reluctant to request assistance, or even to discuss their work, in the fear that this may be interpreted as a disclosure of professional inadequacy (Rosenholtz 1985). Thus, cultures 'conspire to maintain the *status quo*' (Heckman 1987: 77) and for many teachers the classroom becomes a sanctuary, 'preserved and protected through . . . isolation and a hesitancy of parents, administrators and other teachers to violate it' (Bullough 1987: 93).

Privatism is reinforced by the egg-crate architectural structures of schools, with isolated and insulated classroom compartments, and by cellular patterns of organization (Lortie 1975). Weick (1976) characterizes schools as 'loosely coupled systems' in which each element is attached but retains some identity and separateness. While these structures ensure a degree of autonomy for organizational members, they reduce the potential for collaborative action. [. . .]

· The centrality of the classroom in the occupational culture of teaching is an interesting and well-documented phenomenon. Research suggests that teachers rely almost exclusively on practical classroom experience as the main source of their professional knowledge and give little credence to formal educational theory (Hargreaves 1984). It is claimed that teachers' psychic rewards come largely from classroom interactions with pupils (Lortie 1975) despite, it seems, the apparent antagonistic nature of these interactions. Even when opportunities arise for teachers to engage collaboratively with colleagues, many show a marked reluctance to do so. [. . .]

Once the cultural realities of schools are recognized it is possible to conceptualize the process of change in a more sophisticated way. The cultural norms that inform the practice of teachers are deeply rooted but, to a large extent, implicit and intuitive. As Erickson (1987: 18) argues, 'it is precisely that which makes intuitive sense to someone that is evidence of some aspect of the individual's cultural system'. Teachers are too familiar with the cultural norms of their occupation to appreciate the hold they exercise over them. They are blinded by familiarity in the way that the fish, presumably, is the last creature to understand the nature of water. Professional understanding can be enhanced, however, through procedures which help teachers confront the norms embedded in their practice. This requires procedures which distance teachers from their taken-for-granted realities. The familiar has to be made strange. The key to promoting change is through the establishment of collaborative cultures, based on the principles of collegiality, openness and trust (Lieberman and Miller 1990), for 'schools cannot be improved without people working together' (Lieberman 1986: 6). In such cultures a norm prevails 'that favors the thoughtful, explicit examination of practices and their consequences' (Little 1990: 522). In Porter's view (1987: 150), collaborative practices 'break down teacher isolation and give credence to their ideas; make them more receptive to and analytical with new ideas; increase professional confidence; [and] strengthen commitment to the improvement of practice'.

Little (1990) distinguishes between different kinds of teachers' collegial relations on an independent–interdependent continuum. At the independent end collegial relations are confined to 'story telling and scanning for ideas'. While story telling may have some cathartic value, it remains doubtful whether it contributes much to teachers' professional understanding. Moving towards the interdependence end of the continuum, collegial relations become more interactive through 'aid and assistance' and 'sharing'. The greatest degree of interdependence, however, is achieved through 'joint work'. Little (op. cit.: 519) reserves this term for 'encounters among teachers that rest on shared responsibility for the work of teaching (interdependence), collective conceptions of autonomy, support for teachers' initiative and leadership with regard to professional practice, and group affiliations grounded in professional work'. This again implies that substantive change in the curriculum is contingent upon a fundamental reorientation in school culture. As Deal (1990: 9) observes, 'schools will become fundamentally different only when we quit correcting surface deficiencies and recognize that transformation involves a collective renegotiation of historically anchored myths, metaphors and meanings'.

It is doubtful, though, whether collaboration in itself is enough to guarantee significant change in classroom practice. As currently practised, collaboration is largely voluntary and often focuses on those areas of school life that are generally peripheral and uncontested. Alternatively, collaboration may operate at the level of policy-making with policy implementation being carried out on an individual basis. Collaboration, then, is not an end in itself but an important prerequisite to the development of 'a culture of inquiry' (Lieberman and Miller 1990). It is the disposition to enquiry rather than collaboration *per se* that provides the catalyst for change. [. . .]

The micropolitical perspective

A number of writers argue that the perspectives so far examined provide inadequate accounts of schools and, by implication, of the processes that take place within them, including change. These perspectives tend to treat schools as homogeneous entities, thus masking important internal conflicts and tensions. The cultural perspective does acknowledge the possibility of subcultures but these are often perceived as being subordinate to an all-pervasive dominant culture. It continues to privilege consensus over conflict as an explanatory device. Ironically, the move towards more collaborative cultures often has the effect of making the micropolitics of schools more visible. Conflicting interests are often an expression of the competing subculture ideologies 'with proponents of competing views each holding their own to serve the best interest of students' (Little 1990: 521). In collaborative cultures deeply held beliefs – the sacred norms – are more likely to be exposed. It is perhaps in order to minimize conflict that collaboration tends to focus on those areas of school life that are largely peripheral and uncontested. From a cultural perspective collaboration is perceived as a desirable end in itself; from a micropolitical perspective questions are raised concerning the ends and interests it serves.

Hoyle (1982: 88) contends that 'politics is inevitably concerned with interests'. For him, micropolitics 'embraces those strategies by which individuals and groups in organizational contexts use their resources of power and influence to further their interests' (ibid.). Thus, from a micropolitical perspective, the distribution and utilization of power in educational institutions becomes the crucial issue in attempting to understand the process of change. Schools and departments within them are viewed as 'arenas of struggle'. As various factions pursue their conflicting interests, bargains are struck, alliances formed and compromises made. Ideological differences and conflicting interests are brought to the surface when attempts to promote change are instigated.

The micropolitics of schools are manifested, primarily, in and through those aspects of institutional life concerned with the control of territory, the distribution of resources, the acquisition of status and participation in the decision-making process. These provide the material, symbolic and discursive resources and power through which interests can be pursued.

From a micropolitical perspective change is seen as potentially – perhaps inherently – destabilizing in that it invariably leads to a rearrangement of the power relationships between individuals and groups. And, as micropolitical research highlights, often 'desired changes fall short because they threaten the balance of power, create opposing coalitions and trigger conflict' (Deal 1987: 7). Ball (1987: 40) draws attention to the fact that 'change in policy should not be confused with change in practice. In the micropolitics of the school it is often the former which is at stake, although micro-political strategies may also be deployed to promote or defend the other'. Moreover, research shows that in a school the same change may have contradictory effects by increasing the power, both real and perceived, of some groups and rendering others virtually powerless. As Sparkes (1989: 105) observes, in the process of innovation 'some teachers will define themselves as winners, some as losers and some as sideliners'.

From a micropolitical perspective, subject departments are seen as a most significant organizational and political division within the secondary school (Ball 1989). Usually, but not always, they confer on their members a sense of common identity in relation to space, epistemology and pedagogy; some more than others. The relative status and power of departments is, at the same time, a consequence of, and reflected in, the curricular structure of the school. [. . .]

It would be misleading to imply that subject departments are homogeneous units based on collegiate principles and shared values. They have their own divisions and conflicts and [. . .] when engaged in innovation they are not immune from internecine strife. Furthermore, Dalton (1988) demonstrates how, in a humanities department, differences of ideology and personality rather than subject allegiances tended to be the main source of conflict. Neither should it be assumed that in secondary schools the subject department is the main unit to which teachers belong. At a generalized level this may be the case, but from a micropolitical perspective it is important to recognize that teachers' allegiances are often to diverse constituencies. Allegiances to particular educational ideologies may transcend subject department boundaries. In most secondary schools teachers have commitments across the academic–pastoral divide. Some have teaching responsibilities in more than one subject department. Socially, teachers' strongest allegiance may be to colleagues from other departments, forged perhaps through commonality in age and experience, mutual interests or collective involvement in extracurricular activities. In schools, faced with the demands of diverse allegiances, the maintenance of an institutional 'even keel' requires of its members the exercise of considerable political acumen.

[. . .]

The micropolitical perspective provides no clear blueprint for bringing about change in schools, although it does provide useful insight into some of the inherent difficulties. Its contribution to our understanding of the process of change has been largely empirical and somewhat pessimistic. It offers no prescription other than the possibility of devising strategies for uniting factions around common goals. But once the micropolitical realities of schools are recognized, the pursuit of consensus and collegiality as democratic ideals has to be recognized as practically problematic. In sites characterized by value pluralism and unequal access to power, compromise rather than consensus prevails, and as compromise generally favours the powerful and privileged the status quo is maintained (Edwards 1992). However, on a more optimistic note, it is well worth remembering that, in the words of MacIntyre (1985: 164), 'it is through conflict and sometimes only through conflict that we learn what our ends and purposes are'.

The biographical perspective

The biographical perspective emphasizes the way in which change impinges upon the lives and careers of practitioners and how the two phenomena interact. It is centrally concerned with examining change in relation to the biographical experiences of individual practitioners, in terms of their hopes, aspirations, fears, commitments, beliefs and values. Appropriate research involves no less than getting inside the heads of practitioners to gain access to their thought processes in order to interpret the world from their perspective. Its analytical frameworks include personal construct and social interactionist theory; its methodologies utilize interview, questionnaire and observation and, more recently, autobiography, narrative and story.

It is now widely recognized that the success of curriculum innovation, whether internally or externally initiated, is contingent upon the professional development of teachers. Yet we have limited understanding of the teacher characteristics associated with the successful implementation of innovation (Stein and Wang 1988; Rudduck 1988). The tendency has been to examine the process of innovation at the institutional rather than the individual level. As Rudduck (op. cit.: 208) points out, 'dealing with the individual's reaction to the possibility to change is not something that has attracted much attention in the literature of educational innovation'. Huberman (1988: 199) makes a similar observation: 'each innovation has been construed as a time-bound process, with little concern being shown for the prior and subsequent careers of the actors involved'.

The occupational context of teachers' lives is characterized by multi-dimensionality, simultaneity and unpredictability [. . .]. It is a context in which the self is constantly at risk. For example, confrontation with difficult pupils diminishes teachers' sense of efficacy (Webb and Ashton 1987) and, by implication, their self-esteem. It is not surprising, therefore, that teachers expend considerable energy in the classroom attempting to minimize confrontational situations. The need to preserve a sense of self is, understandably, a strong determinant in the way teachers behave. The adherence to tried and tested strategies offers them a degree of reassuring stability and control.

The culture which permeates schools provides the normative beliefs and values through which individuals construct a sense of reality and a sense of self. Substantive change is inherently destabilizing because it challenges these largely taken-for-granted structures of meaning and, by implication, threatens the professional identities of teachers. Change also affects their career opportunities and aspirations and may undermine their ideological commitments. The more radical the change the greater the degree of destabilization.

From a biographical perspective, resistance to change can be explained as a psychological reaction to this loss of meaning. Marris (1974: 8) claims that 'there is a deep-seated impulse in all of us to defend the validity of what we have learned, for without it we would be helpless'. This he describes as 'the conservative impulse'. Any event that brings about a change in personal identity involves feelings of loss, anxiety and conflict. The effect is akin to grieving which Marris describes as 'the psychological process of adjustment to loss' (op. cit.: 4).

[. . .]

Marris's work provides a useful framework for re-examining and, possibly, reinter-preting the change literature. Innovations that are consistent with the belief systems of teachers are readily assimilated into their prevailing 'structures of interpretation'. More radical innovations involve a loss of meaning which triggers 'the conservative impulse' and leads to 'grieving'. Therefore, 'teachers resist changes that do not make sense to them' (Heckman 1987: 67). Research seems to support this interpretation. Innovations are often construed in familiar terms by practitioners and assimilated into their pre-vailing structures of meaning, rather than being allowed to pose a fundamental chal-lenge to them. [. . .]

In recent years increasing attention has been given to the phenomenon of teacher stress. The occupational stress of teaching is described by Kyriacou (1987: 146) as 'the experience . . . of unpleasant emotions, such as tension, frustration, anxiety, anger and depression, resulting from aspects of work as a teacher'. These emotions, similar to those experienced during the grieving process as identified by Marris (1974), are debil-itating to human growth and, by implication, constitute a formidable barrier to change. Lauer and Lauer (1973) provide an interesting analysis of the relationship between change and stress. Following Shibutani (1961: 522), they contend that 'the definition of the situation, the self-concept and the reference group are the social psychological bases for human behaviour'. For the teacher the unpredictability of the reference group, that is 'the audience before which he [sic] tries to maintain his self-respect' (ibid.), could be seen as a particular source of stress. According to Lauer and Lauer, the main cause of stress is not change *per se* but the rate and kind of change. Rapid change generates greater stress in that it undermines the psychological bases of behaviour. However, stress is reduced if the change is perceived by those it affects as controllable and desir-able. Other research seems to support this claim. Evidence indicates that teachers who perceive the 'locus of control' in their lives as external experience more stress (Kyria-cou 1987).

The implications of this are far reaching. In order to minimize the stress on teachers it is essential that they are given greater control over the pace and direction of change. Currently in Britain the reverse is happening. [. . .] Teachers are now required to 'deliver' a centrally determined curriculum and to assess pupils in relation to criteria they had no say in formulating, using tests they have little say in devising. Moreover, schools are expected to respond rapidly and unquestioningly to every idiosyncratic change in government policy. The conditions under which teachers now practise are, therefore, highly inductive of stress. [. . .]

Goodson (1991) argues that attempts to understand and promote change from a bio-graphical perspective have focused too narrowly on the classroom practice of teachers. He argues on strategic and substantive grounds for 'a broadening of focus to allow detailed scrutiny of the teacher's life and work' (op. cit.: 39). There is a respectable and growing body of research available on teachers' lives and careers [. . .] as told by the teachers themselves. This work provides a framework for examining the responses of teachers to change within the wider context of their personal and professional lives. [. . .]

Research, using life history method, suggests that during their career cycle teachers pass through a number of discrete stages or phases, characterized by different attitudes, perceptions, concerns, expectations, commitments, etc. Sikes (1985), following Levinson, identifies a number of age-group phases. Similarly, Measor (1985) identifies a number of 'intrinsic critical phases' within the natural progression of the teachers' careers. Huberman (1988) examines the career cycle of teachers more explicitly in relation to attempts at school improvement. His research [. . .] implies that teachers' careers consist of a number of identifiable phases or stages which are passed through sequentially. [. . .] [F]rom phase to phase the commitment of teachers to innovation varies. In general, having consolidated their basic repertoires teachers enter a phase where the willingness and energy to innovate is at its strongest. At the latter stage of a career teachers may enter a phase characterized by 'a pulling back, a narrowing of interests, a diminution of the energy available for collective innovations' (op. cit.: 130). The reasons for this vary. For some it represents a 'natural' refocusing, for others 'disenchantment' through the failure of past innovations. And a further group had resisted innovation in the past and, in their remaining years, could derive some satisfaction from activities not yet corrupted. The implication of Huberman's findings, and of career cycle research in general, is clear. If a change initiative is 'out of phase' with an individual's career it is likely to be either ignored or resisted.

From a biographical perspective change is contingent upon the professional development of individual practitioners carried out within the context of their wider psychological needs; their hopes, fears, aspirations, etc. The success of an innovation is dependent upon the material and psychological support that individuals and groups are given in constructing new sets of meaning. Innovation is synonymous with learning, and learning is often a painful process. It involves, indeed requires, a certain level of dissonance. The extent to which the dissonance which accompanies change is creative or destructive depends on how it is perceived and experienced by individuals. For effective learning to take place teachers need to feel 'in control of change' rather than to feel 'controlled by change'. In the words of Rudduck (1988: 210), 'If we are interested in substantial change, we may need to find structures and resources to help teachers to reexamine their purposes . . . slough off the sediment of socialization, and feel more in control of their professional purposes and direction'.

It is important to realize that the structures of meaning through which teachers interpret their work are not idiosyncratic; they are social constructions mediated through the occupational cultures and discourses within which teachers' practices are located. These in turn are located within and sustained by wider social, political and cultural structures and discourses. It is these structures that we will now examine.

The structural perspective

The structural perspective has a long history but has undergone numerous revisions and additions over time. Central to this perspective is the assumption that the process of schooling is embedded in, and a reflection of, wider economic, social and political structures. One view sees education as the hegemonous means by which these structures are legitimated and 'reproduced' within capitalist modes of production. Within this view there is an element of structural determinism which denies or minimizes the possibility of human agency. However, the structures that impinge on the work of teachers operate at a number of levels and in different ways. At the macro level there are those social, economic, and political structures that are part of Western industrialized society itself. These find their most explicit expression in the educational policies of national or state governments. During the 1980s and continuing into the 1990s, Britain has witnessed a marked swing to the right of the political spectrum in both social and educational policy-making. This appears to be consistent with a general trend within Western capitalist societies as they endeavour to readjust to the demands of an emerging post-industrial social and economic order. Across the Western world political parties, conservative and socialist alike, are now defining education primarily in terms of producing an 'educated' and flexible workforce through the inculcation in young people of those skills and dispositions which are perceived to be necessary in order for them to respond to post-Fordian modes of production and consumption. Central to these policies are discourses which objectify the human subject as producer and consumer and reduce education to a marketable commodity.

[. . .]

At the level of the school and the classroom – what Ball (1987) terms the meso level – another set of structures, over which teachers have limited control, comes into play. And, it could be argued, these structures themselves are structurally determined. They include the implementation of national and local government policies, resources, group sizes, pupil and parent expectations, wider social expectations, including those related to employment, and examination requirements. Further constraints are imposed by the kind, length and quality of initial and in-service education. Teachers often give the impression that, from their perspective, the major structural constraint on their work is that of time. Teachers, then, do not operate as free agents but within the constraints imposed by these structures. The degree of freedom that teachers can exercise in the school and classroom is not necessarily determined by the structures themselves but by how they are perceived by the teachers. And these perceptions in turn are ideologically structured. What is a frustrating constraint for one teacher is a golden opportunity for another.

The relationship between structure and agency is complex and has been the focus of a long-standing academic debate. It is not our intention to rehearse that debate here. However, we consider that a recognition of these structures, and an appreciation of the ways teachers respond to them, is imperative to an understanding of the process of change. Too often failure to bring about change is laid, uncritically and unfairly, at the teacher's door. It alerts us also to the dangers of accepting too readily over-deterministic explanations of teacher behaviour. For example, it has been argued [. . .] that the individualistic tendencies of teachers may not be a pathological response to the uncertainties of their profession – as is frequently assumed – but an 'adaptive strategy [which] protects the time and energy required to meet immediate instructional demands' (Flinders 1988: 25). Following Flinders, Hargreaves (1990) takes a similar line and suggests that teacher individualism could be explained as 'a rational economizing of effort and ordering of priorities in a highly pressed and constraining working environment' (Hargreaves 1990a: 9).

Despite the constraints imposed by structures beyond their immediate control, teachers in Britain until recently enjoyed a level of autonomy not shared by their American and continental European counterparts. This of course has now changed. Giltin (1987) provides a salutary account of the effect that mandated curricula and compulsory testing have had on teacher behaviour in the USA. These structures are often manifested in a 'rationalized curriculum form' of sequential behavioural objectives such as GEMS (goal-based educational management system) and IGE (individually guided education). In Giltin's view, this kind of structure 'makes it necessary for teachers to spend a great deal of their time using technical skills: skills which give teachers the control and precision necessary efficiently to deliver bits of information to students and increase test scores' (1987: 112). Thus, teachers develop a repertoire of narrow technical skills which, when used often enough, become habitual and 'assume a greater place within the teaching role' (ibid.). The lessons from this are clear and do not need to be spelt out by us.

[. . .]

A number of theorists have examined change from an ecological perspective, notably Goodlad (1987a). The ecological perspective shares many of the assumptions of the structural and cultural perspectives but attempts to resolve some of the deficiencies inherent in these. It also highlights the interdependence of the structural and cultural dimensions of change. From this perspective, teachers' reaction to change proposals 'is seen as an outgrowth of efforts to meet environmental demands imposed by the distinctive ecology of the classroom' (Doyle and Ponder 1977: 5). Their behaviour therefore represents 'a set of adaptive responses which have utility in negotiating classroom contingencies' (ibid.). By seeing teachers' responses to structural constraints as adaptive rather than determined, it envisages a greater degree of human agency in the process of change.

Perhaps the most powerful and pervasive structures that impinge on the work of teachers and influence the extent and direction of curriculum change are those of curriculum and assessment. As we have already seen, the culture of teaching and teachers' occupational identities derive from these structures, and it is in relation to and through these structures that the micropolitics of schools are often played out. It is to a closer examination of these structures that we now turn.

The sociohistorical perspective

In recent years, following the seminal work of Ivor Goodson (1981; 1983), considerable attention has been directed towards an examination of curriculum from a sociohistorical perspective. This perspective offers a useful framework for analysing and interpreting the process of curriculum change. Expressed simply, it represents an attempt to understand 'where subjects came from and why they were as they were' (Goodson 1987: viii). [. . .] His [. . .] analysis is centred on three working hypotheses:

1 Subjects are not monolithic entities but shifting amalgamations of subgroups and traditions.

2 In the process of establishing a school there is a tendency for subject-based subject groups to move from promoting pedagogic and utilitarian traditions towards the academic tradition.

3 In case studies much of the curriculum debate can be interpreted in terms of conflict between subjects over status, resources and territory.

These hypotheses provided the basis for Goodson's (1981) own sociohistorical analysis of geography as an academic discipline and school subject and have been utilized by a number of researchers undertaking similar analyses in other areas of the curriculum (Goodson and Ball 1984; Goodson 1985). They provide a framework for researching and analysing the various elements of the curriculum and how these elements interrelate both in their current manifestations and over time. Consequently, sociohistorical analyses have made a significant contribution to curriculum studies and offer important insights into the process of change. These analyses help explain the persistence of a monolithic academic subject-based curriculum against which the hopes of many innovations have been dashed. They also offer an explanation of the somewhat ambivalent response of the educational establishment to the National Curriculum.

Curriculum histories show that academic subject communities are living cultures through which many teachers construct and express their occupational and personal identities. When a teacher says 'I'm a geographer' or 'I'm a historian' more is implied than a statement about the subject he/she teaches. It is a reiteration of allegiance to a collective learning community which confers upon its members a sense of competence and status and reinforces in an individual a particular view of his/her occupational and existential self.

Moreover, as we have already noted, subjects are closely related to the material base of teachers' occupational and personal lives; their social standings and career prospects are closely linked to the fortunes of their subject. It is not surprising, therefore, that subject subcultures are often the source of micropolitical rivalries and conflicts. The school curriculum, as a sociohistorical construct, is inherently political and the promotion of one area will involve campaigning against the interests of others. Hence Goodson's (1987: 3) assertion that 'much of the curriculum debate can be interpreted in terms of conflicts between subjects over status, resources and territory'. [. . .]

Embedded in subject hierarchies are social relationships between people that constitute powerful determinants of the possibility of change. Young (1971: 34) points out that 'as we assume some social relations associated with any curriculum . . . changes will be resisted in so far as they are perceived to undermine the values, relative power and privileges of the dominant group involved'. Thus, the study of curriculum change from a sociohistorical perspective furnishes important understandings concerning the micropolitics of schools.

[. . .]

Summary and conclusions

This chapter has [. . .] considered some of the theoretical perspectives which have emerged from studies of the realities of change within individual institutions or, rather, the detailed realities of the sources of resistance to change which have been identified as offering explanations of the ineffectiveness of many attempts at change and as factors which must be taken into account if planned change is to 'take' in a school. [. . .] [W]ithout a full appreciation of these [. . .] theories, curriculum change cannot be planned with any hope of real success. It is also [. . .] [evident] that a sound theoretical base is needed for sound practice in all areas of educational planning.

References

Ball, S. J. (1987) *The Micro-Politics of the School*. London: Routledge.

Ball, S. J. (1989) The micro-politics of the school: baronial politics, in M. Preedy (ed.) *Approaches to Curriculum Management*. Milton Keynes: Open University. Press.

Bullough Jr., R. V. (1987) Accommodation and tension: teachers, teacher role, and the culture of teaching, in J. Smyth (ed.) *Educating Teachers: Changing the Nature of Pedagogical Knowledge*. London: Falmer Press.

Corbett, H. D., Firestone, W. A. and Rossman, G. B. (1987) Resistance to planned change and the sacred in school cultures. *Educational Administration Quarterly*, 23(4): 36–59.

Dalton, T. H. (1988) *The Challenge of Curriculum Innovation*. London: Falmer Press.

Deal, T. E. (1987) The culture of schools, in L. T. Sheive and M. B. Schoenheit (eds.) *Leadership: Examining the Elusive*. Alexandria, VA: Association for Supervision and Curriculum Development.

Deal, T. E. (1990) Reframing reform. *Educational Leadership*. 47(8): 6–12.

Doyle, W. and Ponder, G. A. (1977) The practicality ethic in teacher decision-making. *Interchange*, 8(3): 1–12.

Edwards, G. (1992) A strategy for the curriculum: a response. *Journal of Curriculum Studies*, 24(5): 463–8.

Erickson, F. (1987) Conceptions of school culture: an overview. *Educational Adminstration Quarterly*, 23(4): 11–24.

Feiman-Nemser, S. and Floden, R. (1986) The culture of teaching in M. Wittrock (ed.) *Handbook of Research on Teaching*. Washington, DC: American Educational Research Association.

Flinders, D. J. (1988) Teacher isolation and the new reform. *Journal of Curriculum and Supervision*, 4(1): 17–29.

Giltin, A. D. (1987) Common school structures and teacher behaviour, in J. Smyth (ed.) *Educating Teachers*. London: Falmer Press.

Giroux, H. A. (1989) *Schooling for Democracy: Critical Pedagogy in the Modern Age*. London: Routledge.

Goodlad, J. I. (1987) Towards a healthy ecosystem, in J. I. Goodlad (ed.) *The Ecology of School Renewal*. Chicago: University of Chicago Press.

Goodson, I. F. (1981) Becoming an academic subject: patterns of explanation and evolution. *British Journal of Sociology of Education*, 2(2): 163–80.

Goodson, I. F. (1983) Subjects for study: aspects of a social history of curriculum. *Journal of Curriculum Studies*, 15(4): 391–408.

Goodson, I. F. (ed.) (1985) *Social Histories of the Secondary Curriculum: Subjects for Study*. London: Falmer Press.

Goodson, I. F. (1987) *School Subjects and Curriculum Change*. London: Falmer Press.

Goodson, I. F. (1991) Sponsoring the teachers' voice: teachers' lives and teacher development. *Cambridge Journal of Education*, 21(1): 35–45.

Goodson, I. F. and Ball, S. J. (eds) (1984) *Defining the Curriculum: Histories and Ethnographies*. London: Falmer Press.

Hargreaves, A. (1984) Experience counts, theory doesn't: how teachers talk about their work. *Sociology of Education*, 57: 244–54.

Hargreaves, A. (1989) *Curriculum and Assessment Reform*. Milton Keynes: Open University Press.

Hargreaves, A. (1990) Individualism and individuality: reinterpreting the teacher culture. Paper presented at AERA, Boston, April 1990.

Heckman, P. (1987) Understanding school culture, in J. I. Goodlad (ed.) *The Ecology of School Renewal*. Chicago: University of Chicago Press.

Holt, M. (1987) *Judgement, Planning and Educational Change*. London: Harper and Row.

Hoyle, E. (1982) Micropolitics of educational organizations. *Educational Management and Administration*, 10: 87–98.

Huberman, M. (1988) Teacher careers and school improvement. *Journal of Curriculum Studies*, 20(2): 119–32.

Kyriacou, C. (1987) Teacher stress and burnout: an international review. *Educational Research*, 29(2): 145–52.

Lauer, R. H. and Lauer, J. C. (1976) The experience of change: tempo and stress, in G. K. Zollschan and W. Hirsch (eds.) *Social Change: Explorations, Diagnoses and Conjectures*. New York: John Wiley & Sons, Inc.

Lieberman, A. (1986) Collaborative work. *Educational Leadership*, 43(5): 4–8.

Lieberman, A. and Miller, L. (1990) Teacher development in professional practice schools. *Teachers College Record*, 92(1): 105–22.

Lieberman, A. and Rosenholtz, S. (1987) The road to school improvement: barriers and bridges, in J. I. Goodlad (ed.) *The Ecology of School Renewal*. Chicago: University of Chicago Press.

Little, W. A. (1990) The persistence of privacy: autonomy and initiative in teachers' professional relationships. *Teachers College Record*, 94(1): 509–36.

Lortie, D. C. (1975) *Schoolteacher: A Sociological Study*. Chicago: University of Chicago Press.

MacIntyre, A. (1985) *After Virtue: A Study in Moral Theory*. London: Duckworth.

Marris, P. (1974) *Loss and Change*. London: Routledge and Kegan Paul.

Measor, L. (1985) Critical incidents in the classroom: identities, choices and careers, in S. J. Ball and I. F. Goodson (eds) *Teachers' Lives and Careers*. London: Falmer Press.

Ponder, G. A. and Doyle, W. (1977) The practicality ethic in teacher decision-making. *Interchange*, 8(3): 1–12.

Porter, A. C. (1987) Teacher collaboration: new partnerships to attack old problems. *Phi Delta Kappan*, 69: 147–52.

Rosario, J. R. (1986) Excellence, school culture, and lessons in utility: another case against simplistic views of educational change. *Journal of Curriculum Studies*, 18(1): 31–43.

Rosenholtz, S. J. (1987) Political myths about education reform: lessons from research on teaching. *Phi Delta Kappan*, 166(5): 349–55.

Rossman, G. B., Corbett, H. D. and Firestone, W. A. (1988) *Change and Effectiveness in Schools*. New York: State University NY Press.

Rudduck, J. (1986a) Curriculum change: management or meaning? *School Organization*, 6(1): 107–14.

Rudduck, J. (1986b) *Understanding Curriculum Change*. University of Sheffield: Division of Education.

Rudduck, J. (1988) The ownership of change as a basis for teachers' professional learning, in J. Calderhead (ed.) *Teachers' Professional Learning*. London: Falmer Press.

Schön, D. A. (1983) *The Reflective Practitioner: How Professionals Think in Action*. London: Temple Smith.

Schön, D. A. (1987) *Educating the Reflective Practitioner*. San Francisco: Jossey Bass.

Shibutani, T. (1961) *Society and Personality*. Englewood Cliffs, NJ: Prentice-Hall.

Sikes, P. J. (1985) The life cycle of the teacher, in S. J. Ball and I. F. Goodson, (eds) *Teachers' Lives and Careers*. London: Falmer Press.

Sparkes, A. C. (1987) Strategic rhetoric: a constraint in changing the practice of teachers. *British Journal of Sociology of Education*, 8(1): 37–54.

Stein, M. K. and Wang, M. C. (1988) Teacher development and school improvement: the process of teacher change. *Teaching and Teacher Education*, 4(2): 171–87.

Webb, R. B. and Ashton, P. T. (1987) Teacher motivation and the conditions of teaching: a call for ecological reform, in S. Walker and L. Barton (eds) *Changing Policies, Changing Teachers: New Directions for Schooling?* Milton Keynes: Open University Press.

Weick, K. E. (1976) Educational organizations as loosely coupled systems. *Administrative Science Quarterly*, 21: 1–19. Reprinted in A. Westoby (ed.) *Culture and Power in Educational Organizations*. Milton Keynes: Open University Press.

Young, M. F. D. (1971) An approach to the study of curricula as socially organised knowledge in M. F. D. Young (ed.) *Knowledge and Control*. London: Collier Macmillan.

21 | Organizations or communities? Changing the metaphor changes the theory*

THOMAS J. SERGIOVANNI

I feel [. . .] that the time has come for us to take a hard look at the basic theories and root metaphors that shape the way we understand schools and leadership and management within them.

The metaphor of choice is organization. Schools are understood as formal organizations, professional organizations, organic organizations and other kinds of organizations. And what goes on in them is understood as organizational behavior. It is from organizational theory and behavior that educational administration borrows its fundamental frames for thinking about how schools should be structured and coordinated, how compliance within them should be achieved, what leadership is, and how it works. From management theory, itself a derivative of organizational theory, educational administration has borrowed its definitions of quality, productivity and efficiency, and its strategies to achieve them. It is from economics, the parent of organizational theory, that educational administration has borrowed its theories of human nature and human motivation – theories built on the simple premise that as human beings, we are motivated by self-interest and thus seek to maximize our gains and cut our losses.

The phrase 'to organize' provides a good clue as to how the metaphor organization forces us to think about schools. To organize means to arrange things into a coherent whole. First there has to be a reason for organizing. Then a careful study needs to be done of each of the parts to be organized. This study involves grouping the parts mentally into some kind of logical order. Next a plan needs to be developed that enables the elements to be arranged according to the desired scheme. Typically this is a linear process. As the plan is being followed, it becomes important to monitor progress and make corrections as needed. Finally, when the work is completed, the organizational arrangements are evaluated in terms of original intentions. These

*This material has been edited and originally appeared in *Educational Management and Administration*.

principles seem to apply whether we are thinking about organizing our bureau drawers or our schools.

Schools must be considered legitimate in the eyes of their relevant publics. Schools, as formal organizations, seek legitimacy by appearing 'rational'. John Meyer (1984) points out that as organizations, schools must develop explicit management structures and procedures that give a convincing account that the proper means-ends chains are in place to accomplish stated purposes. Organizing schools into departments and grade levels, developing job descriptions, constructing curriculum plans, and putting into place explicit instructional delivery systems of various kinds are all examples of attempts to communicate that the school knows what it is doing. Further, school administrators must convince everyone that they are in control. They do this by using rules and regulations, monitoring and supervising teachers, and other regulatory means. Teachers, in turn, develop similar schemes in efforts to control students.

There is an assumption in organizations that hierarchy equals expertise. Those higher in the hierarchy are presumed to know more about teaching, learning, and other matters of schooling than those lower, and thus each person in a school is evaluated by the person at the next higher level. Not only does the metaphor organization encourage us to presume that hierarchy equals expertise, it encourages us to assume that hierarchy equals moral superiority. As teachers, for example, move up the ranks not only is it presumed that they know more about teaching and learning and other matters of schooling but that they care more as well. Those higher in the hierarchy are trusted with more responsibility, more authority, and less supervision.

Though initially organizations are creatures of people, they tend over time to become separated from people, functioning independently in pursuit of their own goals and purposes. This separation has to be bridged somehow. Ties have to exist that connect people to their work, and ties have to exist that connect people to others with whom they work. In schools as organizations the ties that connect us to others and to our work are contractual. Each person acts separately in negotiating a settlement with others and in negotiating a settlement with the organization itself that best meets her or his needs.

Self-interest is assumed to be the prime motivator in these negotiations. In order for schools to get teachers to do what needs to be done, rewards and punishments must be traded for compliance. Teachers who teach the way they are supposed to get good evaluations. Good evaluations lead to better assignments and improved prospects for promotion. Teachers who are cooperative are in the loop of the school's information system, and get picked to attend workshops and conferences. A similar pattern of trading rewards and punishments for compliance exists within classrooms and characterizes the broader relationships that exist between students and their schools.

Both management and leadership are very important in schools understood as organizations. Since motivation comes from the outside, someone has to propose and monitor the various [exchanges] that are needed. In the classroom it is the teacher and in the school it is the principal who has this job. Both are overworked as a result. Leadership inevitably takes the form of bartering. Principals and teachers and teachers and students strike bargains within which principals give to teachers and teachers give to students something they want in exchange for compliance. As a result everyone becomes connected to their work for calculated reasons. Students behave and study as long as they get desired rewards. Teachers respond for the same reasons. When rewards are no longer available or are no longer desired, both teachers and students give less effort in return.

Not all groupings of individuals, however, can be characterized as organizations. Families, communities, friendship networks, and social clubs are examples of collections of people that are different. Because of these differences, the practices that make sense in schools understood as organizations just don't fit. Metaphors have a way of creating realities. Because different metaphors create different realities, truth is always relative and related to its generative metaphor. As Lakoff and Johnson (1980) explain, truth is both subjective and objective. It is always subjective between conceptual systems and only objective within conceptual systems. Changing the metaphor for the school from organization to community changes what is true about how schools should be organized and run, about what motivates teachers and students, and about what leadership is, and how it should be practised.

In communities, for example, the connection of people to purposes and the connections among people are not based on contracts but on commitments. Communities are socially organized around relationships and the felt interdependencies that nurture them. Instead of being tied together and tied to purposes by bartering arrangements, this social structure bonds people together in special ways and binds them to concepts, images, and values that comprise a shared idea structure. This bonding and binding are the defining characteristics of schools as communities. Communities are defined by their centers of values, sentiments, and beliefs that provide the needed conditions for creating a sense of *we* from a collection of *Is*.

Life in organizations and life in communities are different in both quality and kind. In communities, we create our social lives with others who have intentions similar to ours. In organizations, relationships are constructed for us by others and become codified into a system of hierarchies, roles, and role expectations. Communities too are confronted with issues of control. But instead of relying on external control, communities rely more on norms, purposes, values, professional socialization, collegiality, and natural interdependence. Once established, the ties of community become substitutes for formal systems of supervision, evaluation and staff development; for management and organizational schemes that seek to coordinate what teachers do and how they work together; and indeed for leadership itself.

The ties of community also redefine how certain ideas are to be understood. Take empowerment, for instance. In organizations, empowerment is typically understood as having something to do with shared decision making, site based management, and similar schemes. Within communities, however, empowerment of teachers, students, and others focuses less on rights, discretion, and freedom and more on the commitments, obligations and duties that people feel toward each other and toward the school. Collegiality in organizations results from organizational arrangements (variations of team teaching, for example) that force people to work together and from the team building skills of principals. In communities, collegiality comes from within. Community members are connected to each other because of felt interdependencies, mutual obligations, and other emotional and normative ties.

There is no recipe for building community. No correlates exist to implement. There is no list available to follow, and there is no package for trainers to deliver. If we were to change the metaphor for schools from organizations to community, and if we were to begin the process of community building in schools, then we would have to invent our own practice of community. This would require that we create a new theory of educational administration and a new practice of educational administration – a theory and practice more in tune with children and young adults; sandboxes and crayons;

storybooks and interest centers; logarithms and computer programs; believing and caring; professional norms and practices; values and commitments; and other artifacts of teaching and learning. We would need to create a theory and practice of educational administration more in tune with meaning and significance, and the shared values and ideas that connect people differently. And these new connections would require that we invent new sources of authority for what we do, a new basis for leadership – themes I will return to later.

Political scientists, sociologists, psychologists, and theologians all use the word community but mean different things by its use. For our purposes I offer the following definition: Communities are collections of individuals who are bonded together by natural will and who are together bound to a set of shared ideas and ideals. This bonding and binding is tight enough to transform them from a collection of *I*s into a collective *we*. As a *we*, members are part of a tightly knit web of meaningful relationships. This *we* usually shares a common place and over time comes to share common sentiments and traditions that are sustaining.

The theory of *gemeinschaft* and *gesellschaft* can help us to understand this definition and the forms it might take as schools become communities. Gemeinschaft translates to community and gesellschaft to society. Writing in 1887, Ferdinand Tönnies (1957) used the terms to describe the shifting values and orientations that were taking place in life as we moved first from a hunting and gathering society, then to an agricultural society, and then on to an industrial society. Each of the societal transformations he described resulted in a shift away from gemeinschaft toward gesellschaft, away from a vision of life as sacred community toward a more secular society.

Tönnies's basic argument was that as society moves toward the gesellschaft end of the continuum, community values are replaced by contractual ones. Among any collection of people, for example, social relationships don't just happen; they are willed. Individuals associate with each other for reasons, and the reasons why they decide to associate are important. In gemeinschaft, natural will is the motivating force. Individuals relate to each other because doing so has its own intrinsic meaning and significance. There is no tangible goal or benefit in mind for any of the parties to the relationship. In gesellschaft, rational will is the motivating force. Individuals relate to each other to reach some goal, to gain some benefit. Without this benefit the relationship ends. In the first instance, the ties among people are thick and laden with symbolic meaning. They are moral ties. In the second instance, the ties among people are thin and instrumental. They are calculated ties.

The modern formal organization is an example of gesellschaft. Within the organization, relationships are formal and distant, having been prescribed by roles and expectations. Circumstances are evaluated by universal criteria as embodied in policies, rules, and protocols. Acceptance is conditional. The more a person cooperates with the organization and achieves for the organization, the more likely she or he will be accepted. Relationships are competitive. Those who achieve more are valued more by the organization. Not all concerns of members are legitimate. Legitimate concerns are bounded by roles rather than needs. Subjectivity is frowned upon. Rationality is prized. Self-interest prevails. It is these characteristics that undergird our present policies with respect to how schools are organized, how teaching and learning takes place, how students are evaluated, how supervision is practised, how principals and students are motivated and rewarded, and what leadership is and how it works.

Community, according to Tönnies, exists in three forms: community by kinship, of place, and of mind. Community by kinship emerges from the special kinds of relationships among people that create a unity of being, similar to that found in families and other closely knit collections of people. Community of place emerges from the sharing of a common habitat or locale. This sharing of place with others for sustained periods of time creates a special identity and a shared sense of belonging. Community of mind emerges from the binding of people to common goals, shared values, and shared conceptions of being and doing. Together the three represent webs of meaning that tie people together by creating a sense of belonging and a common identity.

If educational administration were to understand schools as communities, it would need to address questions such as the following: What can be done to increase the sense of kinship, neighborliness and collegiality among the faculty of a school? How can the faculty become more of a professional community where everyone cares about each other and helps each other to learn together, and to lead together? What kinds of relationships need to be cultivated with parents that will enable them to be included in this emerging community? How can the web of relationships that exists among teachers and between teachers and students be defined so that they embody community? How can teaching and learning settings be arranged so that they are more family-like? How can the school itself, as a collection of families, be more like a neighborhood? What are the shared values and commitments that enable the school to become a community of mind? How will these values and commitments become practical standards that can guide the lives community members want to lead, what community members learn and how, and how community members treat each other? What are the patterns of mutual obligations and duties that emerge in the school as community?

Though not cast in stone, community understandings have enduring qualities. They are resilient enough to survive the passage of members through the community over time. They are taught to new members, celebrated in customs and rituals, and embodied as standards that govern life in the community. As suggested by Bellah *et al.* (1985), enduring understandings create a fourth form of community – community of memory. In time, communities by kinship, of place, and of mind become communities of memory.

[. . .]

The ways in which we understand authority in schools and what we believe about leadership differ depending upon which metaphor, organization or community, we accept. Consider, for example, the following leadership questions: Whom should one follow? What should one follow? Why should one follow? When schools are viewed as organizations, *whom* typically means the designated leader. *What* is the leader's vision and the pattern of expectations that derive from the organization's purposes. The reason for following, the *why* question, is that the leader and the organization are able to coax compliance through the use of bureaucratic clout, motivational technology, and interpersonal skills.

When 'follow me because of my position in the school and the system of roles, expectations, and rules that I represent' is the answer, schools rely on bureaucratic authority in the form of mandates, rules, regulations, job descriptions, and expectations, all backed up by consequences for noncompliance. When 'follow me because I will make it worth your while if you do' is the answer, schools rely on the personal authority of the leader. Followers, it is presumed, will respond to the leader's personality and to the progressive motivational environment that is provided. All the leader has to do is negotiate the right contract that exchanges need fulfillment and other benefits for cooperation and compliance.

Though bureaucratic leadership has few advocates, personal leadership is widely advocated in the educational administration literature, but there are problems with this view. For example, the underlying motivational rule behind personal leadership is 'what gets rewarded gets done'. Use of this rule tends to trigger its inverse – 'what does not get rewarded does not get done'. Hence, use of this rule tends to lead to calculated involvement. Compliance is traded for rewards as long as one perceives that the exchange is a fair one. When teachers and students perceive that rewards are no longer worth their investments, or when they are no longer interested in the rewards being offered, they are likely to unilaterally renegotiate the contract by giving less.

Basing leadership practice on personal authority, as Haller and Strike (1986) point out, raises moral questions too. Should we follow our leaders because they know how to meet our needs, and because they are charming and fun to be with? Or should we follow our leaders because they have ideas that we find compelling? Leadership based on personal authority places glitz over substance and results in vacuous leadership practice.

In communities, the sources of authority for leadership are embedded in shared ideas. One source is moral authority in the form of obligations and duties that emerge from the bonding and binding ties of community. Another source is professional authority in the form of a commitment to virtuous practice.

When bureaucratic and personal authority move to the side and moral and professional authority move to the center, our understanding of what leadership is and how it works changes. Professional and moral authority are substitutes for leadership that cast principals and teachers together into roles as followers of shared values, commitments, and ideals. This shared followership binds them into a community of mind.

Implications of community are not limited to issues of authority and leadership. With community as the theory, we would have to restructure in such a way that the school itself is not defined by bricks and mortar but by ideas and relationships. Creating communities by kinship and of place, for example, will mean the dissolution of the high school, as we now know it, into several small schools rarely exceeding 300 or so students. The importance of creating sustained relationships would require that students and teachers stay together for longer periods of time. Teaching in fifty-minute snippets would have to be replaced with something else. Elementary schools would have to give serious consideration to organizing themselves into smaller and probably multi-aged families. Discipline problems would no longer be based on psychological principles but moral ones. This would require abandoning such taken-for-granted notions as having explicit rules linked to clearly stated consequences that are uniformly applied in favor of the development of social contracts, constitutions, and normative codes. In-service and staff development would move from the administrative side of the ledger to the teacher side as part of teachers' ongoing commitment to practice at the edge of their craft. Extrinsic reward systems would have to disappear. The number of specialists would likely be reduced and [suspending or excluding students] would no longer be common as families of teachers and students, like families of parents and children, take fuller responsibility for solving their own problems.

All of these changes would necessitate the invention of new standards of quality, new strategies for accountability, and new ways of working with people – the invention of a new educational administration, in other words. The word *invention* is key. Imported conceptions of educational administration that might make sense when schools are understood as organizations no longer make sense when the metaphor is changed to community.

I imagine that my remarks so far have raised a number of questions in your minds. Let me try to anticipate some of them: 'Aren't you setting up a false dichotomy by referring to gemeinschaft and gesellschaft and by drawing extreme contrasts between communities and organizations?' No, I do not think so. The use of polar opposites along a common continuum is a strategy with a long tradition in sociology. Gemeinschaft and gesellschaft represent ideal types that do not exist in the real world in their pure forms. They are, as Weber (1949) pointed out, polar mental representations that can help us categorize and explain on the one hand and track movement along a common continuum on the other. Thus schools are never gemeinschaft *or* gesellschaft. They possess characteristics of both.

Though I believe that most schools are now too gesellschaft and that we need a realignment in favor of gemeinschaft, it is important to recognize that the gesellschaft perspective is both valuable and inescapable. We live, after all, in a gesellschaft world – a society characterized by technical-rationality, which has brought us many gains. Without gesellschaft, we would not have a successful space program or heart transplant technology. Nor would we have great universities, profitable corporations, and workable governmental systems. There would be no hope of cleaning up the environment, and, as a nation, we would not be able to defend ourselves.

Still, we need to decide which theory should dominate which spheres of our lives. Almost everyone will agree that the family, the extended family, and the neighborhood should be dominated by gemeinschaft values. The corporation, the research laboratory, and the court system, on the other hand, might well lean more toward gesellschaft values. In modern times, the school has been solidly ensconced in the gesellschaft camp with unhappy results. It's time that the school was moved from the gesellschaft side of the ledger to the gemeinschaft side.

'Why do we have to change the theory? Why not just consider community to be another kind of organization – perhaps a social or organic organization? And why reinvent educational administration? If community is just another kind of organization, all we need to do is add some practices to what we have that fit this kind of organization.' Unless the root metaphor for the school is changed, I fear that whatever might be considered new with community will be understood in terms of the already established categories (Mannheim 1940). The concept of uncertainty absorption (March and Simon 1958), the tendency to understand new ideas in old terms, will ensure that despite some surface changes, underneath, the schools and administration within them will remain exactly as they are now.

'What about theoretical pluralism? Why not develop a new theory of school as community and new conceptions of administration but not replace anything with them. Let's add community to all the other theories and models that we now have. Then, using a meta-contingency approach we can select different theories from this menu for different problems or select several theories to heighten understanding of the same problem. Isn't this inclusive approach a better way to build a theory and practice of educational administration?' No, I do not believe an inclusive approach is the way to go. To begin with, even if it did make sense to use a meta-contingency approach, as long as the root metaphor for the school remains organization, we may not be studying the right thing. Root metaphors create theoretical categories that are fixed in our collective minds, and, as suggested earlier, new ideas are absorbed into the categories suggested by the metaphor organization. Applying a theory of community to schools understood underneath as organizations creates meanings, realities, and practices that are different than if the underlying theory itself were community.

The appeal of theoretical pluralism is inclusiveness. Yet it is inclusiveness that contributes to the loss of character in educational administration. Sociology does not include everything nor does medicine, architecture, or baseball. Established fields are not characterized by inclusiveness but by exclusiveness. Established fields are constructed from ideas and conceptions that come from within, not those borrowed and then patched together from the outside. Established fields make up their minds about what counts and what doesn't and they are intolerant of the latter. We need to do the same thing in educational administration. A good place to begin is by *changing* the root metaphor for schools from organization to community.

References

Bellah, R. N., Madsen, R., Sullivan, W. M., Swidler, A. and Tipton, S. M. (1985) *Habits of the Heart: Individualism and Commitment in American Life*. New York: Harper and Row.
Flores, A. (ed.) (1988) *Professional Ideals*. Belmont, CA: Wadsworth.
Haller, E. J. and Strike, K. A. (1986) *An Introduction to Educational Administration: Social, Legal, and Ethical Perspectives*. White Plains, NY: Longman.
Lakoff, G. and Johnson, M. (1980) *Metaphors We Live By*. Chicago: University of Chicago Press.
MacIntyre, A. (1981) *After Virtue: A Study in Moral Theory*. Notre Dame, IN: University of Notre Dame Press.
Mannheim, K. (1940) *Man and Society in an Age of Reconstruction*. New York: Harcourt, Brace and World.
March, J. G. and Simon, H. A. (1958) *Organizations*. New York: John Wiley.
Meyer, J. (1984) Organizations as ideological systems, in T. J. Sergiovanni and J. E. Corbally (eds) *Leadership and Organizational Culture*, pp. 85–114. Urbana: University of Illinois Press.
Noddings, N. (1992) *The Challenge to Care in Schools: An Alternative Approach to Education*. New York: Teachers College Press.
Sergiovanni, T. J. (1992) *Moral Leadership*. San Francisco: Jossey Bass.
Sergiovanni, T. J. (1994) *Building Community in Schools*. San Francisco: Jossey Bass.
Tönnies, F. (1957) *Community and Society [Gemeinschaft und Gesellschaft]* (C. P. Loomis, ed. and trans.). New York: Harper and Row. (Original work published 1887.)
Weber, M. (1949) *The Methodology of the Social Sciences* (E. A. Shils and H. A. Finch, trans.). Glencoe, IL: Free Press.

22 | School culture, school effectiveness and school improvement*

DAVID H. HARGREAVES

[. . .]

School cultures – a basic model

The fundamental problems faced by schools, to which their cultures constitute a solution, can be understood in terms of the twin concepts deriving from Bales's (1952, 1953) studies of group dynamics. To solve a complex problem a group has to maintain pressure to keep members on task and devise social controls to prevent distraction; simultaneously it must seek to maintain in the group some social harmony, which is easily disturbed by pressure to keep on task. For example, a member who proffers suggestions regarded as foolish by others is offended by the controlling comments from others pressing for task completion. Groups, then, deal with an *instrumental* function, or task achievement, but also with an *expressive* function, or maintaining good social relationships. Incompetent handling of either function might disrupt the group and its effectiveness. [. . .]

The distinction can [. . .] also be of value when applied to institutions. [. . .] Schools have various instrumental functions, especially those directed towards student cognitive achievement. Such tasks require social controls over teachers and students so that they work together in orderly ways, concentrate on teaching and learning and avoid the ubiquitous possibilities of distraction and delay. Schools thus require what Lieberman and Miller (1984) call 'control norms'. This is the *instrumental-social control* domain of school life. In the same way, schools have an expressive task of maintaining social relationships so that they are satisfying, supportive and sociable – the *expressive–social cohesion* domain of school life. In the present model it is assumed that these two domains, always in potential tension, constitute the core of school cultures.

*This material has been edited and originally appeared in *School Effectiveness and School Improvement*.

An additional assumption is that in each cultural domain there is an *optimal* level for the effective functioning of the school. [. . .] Every school has to find some combination of, and balance within and between, the cultural domains of control and cohesion.

A first typology of school cultures

From this basic model a typology of school cultures is developed (Figure 22.1). At some point along each axis lies a theoretical optimal position between the extremes of the corners.

The school culture of type (A) in the south west corner is high in the instrumental domain, with exceptional pressure on students to achieve learning goals (including examination performance) and perhaps athletic prowess, but with weak social cohesion between staff and students. School life is orderly, scheduled, disciplined. [. . .] The tone (ethos) of the institution is custodial: in hard forms (a military academy) it could be described as coercive; in softer versions (the grammar school) as 'a tight ship' fostering 'traditional values'. Reflecting the institutional inheritance from the nineteenth century, this [is a] *formal school culture*[.]

In the north east corner school culture (B) is characterised by a relaxed, carefree and cosy atmosphere. It places high emphasis on informal, friendly teacher–student relations. The focus is on individual student development within a nurturing environment. [. . .] The 'child-centred' primary school or the 'caring' inner-city secondary school with a strong pastoral system exemplify this type .[. . .] In this *welfarist school culture* the students are happy at the time but in later life look back on their experience with resentment at the teachers' failure to drive them hard enough. In the formal school, by contrast, students are often unhappy at the time, but later recall their experience with gratitude.

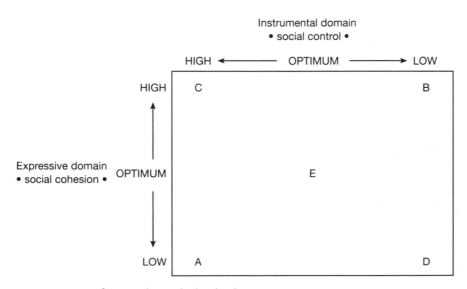

Figure 22.1   A first typology of school cultures

In culture (C) in the north west corner the high instrumental and expressive emphasis creates a frenetic ethos. All are under pressure to participate actively in the full range of school life. Expectations of both work and personal development are high. Teachers are enthusiastic and committed, being pedagogical experimenters and innovators. In this pervasive intimacy, everyone seems to be under surveillance and control. [. . .] This [is a] *hothouse school culture*. [. . .]

In the south east corner (D) is a culture where both social control and social cohesion are exceptionally weak. For both teachers and students the school is close to breakdown – a classic 'at risk' situation. This is a *survivalist school culture*. Social relations are poor, teachers striving to maintain basic control and allowing pupils to avoid academic work in exchange for not engaging in misconduct. [. . .] The ethos is one of insecurity, hoplessness and low morale.

Few actual school cultures fall into the extreme positions described in these cameos – Weberian 'ideal types' of cultures that do not exist but help to interpret those that do. Real schools are locatable at any point in the space between the corners. Since schools are 'loosely coupled' institutions (Weick 1976), different parts of the school (including teacher subcultures and individual classrooms) could be located in a different segment from the rest of the school. In this model, the ideal school of the effectiveness literature is around the centre (E), striving to hold its chosen optimal position in the social control and social cohesion domains. Expectations of work and conduct are high – the principal's expectations of staff and the teachers' of students. Yet these standards are not perceived to be unreasonable; everyone is supported in striving for them and rewarded for reaching them. For both teachers and students, school is a demanding but very enjoyable place to be. It must be recognised, however, that the staff and clients of schools in many other positions (except the south east corner) may well consider their school to be effective.

[. . .]

Nevertheless, the conceptual economy of the basic model provides too restricted a range for an adequate description of the dynamics of schools in their considerable variety of cultural forms. To capture the dynamics of school cultures, and in particular the complex interactions among teachers, a model of greater conceptual complexity is required.

A second typology of school cultures

Institutional cultures (members' values, beliefs etc.) stand in dialectical relationship to their underlying architecture (social structures or patterns of members' social relationships). A structural change often has cultural consequences; a shift in culture may alter social structures. Cultures and their architecture are subject to constant pressure towards change by internal and external factors. When for schools such pressure is unsought and unwelcome, it is this dynamic relationship between structure and culture that illuminates school change, be it improvement or deterioration. The impact of much externally imposed change is structural rather than cultural, since it is easier to legislate about people's work situation and practices than their values and beliefs. Structures can often be determined by fiat; cultures cannot, for they are like corals – living, fragile, slow to form, sensitive to their ecology, easy to destroy, difficult to replace.

The second typology proposes an architecture of five underlying social structures – political, micropolitical, maintenance, development, and service. (The present analysis does not fully explore other structures, such as the moral.) The *political structure* refers to the character and formal distribution of power, authority and status. Beneath the formal organisation and its official positions is an informal network of individuals and groups who plot, plan and act together to advance their interests – the *micropolitical structure* (Hoyle 1982, 1986; Ball 1987; Blase 1991). The political and micropolitical structures interlock, often as a contest between the official functioning of the school and the unofficial manoeuvring of the staff groupings with distinctive subcultures.

Maintenance and development (Hargreaves and Hopkins 1991) are structures that arise from the school's dual needs for stability and change. Some aspects of an organisation must persist over time: they become the taken-for-granted routines of social life which provide order and continuity for the community. Though *maintenance structures* are often hardly noticed because of their sheer familiarity, they are powerful in their impact; to challenge and disrupt them is often to alarm and confuse community members. At the same time, some aspects of school are subject to change, and to manage change requires structures of various kinds. The enduring bureaucratic systems designed for maintenance, such as committees and posts of responsibility, are often the first choice as *development structures*. To cope with change effectively, however, an organisation may have to devise different structures or temporary systems for specific, short-term development tasks. Maintenance and development structures, like political and micropolitical structures, are often in tension.

The *service structure* forges the social relations between the organisation's staff and its clients – in the case of schools, the relations between the teachers, students and their families, and governing bodies – including the distribution of rights and duties of each.

This typology organises the possible variations in this architecture around two (Weberian ideal) types of school here called *traditional* and *collegial*. In the literature about school cultures the terms collegial and collaborative are used interchangeably. This is unfortunate and potentially confusing. Collaboration does not necessarily involve an institutional base to its structure, but refers to a disposition towards, or the enactment of, a style of relationship which may take place in a very wide range of structural conditions – total strangers can collaborate in brief and transient encounters, as when one helps an old lady across the road. Collegiality, far from being a synonym for collaboration, invokes an institutional structure – the *collegium*, or 'organised society of persons performing certain common functions', in dictionary language. In this typology the term collegial refers to a type of institution, where particular forms of both structure *and* culture exist. This helps to avoid the danger of talking about school cultures as if they existed independently of structural bases.

By cross-tabulating five elements of architecture with two types of school, as in Table 22.1, ten structure-culture complexes are exposed. Each is expressed through a dual descriptor.

The traditional school culture

In the traditional type, the *political structure* is essentially *feudal*, the principal and senior teachers (including heads of subject departments in secondary schools) being like a monarch surrounded by barons. In describing its 'despotic political structure', Waller

Table 22.1   A second typology of school cultures

	Traditional school	Collegial school
Political structure	feudal-consultative	egalitarian-participative
Micropolitical structure	fissile-ingratiative	integrative-exclusive
Maintenance structure	bureaucratic-positional	delegative-rotational
Development structure	individualist-hierarchical	institutional-collaborative
Service structure	autocratic-deferential	contractual-accountable

(1932) captured the essence of the traditional school. This power is never absolute: the despotism is 'in a state of perilous equilibrium . . . threatened from within and exposed to regulation and interference from without'. [. . .] The style for conducting relations between principal and teachers (and between teacher and students) is therefore *consultative* as well as feudal, to keep challenges at bay and temper accusations of tyranny or authoritarianism. The consultation may be explicit, a seeking of views followed by a discussion before the monarch's decision is made; but often it is implicit, a checking out of what people will accept without risk of rebellion. Today the feudal structure commands less assent from most teachers than it did in Waller's time.

The *micropolitical structure* is *fissile*, inherently liable to break into groups as the barons quarrel over status, power and resources (Cf. A. Hargreaves 1992). The constant need for the courtiers to curry favour with the monarch (or to retire from court to social and physical isolation in distant parts of the kingdom) promotes a culture that is *ingratiative* (D. H. Hargreaves 1972); the teachers have to learn the art of pleasing, and avoiding displeasing, the principal by a variety of tactics – which simply replicates how students seek to control their relationships with teachers (Jackson 1968). [. . .]

The daily routines of the traditional school are conducted not in feudal terms but according to *bureaucratic* principles and procedures that provide the *maintenance* structure of most modern organisations. Rules and regulations guide decision making and the handling of problems. Action to maintain the system is controlled on a *positional* basis: teachers have assigned offices with a designated sphere of authority and clear labels that indicate both the standing of the position and the specialist competence. Members know (or are supposed to know) who is in charge of what and to whom every one is accountable: to neglect one's specialised duties is as dangerous as to arrogate to oneself the powers and privileges of another. [. . .]

In the traditional school, as in all bureaucracies, innovation is introduced with difficulty. Teachers are, on an *individualist* basis, free to innovate within their own classrooms, provided that either this does not break the system's rules and regulations or breaches can be protected from the knowledge of superiors. [. . .] The most successful ways to innovate are from, or with the support of, the top of the hierarchy: principals purport to have the best ideas for change. Much as a principal may enthuse about the innovation, teachers have to implement it; if they do not actively support it, they may use their potential to undermine or pervert it. In short, there is a weak *development structure*, which is often simply a *hierarchical* appendage to the more effective maintenance structure. Since levels of trust between staff are relatively low, change is accompanied by increases in paperwork: records and minutes are required to keep everyone informed and to allay suspicions that changes might be made without consent. [. . .]

Teacher–parent relations are a variant of the *autocratic* principle governing teacher–student relations. A sharp boundary exists between professionals and lay persons. [. . .] Teachers have specialised knowledge and skills to which clients are expected to defer: the *service structure* of autocracy (which is about the distribution of power) does not necessarily entail an authoritarian manner to the client, but does require *deferential* compliance. If clients (parent or child) prove to be intractable, lacking in sufficient deference, they may be invited to seek educational services elsewhere.

The collegial school culture

The *political structure* of the collegial school is really quasi-collegial (Hoyle 1986). In pure collegial systems, member elect their head, power is shared subject to the statutes and ordinances, and responsibility for the college is a collective one. The headteacher in England and Wales is appointed, has legal responsibilities and is accountable for the conduct of the school to a governing body and so staff relationships cannot be fully *egalitarian*. Nevertheless, in a collegial school the principal acts in practice as *primus inter pares*, allowing – or purporting to allow – all teachers equal rights to be *participative*, always in discussion and sometimes in decision making.

There is here the possibility in the *micropolitical structure* of fission into competing interest groups, but (in contrast to the traditional type) this is counteracted by the *integrative* culture's centripetal drive towards consensus. As the culture is participative rather than democratic, voting on key policy matters is avoided. If, through voting, a simple majority view were to prevail, there would be a risk of creating a ruling group with a substantial disaffected minority. [. . .] There may emerge a small deviant group of members who, if they cannot be integrated, are quietly excluded, being ignored or tolerated as eccentrics. Newcomers to the school are checked not just for their technical expertise (as in the traditional school) but also for their 'fit' in terms of the ideological stance of the school – and so may be offered an initial short-term contract before entry into this essentially *exclusive* culture.

A close integration of the social control and social cohesion domains is evident in the way the collegial schools defines its mission. Policies tend to be whole-school policies which are not accepted without substantial consensual support and commitment. The implementation of such policies is achieved by the trustful *delegation* of responsibilities and the regular but non-permanent *rotation* of duties among members, in place of the 'allocation by position' in the traditional school. The high level of trust leads to low levels of written communication and paperwork. [. . .] The looser framework of teacher role distribution provides a *maintenance structure* within which boring jobs of a routine but professional character are shared rather than falling to the lot of low status members. [. . .]

For teachers, the *development structure* is clearer, stronger and more salient than the maintenance structure; innovative initiative is not linked to hierarchical standing. The whole-school or *institutional* focus is supported by *collaborative* relationships through which members work together to implement any change designed to realise shared goals compatible with the school's mission. Leadership is distributed non-hierarchically, a match being sought between opportunities and individual talent and interest, wherever they lie, irrespective of status. Innovation is public and team-focused; it transcends individual teachers and survives their departure. [. . .]

Finally, in the *service structure*, relations with clients (students, parents, governors) tend towards the *contractual*, in recognition that all parties have both rights and duties, and that sound working relationships spring from explicit acceptance of such partnerships. Contract entails being *accountable*, but in a mutual and comfortable form, based on relationships characterised by openness, confidence and trust.

Cultures in transition

Over the last hundred years or so, the general drift seems to be from the traditional towards the collegial, spawning many mutant forms on the way. This evolution reflects many of the wider changes in society and other social institutions especially between 1960 and 1980. Most schools, perhaps, are in some aspects traditional and in others collegial. Official policy may favour mixed types – contemporary British policy on schools favouring traditional political structures but collegial service structures. In Britain, cultures in transition are common under the impact of the unprecedented scope and peace of educational reform. [. . .]

Current changes in school cultures and architectures are often understood, experienced and interpreted by teachers as a tension between the traditional and the collegial since these [. . .] are the roots of, and remain deeply embedded within, the professional conceptual frameworks used to make sense of school. As a result, some teachers, and especially principals, continue to strive towards either one of the ideal types or a pragmatic admixture.

School cultures – effectiveness, change and improvement

How might the two typologies contribute to the development of theory or research into school effectiveness and improvement? One of the key criteria for the quality of theory is its fertility in generating hypotheses for empirical test. The remaining section of the chapter is devoted to suggesting hypotheses that might be tested if operational and measurable versions of the typologies can be devised.

School effectiveness

Is one type of school culture more closely associated with school effectiveness than another? The answer depends on the criteria by which effectiveness is judged. In the first typology, the survivalist school least meets criteria for effectiveness, almost by definition. The other three types pose problems.

The school with a welfarist culture is weak by academic criteria, with poor learning outcomes, but staff would assert their achievement in terms of expressive outcomes, which might include low rates of delinquency. The formal school culture, by contrast, is associated with high academic press, but assigns little value to the expressive domain. It could be hypothesised that where the students come from families committed to the school's high academic expectations and are capable of meeting the academic targets, the school will be effective by the relevant criteria – fee-paying boarding and selective schools especially. On the other hand, where the students and their families have low academic interests, aspirations and commitments, and the students display low self-esteem, the failure to provide supportive social cohesion could make a formal school less effective in terms of academic outcomes – some inner-city schools, perhaps. The hothouse culture might be associated with selective or differential effectiveness: for pupils wilting under excessive instrumental and/or expressive pressures, the school would be ineffective, but others might cope well with, or even flourish in, this ethos. Indeed, whilst there is a general question of whether school effectiveness correlates with school culture, there is an equally important question of whether some cultures are more effective with certain kinds of teacher and certain kind of student.

The school of a 'balanced' culture achieving some optimum position in both domains might claim to be the most effective, *but only when the criteria of effectiveness assign equal weight to both instrumental and expressive outcomes*. It could be argued, of course, that many parents and politicians give more weight to the instrumental. The popular conception of the effective school in contemporary Britain would be to the west (and perhaps south west) of the E space in Figure 22.1. E is not necessarily the correct location for the collegial school culture, which with its emphasis on agreement, consistency and working together could in some variants assume hothouse and welfarist forms. Collegial cultures vary sharply in terms of culture content (Cf. Campbell and Southworth 1992) and mission, and so can be located anywhere to the north of E.

These tentative suggestions may be regarded as hypotheses: whether and in what ways school culture is associated with effectiveness needs to be put to empirical test. School cultures of particular types may be more attractive and satisfying than others to teachers and/or students and/or parents, and that may be important in itself. Research should test whether and in what ways school culture relates to a variety of outcome measures, especially cognitive ones, but not excluding the possibility that school culture might [. . .] be a variable irrelevant to some or all outcome measures. Linking school culture to variations in teacher values and practices is insufficient to throw light on school effectiveness. As Huberman (1992) sharply points out,

> innovations are not introduced to improve professional capacity; they are introduced to heighten pupils' skills and capacities. True, we are not likely to get the second without the first, but by getting different instruction, we may not necessarily get more learning. [. . .]

Indeed, Huberman indirectly points to the fact that it is easier to make hypotheses about the relationship of school effectiveness with cultures of the first typology than with those of the second typology. One of the strengths of the first typology is that it embraces both teacher and student levels, since both are affected by the pervasive institutional dimensions of social control and social cohesion. The second typology is concerned with teacher rather than school cultures: its greater sensitivity at the teacher level is achieved at the cost of neglect of the student level. Indeed, while it is possible to investigate both teacher and student versions of school culture in the first typology, it is difficult to imagine a student version of the cultures in the second typology that would be anything more than their perceptions of cultures and structures operating at teacher level. It is thus more difficult to make hypotheses about student cultures or student outcomes that might be associated with traditional or collegial cultures. Any linking of better student cognitive outcomes with the traditional and better student social outcomes with the collegial are likely to be weak. As we shall see below, when it comes to making hypotheses about student outcomes, the two typologies combined are more suggestive than either alone.

School change

Which type of culture most helps schools to cope with change, in what ways and under what conditions? In the first typology, survivalist schools are on the edge of breakdown, barely coping at all. Of the remaining three types, there is nothing to indicate whether one type is inherently more able to cope with change than others. Clearly if the external pressure is towards higher social control, traditional and hothouse cultures have the advantage; if the trend is towards greater social cohesion, welfarist and hothouse cultures have the edge.

The advantage of any school in the more central locations in Figure 22.1 over the corner locations is that it has, so to speak, less distance to move, and so fewer destabilising adjustments to make, to adapt to external shifts in instrumental and expressive emphases. But schools in central positions are not necessarily flexible; their more central position may reflect confusion or incoherence over the two domains. But if the culture is intentionally balanced, then school leaders are likely to be alert to any impending change and to the need for any adjustment to unavoidable problems. Schools with organisational flexibility of a high order linked to an acute sensitivity to changes in the external environment seem to exist. In theory, a school with this capacity to detect, respond to and control change, whilst retaining some balance between social control and social cohesion, should be in a central position in Figure 22.1. It is a hypothesis to be investigated.

In the second typology, the advantage enjoyed by each type is again relative to circumstances. The traditional school type, with its strong maintenance structure, prospers well in stable circumstances; and if the principal's authority is accepted and seen as the legitimate source of innovation, there can be a positive and effective response to externally imposed change. If these conditions do not apply, then the weak development structures may not bear the weight of innovation. The collegial school type, with its stronger development structure and collaborative relationships that sustain teachers under stress, may be better placed to handle rapid change. This is one criterion of effectiveness – which may or may not correlate with effectiveness defined as student outcomes. Emergent collegial cultures in British schools may indeed have the edge in successfully implementing the changes following the Education Reform Act 1988, but if their student outcomes remain unaltered then the schools, though changed, cannot be said by standard criteria to be more effective.

Collegial cultures may handle many types of change well but only under specific conditions. For example, when there is collective agreement to the externally imposed change, it may be filtered through the school's vision or mission and so implemented. But if there is no such agreement to the change, the staff may become bogged down in discussion or even division, with the effect of delaying implementation, allowing only partial implementation or even forcing rejection of implementation on the grounds that the damage to staff cohesion is too great a price to pay. The traditional school, by contrast, is more comfortable with partial or selective implementation, since whole staff agreement to a change is not a pre-condition of acceptance.

Indeed, the now common assumption that collegial cultures support change must be qualified by a recognition that the collegial school's egalitarian-participative structure may become a strong source of resistance to any externally driven change when staff are hostile to it. Welfarist and hothouse cultures that are strongly collegial are likely to be highly resistant to external change that is incompatible with their missions. Where collaboration among teachers takes the form of ideological convergence (rather than trust), where there is low toleration of divergent views (rather than respect for difference), then there are within the school reduced resources for accommodating unwelcome outside pressures. It is hypothesised that, given the emphasis of recent education policies, collegial welfarist schools will be most resistant to current demands for change – and some of those may be the low-achieving schools in inner-city areas (Ofsted 1993) where politicians are expecting reforms to have their greatest impact. A headteacher could revert to a feudal-consultative style to change the direction and philosophy of the school, but this would be perceived as reneging on the collegial culture, which could in itself provoke resistance. Even the introduction of a new head might have limited effects, since collegial cultures are averse to strong, charismatic leaders seeking to move the school to new values.

School improvement

School culture may be a *cause*, an *object* or an *effect* of school improvement: indeed, all three are possible. It is said that school culture should be a target for change, on the grounds that in due course it will exercise an improving causal influence on other variables, and eventually on student outcomes, which in turn reinforce the culture. Indeed, the principal task for a school leader may be the management of the culture to such ends (Schein 1986).

For [many years] it has been urged, especially in North America, that collaborative cultures (variously defined) are superior to non-collaboration and better able to support school improvement. [. . .] Consequently teachers are enjoined to become more collaborative; and administrators may be tempted to contrive to promote teacher collaboration as a means of implementing politically and administratively led reforms (A. Hargreaves 1991). More recently, collaboration has been subjected to a more sceptical and analytical treatment (Little 1990); it has been argued that collaboration can be excessive and therefore damaging, and has been assigned undue importance as a means of increasing school and teacher effectiveness (Huberman 1993; A. Hargreaves 1993). Certainly the emphasis given to social cohesion in extreme hothouse and welfarist cultures can be excessive; 'collaboration for its own sake' without regard to context or purpose makes a dangerous educational principle. But then the inadequate social cohesion characterising extreme formal and survivalist cultures also carries debilitating penalties. Schools need to find some optimal version of social cohesion – and of social control too. [. . .]

In the models offered here, collaboration is possible in both traditional and collegial cultures. No school culture, and certainly not the collegial, can make exclusive claims to collaboration, but collegial schools have a firm architecture that fosters collaboration. Collegial cultures are, however, not reducible to collaborative relations, and it is dangerous to imagine that either collegial cultures or collaborative teacher styles necessarily entail certain structures, such as team or joint teaching. If the relationships between school culture and school improvement are to be tested empirically, it will be essential to look beneath the cultural features, such as collaborative attitudes, to their underlying structures. In the collegial culture there are likely to be found not just examples of collaboration but also other cultural and architectural features such as:

- commitment to a shared vision for the school, providing teachers with clear purpose and direction, and so potentially strong morale;

- co-ordination of policy to create a consistent environment and expectations for teachers and students;
- methods for improving curriculum continuity and progression for students, so that unplanned repetitions or omissions are avoided and teachers build on the foundations established by colleagues in related subjects or in earlier classes;
- practices that support mutual classroom observation and discussion of teaching and learning, allowing the sharing of both problems and good practice, experimentation with new ideas, and the encouragement of reflection;
- a means of reconciling the demands of professional development with those of school development.

Since these features seem less common (but not entirely unknown) in traditional school cultures, it seems reasonable to hypothesise that collegial cultures will be more supportive of school improvement. Though the warning voices from North America should be heard, British empirical evidence on collegial cultures (Southworth 1987; Nias, Southworth and Yeomans 1989; Campbell and Southworth 1992) offers few indications that schools are de-stabilising themselves and stifling teacher initiative by excessive indulgence in or pressure towards collaboration. There are important exceptions, as in the case of the collegial welfarist culture noted above; but these merely qualify rather than wholly falsify the general hypothesis. In most circumstances collegial cultures should favour the self-improving school – and also external consultancy, since they should foster staff co-operation with advisers, if the intervention is designed as a collaborative venture. Whether the collegial, improving school will be more effective in terms of the quality of teaching and student achievement has yet to be firmly established, but the factors highlighted in the previous paragraph contain what might be key structural links between teacher cultures and student outcomes. No school or teacher culture can be shown to have a *direct* impact on student learning and achievement, and claims to that end are vacuous. But the effects of culture can be conceptualised as trickling down, so to speak, through the architecture – political and micropolitical, maintenance and development, and service – until they eventually make some impact on what goes on in classrooms – and the ways in which that is [. . .] conceptualised and investigated (Brown and McIntyre 1993). Is the flow of culture trackable through research?

At a time when in Britain, as in other countries, there is a political interest in the detection and improvement of under-achieving or 'failing' schools, the relationship between school culture and school effectiveness/improvement needs closer investigation. Improved techniques for depicting and measuring school cultures are needed. At the same time better methods for mapping the process of change, including the change from one type of culture to another, are also essential. Only then can hypotheses on the possible forms and extent of advantage for collegial cultures be tested; only then can the possibilities and limitations of school improvement through cultural change be uncovered. Teachers are beginning to use culture within their professional vocabulary to discuss school improvement and are increasingly being influenced by the growing academic literature. But, like the researchers, they lack adequate conceptual frameworks and investigative tools to explore school culture. For both researchers and practitioners, better models and techniques would generate enhanced conceptual, methodological, heuristic and explanatory links between school effectiveness and school improvement as well as hypotheses about their relationships that could be put to empirical test.

References

Bales, R. F. (1952) Some uniformities of behaviour in small social systems, in G. E. Swanson, T. Newcombe and E. L. Hartley (eds) *Readings in Social Psychology*. New York and London: Holt, Rinehart and Winston.

Bales, R. F. (1953) The equilibrium problem in small groups, in T. Parsons, R. F. Bales and E. A. Shils (eds) *Working Papers in the Theory of Action*. Glencoe, IL: Free Press.

Ball, S. J. (1987) *The Micro-Politics of the School*. London and New York: Methuen.

Berger, P. and Luckman, T. (1967) *The Social Construction of Reality*. Harmondsworth: Penguin.

Blase, J. (1991) *The Politics of Life in Schools*. Newbury Park and London: Sage.

Brown, S. and McIntyre, D. (1993) *Making Sense of Teaching*. Buckingham and Philadelphia: Open University Press.

Campbell, P. and Southworth, G. (1992) Rethinking collegiality: teachers' views, in N. Bennett, M. Crawford and C. Riches (eds) *Managing Change in Education: Individual and Organisational Perspectives*. Buckingham and Philadelphia: Open University Press.

Hargreaves, A. (1991) Contrived collegiality: the micropolitics of teacher collaboration, in J. Blase (ed.) *The Politics of Life in Schools*. Newbury Park and London: Sage.

Hargreaves, A. (1992) Cultures of teaching: a focus for change, in A. Hargreaves and M. G. Fullan (eds) *Understanding Teacher Development*. London and New York: Cassell.

Hargreaves, A. (1993) Individualism and individuality: reinterpreting the teacher culture, in J. W. Little and M. W. McLaughlin (eds), *Teachers' Work*. New York and London: Teachers' College Press.

Hargreaves, D. H. (1972) *Interpersonal Relations and Education*. London and Boston: Routledge and Kegan Paul.

Hargreaves, D. H. and Hopkins, D. (1991) *The Empowered School*. London and New York: Cassell.

Hoyle, E. (1982) Micropolitics of educational organisations. *Educational Management and Administration*, 10(2).

Hoyle, E. (1986) *The Politics of School Management*. London and Toronto: Hodder and Stoughton.

Huberman, M. (1992) Critical introduction, in M. G. Fullan (ed.) *Successful School Improvement*. Buckingham and Philadelphia: Open University Press.

Huberman, M. (1993) The model of the independent artisan in teachers' professional relations, in J. W. Little and M. W. McLaughlin (eds) *Teachers' Work*. New York and London: Teachers' College Press.

Jackson, P. W. (1968) *Life in Classrooms*. New York and London: Holt, Reinhart and Winston.

Lieberman, A. and Miller, L. (1984) *Teachers – their World and their Work*. New York and London: Teachers' College Press.

Little, J. W. (1990) The persistence of privacy: autonomy and initiative in teachers' professional relations. *Teachers' College Record*, 91(4).

Nias, J., Southworth, G. and Yeomans, R. (1989) *Staff Relationships in the Primary School*. London and New York: Cassell.

Office of Her Majesty's Chief Inspector of Schools (1993) *Access and Achievement in Urban Education*. London: OFSTED.

Schein, E. H. (1986) *Organizational Culture and Leadership*. San Francisco: Jossey Bass.

Southworth, G. (1987) Primary headship and collegiality, in G. Southworth (ed.) *Readings in Primary School Management*. London and Philadelphia: Falmer Press.

Waller, W. (1932) *The Sociology of Teaching*. New York and London: John Wiley.

Weick, K. E. (1976) Educational organisations as loosely coupled systems. *Administrative Science Quarterly*, 21(1).

23 | Linking school effectiveness knowledge and school improvement practice*

DAVID REYNOLDS

If a Martian, that value-free creature so beloved of social scientists, were to visit the planet to take a look at its educational arrangements, the most remarkable thing that would probably strike him or her about our educational research and practice would be the lack of mesh between the enterprises of *school improvement* and *school effectiveness*. With the exception of North America which now exhibits the beginnings of links between these two disciplines or sub-disciplines, in virtually all other societies around the world there are few points of intellectual or practical contact between scholars in the two disciplines. In addition, the take up of school effectiveness knowledge not just directly into the mechanics of school improvement programmes but indirectly into school practice through influence upon the practitioner and policy maker communities is comparatively rare.

[. . .]

The school improvement paradigm

Underlying the two distinctive bodies of scholarship and the separation of the two groups of scholars are two very distinctive intellectual traditions and histories. School improvement in the 1960s and 1970s had a number of paradigmatic characteristics, as shown in Table 23.1

This early approach adopted a technological view of school improvement, in which innovations were brought to schools from outside of them and then introduced *top down*, in which the innovation was based upon the knowledge produced by persons outside the school, in which the focus was the school's formal organization and curriculum, in which the outcomes were taken as given, in which the school was the focus of the innovation more than the individual practitioner and in which the goals were

*This material has been edited and is from *School Based Management and School Effectiveness*.

Table 23.1   Characteristics of two school improvement paradigms

	1960	1980
Orientation	Top down	Bottom up
Knowledge base	Elite knowledge	Practitioner knowledge of 'folk lore'
Targeting	Organization/curriculum based	Process based
Outcomes	Pupil outcome orientated	School process orientated
Goals	Outcomes as given	Outcomes problematic, to be discussed
Focus	School focused	Teacher focused
Methodology of evaluation	'Hard' quantitative evaluation	'Soft' naturalistic, qualitative evaluation
Site	Course, outside school	School
Focus	Part of school	Whole school

learning outcomes. The whole improvement edifice was based upon a positivistic, quantitative evaluation of effects.

The worldwide failures of this model of school improvement to generate more than very partial take up by schools of the curricular or organizational innovations (see Reynolds 1988) became established findings within the educational discourse of the 1970s. Out of the recognition of this failure came, reactively, the new improvement paradigm of the 1980s which is still reflected in much of the writing on school improvement that is current and in evidence today. This new movement has celebrated *bottom-up* school improvement, in which the improvement attempts were 'owned' by those at school level, although outside school consultants or experts would be allowed to put their knowledge forward for possible utilization. It celebrated the *lore* or practical knowledge of practitioners rather than the knowledge base of those who had conducted research. It wished to change educational processes, rather than school management or organizational features which it saw as reified constructs. It wanted the outcomes or goals of school improvement programmes to be debated and discussed, rather than accepted as given. Indeed, the process of school development was often seen by school improvers as a process of making value choices explicit rather than implicit, in which the resultant values debate aided the improvement process. The paradigm also wished to operate at the level of practitioners rather than at school level, with a qualitative and naturalistically oriented evaluation of the enterprise being preferred to a quantitative evaluation. The improvement attempt was *whole school* rather than *part of school* oriented and it was also school based rather than outside school or course based (this material is developed in Reynolds (1988)).

[. . .]

There is little doubt that the reactive nature of the new school improvement paradigm outlined above was deficient in terms of it actually generating school improvement, as some of its proponents began to realize. Hopkins and Holly (in Reid *et al.* 1987) were already recognizing by the late 1980s that although schools should *own* their improvement attempts, outsiders could perform a valuable function in bringing *excellent* or *elite* knowledge to the attention of teachers in the schools. The process-oriented *journey* of school improvement was still stressed, but by the late 1980s the journey was also undertaken in order to enable schools to evaluate their processes and outcomes. Qualitative techniques were still the approved methodology for the measurement of programme impacts, processes and outcomes, but a rigour shown by a concern to check the validity of findings had now appeared in this work.

However, in spite of the signs of intellectual movement within the school improvement paradigm itself noted above, the description of the paradigm in the above paragraphs would not seem to be an unfair description of its core beliefs. Certainly there would be variation between and within countries in their reactiveness against the old paradigm, with the British sociology of education and teacher researcher movement as the most extreme (Elliott 1980; Woods and Pollard 1987), but overall it is clear the paradigm was substantially accepted internationally.

The school effectiveness paradigm

The school effectiveness research paradigm has a very different intellectual history and has exhibited a very different set of core beliefs concerning operationalization, conceptualization and measurement by comparison with the approaches of the school improvers. It has been strongly quantitative in orientation with researchers arguing that the dominant, psychologically oriented beliefs in the importance of outside school factors (for example, Coleman *et al.* 1966; Jencks *et al.* 1971) had to be destroyed by utilization of the same quantitative paradigm rather than a more qualitatively oriented approach.

Adherents to the paradigm are concerned with pupil outcomes primarily, which is not surprising given the political history of school effectiveness research in the United States, where it has grown and built on the beliefs of Ron Edmonds and his associates that all *children can learn*. Processes within schools only have an importance within the school effectiveness paradigm to the extent that they affect outcomes – indeed, one *back maps* with the paradigm from outcomes to processes. The school effectiveness paradigm furthermore regards pupil and school outcomes as fundamentally unproblematic and as given; indeed, in the great majority of the North American effectiveness research the outcomes used are only the very limited, official educational definitions of the school as an academic institution. School effectiveness researchers, indeed, often talk of a *good* or *excellent* school as if the definition of good or excellent is unproblematic. Lastly, the school effectiveness paradigm is organizationally rather than process based in terms of its analytic and descriptive orientation, preferring to restrict itself to the more easily quantifiable or measurable. As an example, Fullan's (1985) process factors such as 'a feel for the process of leadership' or 'a guiding value system', or 'intense interaction and communication' are largely eschewed in favour of organizationally and behaviourally oriented process variables such as 'clear goals and high expectations' and/or 'parental involvement and support'. Additionally, the focus within the school improvement paradigm on the attitudinal and on personal and group inner states is replaced within school effectiveness research by a focus on the more easily measured behaviour of persons.

From the outline of the history of the two paradigms above, it can be seen that the two disciplines of school effectiveness and school improvement are coming from very different places intellectually, methodologically and theoretically. The school improvement paradigm was a reactive one from the early 1980s, reacting against the top-down imposition of elite defined knowledge in schools towards a celebration of practitioner lore, and an acceptance of the ensuing goals debate rather than an acknowledgement of predetermined school goals. In this reactive phase, school improvement is very different in its orientations to the school effectiveness paradigm which began to emerge in the early to mid 1980s, with its outcome focus, its quantitative methodology, its concern to generate truthful knowledge about schools (whether practitioners agreed with it or not!) and its concern with reified school organizations and easily measured behaviours, rather than with the attitudes of teachers and pupils.

There is [. . .] evidence that some of those appreciative of aspects of the school improvement tradition have realized the necessity for paradigmatic change, if only within that same paradigm, as noted earlier by Holly and Hopkins. Fullan (1991), too, in his more recent writing pays considerably more attention than before to the *recipes* of school effectiveness knowledge. [. . .] Hopkins (1990) talks about 'the necessary synthesis between improvement and effective schools knowledge'.

Some scholars within the school effectiveness community have also argued for the interpenetration and synthesis of both bodies of knowledge in the interests of improving pupil performance and school quality. Mortimore (1991) argues for transferring 'the energy, knowledge and skills of school effectiveness research to the study of school improvement'. Elsewhere, I have also argued that school improvement attempts need to understand the complex psychological abnormality that is exhibited within ineffective schools (Reynolds, 1992), evidence of which should be taken from the effective schools literature. The mission statement of the journal *School Effectiveness and School Improvement* (Creemers and Reynolds 1990) also argued for the still, small voice of empirical rationality being jointly utilized to assess the validity both of existing models of school improvement and the validity of our existing simplistic factor-based theories of school effectiveness. In all these respects the historical divisions between effectiveness and improvement may be considerably diminishing in importance.

How the school effectiveness research contributes to school improvement

If closer relationships between the two specialities were to be formed there is much ground for believing that both specialities could contribute greatly to the academic and practical needs of the other. To take school improvement first, the clear need is for school improvers to have knowledge of those factors within schools and within classrooms that may be manipulated or changed to produce higher quality schooling. At the moment, school effectiveness researchers are failing to generate that knowledge that is relevant to the school improvement enterprise in the following specific ways:

• There are very few case studies of the effective, or for that matter the ineffective, schools that would show the interrelationships between school process variables and which would paint a picture for practitioners of the fine-grained reality of school and classroom processes. The American study by Rosenholtz (1989) and some of the recent *mixed methodology* work from the Louisiana School Effectiveness Study of Stringfield and Teddlie (1990) are exceptions to this trend internationally. In Britain, however, there are still no in-depth, qualitative portraits of effective schools following the pioneering work of Rutter *et al.* (1979) or Mortimore *et al.* (1988).

The explanations for the absence of rich case study data are simple, of course, since school effectiveness researchers have probably feared the identification of schools, which would follow the publication of rich descriptions, when they have customarily promised schools anonymity in the research process. The effect of this absence, though, is to reduce the practitioner relevance of the effectiveness research and to make the transfer of knowledge to the improvement community (with its qualitative orientation) more difficult:

- School effectiveness studies are deficient at the level of *processes* rather than factors, since effectiveness researchers have considerably more experience at the level of school organizational factors. School processes defined in terms of attitudes, values, relationships and climate have been neglected therefore, even though the school improvement community needs information on these factors within schools, given their centrality to the process of improvement and development.
- School effectiveness studies customarily show a snapshot of a school, at a point in time, not an evolutionary and moving picture of a school over time, a neglect which hinders the usefulness of the knowledge for purposes of school development. School improvement needs to have ideas about how schools came to be effective (or for that matter ineffective) in order to replicate (or for that matter eradicate) the process, which necessitates a dynamic, evolutionary, evolving and *change over time* orientation within school effectiveness research.
- School effectiveness studies from outside North America, particularly those from Britain (for example, Rutter *et al.* 1979; Reynolds *et al.* 1987), neglect the detailed study of the crucial variable of the principal or headteacher. Both these early British studies of school effectiveness, for example, have few headteacher variables because the researchers had to promise their sponsoring educational authorities that they would not concentrate in detail in this area, which in the context of the professional headteacher autonomy customarily prevailing in the 1970s and 1980s was hardly surprising. When the Rutter team later sought to translate their findings about effective school factors into their schools, it is not surprising that their knowledge-deficient improvement programmes failed to generate much overall improvement in educational processes or pupil outcomes (Maughan *et al.* 1990).
- School effectiveness studies have thus far (with the notable exception of work by Coleman and LaRoque (1991) neglected greatly the other educational institutions, arrangements and layers above the level of the school.

   [. . .]

   School improvement needs clearly to be informed by knowledge as to what conditions outside the level of the school are necessary to generate process and/or outcome improvement – currently school effectiveness research tends to generate knowledge only about school-level variables.

- School effectiveness research, whether of North American, British or Dutch origin, tends towards the generation of lists of organizational process factors within schools that are associated with pupil outcomes. Yet what school improvers need to know is not what 10, 20 or 30 factors may be useful enhancers of outcomes if changed, but which one or two factors should be changed. Given the difficulty of focusing upon large numbers of changes simultaneously and the importance of ordering temporally the change attempts in schools (Hargreaves and Hopkins 1991), this need for change strategies that relates to a small and discrete number of factors is magnified by the need to alter those variables within schools which are the key determinants of other process variables. No school effectiveness study so far has attempted to isolate the direction and strength of the influences that link school process variables together.

- School effectiveness research, to compound the difficulties noted above, cannot even prove conclusively which process variables are causes of school effectiveness and which effects. If we take as an example the well established link between teachers' high academic expectations of their pupils and their pupils' good results in examinations or tests of attainment, it may be that the direction of the relationship is a positive one from academic expectations, to academic success, or that academic success may by contrast influence academic expectations since the experience of high examination passes at school level may lead to an expectation of them continuing, or there may be interactive influences. The directionality of the relationship – crucial for school improvers wishing to decide what to target for improvement – is not established within the research base for this variable and for many other groups or pairs of variables within the school effectiveness knowledge base.

- School effectiveness knowledge also misses the chance of satisfaction of the needs of the school improvement enterprise by being thoroughly dated. Improvement schemes [. . .] need to be based on knowledge that is generated from school systems that reflect the [current] characteristics of schools [. . .], not the schools of the 1970s and 1980s. At the level of what makes for effective schooling, process factors such as the assertive principal instructional leadership that was associated with effectiveness in the 1980s may not be associated in the same way [now], when demands for *ownership* by teachers may have changed the educational cultural context. Outcomes appropriate for measurement in the 1980s such as academic achievement or examination attainment may not be the only ones appropriate to the [current context], where new goals concerning knowledge of how to learn or knowledge in mastering information technology may be necessary.

  Even those process factors associated with effectiveness in the 1970s and 1980s may not be, on their own, sufficient to generate effectiveness in the [current context]. The principal, for example, who was an effective leader in the 1980s now finds a bewildering variety of new aspects to the role in the case of British schools [. . .]. He/she is now expected to sell the school as a product, to motivate staff without instrumental rewards, to translate the externally imposed policy agenda into internally driven programmes and to possess psychological resilience in the face of considerable anxiety, uncertainty and concern. The person able to do this [now] may well not be the principal or headteacher described in the school effectiveness research of the 1980s, yet school effectiveness researchers [. . .] are still operating within a strangely aged paradigm in terms of what school variables, and what dimensions of school variables, to collect data on (for further speculations on this theme see Reynolds (1992)).

- School effectiveness research has rarely been 'fine grained' enough to provide the school improvement enterprise with the information it needs, since the variation in *what works* by context has been a focus only of a very limited amount of North American work (Hallinger and Murphy 1986; Wimpelberg *et al.* 1989). School improvers need more than the notion of what works across context in the average school, and need more than data upon the relationships between school processes and outcomes for all schools – they need knowledge of the factors that will generate improvement in particular schools in particular socio-economic and cultural contexts. Since only a small amount of our school effectiveness knowledge base is disaggregated and analysed by context, the delineation of the precise variables that school improvement needs to target to affect outcomes is clearly impossible at present.

- School improvement researchers often find themselves working in historically ineffective educational settings yet the knowledge base within school effectiveness may not be necessarily easily applicable to those settings. Researchers seem to have worked with an implicit (and in the case of some of the earlier advocates within the school effectiveness movement, an explicit) deficit orientation towards the ineffective school, in which it is seen as not possessing the factors that make other schools excel. The possibility, which is my own view (Reynolds 1992), that the ineffective school may possess variables at the level of interpersonal problems, projections, defences and the like, which in turn do not exist in the effective school, seems to be rarely considered by researchers. The knowledge of these areas, of these *ghosts* or *shadows* on the change process that improvers of the ineffective schools would naturally need, will not be found in a school effectiveness paradigm in which the good practice of effective schools is simply *back mapped* on to the ineffective schools and then assumed to be sufficient to help the ineffective improve.

How school improvement could help school effectiveness research

At its simplest level, school improvement strategies provide the ultimate test for many of the theories posited within the school effectiveness research enterprise, since the change in school outcomes identified by research as being linked to school processes is the way of testing whether there is a causal link between processes and outcomes. School improvement schemes and strategies based upon the school effectiveness research communities' identified characteristics are therefore of crucial importance to the development of school effectiveness research.

A number of further tasks for school improvement practitioners to facilitate the further development of school effectiveness research also suggest themselves:

- School improvement studies all too rarely measure the impact of changes in improvement programmes upon the outcomes of pupils or students. Part of the explanation for this may be the historical tendency of school improvement to celebrate certain styles of professional practice because of its association with the training needs and desires of the teaching profession within schools, and part of the explanation may be the reluctance of many within the school improvement paradigm to be explicit about what the nature of the school outcomes or the educational goals of their programmes really are. The absence, though, of these data as to programme effects restricts the ability of those within the school improvement paradigm to help the school effectiveness research base expand in terms of further understanding the possible relationships between school processes and school outcomes.
- School improvement programmes need to cease their *grapeshot-* or *multiple-factors-* based approach to school development and change, since changing more than one school factor at a time (which is what most attempt) makes it impossible for school effectiveness researchers to judge which of the factors concerned may be those factors accounting for any sources of increased pupil outcomes. The school effectiveness knowledge base is again clearly impoverished by an inability to elucidate what, or what not, at the level of the processes of the school has an impact upon outcomes.

- School improvement programmes need urgently to pay attention to the implications of multi-level modelling procedures for their programmes. The evidence from effectiveness research that schools can have differential effects upon their pupils (Nuttall *et al.* 1989) and that schools effective for some groups of pupils may actually be ineffective for others, has wide ranging implications for school improvement, since these results imply that improvement attempts need urgently to move away from the much vaunted whole-school strategies towards more finely targeted programmes that may vary within the school in terms of their focus and their target group. By focusing improvement at the level of boys/girls, high ability/low ability pupils, and pupils from ethnic minorities/pupils from *host* cultures it would be possible for school improvement persons to generate more appropriate school change strategies, but most importantly it would be possible for school improvement to generate evidence about differentially effective school processes as the effects of their change attempts were targeted within schools, an area where school effectiveness knowledge has been historically non-existent.

School improvement research needs to refocus its activities away from the level of the school to that of the classroom if it is to generate the possibility of increased school outcomes and if it is to generate knowledge of use to the school effectiveness research enterprise. A considerable volume of research now exists that shows teachers' focal concerns to be with the content of their curricular and instructional practices rather than with the wider area of the school, yet school improvement rarely has an instructional focus (see, for example, Fullan, 1991). Within centring itself upon the instructional level, school improvement runs the risk of manipulating variables only at the level of the school, which in most recent research explain much less of the variation in student outcomes than do those variables at the instructional or classroom level (see, for a review, Creemers 1992). School improvement also runs the risk of not helping the development of school effectiveness research by not manipulating, and giving information about, the characteristics of the instructional level.

Conclusions

We have seen in this chapter that there are wide divergencies in the orientation, methodology and theoretical approaches of the specialisms historically known as *school effectiveness* and *school improvement*. These differences are the result of the historical nature of each group of scholars' and practitioners' development, with school effectiveness researchers desirous of remaining within a positivistic framework to disprove the findings from positivistic educational psychology and with school improvement practitioners reactively moving to a qualitative, appreciative stance rather than an evaluative one because of the nature of their reaction against the failed improvement paradigm of the 1960s and 1970s. We noted, however, some movement by both groups towards a blending of what had been seen as oppositional approaches.

We have continued by arguing, though, that there is much that school effectiveness researchers can do to develop the school-based knowledge base which school improvers need in their possession as they relate to their schools, and we have concluded that there is much that school improvement attempts can do to improve the validity and reliability (and in fact the transferability) of the school effectiveness knowledge base into schools, by means of testing the findings of school effectiveness research and their resulting propositions within schools.

All our discussions so far assume, though, that the intellectual and practical enterprises of school improvement and school effectiveness remain separate, yet that separation in itself may be undesirable, when compared with the potential benefits for knowledge and practice of an integrated, coherent and coordinated intellectual and practical enterprise that would be concerned jointly with research and practice on school effectiveness and school improvement. [. . .]

References

Coleman, J. *et al.* (1966) *Equality of Educational Opportunity.* Washington, DC: US Government Printing Office.

Coleman, P. and LaRoque, L. (1990) *Struggling to be Good Enough.* Lewes: Falmer Press.

Creemers, B. (1992) School effectiveness and effective instruction – the need for a further relationship, in J. Bashi and Z. Saff (eds) *School Effectiveness and Improvement.* Jerusalem: Hebrew University Press.

Creemers, B. and Reynolds, D. (1990) School effectiveness and school improvement: A mission statement. *School Effectiveness and School Improvement,* 1(10): 1–3.

Elliott, J. (1980) Implications of classroom research for professional development, in E. Hoyle and J. Megarry (eds) *World Yearbook of Education 1980.* London: Kogan Page.

Fullan, M. (1985) Change processes and strategies at the local level. *Elementary School Journal,* 85(13): 391–421.

Fullan, M. (1991) *The New Meaning of Educational Change.* London: Cassell.

Hallinger, P. and Murphy, J. (1986) The social context of effective schools. *American Journal of Education,* 94: 328–55.

Hargreaves, D. and Hopkins, D. (1991) *The Empowered School.* London: Cassell.

Hopkins, D. (1990) The international school improvement project (ISIP) and effective schooling: Towards a synthesis. *School Organization,* 10(3): 129–94.

Jencks, C. *et al.* (1971) *Inequality.* London: Allen Lane.

Maughan, B., Ouston, J., Pickles, A. and Rutter, M. (1990) Can schools change 1: Outcomes at six London secondary schools. *School Effectiveness and Improvement,* 1(3): 188–210.

Mortimore, P. (1991) School effectiveness research: Which way at the crossroads? *School Effectiveness and School Improvement,* 2(3): 213–29.

Mortimore, P., Sammons, P., Ecob, R. and Stoll, L. (1988) *School Matters: The Junior Years.* Salisbury: Open Books.

Nuttall, D., Goldstein, H., Prosser, R. and Rasbash, H. (1989) Differential school effectiveness. *International Journal of Educational Research,* 13(7): 769–76.

Reid, K., Hopkins, D. and Holly, P. (1987) *Towards the Effective School.* Oxford: Blackwell.

Reynolds, D. (1988) British school improvement research: The contribution of qualitative studies. *International Journal of Qualitative Studies in Education* 1(2): 143–54.

Reynolds, D. (1992) School effectiveness and school improvement in the 1990s, in D. Reynolds and P. Cuttance (eds) *School Effectiveness.* London: Cassell.

Reynolds, D., Sullivan, M. and Murgatroyd, S. J. (1987) *The Comprehensive Experiment.* Lewes: Falmer Press.

Rosenholtz, S. (1989) *Teachers' Workplace.* New York: Longman.

Rutter, M., Maughan, B., Mortimer, P. and Ouston, J. (1979) *Fifteen Thousand Hours: Secondary Schools and their Effects on Children.* London: Open Books.

Stringfield, S. and Teddlie, C. (1990) School improvement effects: Qualitative and quantitative data from four naturally occurring experiments in phases 3 and 4 of the Louisiana school effectiveness study. *School Effectiveness and School Improvement,* 1(2): 139–61.

Wimpelberg, R., Teddlie, C. and Stringfield, S. (1989) Sensitivity to context: The past and future of effective schools research. *Educational Administration Quarterly*, 25: 82–107.
Woods, P. and Pollard, A. (eds) (1987) *Sociology and teaching: A New Challenge for the Sociology of Education*. London: Croom Helm.

24 | School improvement – propositions for action*

DAVID HOPKINS, MEL AINSCOW AND MEL WEST

In the 1990s, the educational agenda has increasingly been dominated by a concern to make sense of, and implement, the radical reform agenda of the previous decade. This quest for stability, however, has been sought against a background of continuing change, as expectations for student achievement rise beyond the capacity of the system to deliver. It has also become increasingly apparent that change and improvement are not necessarily synonymous. Although it is true that external pressure is often the cause, or at least the impetus, for most educational change, this is not to imply that such changes are always desirable. Indeed in our opinion, some externally imposed change should be resisted, or at least adapted to the school's own purpose.

As we work with schools within the framework of the national reform agenda we are committed to an approach to educational change that focuses on student achievement *and* schools' ability to cope with change. We refer to this particular approach as *school improvement*. We regard school improvement as a distinct approach to educational change that enhances student outcomes *as well as* strengthening the school's capacity for managing change. In this sense school improvement is about raising student achievement through focusing on the teaching–learning process and the conditions which support it (Hopkins *et al.* 1994).

Improving the Quality of Education for All

Since the early 1990s, we have been working closely with some 40 schools in East Anglia, North London, Yorkshire and Humberside on a school improvement and development project known as *Improving the Quality of Education for All* (IQEA).

* This chapter is based in part on a paper prepared by David Hopkins as the keynote address at the Secondary Heads Association (SHA) President's Inaugural Conference on 'Improving Secondary Schools', 18 October 1995.

The overall aim of the project is to strengthen a school's ability to provide quality education for all its pupils by building upon existing good practice. In so doing, we are also producing and evaluating a model of school development, and a programme of support. IQEA works from an assumption that schools are most likely to strengthen their ability to provide enhanced outcomes for all pupils when they adopt ways of working that are consistent with their own aspirations as well as the current reform agenda.

At the outset of IQEA, we attempted to outline our own vision of school improvement by articulating a set of principles that provided us with a philosophical and practical starting point. Because it is our assumption that schools are most likely to provide quality education and enhanced outcomes for pupils when they adopt ways of working that are consistent with these principles, they were offered as the basis for collaboration with the IQEA project schools. In short, we were inviting the schools to identify and to work on their own projects and priorities, but to do so in a way which embodied a set of 'core' values about school improvement. These principles represent the expectations we have of the way project schools pursue school improvement. They serve as an *aide-mémoire* to the schools and to ourselves.

The five principles of IQEA are:

- School improvement is a process that focuses on enhancing the *quality of students' learning*.
- The vision of the school should be one which embraces *all* members of the school community as both learners and contributors.
- The school will see in external pressures for change important opportunities to secure its *internal priorities*.
- The school will seek to develop structures and create conditions which encourage collaboration and lead to the *empowerment* of individuals and groups.
- The school will seek to promote the view that *monitoring and evaluation of quality* is a responsibility which all members of staff share.

We feel that the operation of these principles creates synergism – together they are greater than the sum of their parts. They characterize an overall approach rather than prescribing a course of action. The intention is that they should inform the thinking and actions of teachers during school improvement efforts, and provide a touchstone for the strategies they devise and the behaviours they adopt.

So far, we have summarized our broad approach to school improvement. There is now the issue of how best to support schools through this complex process. Our current thinking and practice is best summarized by describing what we do *within* and *outside* school (Hopkins 1994).

Our *within*-school work concerns the nature of our own intervention. As is by now quite obvious, we have explicitly chosen an interventionist role. Our roles vary from time to time and from place to place. On some occasions this may involve us in questioning our school-based colleagues in order to encourage them to 'think aloud' about their work. Often they tell us that simply having an outsider who poses questions in a supportive way and then helps to set deadlines is helpful. Having established a long-term agreement to collaborate with colleagues in a school, and then invested time in creating a working relationship with those colleagues, it is appropriate that we should be prepared to offer a critique of their proposals and actions. In this way we are seeking to balance our support with a degree of pressure that is intended to push their thinking forward.

Our *outside*-school role focuses mainly on the training sessions we hold for the various cohorts of schools involved in the project. There is a strong emphasis on 'reflection and enquiry' within these sessions. Reflection is the essential building block of professional competence and confidence. The training is based around the conditions we regard as necessary for successful school improvement which are described later in this chapter.

School improvement of course is not a 'quick-fix' approach to change. In attempting to work with schools in this way one is immediately confronted with staggering complexity, and a bewildering array of policy and strategy options. Through our engagement with schools we have begun to develop a series of propositions that attempt to unravel the complexities of school improvement. These reflections are based on our recent work in schools, in particular on our experience on the then DES 'School Development Plans' project (Hargreaves and Hopkins 1991), as well as the 'Improving the Quality of Education for All' (IQEA) school improvement network (Hopkins *et al.* 1994).

Proposition one: Without a clear focus on the internal conditions of the school, improvement efforts will quickly become marginalized

One of the great fallacies of educational change is that policy directives, from any level, have a direct impact on student achievement. What we do know from experience, as well as the research on student achievement and school effectiveness, is that the greatest impact on student progress is achieved by those innovations or adaptations of practice that intervene in, or modify, the learning process. Changes in curriculum, teaching methods, grouping practices, and assessment procedures have the greatest potential impact on the performance of students. The main point that we wish to make here however, is that *school improvement works best when a clear and practical focus for development is linked to simultaneous work on the internal conditions within the school.* Conditions are the internal features of the school, the 'arrangements' that enable it to get work done. Without an equal focus on conditions, even development priorities that directly affect classroom practice quickly become marginalized.

Within the IQEA project, we have begun to associate a number of 'conditions' within the school with its capacity for sustained development. At present, our best estimate of these conditions which underpin improvement efforts, and so therefore represent the key management arrangements, can be broadly stated as:

- a commitment to *staff development*;
- practical efforts to *involve* staff, students and the community in school policies and decisions;
- 'transformational' *leadership* approaches;
- effective *coordination* strategies;
- proper attention to the potential benefits of *enquiry and reflection*; and
- a commitment to *collaborative planning* activity.

Taken together, these conditions result in the creation of opportunities for teachers to feel more powerful and confident about their work. This is particularly important because difficulties often occur for both individual teachers and the school when development work begins. Teachers, for example, may be faced with acquiring new teaching skills or with mastering new curriculum material. The school as a consequence may be forced into new ways of working that are incompatible with existing organizational structures. This phase of 'destabilization' or 'internal turbulence' is as predictable as it is uncomfortable. Yet many research studies have found that without a period of destabilization successful, long-lasting change is unlikely to occur.

Proposition two: School improvement will not occur unless clear decisions are made about development and maintenance

It is all well and good to talk about development in broad terms, but given current concerns about overload in our change rich environment, such a general and unfocused agenda is unrealistic. Decisions need to be made about what changes need to be implemented and how they are to be selected. This is a profound question, and one that reflects what is perhaps the most crucial challenge facing schools today – how to balance change and stability effectively. How on the one hand to preserve what is already admirable and fine in a school, and on the other, how to respond positively to innovation and the challenge of change.

Bearing this conundrum in mind we introduced in the *empowered school* (Hargreaves and Hopkins 1991) the distinction between a school's development and maintenance activities:

- *Maintenance* refers to the school carrying out its day-to-day activities, the fulfilling of its statutory obligations, and to supporting teaching and learning within the context of the National Curriculum, all to the best of its ability.
- *Development* on the other hand refers to that amount of resource, time and energy the school reserves from the total it has available, for carrying forward those aims, aspirations and activities that 'add value' to what it already does. It is through its development activities that a school continues to make progress in times of change.

The effective use of those resources devoted to development obviously implies a high level of prioritization. A common problem is that many schools overload their development plans. Because there is insufficient distinction between plans for development and plans for maintenance (e.g. those devoted to budgets, timetable, staffing), there is a tendency to put all external changes into development, thus ensuring that nothing gets done properly. The distinction between development and maintenance should allow the school to make more coherent decisions about the focus of its developmental energy irrespective to some extent of the external reform agenda.

Although some external changes need to become developmental priorities in their own right, more often it is better to select priorities that cut across a range of external or curriculum changes. It is becoming apparent from our work in schools that the more 'generic', yet focused, a priority for development is, the more impact it will have on the maintenance system. A priority on teaching and learning, for example, will inevitably spread across a school's curriculum activities to the darkest realms of its maintenance activities, when teachers realize that a new approach 'works' and can be used in another unit of study or scheme of work.

At the heart of the issue regarding maintenance and development is the question of how people's time is used. Indeed, it can be argued that this is the best indicator of what is of greatest importance in a school. The innovative responses required for sustained development (e.g. delegation, task groups, high levels of specific staff development, quality time for planning, collaborative classroom activity) are inimical to successful maintenance. What is required are complementary structures for both maintenance and development, each with their own purpose, budget and ways of working. Obviously the majority of a school's time and resources will go on maintenance, but unless there is also an element dedicated to development, then the school is unlikely to progress in times of change. It is interesting to note that the school level conditions referred to in Proposition One constitute an archetypal development structure.

Proposition three: Successful school improvement involves adapting external change for internal purposes

The distinction between development and maintenance underpins our approach to development planning. Development planning itself is commonly regarded as an important preliminary to school improvement. Working through the planning cycle is likely to involve the school in generating a number of 'priorities' for action – often too many to work on. This means that decisions about 'priorities' must be made – moving from the separate, perhaps even conflicting priorities of individuals or groups, to a systematically compiled set of priorities which represent the overall needs of a whole school community. Previously, we have suggested that two principles should guide this process of choice amongst priorities (Hargreaves and Hopkins 1991: 42):

- *manageability* – how much can we realistically hope to achieve?
- *coherence* – is there a sequence which will ease implementation?

More recently (Hopkins *et al.* 1994), we have noted that a third principle can help to guide schools through what is often a difficult series of choices.

- *consonance* – the extent to which internally identified priorities coincide or overlap with external pressures for reform.

We believe that there is empirical evidence to suggest that those schools which understand consonance, and therefore see externally generated change efforts as providing opportunities, as well as (or instead of) problems, are better able to respond to external demands. It is through such an understanding of how to approach planning that schools begin to see the potential in adapting external change to internal purpose.

We have previously outlined a theoretical model, 'A framework for school improvement' that informs our work with schools (Hopkins *et al.* 1994; Hopkins 1996). The framework provides the setting for a series of assumptions upon which our generic approach to school improvement is based. There are essentially two major components to the framework – the 'capacity building dimension', which has already been discussed in relation to the conditions for school improvement, and the 'strategic dimension'. It is when the school is making strategic decisions that the three principles of manageability, coherence and consonance are likely have most significance.

In essence, the *'strategic dimension'* reflects the ability of the school to plan sensibly for development efforts. In line with the argument so far, we encourage project schools to select *developmental priorities* that are related to some aspect of curriculum, assessment or classroom process which the school has identified from the many alternatives that have emerged from the consultations with staff that characterize whole-school development planning. But we have also encouraged them to consider the degree to which opportunities in the external environment can be exploited, or demands from the external environment met, while pursuing priorities which are appropriate to the school's internal needs.

At its simplest, the school improvement *strategy* is a deliberate action or sequence of actions taken by a school staff in order to implement identified curriculum or organizational priorities. However, the strategy is likely to be more powerful in those situations where it brings harmony between external and internal forces for change.

Most schools currently attempt some form of rational planning, but all too often this planning begins with abstract goals or managerial preferences. The strategic approach which we have described differs in that it encourages schools to begin at the other end of the sequence – working from the outcomes currently achieved and seeking ways to improve those which relate internal needs to external circumstances. Our observation is that the capacity for continual improvement at school level is closely bound up with such strategic thinking, which transforms a series of perhaps sensible but nevertheless 'one-off' goals into a coherent and managed series of priorities which establish a balance between internal and external pressures for change.

Proposition four: School improvement will remain a marginal activity unless it impacts across all the levels of the school

One of the things that we know from research and experience is that change will not be successful unless it impacts all levels of the organization. Specifically, our focus is on three levels within the school and the ways in which these interrelate:

- The *senior team* level is responsible for overall management and the establishment of policies, particularly with respect to how resources and strategies for staff development can be mobilised in support of school improvement efforts.
- The *department* or *working group* level comprises those established groups within the school responsible for curriculum, teaching and learning.
- Finally, at the *individual teacher* level, the focus is on developing classroom practice through professional growth.

In very effective schools these three levels are mutually supportive. Consequently, a specific aim of our work is to devise and establish positive conditions at each level, and to coordinate support across these levels. It is in this connection that we require the establishment of a team of coordinators in each school whose task includes the integration of activities across the various levels. We refer to these coordinators as the project *cadre*. They are responsible for the day-to-day running of the development project in their own school, and for creating links between the ideas of the overall project and practical action. In many schools, members of the cadre establish an *extended cadre* which serves to widen the impact of the project in a more formal way within the school. As the cadre stands outside of the normal hierarchical structures, it is able to act in a more focused and flexible way. In one sense, they act as the manifestation of a development structure within the school. The role of the cadre is of crucial importance in our approach to school improvement. They are the key to integrating the various levels within the school.

Proposition five: Data about the school's performance creates the energy for development

As a consequence of our work on the IQEA project, we have realised that those schools which recognize that enquiry into and reflection on the school's performance are important elements within the improvement process possess additional momentum for change. This seems to be particularly true where there is widespread staff involvement in these processes, and when there are good reasons for such participation. For example, it is much easier to focus efforts around the school's priorities when every member of staff sees himself or herself as playing a role in the evaluation of the related policies and practices. Similarly, it is often only teachers who possess vital knowledge about classroom outcomes, so any attempt to evaluate on the basis of senior manager's perceptions is at best partial. As we have outlined elsewhere (Ainscow *et al.* 1994: 12) enquiry and reflection as development 'tools' are at their most effective when there is:

- systematic collection, interpretation and use of school-generated data in decision-making;
- an effective strategy for reviewing the progress and impact of school policies and initiatives;
- widespread staff involvement in the processes of data collection and analysis;
- a clearly established set of 'ground-rules' for the collection, control and use of school generated data.

The need to ground policy decisions in data about how the school is functioning is paramount.

Of course, there is a feedback role to be filled by data gathering to determine whether or not policies are having impact in the areas they seek to address. But here the focus needs to remain on the collection of evidence on impact, and not merely of implementation. It is vital to keep this distinction in mind, or we can convince ourselves that we are improving the school whilst in reality we are merely changing its policies. Effective strategies again depend on the level of involvement of classroom teachers, since it is the teacher who is best placed to detect whether it is improvement rather than simply change. Involving teachers in this process also provides them with a stimulus to make changes work for the benefit of students.

Establishing such a climate requires careful planning, and often needs to be supported by staff development activities, particularly where we wish to encourage staff to work together in each other's classrooms, acting as observer and 'critical friend' to a colleague. It also needs clear understandings about what data will be gathered, how data will be gathered and who will be the audience.

Once teachers begin to participate in these activities, they quickly become fascinated by the data they produce and the meaning which can be attached to it. Indeed there is a detectable increase in commitment to aspects of the improvement programme as data relating to them becomes available. Teachers seem to draw new energy from feedback which relates specifically to their own contexts and efforts, and levels of motivation increase with the feeling that they are 'coming to grips' with real issues. This seems to be equally true whether the data is positive or negative – we have seen a number of cases where negative data has apparently reaffirmed teachers' commitment to change.

Proposition six: Successful school improvement efforts engender a language about teaching and change

The framework for school improvement, described in previous sections, is highly consistent with Joyce's analysis of the characteristics of effective large scale school improvement initiatives (Joyce *et al.* 1993: 72), in so far as these have tended to:

- focus on specific outcomes which can be related to student learning, rather than adopt laudable but non-specific goals such as 'improve exam results';
- draw on theory, research into practice and the teachers' own experience in formulating strategies, so that a rationale for the required changes is established in the minds of those expected to bring them about;
- target staff development, since it is unlikely that developments in student learning will occur without developments in teachers' practice; and
- monitor the impact of policy on practice early and regularly, rather than rely on 'post-hoc' evaluation.

There are two respects in which these characteristics are particularly relevant to the theme of this chapter. First, they provide an example of how the priority for development (the first two points) links together with simultaneous work on the school conditions (the second two points). As we have argued, this marriage is a vital component of sustainable improvement efforts. Second is the emphasis on specifications of teaching and learning. There is mounting evidence that the content of a lesson notwithstanding, the use of appropriate teaching strategies can dramatically increase student achievement (Joyce *et al.* 1992). A major goal for school improvement, therefore, is to help teachers become professionally flexible so that they can select, from a repertoire of possibilities, the teaching approach most suited to their particular content area, and the age, interests and aptitudes of their students.

It is our firm belief that one of the characteristics of successful schools is that *teachers talk about teaching*. There is a growing literature about classroom practice (see for example: Joyce *et al.* 1992; Creemers 1994; Hopkins *et al.* 1994: chapter 4; West *et al.* 1995) to help focus such discussions: drawing on research about teaching approaches can help to initiate the dialogue. School improvement strategies need to help teachers create a discourse about, and language for, teaching. In our experience this is achieved when development priorities on teaching and learning are based on the best advice and experience around. Such advice begins with, and leads from, the practice of teachers and their perceptions of the world of the classroom. Some complexity is inevitable once teachers begin to engage seriously with one another's practice by sharing their own experiences and searching for shared meanings. But working towards a common vocabulary, both facilitates sharing and empowers practice. At the heart of this empowerment are a number of activities which we have found to be helpful. These include:

- teachers discussing with each other the nature of teaching strategies and their application to classroom practice and schemes of work;
- establishing specifications or guidelines for the chosen teaching strategies;
- agreeing on standards used to assess student progress as a result of employing a range of teaching methods;
- mutual observation and partnership teaching in the classroom.

It is in this way, as Judith Little once remarked, that 'teachers teach each other the practice of teaching'.

CODA: The ultimate achievement of school improvement is a transformation to the culture of the school

Change is disruptive; the phase of 'internal turbulence' referred to earlier is as predictable as it is uncomfortable. Many research studies have found that without a period of destabilization, successful, long-lasting change is unlikely to occur (Fullan 1991). Yet it is at this point that most change fails to progress beyond early implementation. In these cases, when the change hits the 'wall' of individual learning or institutional resistance, turbulence begins to occur and development work begins to stall.

Many of the schools that we have been working with survive this period of destabilization by either consciously or intuitively adapting their *internal conditions* to meet the demands of the agreed on change or priority. We encourage schools to diagnose their internal conditions in relation to their chosen change *before they begin developmental work*. They can then begin to build modifications to conditions into the strategies they are going to use. When this happens, we begin to see changes occurring to the *culture* of the school. For example, classroom observation becomes more common in many schools as a result of development work. When this happens, teachers also begin to talk more about teaching, collaborative work outside of the particular project increases, and management structures are adapted to support the work. When taken together, these changes in attitudes, practice and structure create a more supportive environment within the school for managing change. The school's 'change capacity' is increased and the groundwork is laid for future change efforts. A virtuous circle of change begins to be established. Schools who have been through similar 'change cycles' either experience less internal turbulence, or are able to tolerate greater levels of turbulence, because they have progressively enhanced their capacity to change as a result of this developmental process.

One can summarize this process using the following notation: 'P' stands for the priority the school sets itself, 'S' the chosen strategy, {} the period of destabilization, 'Co' the school's internal conditions that are modified in order to ameliorate the destabilization and 'Cu' the resulting change in culture.

$$P \rightarrow S \rightarrow \{\} \rightarrow Co \rightarrow Cu$$

Real life of course is not as simple or as linear as this formula suggests, but this way of describing the process of development resonates with the experience of many of those that we talk to and work with. The process of cultural change is also not a 'one-off' as is implied by the notation, but evolves and unfolds over time. Often many sequences have to be gone through before a radically different culture emerges in a school (Hopkins 1996).

Many of the headteachers we have interviewed and work with, adopt, albeit intuitively, such an approach to the management of change. They seem to agree with Schein (1985: 2) when he wrote that, 'the only thing of real importance that leaders do is to create and manage culture'. These headteachers realize that the impact of successful change needs to be on the culture of the school, for it is the culture that sustains the changes in teaching and learning that consequently enhance the achievement of students. It is almost as if they begin the development process by asking, 'What cultural changes are required?' and then, 'What priorities, strategies, and changes in conditions can bring this about?' In our experience, outstanding headteachers manipulate priorities, strategies and conditions in order to affect culture, for they know that ultimately this is the only way of enhancing the quality of educational outcomes and experience for all pupils.

The link between school improvement strategies and the culture of the school is of crucial importance. Our approach to school improvement as we have described it in this chapter, and expressed it in the six propositions, is not about the implementation of centralized reforms in a more effective way. It is, as we have seen, more to do with how schools can use the impetus of external reform to 'improve' or 'develop' themselves. Sometimes, what a school chooses to do in terms of school improvement will be consistent with the national reform agenda, at other times it will not. Whatever the case, the decision to engage in school improvement, at least in the schools that we work with, is based on an aspiration to create cultures that enable teachers to effectively pursue what is the best for the young people in that school. When this occurs we not only begin to meet the real challenge of educational reform, but we also create classrooms and schools where both our children and their teachers learn.

References

Ainscow, M., Hopkins, D., Southworth, G. and West, M. (1994) *Creating the Conditions for School Improvement*. London: David Fulton Publisher.

Creemers, B. (1994) *The Effective Classroom*. London: Cassell.

Fullan, M. (1991) *The New Meaning of Educational Change*. London: Cassell.

Hargreaves, D. H. and Hopkins, D. (1991) *The Empowered School*. London: Cassell.

Hopkins, D. (1994) The yellow brick road. *Managing Schools Today*, 3(6): 14–17.

Hopkins, D. (1996) Towards a theory for school improvement, in J. Gray, D. Reynolds and C. Fitz-Gibbon (eds) *Merging Traditions: The Future of Research on School Effectiveness and School Improvement*. London: Cassell.

Hopkins, D., Ainscow, M. and West, M. (1994) *School Improvement in an Era of Change*. London: Cassell.

Joyce, B., Showers, B. and Weil, M. (1992) *Models of Teaching*, 4th edn. Englewood Cliffs, NJ: Prentice-Hall.

Joyce, B., Wolf, J. and Calhoun, E. (1993) *The Self Renewing School*. Alexandria, VA: ASCD.

Schein, E. (1985) *Organizational Culture and Leadership: a Dynamic View*. San Francisco: Jossey Bass.

West, M., Hopkins, D. and Beresford, J. (1995) 'Creating the conditions for classroom improvement. Paper given at the BERA/ECER Conference, Bath, England, 17 September 1995 (mimeo).

25 | Fair Furlong Primary School[*]

AGNES McMAHON, JEFF BISHOP, ROGER CARROLL AND BRIAN McINALLY

This is a study of a primary school in Bristol, a school which has a vibrant, exciting atmosphere, where pupils and teachers work hard and effectively. A school described by governors, parents and teachers as 'marvellous', 'absolutely brilliant', 'exciting', 'inviting' and about which the chair of governors said 'it's all buzzing in the school now'. The classrooms and corridors are filled with displays of children's work, there is a school choir which has sung in Bristol Cathedral, children study the violin, participate in workshops with artists in residence, enter and win competitions, put on excellent, high-standard performances for their parents at Christmas, look after an area of woodland as part of an environmental project, enjoy and experience success with their academic work and above all are valued as individuals. The school prospectus states:

> We try to be a caring school where every child will feel secure, happy and valued and where purposeful learning can take place. We want the children to be happy at school and we want learning at school to be a positive experience . . . we aim at happy and hardworking children who are proud of their achievements.

In [our] opinion [. . .] these aims are being achieved. Teachers in schools like this can be justifiably proud of their work, but the achievements here are greater, since this is a school that can accurately be described as one which is succeeding against the odds.

The school community

The data that follow are drawn from 1994 statistics supplied by Bristol City Council and from the bid for government funding by the Bristol City Challenge Steering Group (1992). The school is situated in one of the areas with the highest incidence of poverty

*This material has been edited and was originally published in National Commission on Education (1996) *Success Against the Odds*.

in Bristol. Using six indicators – unemployment; free school meals; community charge rebates; children in households with no earners/in households with one lone parent working part-time; long-term illness; mortality rates for those under sixty-five – it is in the quintile of city areas with the highest incidence of poverty. The social characteristics of the area have been summarised as 'very high proportion of lone parents; clear evidence of poor health and premature death; poor community facilities; low educational expectations of young children; unemployment fifty per cent higher than the local average; long term unemployment worst in the city and remoteness from the areas of growth'. [. . .]

What is the school like?

The school is a large, mixed primary school, taking children from ages three to eleven. In September 1994 there were 382 pupils on roll including a forty-five-place nursery class. The nursery operates in two sessions and these children do not stay for lunch; 166 (49 per cent) of the children in the infant and junior classes are registered for free school meals. All the children are white and none of them has English as a second language. The average class size is twenty-seven. In the 1994 autumn term four pupils had statements of special educational needs though this number has since increased. There are twenty-two full-time and part-time teachers (16.2 full-time equivalents (fte)).

The school is predominantly a female environment. The headteacher is a woman and there is only one male teacher; the caretaker and cleaners are all women. This gender balance is not the result of any deliberate policy; on the contrary, the headteacher said that she would like to have some more male teachers on the staff. However, the headteacher and the governors had developed a rigorous selection and appointment process and she said that the quality of male teachers who had come forward for interviews had been disappointing.

[. . .]

The school as a workplace

The teaching and non-teaching staff all said that the culture and ethos of the school was positive and supportive, that it was a very good place in which to work and that they enjoyed being there.

[. . .]

The school governors were also all very positive about the school. Two parent governors said that the school was inviting and that more parents were now coming into the school, while previously they would have found it threatening. The whole atmosphere was 'brilliant', the children felt secure and valued. They particularly cited the fact that children were encouraged to take reading books home, as this was something that had not happened previously.

What is being achieved?

Is there any hard evidence that this is a successful school? The headteacher is clear that while pupil learning has improved across the board there is still progress to be made.

Reading scores and pupil work are carefully monitored and show signs of improvement from year to year. The teachers are now assessing children on entry and intend to use these data as one means of measuring added value when matched against the SATs (standard attainment task) scores at Key Stages 1 and 2. For the last two years a reading audit has been conducted across the school and pupil reading scores have been carefully recorded; the staff are now considering also conducting a maths audit. These data, together with SATs scores, will give a broad indication of pupil progress, individually and as a group from year to year. The standard of pupil behaviour is very high and has improved immeasurably in the last four years. There are no unexplained pupil absences because the staff carefully implement the school policy on this issue. The staff provide a lot of extension and enrichment activities for the children: working with an artist in residence; a link scheme with a school in a very middle-class area of the authority; involvement in link projects with schools in Ghana and Malaysia; environmental projects. The children also participate in activities which in a middle-class school would be unremarkable but which in this community are unusual. For instance, the governors all commented upon the fact that pupils now take reading books home; that they can learn to play the violin; that there is a school choir which sings in public concerts; that the pupils enter and win art competitions at local and national level; and that they are polite and well behaved in school. Other indices of the school's effectiveness are that teacher turnover is low, that the staff absentee rate is very low and that the staff enjoy working in the school. The pupil roll has increased by approximately 100 in the last four years. Parental support for the school is strong, with approximately 98 per cent attending parents' evenings and excellent support for any activities – for example, concerts and fairs – organised by the school.

Has the school always been successful?

The present chair of governors has been a governor of the school for some twenty years and has experience of working with several headteachers. He has seen the school go through good and bad times but is open about the fact that before the appointment of the present headteacher, in June 1990, things were at a very low ebb. [. . .]

The most obvious and immediate problem was that the children's behaviour was very poor and this made teaching a difficult and stressful experience for the staff. [. . .] [The headteacher's] perception of the situation when she arrived was that:

> there was no structure in the staffing, no senior management team, no roles that people fulfilled in any way – no feeling of working as a team or to whom to go if you had problems. Staff in order to survive operated within the four walls of the classroom. What happened in the corridor and the playground they couldn't cope with.

Some four and half years later conditions in the school are very different: there is a sense of direction and purpose, clear evidence of team work on the part of the teaching and non-teaching staff and considerable evidence of pupil achievement. Yet the community has not changed, indeed some would argue that the social problems have worsened, and several of the original governors and teachers are still in post. What has brought about this transformation?

What are the factors that are contributing to the school's success?

The staff and governors who were interviewed were agreed that three factors had made a difference to the school. These were:

- the behaviour policy;
- the display policy;
- the leadership provided by the headteacher and the management systems that she has put in place.

The behaviour policy

The school has a 'good behaviour' policy, which is based on assertive discipline. [. . .] There is one key rule for everyone, which is that everyone will act with courtesy and consideration to others at all times, and this is elaborated in seven supporting statements. The behaviour policy was developed collaboratively by the staff, and they now have a system in place which links the rules to a system of rewards and sanctions and which is clearly understood by the pupils and themselves. All the staff said that this policy has worked extremely well.

The headteacher said that, on taking up her post, she had immediately recognised the high level of stress that pupil behaviour caused the teachers and she was determined to do something about it. [. . .]

The children are expected to behave as well with the non-teaching staff as with the teachers and these staff operate the same policy of rewards and sanctions. The LEA (local education authority) adviser, who had reviewed the implementation of the policy, said that he had been pleased that it was not crudely behaviourist but focused upon children's self-discipline; it was about children valuing themselves and raising their self-esteem and staff valuing them as people and forming relationships with them. Teachers spoke positively of the way the behaviour policy provided a framework for them. [. . .]

The headteacher and the staff strive to create a calm and orderly atmosphere in which the children behave well because they are learning self-discipline rather than because they are constantly chided; the staff in turn model patterns of good behaviour for their pupils. Considerable emphasis is placed on praising and rewarding children for their work and general effort and for good behaviour. The school assembly every Friday morning is used as an opportunity publicly to praise pupils who have been identified by their teachers for good work and behaviour. They come to the front of the hall and receive a certificate from the headteacher which they can take home and keep. Whereas some are rewarded for merit in their work, the efforts of a child who comes to school on time every day after a period of late arrivals will also be recognised. The pupils in Year 6, the leaving class, are given special responsibilities around the school. Each child has a special task which changes every term; they help in the school office, photocopy material for the teachers, act as library monitors and they are also given a pastoral role in relation to the younger pupils, sitting with them at lunch and spending time with them in the classroom on wet playtimes. This pastoral role not only gives the older pupils a sense of responsibility but also reduces the likelihood that the infant pupils will be intimidated or bullied. The intention is that, rather than being intimidated by them, the younger children will see those in Year 6 as people who will take care of them.

The headteacher and the staff are very pro-active when any discipline problems arise. Every effort is made to sort the issue out immediately and parents are asked to come into the school to discuss the matter. The rationale for this is that the child will be helped to overcome the problem if the teacher and the parent are working together.

The display policy

The impression gained on entering the school is of a clean, bright and stimulating environment in which to work. The hall, corridors and classrooms contain brightly coloured displays of children's work which are changed on a regular basis; there are interesting and beautiful objects on show and, in so far as this has been possible, the furniture and fittings in the school have been chosen with an eye to their aesthetic qualities. All the space in the building is utilised and it is used well. It was not always like this. The quality of display was reported to be relatively poor before the appointment of the present headteacher, and teachers were sometimes reluctant to mount displays of work because they would be torn down or disfigured by the pupils. One of the governors said that there used to be mess and paper everywhere: 'going into the classrooms was like an obstacle course'. The changes have not occurred accidentally but are a result of a specific policy on display, developed by the art and craft coordinator and the headteacher, in consultation with the staff. Three aspects are worthy of mention. First, the policy itself sets out clear expectations about the way in which pupil work should be presented and how frequently displays should be changed. Individual teachers are responsible for their own classrooms and groups of teachers form 'corridor teams' and have responsibility for the displays outside their rooms. [. . .]

A second aspect of the policy is that beautiful and interesting things should be seen around the school. For example, in the reception areas and corridors there are framed pictures and photographs, fish tanks, plants and flowers; albums of photographs of school events are available for parents and visitors to browse through. [. . .]

Third, the headteacher has been concerned to make the school environment welcoming for staff as well as for pupils. The staffroom is a large, comfortable room in which the teachers can relax. Though these facilities are well appreciated, some of the teachers initially questioned whether improving the facilities should be a priority. [. . .]

In August 1991, when the present headteacher had been in post for little more than a year, there was a major catastrophe when one whole section of the school was destroyed by fire. This was a devastating experience for the staff. As one of the governors said, 'At the time we could all have cried.' Many of the practical improvements that had already been made to the building were destroyed. The headteacher spent the whole of her summer holiday that year supervising the clearing of the site and the installation of Portakabins so that the school could reopen in September. This was a crisis period for the school, but, nearly three years later, several people said that this terrible experience had had positive outcomes. The year spent working in Portakabins while the school was rebuilt had brought the staff together as a team and it had also given the headteacher the opportunity to put in place the high-quality learning environment that she wanted for the children. One of the staff said of the headteacher at this time: 'I would never have dreamt of asking for some of the things that she asked for – she paid constant attention to detail.' The LEA adviser's assessment was that the headteacher has been able to illustrate her philosophy of education in the building. [. . .]

The leadership provided by the headteacher

The headteacher is highly experienced and is in her second headship. She had previously spent ten years as a very well-respected headteacher in a primary school in a middle-class suburb in Essex, a school which she had opened. On moving to Bristol, she deliberately chose to work in a different type of school. Her mission for the school is essentially very simple; she says that she was unhappy about the low level of expectations of the children when she first arrived and felt that they were not getting their entitlement. [. . .]

The interviews with teaching and non-teaching staff highlighted three sets of factors which have enabled her to make a big impact upon the school: she has clear ideas about what she wants to achieve; she is perceptive and caring and has abundant energy; she has excellent managerial skills.

Several people spoke about the headteacher's clear sense of direction. The staff recognised and welcomed the fact that she had clear aims and goals but they did not feel that these were being imposed upon them against their will. There were opportunities to talk things through, and if they disagreed with something they said so and the headteacher would listen. A teacher commented: 'She puts it over in a way that makes you want to do it.' One of the general assistants said of the headteacher: 'She wants the best – things as perfect as possible and she strives for that. She deals with problems and she doesn't lose her head. She can be sympathetic, she has to be tough.' The adviser's judgement of the headteacher was that she was 'A very focused leader, she knows where she is going, she knows what she wants, she takes action, she tries things – she doesn't always succeed but by that process she learns.'

Many people commented upon the headteacher's hard work and energy and her caring qualities. Staff said that they felt valued, that the headteacher recognised their contribution to the school and thanked them for their work. [. . .]

Her managerial skills are seen as being excellent:

> The head is an extremely organised person, a super manager, she seems to know what is going on everywhere. I have never known anyone who can juggle so many balls at once.
>
> (Class teacher)

[. . .]

The headteacher is conscious of the fact that she will be seen as a role model and tries always to demonstrate her philosophy of education through her practice. This can be seen in numerous ways – for instance, by the style of her conversations with and her behaviour towards the children, the staff and the parents; by her high personal standard of organisation and time-keeping; by the fact that her room is welcoming, tidy, decorated with pictures and flowers and that she is always well groomed and especially that she works extremely hard for long hours. She commented that she felt guilty if she was not the last one to leave the school although she realised that this was unnecessary. She said that she always tries to make time to talk to people when they want to see her and not to make them aware of the other pressures on her time.

School management in practice

It is difficult in a short case study to convey a full picture of the school. Three key aspects of the organisation have been selected to illustrate the quality of work that takes place: the management of staff; teaching and learning; and the school's relationship with governors, parents and the wider community.

Staffing issues

When the headteacher took up the post she found that there were no effective management procedures for teaching and non-teaching staff. Teachers did not have job descriptions; the responsibilities of incentive post-holders were unclear; there was no senior management team; teachers did not work together and the infant and junior staff were somewhat divided; there was no tradition of staff participation in decision-making. One of her immediate goals was to get the staff to work together as a team and in this she has clearly been successful. During the first few weeks in the school, beginning in June 1990, weeks which were difficult and emotional ones for her because she found the situation worse than she had anticipated, the headteacher conducted a form of needs analysis, making out a check-list of what was good about the school and what needed attention. Her key decision was that she would establish a senior management team (SMT) and this was put in place the following September. She has said that she did not have time to consult about this but just told staff that was what was required. The SMT consists of the headteacher, the deputy and the four senior incentive post-holders, two of whom were new appointments that she was able to make in September 1990. The SMT meet weekly and the headteacher says that she sees it as one of the main levers in taking the school forward. There are set agenda for the meetings, and the minutes, which detail the action that will be taken, are published on the staff notice board. Full staff meetings also take place on a weekly basis, again with agenda and minutes. These meetings usually contain discussion about school policy issues and are often led by a teacher who has specific responsibility for a particular policy area. Discussion is actively encouraged; indeed initially the headteacher would deliberately ask people for their views, but this is now unnecessary as everyone participates. Her policy is to consult the staff as fully as possible, but to be aware of the demands consultation can make on staff time. On a procedural matter, for example, on how milk should be distributed to the classrooms, a suggested strategy might be presented to the staff just to check that they all agree with it. In contrast, a draft policy on language would be put forward for full discussion. The procedures adopted for these meetings act as a model for the staff about how they can conduct their small group meetings about curriculum matters and display. Staff regularly discuss issues about teaching and learning formally and informally; a newly qualified teacher commented that: 'the meetings are long enough for individuals to contribute – people don't say "don't bring that up it's time to go home"'.

[. . .]

Each member of staff now has a clear job description and everyone, with the exception of new members of staff who are given a year to settle in, has a specific, school-wide responsibility. This process started with the headteacher conducting a professional development meeting with every member of staff, raising questions such as these. What skills have you got that the school is not using? What are your INSET (In-Service Education and Training) needs? What do you hope to do? From this initial meeting she negotiated a job description with that person. The practice of holding an annual professional development meeting with every member of staff has continued and these meetings enable the headteacher to keep in touch with staff needs and aspirations. The appraisal system is carried on independently and is used primarily as a means of identifying success and ways forward for development. All the job descriptions are published in the comprehensive staff handbook. A very simple strategy that she introduced as a means of breaking down barriers between infant and junior staff was to mix infant and junior classes on the same corridor. One of the rooms close to the staffroom has been turned into a resource and preparation room for the staff. As well as being generally useful, this has served a dual purpose in that resources are shared rather than being stored in individual classrooms and the informal exchange of teaching materials and ideas between teachers has been facilitated.

Teacher professional development is given a high priority. Many INSET activities are organised by the local federation of schools but individual teachers are given support to attend other programmes. [. . .]

Teaching and learning

The core purpose of the school is to provide high-quality learning experiences and opportunities for the children, and much is done to try to ensure that these are made available. Several strategies can be identified. First, priorities and targets are identified through the school development planning process and progress in achieving these is monitored over the year. Decisions about the allocation of resources, the selection of topics for discussion at staff meetings and the focus for professional development days are influenced by the priorities identified in the development plan. Second, priority is given to curriculum planning. Teachers meet in year groups to plan their work for the term, and each teacher has a file containing proformas on which they enter their individual lesson plans for the week; these files are then given to the headteacher weekly for comment and feedback. Third, there are detailed procedures for record-keeping and for monitoring the children's work. All children have portfolios which they build up as they progress through the school and which contain examples of their work; the teachers have recently instituted a system of moderating examples of pupils' work to try and ensure that they are operating a consistent standard. The children's work is valued and they receive positive feedback from their teachers; twice a day, at lunchtime and the end of the afternoon, pupils who have done a good piece of work are sent to show their work to the headteacher and receive her commendation. Fourth, the staff, as early as possible, try hard to identify any pupils, even in the nursery class, who have special educational needs, and to provide additional help and support where necessary. Several people praised the work done by the special needs teacher.

A fifth strategy that the headteacher has introduced is that, each Monday morning, she spends a couple of hours in a different class, observing the teacher and talking to the children about their work, and she follows this up with a feedback discussion with the teacher. Over the course of a school year she will observe each teacher on three occasions. Sixth, efforts are made to support the teachers in the classroom; every teacher has a period of release time each week which they can use for planning and they have the support of a general assistant for three half-sessions per week. In addition, curriculum coordinators get some limited time – for example, half a day a term – to work with their colleagues in the classroom, and also have one and a half days to attend subject specific INSET organised through the local federation of schools. This is an innovative strategy for a primary school since teachers in these schools frequently have no free time during teaching hours. A further distinguishing feature of the school is that the headteacher and staff are pro-active in seeking out opportunities to enrich the curriculum for the children. There are numerous extra-curricular activities, such as choir, recorder groups, football and rounders teams, swimming galas, art workshops and environmental projects, and the staff are prepared to enter competitions and take up initiatives that they feel will be valuable for the pupils. [. . .]

The school's relationship with governors, parents and the wider community

Several members of the governing body have been governors for many years. They are committed and very loyal to the school and very supportive of the developments that are taking place. The governors meet twice a term and there are a number of sub-committees (finance, personnel, curriculum), which also usually meet twice a term. The head-teacher attends practically all of the sub-committee meetings as well as the full meetings of the governing body. The chair of governors said that he feels that the government is currently expecting too much of school governors, that the role is becoming too demanding. He also pointed out that, because of the high rate of unemployment in the community, there are plenty of people who have time to devote to being a governor but many of them lack relevant experience: 'we don't have business people wanting to be governors'. Nevertheless, the governors are fully involved in decision-making about school policy and are active organisers and supporters of school initiatives. Recently, they have started the practice of formally visiting classrooms for a day, focusing on a specific area, so that they can be better informed about particular aspects of the school curriculum. For example, two governors will come into school to look at the implementation of the maths policy, and then report back to their colleagues at the next meeting.

Relationships with parents have improved immeasurably. The main indicator of this is that many more parents are now coming into the school to talk to the teachers and to see the work that their children have produced. The number of parents attending school productions has greatly increased. [. . .]

The teachers are in their classrooms from 8.45 a.m. and the parents are encouraged to bring any queries or concerns to them then or after school. The parent governors said that parents now found the school much more welcoming and felt comfortable about entering it. In return, the parents have learned how to help their children with reading and are very supportive of school activities. [. . .]

Conclusion

This is a dynamic school which is moving forward and making progress. Neither the headteacher nor the staff feel that they have achieved their goals in relation to the quality teaching and learning experiences that they want to provide for the pupils. The headteacher's own assessment is that, though a great deal has been achieved, much still remains to be done. She feels that the necessary structures are now in place, that the school is well supported by the parents, that staff morale is high and that this has placed the school in a position where everyone can move forward on teaching and learning:

> The minute I feel the school has gone as far as it can, I should go. The minute we say we have achieved [our vision for the school] we should do some soul-searching.
> (Headteacher)

Several of the people interviewed had clear ideas about what were the school's future priorities: improving the external environment; developing the library; developing the use of information technology. Staff were agreed that the school was succeeding and was effective, citing as evidence the behaviour policy; the display policy; the fact that they set themselves targets and were able to meet them; the fact that they regularly reviewed and developed their policies and planning mechanisms; that they worked well together as a team; above all, that their expectations of the children were high. [. . .]

None of the changes that have taken place in the school have occurred overnight. The present position of the school is the result of hard work by the headteacher, the staff and the governors over some four to five years. They hope to be able to sustain the momentum and to continue to make improvements in teaching and learning in the years ahead. In examining why this school is succeeding against the odds, this hard work over a number of years must be seen as a major explanatory variable. However, it is also important to note that this work and effort has had a clear focus and has been carefully planned by the headteacher in consultation with her staff. [. . .] The head-teacher has been able to build her staff into a strong team, help them develop a clear sense of direction and purpose, and together they have turned the school around. It is for these reasons that the school is succeeding against the odds.

Index